# The Directors—
# Take One

# The Directors
## Take One

## Robert J. Emery

ALLWORTH PRESS
NEW YORK

06   05   04   03   02            5   4   3   2   1

Published by Allworth Press
An imprint of Allworth Communications
10 East 23rd Street, New York, NY 10010

Emmy® is a registered trademark of the National Academy of Television Arts and Sciences. Academy Awards® and Oscar® are registered trademarks and servicemarks of the Academy of Motion Picture Arts and Sciences.

Photos provided courtesy of Media Entertainment and the directors interviewed.

Cover design by Douglas Design Associates, New York, NY

Interior design by Rachel Reiss

ISBN: 1-58115-218-3

Library of Congress Control Number: 2002101256

Printed in Canada

Previously published by TV Books, L.L.C.

# Contents

For Sue, Kevin, and Kelly

# The Directors—
# Take One

# Introduction

The interviews contained in this book were conducted for the television series *The Directors* (Encore Movie Channel), which was produced in cooperation with the American Film Institute. Presented here are the first thirteen interviews, *Take One*, to be followed in the future by several new volumes that will present additional interviews conducted for the series. To date fifty-two episodes have been completed accounting for well over two hundred hours of videotape. Twenty-six additional episodes are in production. Each one-hour episode featured a single director along with guests and extensive use of film clips from the director's movies. However, only about twenty-five minutes of each director's interview actually made it into the completed hour. It occurred to me that film enthusiasts and film goers, as well as film students, should not be deprived of the opportunity to read and learn from what each of these outstanding directors had to say in his or her entire interview. Hence, the birth of this book and subsequent books to come.

I have been associated with film and video production all of my adult life. My interest in films and film directors goes back to the days when I first began directing feature films. Between 1969 and 1975 I wrote, produced, and directed seven small features before turning to documentaries, which I dearly love. However, I returned to feature film writing and directing with the 2000 production of *Swimming Upstream,* a coming-of-age story based on the novel *The Greatest Thing That Almost Happened* by the late Don Robertson. I can honestly say, however, that one of the most rewarding projects I have ever been involved with has been *The Directors,* a project that I originated.

Movies are magic and the directors who make them are magical. I truly believe that the successful ones are members of an exclusive and rare breed.

To be in the film business takes dogged determination unlike any other business one can be in, because getting a film made is not easy, to put it mildly. Just about all of the directors interviewed will tell you it helps to be a bit of a masochist because the work is very, very difficult. Have you ever heard the quote "You are only as good as your last film?' Yet, all of these directors are passionate about what they do, and perhaps that is why they do it so very well.

I wish to thank my dear friend Milt Felson. As I write this Milt is about to turn ninety years young, going on seventy. He is an extraordinary man who has had an extraordinary career as a producer (*The Bell Jar, Saturday Night Fever*) and was a long time member of the board of directors of the Directors Guild of America. It was Milt who opened the doors for me and graciously agreed to come out of retirement and act as Executive Producer for the series.

I sincerely thank all of the wonderfully talented directors who participated and gave of their valuable time, along with over 200 Hollywood actors, writers, producers, and cinematographers who appears in the television series as guests. I would also like to thank Jean Firstenberg and James Hindman, Co-Directors of the American Film Institute, for their assistance in making this series a reality. And my sincerest thanks to director Robert Wise who allowed himself to be my first "victim." If it were not for Bob's willingness to participate I seriously doubt if I could have gotten this project of the ground to begin with. His involvement brought us the credibility we needed to go forward. In the process I was fortunate enough to become his friend.

In transcribing the on-camera interviews into this book some editing was necessary. However, I have retained as much of the original interviews as possible.

Robert J. Emery

# The Directors—
# Take One

# The Films of Robert Wise

Robert Wise was born on September 10, 1914, in Winchester, Indiana. The youngest of three brothers, he moved to Los Angeles at the age of nineteen and began working at RKO Pictures at a job his brother was able to obtain for him.

Wise entered the directorial ranks after an apprenticeship as a film editor. He is credited with editing twelve features, but his most famous editorial assignment was for Orson Welles on *Citizen Kane*, considered by many to be the greatest film of all time. He went on to edit another Welles film, *The Magnificent Ambersons*, and also directed some additional scenes for that movie while Welles was away on an assignment in Brazil.

Wise's pictures have garnered sixty-seven Academy Award nominations and nineteen Oscars. Wise himself has been nominated seven times and has won four Oscars. He became a double Oscar winner twice, as both Best Director and producer of the year's Best Picture, for two films that have become recognized as all-time classics—*West Side Story* (co-directed with Jerome Robbins) and *The Sound of Music*.

Reams of copy has been written about this man who is held in high esteem in the industry and considered one of Hollywood's most prolific directors. He is known as one of the nicest men in Hollywood, a well-deserved title. He tirelessly gives of his time to the industry and to young filmmakers. His involvement in the Directors Guild of America, American Film Institute, National Council on the Arts, Motion Picture Country House and Hospital, USC School of Film and Television, Museum of Modern Art (New York), National Education Film Festival (Oakland), and the Academy of Motion Picture Arts and Sciences is well documented.

---

NOTE: Robert Wise was the first director to be interviewed for this series. For that the author of this book will be forever grateful.

*He was probably the most expeditious, one of the most efficient directors ever. He didn't shoot a lot of extra film, and he didn't protect himself with a lot of other shots. He knew exactly what he was doing and he did it with expedience and efficiency and with great harmony on the set.*

*Robert Mitchum—Actor*

# The Conversation

I came out to Hollywood in August of 1933 and started working at RKO Studios the next month and have not stopped working in the business since—more than sixty years now. I didn't know what was going to happen to me when I came out. I had no idea of how far my future would go and now that I look back I don't know where the more than sixty years have gone. They seem to have just vanished.

I grew up in Indiana in a little town of about twelve thousand people and I used to go to the movies. We had three movie houses and I would go as often as I had the money for it. I was a Depression dropout from college. I managed to get one year in at Franklin College near Indianapolis on a scholarship. I just eked through. It was the height of the Depression, everything was terrible and my dad's business was on the rocks. I couldn't get a job in Franklin. That turned out to be a fortunate thing for me because my older brother Dave, who was seven years older, had come out here to Los Angeles in the late 1920s. He had kind of wanderlust and started working at RKO Studios as a labor guy. By the summer of 1933 he had worked his way up to the accounting office, which was his field. It was decided by my family that if I couldn't go back to college I should join Dave and he'd help me get a job and I'd earn my living.

## Los Angeles Beckons

He got me an appointment with the head of the film-editing department at RKO, who had happened to say that, well, he could use a young eager kid. I was not quite nineteen. I worked in the film-shipping department, carrying films up to the projection room for the executives to look at, and that was my first job in the business.

I went around that lot just watching and looking at the stages—eyes that big, you know. I went by one of the office buildings and outside there was a rather stocky, little, chunky man in white ducks and white shirt and very heavy glasses talking to a couple of women who were in pantaloons and skirts and parasols, and it was fascinating. This man was talking very animatedly to them. I walked by, kind of hanging around, watching this scene, and later on I described it to somebody and they said, "Well, that must have been George Cukor, the director, talking to Katharine Hepburn and Joan Bennett. They're making *Little Women*." Many years later I told George that he was the very first live movie director I ever saw.

After I got out of the shipping room, P.K. Wood, who was the head of sound effects editing, spotted me and thought maybe I had some possibilities and asked for me to be put in his department to become a sound effects editor. I went out on a couple pictures doing that. Then I became a music editor and I thought that was fine. But after a couple of years I looked around and I saw there were men there that had been doing that for twenty or twenty-five years, and I realized that was a dead end and I didn't want to stop there. I went to my boss, Jimmy Wilkinson, and asked to be put over on the picture side so I could become an assistant film editor. I got put with a fine master editor who let me move ahead just as fast as I could. On the last three films I worked on with him I was doing so much of the work that he insisted I share credit with him. So I got credit on *The Hunchback of Notre Dame*, *5th Avenue Girl*, and *The Castles*.

Back then the editing rooms were fairly simple, with benches all around and an old-fashioned Moviola—I'm going back to 1934 or 1935 now— which sat on a kind of wooden stand with the picture head on one side and the sound on the other. You'd attach them together, and your picture ran up one side on the little viewer of the Moviola and your soundtrack was running on the other side. Over on the bench you'd have your rewinds and your slate machines that you could synchronize your picture and your track with. You would mark the film and cut it. Those were the days before tape came in, so you'd get a whole reel clipped together, then go down to the end of a hall and splice them by hand on this hot splicer.

I worked as assistant editor on one film that George Stevens directed, but I didn't have a lot of direct contact with him in those days. But I learned from him. I learned the importance of the director, how vital he was, what his job was, but it took me a little while to get that all sorted out. George Steven Sr., Willie Wyler, John Ford, Howard Hawks, and people like that were all my idols in terms of directors. I looked up to them constantly and repeatedly and saw their films time and time again.

# Curse of the Cat People (1944)

*Simone Simon; Kent Smith; Jane Randolph; Ann Carter; Eve March;*
*Julia Dean; Elizabeth Russell; Erford Gage; Sir Lancelot.*

I had been wanting a chance to direct. Those were the days when studios were making a lot of B pictures, low-budget pictures with short scripts. I was editing a small B picture called *Curse of the Cat People*. The director got terribly behind schedule and they couldn't seem to speed him up. He had used up the whole schedule and only shot half of the script. I got a call on a Saturday to go meet the executive producer. He said he wanted me to take over on Monday morning. So that was it. I took over on Monday morning.

It happened then that another director, Dick Wallace, heard that I had gotten my break. He was shooting on the lot. He took time out between his sets to congratulate me and wish me well. I'll never forget one thing he said to me. "Bobby," he said, "I only have one bit of advice to give you. If a scene seems a trifle slow on the set, it'll be twice as slow in the projection room." And boy, was he ever right. I've tried to remember that all through my career. Sometimes I forget and kick myself in the fanny.

Now, the truth is I showed a little bit of hesitancy about taking that first film for this reason: I was scheduled to go back that very night and work with the director that I was replacing while he did some special effects. I felt awkward about working with him that night knowing I was going to take over on Monday morning. So when I showed this bit of hesitation, the executive producer said to me, "Bob, he's not going to be there Monday morning directing that film. Somebody else is going to be there doing it. Now, it could be you or somebody else, but he's not going to be there. So what will it be?" And I said I'd be there, and that's how I got to direct my first picture.

## Wise meets Welles

Let me tell you how *Citizen Kane* came about. I had just finished editing a film called *My Favorite Wife,* so I was between pictures. I got a call from my boss, Jim Wilkinson, and he said, "Listen Bob, you know that Orson Welles fellow? Well, he thought he'd make this picture and he got the front office to let him go ahead and shoot two or three test scenes. Well, he's done three of them and they realize he's actually shooting this picture, so they give him the green light to go ahead and make the film, and he wants another editor."

They had given Orson an old-time hack editor to work with because he was supposedly just shooting tests. So I went down to see him. He was in the midst of shooting the scene at the beach in the tent. During a break in the shooting he came out to meet me, so the first time I ever saw Orson was as old man Kane. We chatted for a few minutes, and evidently he liked the cut of my jib and I had a decent enough record of editing jobs, so when I got back to Hollywood my boss called and said, "You got it, kid." Of course I was thrilled. I thought it would be a very rare episode in my life, and it was.

Orson had come out to Hollywood with the most extraordinary contract that had ever been seen up until that time. It gave him complete power over his production in every way imaginable. I guess there was a little resentment around town by the established people—directors, producers, and others— who hadn't had that kind of carte blanche in their contracts. So I think a lot of them were kind of looking for him to stumble and not make it. But I don't think Orson was concerned or aware of it because he had such complete concentration on *Kane*. That became his whole life and I don't think he cared about the rest. I seriously doubt that Orson had as complete concentration on any of his other films than he did on *Kane*. When we did *The Magnificent Ambersons* a year or so later, there were other distractions.

Kane's death scene has been discussed many times over the years. The nurse comes through the door, and Kane appears to be dead, so the question has come up many times: Who was in the room to hear him say "Rose-bud?" I don't know whether that was done deliberately by Orson, just to muddle things or make people wonder about it or look for it or what. I don't know. But we've accepted over the years that somebody was around in some way to hear. We just bought into it.

## More Tales of Welles

Orson was extraordinary in many ways. He was also an extremist. Let me say right now that he was as close to being a genius as anybody I've met in the business. He was absolutely brilliant, but maddening at times. He would do something outrageous and you'd want to tell him to shove it and walk off. Then he'd have an idea that was so brilliant that your mouth fell open and you wouldn't walk. He was very exciting and very stimulating to work with. But, as I say, he was an extremist.

I finally got him to do some looping on the end of *Kane*, but he resisted it for weeks. I don't know why he was afraid of it. I almost had to literally push him through the door of the dubbing room, put the earphones on him, and get ready to go. Once he did it, he was brilliant at it, of course, because of all his previous radio experience. But from that point on, the soundtrack, as far as dialogue on the set goes, didn't mean anything to him. If he was doing a scene in *Ambersons* and an airplane went over and ruined a good take, he'd say, "We'll loop it later."

Orson had done a radio show of *The Magnificent Ambersons* a year or so before and it was brilliant. When I heard that he was going to do a movie out of it I was delighted, because I thought it would show another side of Orson. Unfortunately, it ran into some problems. He was doing a *Lady Esther* radio show, and all of his Sundays were spent on that because we were shooting six days a week on *Ambersons*. We were weeks away from finishing shooting when the war started, and Orson was approached by our government to go down to Brazil and make a picture with Brazilians as part of our good neighbor policy, to keep the South American countries on our side in the war. Orson jumped at that. But we went on filming *Ambersons*.

Suddenly he got a wild idea that he wanted to make another picture before he finished *Ambersons*. I think he owed RKO another film. He had a script called *Journey into Fear*. He put that into the works. Then he put Delores del Rio, who was his girlfriend at the time, in the female lead, and then he decided that the only person to play the Turkish gentleman was he himself. So Orson was directing *Ambersons* during the day and acting all night in *Journey into Fear.* He would come in during the screening of *Ambersons* rushes and he would be groggy. I think he kept himself alive on all kinds of drugs and amphetamines. When we finished shooting he had to go to Washington for a briefing on the Brazil film, and I had not finished editing with him yet. Then I took reels of film down to Miami where he was scheduled to take off for South America. We spent three days and nights in a studio down there doing all this work and then he took off for South America. I literally took him right down to the dock to catch his flying boat over to Rio. He took off and I didn't see him again for many years.

I went back and finished up the film. I was scheduled to take a print down to show to Orson in Rio but they put an embargo on any civilians flying down there so we sent him a print. After he saw it we had long phone conversations about what he liked and didn't like. Unfortunately, I've lost it along the way, but he later sent me a thirty-seven page cable that suggested more changes and improvements. We did as many of those as we could as long as they made any sense to us. By now the studio was getting a little nervous. They had a lot of money in this picture and they were determined to have a sneak preview. They held the preview but the audience just didn't like the picture at all. They walked out in droves. They laughed in the wrong places. It was a disaster. So we started the whole process of editing all over again and held another preview that was a little better. Then we did more cutting and had to shoot an added scene, which I directed because I had a little experience. Finally, on the fourth preview, with forty-five minutes to an hour cut out of it, we had a preview down at Long Beach and the audience sat for it and they didn't laugh and they didn't walk out.

Our paths didn't cross again until 1953, in London of all places. I was there making tests of talent for *Helen of Troy*. He was working on another stage as an actor. I went over and we had a nice reunion. He was very warm and very happy to see me. We chatted for a few minutes, then he was called to the set and I went back to my stage. He told me he would come by to see me on my set. When he came by I was involved in a big scene and he couldn't wait. I didn't see him again for ten years.

## Preparing to Direct a Film

I was very nervous about taking over on *Curse of the Cat People*. I was glad I didn't have weeks to work up to that. I got to the studio at 4:30 in the morning with my little viewer finder. I had to go into this empty stage and find the lights so I could see what I was doing. I would use my finder and start making notes about how I wanted to cover the scene and how I wanted to stage it. I continued to do that for many years and then later on I got into storyboarding. But the more preparation you do before you start to shoot, the better your picture is going to be, because the expensive time, the pressure time, is when you're shooting. And if you are prepared you have much more time to spend with your actors. You get better scenes and better results than if you haven't prepared enough. There are two important words—participation and communication—that I always tell the students when I go out to the universities.

## Blood on the Moon (1948)

*Robert Mitchum; Barbara Bel Geddes; Robert Preston; Walter Brennan; Phyllis Thaxter; Frank Faylen; Tom Tully; Charles McGraw; Clifton Young; Tom Tyler; George Cooper; Tom Keene; Bud Osborne; Zon Murray; Robert Bray.*

An editor friend of mine actually found a script sitting on a shelf at RKO and brought it to me and said, "Gee, I think this has got possibilities. I don't know why it's on the shelf." I got an okay from the front office to spend a minimum amount of money for a writer. We got a writer and she developed the script and it was called *Blood on the Moon*. So we sent it up to the front office and they liked it. The idea was that my friend would be the producer and I would be the director. Then a couple of agents came in and tried to undo me. They wanted to sell another director along with a star as a package deal. But the head of the studio turned them down flat and let us do it.

Actually, the people that tried to do me in were from my own agency. After I got the assignment to finish up *Curse of the Cat People,* I was signed to a standard seven-year contract with RKO. I was then approached by this big agency that offered to represent me. They said, "We won't take any commission from you until we better your contract." I said fine. Well, it was men from this very agency that were trying to sell another director. My own people were undercutting me. I found this out from a friend. They were trying to sell another guy who was getting seventy-five thousand dollars a picture, which meant they would get more in commissions. I, on the other hand, was getting peanuts and their commissions would have been much smaller if I directed the picture. That's the way it worked sometimes. Fortunately, it did not happen that time and I went on to direct *Blood on the Moon*.

In that film we had a fight scene in a bar between Bob Mitchum and Bob Preston, who was the heavy in the piece. I wanted to have a fight that was not full of all the marvelous stuntmen in town crashing through tables and out windows and all. I wanted a real fight to the death between these two men, which meant it had to be much closer, much tighter, much more vicious, in a tight spot. I had a lot of trouble with the stuntmen. They wanted to break it wide open. But instead I had Mitchum and Preston do the fight themselves. If people see the film, they'll see a real fight almost to the death, with guys down on the floor punching each other, trying to strangle each other, do each other in, and being, when they finished, absolutely exhausted. When Mitchum finally won he could barely get up on his feet. He was all out of breath and worn out from this struggle. I've had many people tell me they think it's one of the most effective fight scenes of that nature they have ever seen. But that was my concept going in.

## Moguls, Moguls, and More Moguls

I've had some knock-down-drag-out fights with some studio bosses in my time, one in particular with Darryl Zanuck. Darryl, by the way, was somebody I had tremendous respect for. He was a fine producer and fine filmmaker.

I like to shoot a lot of coverage when I can. As a former editor, I know how marvelous it is to have a lot of coverage. In this one picture I had a particular scene around a table. Table scenes are always very challenging for directors. I had planned it very carefully, with certain kinds of setups, and I knew just how I wanted it to go. Well, Darryl saw the rushes and he wrote me a very strong note saying that this had to stop. He said, "I saw that break-fast table scene and it's over-covered and it must stop or I'm going to have to take some action," which meant take me off the picture. So I sat down and wrote a memo to him and outlined exactly how I planned it, what the different angles were for, why it wasn't over-covered, and how I was using them and never heard another thing from him. That calmed him down.

Besides a certain crudeness attributed to some of them, the men who ran the early studios loved films. They had grown up with films. They may not have expressed it in the most delicate of terms, but I think that's one of the differences between them and the current studio heads. I don't know many of those running the studios now. I don't know how many of them have that pure love for film running through their veins that I think Louis B. Mayer, Harry Cohn, and Jack Warner had.

I had an opportunity to go out to Jack Warner's house once, to run a first cut of a film I had done over there. He had a lovely projection room lined with bound scripts of films he'd had done. I walked along and looked at some of those titles and I was reminded of what a marvelous series of films they had made. I was taken aback.

But as I said, those men loved movies. I remember when I was at Fox under contract—not an exclusive contract—and I was given a script by Zanuck that Bob Baxter was going to produce. I read the script and I thought it was all right but I didn't think it was anything exceptional or un-usual and I didn't really have too much enthusiasm for it. So I told Mr. Baxter that I really didn't feel that I wanted to do it. I got a call from Zanuck, and of course I knew what it was going to be about. Zanuck said, "I understand you don't like the script." I said, "Well, it's not that I don't like it, I don't think it's anything special. I think it's going to take a lot of time, energy, and money and I'd like to do something more stimulating." He said, "Well, Bob, I've been in this business a long time." He said, "I think, if you get one picture out of three or four that you're really excited about, you're gonna be very lucky." He said, "I have a whole program of pictures that I have to make for the studio. I have to fill that distribution and I really would like you to make this picture." And I said, "Well, as long as you know how I feel about it, I will do it and give it everything I can."

That's pretty much gone now. I'm talking back in the days when the studios had big contract lists and each of them was making fifty or sixty films a year. The studios had a great sense of continuity and had actors and writers and directors and all under contract. But as you know, it has all changed. The studios don't have people under contract now, so almost anybody, unless he just wants any kind of a job, has a choice. If the studio comes to you now with a project, you either like it or don't like it, say yes or say no. The last studio contract I had was with MGM. I had done *Executive Suite*, which came out in 1953. Then I went abroad to do *Helen of Troy* for Warner Bros. *Executive Suite* came out, was successful, so MGM wanted to sign me. I signed a straight three-year contract. I got out of that contract before I finally finished it. I had to give them another picture and that's the last contract I've had. All my other pictures were individual deals. All things that I chose to do—nothing I had to do.

# The Set-Up (1949)
*Robert Ryan; Audrey Totter; George Tobias; Alan Baxter; Wallace Ford;*
*Percy Helton; Hal Baylor; Darryl Hickman; Kenny O'Morrison;*
*James Edwards; David Clarke; Phillip Pine; Edwin Max.*

I had finished *Blood on the Moon* and the head of the studio called me up to his office. He said, "I've got a script here, and I think this might be something that you'd be interested in." He threw it across to me and it was *The Set-Up*. I went away to read it right away and absolutely flipped out. I loved it. I called him immediately and said, "I want to be on this." Robert Ryan was set as the lead, but we had a little delay because Ryan was doing a picture at some other studio as a loan-out. So we had time to do our pre-production planning. Then Howard Hughes bought the studio and immediately put everything on hold—stopped everything we were doing on *The Set-Up*— and I was put on layoff. Our contracts included a period of time that they could put you on layoff and not use you. All I wanted to do was to get back in the studio and get that picture going. The whole lot was going to pieces because there was no production, so since we were further along, easier to get into production, they just gave us a green light to go ahead.

This was not a story of Madison Square Garden and the Championship Bout, but a small tank town arena with third-rate fighters some place back in Pennsylvania. I wanted to capture the feeling of that. So I had them find me an old, run-down, fight arena down in Long Beach, and I would go down there on fight night. I would get down there before anybody was there. I'd watch the fighters come in and I would watch the handlers come in and watch their attitudes, make notes of their wardrobe. I spent a whole night in the dressing room watching how the fighters comported themselves and how they went out into the fight and how they came back, having won, maybe, or having been knocked out. I spent the whole evening there soaking up as much detail about the atmosphere, the ambiance, the feeling of that place as I could. I went down the next night and stayed out in the front watching the fighters and the handlers. I studied all of that and made my notes.

It's the first time we worked with a zoom lens and storyboards. We'd have a sketch of the set and a layout, a plan. We did that on the whole show except for the fights. You don't do the fights that way because those are rehearsed anyway, and choreographed before you shoot, and then you just shoot it with a lot of cameras.

# The Day the Earth Stood Still (1951)

*Michael Rennie; Patricia Neal; Hugh Marlowe; Sam Jaffe; Billy Gray; Francis Bavier; Lock Martin; Drew Pearson; Frank Conroy; Carleton Young; Fay Roope; Edith Evanson; Robert Osterloh; Tyler McVey; James Seay.*

While I was under contract with Twentieth Century Fox, I got a call from Darryl Zanuck one day and he said, "I want you to go see a producer named Julian Blaustein, I think he has a script you might find interesting." So I went down to meet Blaustein, whom I had never met, and he handed me the script of *The Day the Earth Stood Still.* He told me briefly what it was about. I went away and read the script and loved it. I loved what it was about. I loved what it had to say in its approach against war. I thought it was something I very much wanted to do.

There were some people that were surprised that a picture with that kind of content would be made under Zanuck, because he had been a big Army man. I think he was a colonel or a general in the war and very pro-military. I simply have to say he was a filmmaker above everything else. He loved the script and the completed film. He thought it was a fine piece of work and no problem at all.

The one place that we did have a little problem was getting any kind of help from the Defense Department. We needed those troops and the jeeps and a few tanks. To get anything like that from the Defense Department you have to submit the script. They read the script and we got turned down. They didn't go for that message and didn't want any kind of indictment of what we might be doing militarily. But we had an ace up our sleeve. Fox had a representative in Washington who knew his way around, so we went over to the National Guard and they didn't seem to have any problem with it. So all the troops and equipment we shot at our Washington location was not real Army but National Guard.

The same thing happened years later on *The Andromeda Strain*. We needed a helicopter, a few jeeps, and things like that. We knew we could always rent those if necessary, but if we could get help from the Air Force and Army it would save us forty or fifty thousand dollars. It was an anti-biological warfare piece and they didn't approve, so we didn't get the equipment.

For the lead in *The Day the Earth Stood Still* we all had in mind the fine English character actor Claude Raines. He was a brilliant, marvelous actor and we always felt he was the man. But unfortunately, or fortunately, as it turned out, he was tied up with a play in New York. Darryl Zanuck said, "Hey, I've just come back from London, and while I was over there I saw a young man on the stage that I was very impressed with. He hasn't been seen on film here, but I thought he had such potential I signed him to a contract and I think you should take a look at him." It turned out his name was Michael Rennie and he was just absolutely perfect for us. Here was a young man who had never been seen on the screen before so he was fresh and new and he had kind of a tall, sensitive look, and all in all I think it was one of those things where we just lucked out.

There was never any question that I would shoot the film in black and white. This was the early 1950s and some color was being shot, but very sparsely because it was more expensive and they still were using the big, cumbersome, three-strip color then. So there was never any question. I intended it to be black and white right from the beginning.

## Executive Suite (1954)

*William Holden; June Allyson; Barbara Stanwyck; Fredric March; Walter Pidgeon; ·*
*Shelley Winters; Paul Douglas; Louis Calhern; Dean Jagger; Nina Foch;*
*Tim Considine; William Phipps; Lucille Knoch; Edgar Stehli; Mary Adams.*

John Houseman, a good friend and dear, marvelous, creative man, was the producer of the film. He had been a partner with Orson Welles in Mercury Theater. He came to visit the *Kane* set·a couple of times in New York and that's how I met him. I hadn't seen him much over the years, but all of a sudden, out of the blue, I got a call from my agent that John Houseman wanted to talk to me about directing *Executive Suite*. He remembered my work with Orson and had seen some of my subsequent work as a director.

John was very creative and very sensitive of script, of writing, of casting—just every detail of filmmaking. He was always very involved in his productions without trying to over-push the director or look over his shoulder or second guess him or anything like that. He was just very supportive.

Doing *Executive Suite* in black and white, as well as *The Day the Earth Stood Still*, was very deliberate. I wanted to have a strong sense of reality, believability, and credibility in it. So from the beginning we didn't think about anything but black and white. This is before color television came in, where the need to have a color negative for television was not as strong as it became later.

We had William Holden, June Allyson, Barbara Stanwyck, Paul Douglas, and Fredric March. I was delighted to have Fred for this part. It was a very rich part. Fred was a fine actor but he had just come out in the film before ours was due to go, in which he was kind of criticized for being overboard too much. So I knew that this part he was going to play for us was very susceptible to an over-rich performance. My feeling was the less he did the better. Before we met I had only talked to him on the phone. I was wondering to myself how he was going to approach the level of his performance. He said to me, "You know Bob, when I first read the script I thought of all the wonderful, marvelous pieces of business I could do with this character." Well, my heart sank. Then he said, "You know, I read it again and I changed my mind. I think that the least I do with the character, the more effective it will be." I said, "Freddie, I could lean over and kiss you because that's exactly what I wanted to tell you." He said, "You know all the actors tend to get carried away and go." He said, "If you find me getting overboard or too much of anything, just come up and whisper in my ear, 'too much,' and I'll bring it down."

# Helen of Troy (1956)

*Rossana Podestà; Jacques Sernas; Cedric Hardwicke; Stanley Baker; Niall MacGinnis; Nora Swinburne; Robert Douglas; Torin Thatcher; Harry Andrews; Janette Scott; Ronald Lewis; Brigitte Bardot; Eduardo Ciannelli; Marc Lawrence; Maxwell Reed.*

I had directed a film or two for Warner Bros. with my free time from Twentieth. I got a call out of the blue from Jack Warner saying he had this film, this spectacle, that is being done in Rome, and would I be interested in taking a look at it. That kind of intrigued me because Cinemascope was becoming popular and I had never done a picture in Cinemascope color. I thought maybe it was time I got into that sort of genre, and that's what compelled me to take it. It was fascinating to do.

I spent almost a year in Rome working on it. It was not an easy film. It was a difficult film and we had some problems on it. But I think it came out quite well. It was not the most popular film I've ever made although, interestingly enough, some of the younger directors like it. Martin Scorsese and Oliver Stone told me on different occasions that the film had a great influence on them. Marty liked it so much that he had Warner Bros. make a brand new 35mm print, which he donated to the Museum of Modern Art in New York. I felt good about that.

## Tribute to a Bad Man (1956)

*James Cagney; Don Dubbins; Stephen McNally; Irene Papas;*
*Vic Morrow; James Griffith; Onslow Stevens; James Ball; Jeanette Nolan;*
*Chubby Johnson; Royal Dano; Lee Van Cleef; Peter Chong.*

I was still fairly young as a director then, and Spencer Tracy was such a legendary character and actor that I was a little nervous when I walked into that first meeting. Sam Zimbalist was the producer and we met in his office and talked about the script. Tracy was committed and was very enthusiastic about the film, and we talked at some length about the script. At that point we only had the first two acts. Michael Blankfort was writing and he was working on the third act and we all seemed to like it.

It was a story about horses, and the producer thought we should set it someplace with a marvelous scenic background, maybe up high in the mountains with a lot of green rather than the usual sort of western horse country. I agreed with that right away, and Tracy and I left very high on the prospects of the film.

But the next morning he called me from New York and said, "Do you think we should really do this? Do you really like the script that much? Should we do this or not?" I didn't know what to make of that.

We finally found marvelous locations about nine thousand feet up on the west side of the Rockies with great snow-covered mountains in the background and beautiful green meadows. Tracy had developed a little cyst on his cheek and was very worried about it. He tended to be a bit of a hypochondriac and he felt he should have it tested and taken care of before coming up to the location. I went on ahead with the rest of the troupe while he stayed down below. I started to shoot the film with the other cast members and I shot everything I could without Tracy. He finally showed up one day and I went to see him at the motor lodge motel where we were staying. He had a little patch on his cheek where this cyst had been removed. He pulled the tape off to show it to me and was almost in tears, saying, "Do you think this is going be all right? Am I going be okay?" He seemed really concerned about it.

He didn't have to work the first day or two because we wanted him to get acclimated to the climate, but he came up to visit our set. The next day he did a couple of scenes and I let him go early because I didn't want to push him too much. Right away he began to complain about the altitude and shortness of breath. About the third morning, while we were rehearsing, he said several times, "I don't know whether I can really make this show. I don't know whether I can complete this. This is tough up here in this altitude. Bob, I can't do the show."

Well, by this time I'd just about had it so I said, "Thank you very much." We just closed the troupe down and went down to the motel and I called the studio and I told them what the situation was. I said, "I don't think we'll ever get him through this show. We'll just be spinning our wheels. Do we replace him or what?" A couple of hours later the studio called back and said, "Okay, he's out of the picture. We'll try to get you Clark Gable."

I went over to see Tracy and to tell him this. He said, "That's the end, my career is finished. I'll never work again." Needless to say, he was distraught. No one had ever done this to him before. He had complained on other pictures but they had never pulled him out of one before and he just hadn't expected them to do it this time. I think what he had in mind was that we would get another location down five thousand feet and restart in a few months. Something like that, I don't know. That's just my conjecture. But as angry as I was at him, with this scene he was playing about this being the end of his career, I was almost sorry for him. It was very touching. And of course it wasn't the end of his career, it was just the end of him on that picture.

Jimmy Cagney read it and said he would do it but he couldn't do it for a couple of months. So we had to wrap it up and go down the hill and go back to the studio to wait for Jimmy. During the interim Bob Francis, who was a rising young leading man then and a principle in our picture, was taking flying lessons and got killed. So they had to recast that part also. That meant that I had to go back up into the mountains and redo his scenes with a new actor.

# Somebody Up There Likes Me (1956)

*Paul Newman; Pier Angeli; Everett Sloane; Eileen Heckart;*
*Sal Mineo; Harold Stone; Joseph Buloff; Sammy White;*
*Arch Johnson; Robert P. Lieb; Theodore Newton.*

This was only Paul Newman's second feature. His first was a costume piece called *The Silver Chalice* for Warner Bros. I met with him and I thought he just seemed right, and I also was familiar with his work on the stage in New York. So Paul was signed for the part.

One of the better things we had in addition to Ernie Lehman's fine script was that we had a chance to spend a lot of time with the middleweight fighter Rocky Graziano, whose story we were telling. Paul and I and Rocky went around the Lower East Side of New York City where Rocky grew up and saw his haunts and met his buddies. He also got us a lot of stills of the period, and a lot of the clothes Paul wore in the film came from Rocky. Also, Rocky had done a *Look* magazine interview on tape. We were able to get that so Paul could listen to Rocky and get the cadence of his delivery. We decided early on that whatever Paul could do honestly that accurately portrayed Rocky, he would do it. If anything were false, then he wouldn't do it. So Paul studied Rocky and I think he came off with a brilliant performance—really good and a real characterization.

I had a scene that took place on the Lower East Side's rooftops and I couldn't do that at the studio. I needed a few extra gang members, hoodlum kind of types. So I was interviewing in the office of MGM in New York and in came this character with a little straight cap on his head, all kind of cocky, and it was Steve McQueen. I was somehow just taken by his whole attitude and his look and so I put him in the scene. Somehow I got him established in such a way in the scene in New York that I had to bring him out to the coast to do another added little scene with Paul and Sal Mineo. So I did the one little scene with him and that was it until we worked together years later in *The Sand Pebbles*.

I cast Robert Loggia, too. He played a cheap gangster. He was just getting started back then. We're talking about 1956, or something like that. I liked him very much when I met him and I thought he did a very, very good job for us. He eventually came out to Hollywood from New York. I've been so pleased to see how his career has grown over the years.

He and Steve had that chemistry for the screen, and of course Paul had it also. That's something that you can't study, you can't learn. I don't mean to say that actors shouldn't learn technique. They should study acting, but some have and some don't have that gene, that chemistry, that connects with that silver screen. And as I say, it's nothing you can study, you either have it or you don't have it. Bogart had it in spades and could hold the screen no matter what. I wish I knew what it was. I wish we could give somebody a shot for it. I can't define it. It's something in the genes.

# Run Silent, Run Deep (1958)

*Clark Gable; Burt Lancaster; Jack Warden; Brad Dexter; Don Rickles; Nick Cravat; Joe Maross; Mary LaRoche; Eddie Foy III; Rudy Bond; H.M. Wynant.*

I went down to San Diego to see one of the World War II subs that was a museum. When I first stepped in it, I was absolutely amazed at the small size of it. You're kind of cramped, tight, close, and I was determined to get that on the screen. Up to this time, most films made about submarines were opened up a little. The interiors were a little bit wider for the convenience of working. I said to my art directors, "I want you to go down to that real sub, photograph and measure it, and then you give me every set the same size of that submarine." I wanted the actors to feel the pressure of living in that kind of condensed atmosphere. I think that helped contribute quite a lot to all the performances.

# I Want to Live! (1958)

*Susan Hayward; Simon Oakland; Virginia Vincent; Theodore Bikel; Wesley Lau; Philip Coolidge; Lou Krugman; James Philbrook; Bartlett Robinson; Gage Clarke; Joe De Santis; John Marley; Raymond Bailey; Alice Backes; Gertrude Flynn.*

This was a real life story about Barbara Graham, who was convicted, along with a couple of men, of being involved in beating an old lady to death. She was sentenced to death and was the last woman, I believe, to go to the gas chamber in California. This was back about 1956. Walter Ranger was the producer and I called him and said, "Well, Walter, people seem to like horror stories, and this is a real-life horror story if I have ever read one, so let's do it."

Once we decided to do it I went up to San Quentin. Once again, in my determination to do things as they actually are, I wanted to see an execution. I wanted to know what it was like. I wanted to know everything about it because I didn't want critics to be able to say that's some Hollywood writer/director's version of what it's like to go to the gas chamber. So I went to the warden and I explained to him why I wanted to see an actual execution. He said, "Well, Mr. Wise, I know where you're coming from. Capital punishment is the law of the State of California and I think it's well for the citizens to know what it's like. I'll let you do it."

He called me a couple of weeks later and said, "If you'll come over here early Friday morning we will have an execution going on." So I went. Once you are in there it's divided. One side of the chamber has windows all around it and the witnesses are outside. Inside would be the warden and the doctor with the stethoscope. I was inside with the warden. I didn't know if I would be able to watch it all or whether I'd get sick or have to turn away. Fortunately, it turned out to be very quiet and a very unemotional scene. The victim was a young black man who had been convicted of murder a couple of years before and had run out of appeals. There were no hysterics, no emotion. It was very solemn, very quiet, and I found I was able to stand there with the warden and watch the whole thing. But it's awful.

When I did the film, with Susan Hayward playing the part, once she got the fumes in there, you could see that she started to go. I had her hands strapped down and she did some twitches and then I cut away. But in actuality, during the real execution I saw, that boy twisted and turned and struggled for about seven or eight minutes before he was pronounced dead. It's just ghastly to see.

Susan Hayward was just marvelous in the role. She had such sympathy and empathy for that character. Not because of the criminal thing, but because Susan's marriage at that time was very rocky and there was a lot of press. Barbara Graham had a lot of problems with the press in her trial. So I think right from the beginning, Susan had a lot of empathy, a lot of feeling for Barbara, particularly her problems with the press.

# West Side Story (1961)

*Natalie Wood; Richard Beymer; Russ Tamblyn; Rita Moreno; George Chakiris; Simon Oakland; Ned Glass; William Bramley; Tucker Smith; Tony Mordente; David Winters; Eliot Feld; Bert Michaels; David Bean; Robert Banas.*

I originally accepted the job as both the director and producer on *West Side Story*. Then I was approached by Harold Mirisch, whose company was presenting the film for United Artists. He said, "Hey, what would you think about having a co-director?" I said, "No way. That can't be. It's silly." He said, "Well, Jerome Robbins, who directed and choreographed the New York show as well as the national company, feels that unless he can be more involved in the picture he doesn't want to come out and do the choreography." I said, "I don't think that makes any sense. Why don't you let him direct it?" He said, "No, no, this is a big picture and he's never done a film." I said, "Well, that doesn't make any sense to me. Forget it."

I went home that night and almost literally took my director's hat off and put on my producer's hat and said to myself, "What's the best thing for this picture?" And I decided that if there were any way to work with Robbins that would be best. I knew that I could always get some of his dance assistants to come out and reproduce what was done on the stage, but I knew that Jerry, being as brilliant as he was, would find the adaptation and changes needed to put it on the screen. So I went back and said, "Okay, I'll consider pursuing this."

This started a series of talks between Jerry and myself. We decided that he would be in charge of the musical numbers, both to direct and edit. I would be there to help him on those, and I would direct the book and he would be there to give me his suggestions, and that's the way we did the film.

The difference in the two mediums—film and stage—is that on the stage you're not quite into reality. Once you are removed from reality people can go from dialogue into song without you feeling a little twinge of embarrassment. Film is a very real medium and it doesn't take kindly to stylization or ultra-theatrical things or poetic things.

Our challenge was how to take the highly stylized dancing and the highly theatrical moments, like the meeting of the boy and the girl in the gym, and the poetic moments, like the fire escape number, and translate those into the realism of the screen in a way that would be acceptable. And that's what we spent months and months working out before we started shooting.

I insisted that we had to open the picture in New York on the streets. There was no way I could try to do that in Hollywood. I had a battle with the studio because that was going to cost a lot more money, but I said that's the only way we could do it.

I didn't want to do that same old shot of New York from across the river. I had to deliver it in a fashion that would help people accept the dancing in the streets very early in the film. So I got to wondering what it would look like straight down from a helicopter. We rented one of those old New York Airways choppers and went and looked at that marvelous city from the sky. The shot gives you a look at a real New York, but in an abstract way.

I felt that helped put the audience in a frame of mind to accept these kids dancing on the real streets just a few minutes later.

We had shot about 60 percent of the film and the front office got very concerned that we were getting farther and farther behind schedule and over budget, and they decided that the co-direction was the problem. I tried to convince them that I didn't think that was the case, but they prevailed and they said, "Jerry's got to go." It was a very touchy and difficult time. Fortunately for me, Jerry had rehearsed all the other dance numbers and his rehearsal people stayed on the film to help me do those numbers. So I was able to photograph what he had rehearsed and get it on the screen successfully. Later, when I got the picture cut, I asked Jerry to come out and look at it with us, and he did and he seemed to like it very much. He had some very cogent suggestions about how things might be improved here and there. I believe that, despite the problems, Jerry was very happy with the film. I received two Academy Awards, one for co-directing—and Jerry got one for his co-directing—and one for producing the best picture of the year.

## Two for the Seesaw (1962)
*Robert Mitchum; Shirley MacLaine; Edmon Ryan;*
*Elisabeth Fraser; Eddie Firestone; Billy Gray.*

That's about the only incidence of any major picture I did where the cast was already set. But I loved the script. Isabelle Leonard wrote it and it was a lovely, lovely script. Of course, a marvelous play had been done first. I went with the cast that had been already selected. I liked Shirley MacLaine particularly. I thought Bob Mitchum was a little off somehow. I always felt he was a little more at home in a kind of rougher role. But I was very pleased with the job he turned in. I thought it was very believable, very real, and people reacted well to it.

One of the biggest difficulties I had on that picture was working with Shirley and Bob. Not in the scenes but in getting them into the scenes. They just liked each other very much and they sparked each other, and they kidded each other, and they told jokes and ribbed each other, and were constantly telling jokes. The two of them were truly funny. They were breaking us all up, the crew as well as myself. Sometimes it would take as much as ten minutes to calm them down and get them onto the set to do a scene.

Finally one day I got the crew back from lunch and I lectured them. I said, "Now listen gang, we've got to stop being such a good audience for these two or we'll never get this picture done. I'm as guilty as you are, so let's not be such a good audience for them. Let's settle down so I can get this picture done." But I loved working with both of them.

## Cast Right and Your Job Will be Easier

Let me say that I think any director with any honesty will admit that 80 percent of his or her job in getting a performance from an actor is having the right actor in the right part. You have to have a meeting of minds about how you see the character in relation to the script and the other characters, so that you know that you and the actor are in accord with the interpretation that's going to come out. Then it's simply a matter of day-to-day working and rehearsing and trying things and experimenting to improve and extend and expand as much as you can on that basic performance.

I don't like cold readings. I rarely ever have them, even in small parts. I like to have the actor take the scene away, whatever it is, and work on it for a little while, and then come back and read it for me. I don't think you really can judge what an actor can do in a cold reading. Occasionally you're in a tight spot and in a hurry and something comes up and you have to have a cold reading, but I don't think they're really helpful to either the director or the actor.

## The Value of Preproduction

Preproduction—I can never get enough of it. You plan everything possible. You need to have everything set and ready—your sets and, of course, the casting. But all the details—the props, the wardrobe, everything that goes into making a picture—you want to have all prepared and ready when you start to shoot, because that's the expensive time. That's when everybody's on the payroll, what with the actors' expensive salaries and all. So you want to have everything ready to go and not have any holdups because you failed to prepare yourself. Don't ever skimp on preproduction.

## The Sound of Music (1965)

*Julie Andrews; Christopher Plummer; Eleanor Parker; Richard Haydn; Peggy Wood; Charmian Carr; Heather Menzies; Nicholas Hammond; Duane Chase; Angela Cartwright; Debbie Turner; Kym Karath; Anna Lee; Portia Nelson; Ben Wright.*

When I started to prepare for *Sand Pebbles* I had to go to Taiwan and Hong Kong to look for locations. Early on it became very, very apparent that this film was going to take a long time to put together. We went to Taiwan to shoot because I couldn't go to mainland China. We weren't allowed there because it was under Communist rule. I looked at my schedule said, "Gee, this is going to be a year before I can start really getting this thing underway. I really think I ought to do another picture in between if I can." So I let it be known that I was interested in maybe doing another film before I did *Sand Pebbles.* That's when I was asked if I would be interested in doing *The Sound of Music.* And that's how I got into that.

Before we talk about *The Sound of Music,* there's a story I want to tell about McQueen. When all this was happening we didn't have a cast yet for *Sand Pebbles.* When I first sent a list of people up to the front office for casting ideas for *Sand Pebbles,* I had six or eight people on that list. One of them was Steve McQueen, but he was way down on the list. Twentieth Century Fox thought he was good, but he didn't have a big enough name to carry the picture at that time, so we forgot about him. Time goes on, and I've done *Sound of Music,* and we come back to *Sand Pebbles* and about a year and a half has gone by. In the meantime, Steve had a successful TV series and had starred in *The Great Escape.* So when we started talking casting again he was up at the top of the list.

I had not seen *The Sound of Music,* but I knew about it. Ernie Lehman, who did the screenplay for me on *West Side Story,* had done a first draft script on it, and so it was sent over to me and I read it and loved it and thought it was just marvelous. Then I got a record of the score of the show and heard all of those marvelous songs of Rodgers and Hammerstein and I thought, "Well, this is for me." There wasn't any question in my mind. Willie Wyler had actually been on it for a while, working with Ernie on that first script. But he got into some kind of dispute with the studio about his interpretation of it, and they took him off or he left. So it became free just about that time and that's when I took it on.

I'm always asked about that opening shot. Interestingly enough, I read Ernie's script and he had described this aerial shot in the script. I called him and I said, "I love your script, but we can't do that."

I felt people would say we were swiping from ourselves, copying the opening helicopter shot from *West Side Story.* I thought we'd be accused of plagiarizing ourselves. He said, "Okay, fine. I can't think of a better opening. If you can find a better opening, fine." I couldn't find a better opening, so that's what I shot.

From the beginning we always thought about Julie Andrews as being ideal for our show, but there was some question about whether she was photogenic because she hadn't been seen on the screen before. She had already shot *Mary Poppins* at Disney but it hadn't been released yet, so we got permission from the producer to go over there and to see some of their film. The minute she came on the screen there was no question in our minds that we had found our lady. She was marvelous in it. She's a tremendous talent, has great range, but she seemed to be most popular, unfortunately for her career, with things like *Mary Poppins* and *The Sound of Music*. She is a marvelous lady, a great talent, marvelous to work with, a perfectionist, couldn't work too hard to get it better and better and better, and yet with a great sense of humor and a lot of fun.

I always felt that the part of the captain was kind of dull, kind of stock. I had seen Chris Plummer on the stage in New York a couple of times and was impressed with his qualities and abilities as an actor. I wanted Chris because I knew he'd add a kind of edge and color and a bit of darkness to the role. I had to fly to London to convince him to do it because he didn't think it was his kind of thing. He finally accepted and I think he was a big, big asset to the film.

Some of the critics didn't like the picture all that well. You learn to survive these things, you know, but they still hurt. Even Bosley Crowther of *The New York Times* came down on us, saying it was too sweet, too sticky. I think that we did cut down considerably on what I thought was excessive saccharin sweetness from the stage show. But there was a story to tell, a certain kind of story, and that was what we had to do. With all due respect to some critics, we did get fine reviews in other places. The *LA Times* here gave us a smashing review and I think the most telling fact is that it's lasted now over twenty-five years. Everyplace I go in the world, people are delighted to hear that I did *The Sound of Music*. It was the highest grossing picture of all time. Now, of course, it's way down the list since the big blockbusters have come along.

# The Sand Pebbles (1966)

*Steve McQueen; Richard Attenborough; Richard Crenna; Candice Bergen; Emmanuelle Arsan; Mako; Larry Gates; Charles Robinson; Simon Oakland; Ford Rainey; Joe Turkel; Gavin MacLeod; Joe Di Reda; Richard Loo; Barney Phillips.*

Logistically, *The Sand Pebbles* was a difficult film to do. I had trouble getting into Taiwan to shoot, and then, when we finally did, we had all kinds of weather problems. It was stormy, rainy weather, winds changing from one way to another. I had this ship and I'd shoot part of a sequence and have the smoke coming out of the stacks going one way, and we'd go down the next day to finish the sequence and the wind's blowing the other way, which meant I had to change my day's work right away. We used to go out on our locations with six different shooting calls. If the weather was sunny and good, we'd do these scenes. If it were overcast, we'd do these scenes. If it were a little misty, we'd do these scenes. If the wind were blowing right to left, we'd do these scenes and if it were blowing the other way, we'd do these scenes. We had to keep adjusting all the time.

I love the story and the way it caught the period and the fascinating characters, and I also liked what it had to say. I felt maybe it was time that we were all reminded, the American public particularly, of the phrase "Yankee Go Home" that people thought started in World War II. Of course, we were not the only ones in China that ran the gunboats. The French, the English, and the Germans did, too. All the major powers really kind of ran China in those days until the revolution. In the film, the character that Steve played goes through a change. He goes from the man who called the Chinese soapheads to a man who was very much in sympathy with them. In the end he wanted to stay there in China.

This was Candice Bergen's second picture. She had done a picture called *The Group* and I think she was only about nineteen when she did that. She was only twenty, twenty-one, when she did my film. We had a marvelous time working together. I'm so pleased at the great success she enjoyed in films after that, and of course with her renowned TV show *Murphy Brown*.

I mentioned earlier that when you want to do something with the military you have to go to the government with your script. Fortunately we didn't need anything on this picture from the Defense Department because this was a period piece; they couldn't provide the gunboat, they couldn't provide uniforms or anything. They didn't have anything that we wanted. I'm sure if we had had to go to them for anything they would have probably disapproved of the script. When we got to Taiwan to begin shooting I did go to see our ambassador there and tell him of our project and what it was about, just so he would be aware of what we were doing there. But there were no consequences.

There is one other important element about the film that I really want to mention and that is McQueen himself. Working with Steve was a rare experience. I had met him before getting started on the film. I never worked with an actor, a star, that knew as well what worked on the screen for himself. Steve knew what worked for Steve McQueen on that screen. For instance, he might be in a rehearsal and he would say, "I think maybe I can get that over without that line and with just a reaction." Every so often something would come along where McQueen's knowledge of himself really helped the scene and paid off.

## Why He Decided to Produce His Own Films

I've been asked many times why at a certain point in my career I became a producer as well as a director. I did that primarily to bring much more continuity to my pictures. When I was directing for the major studios, when I was under contract, I would make a picture, then go on to another picture. The next thing I would hear about my last picture was when I would read an ad in the paper that it would be playing at the Pantages Theater the next day or the next week. I had no say about how it was released or distributed or anything to do with the advertising or how it was sold. So I decided that I'd like to be a producer as well. I could be in at the very beginning, in the writing stage, developing the script and following the film all the way through production. When I finished postproduction I was able to follow through on how it was distributed and how it was sold and what the advertising would be like. Now, I couldn't dictate that and I didn't want to. But I wanted to be consulted about it. I wanted to have some voice in what happened to my pictures after I made them. Becoming my own producer allowed me to do that.

## Do It By Suggestion

When I read the book *The Haunting of Hill House,* it was full of suspense. I wanted to do this film very badly. I've had many people tell me that I made the scariest picture they had ever seen, but they say, "You didn't show anything—how'd you do it?" It's all by suggestion and little bits and pieces of things that might have something behind them, that might be scary, and it does work on people. It works very effectively on them.

I think this obviously stems from my training with producer Val Lewton. I just think it's more fun, somehow, to accomplish the sense of concern, fear, and terror in an audience without having to hit them in the face with it. You don't have to use all those optical devices and special effects and make up things that we can do. Do it by suggestion. Leave something to the imagination.

I much prefer the more subtle approach, which I think is more terrifying than all the gore you see now. The greatest fear that people have is the fear of the unknown, so I much prefer that to horror films that are done with all the special effects and the monsters and the gore. I think that's too easy.

# Star (1968)

*Julie Andrews; Richard Crenna; Michael Craig; Daniel Massey; Robert Reed;*
*Bruce Forsyth; Beryl Reid; John Collin; Alan Oppenheimer; Richard Karlan;*
*Lynley Laurence; Garrett Lewis; Elizabeth St. Clair; Jenny Agutter; Anthony Eisley.*

Well, when Twentieth Century Fox signed Julie Andrews for *The Sound of Music*, they signed her for two pictures. After working with her on *The Sound of Music*, I very much wanted to do another film with her. We were looking around for something and my story editor, Max Lamb, came in one day and suggested she would be a great Gertrude Lawrence, who was, of course, a very famous stage, film, and musical star. And that's how it all started, as a vehicle to star Julie for the second commitment to Fox.

We were so surprised when it did not do all that well, because when we previewed it in the Midwest we received as good a preview as we had on *The Sound of Music*. It seemed like we had another solid hit. We opened in London at the Dominion Theater where *The Sound of Music* had played for four years. I remember the London paper saying, "There goes the Dominion Theater again to Julie Andrews for another four years." But, boy, it just didn't work. I think part of it was that it was out of its time.

I've seen the picture within the last year and a half, one time in New York at a movie house and once in San Jose with an audience. The audience absolutely adored it and ate it up. They just loved every moment of it. I think it's got some marvelous work in it. Julie's performance is some of the best work she's done, just some extraordinary and stylish musical numbers that Michael Kidd choreographed. I think it's too fine a picture to be just languishing on a shelf in a vault someplace so I'm trying to get Twentieth Century Fox at least to put it out on cassette and video disc so it can be seen by people. It's too good to be sitting there.

# The Andromeda Strain (1971)

*Arthur Hill; David Wayne; James Olson; Kate Reid; Paula Kelly;*
*George Mitchell; Ramon Bieri; Kermit Murdock; Richard O'Brien; Eric Christmas;*
*Peter Hobbs; Mark Jenkins; Peter Helm; Joe Di Reda; Carl Reindel.*

I got a call from Universal. They had optioned a new book and if I was interested they would go ahead and purchase it for me. It turned out to be

Michael Crichton's *The Andromeda Strain.* That fit right into what I was looking for. It was today, it was modern, although it was classified as science fiction. It really was more science fact than fiction. I was delighted because that brought me into today's world of technology.

I was fascinated by the whole story and the explanation of what might have come back in this capsule that had been shot up into space. It was, in a sense, an indictment of biological warfare, and it was that underlying note that appealed to me very much. So it was going to be an interesting and fascinating and very intense and suspenseful science-fiction film. But the film was also going to have something important to say about the area of biological warfare and chemical warfare and nuclear warfare.

# The Hindenburg (1975)

*George C. Scott; Anne Bancroft; William Atherton;*
*Roy Thinnes; Gig Young; Burgess Meredith; Charles Durning;*
*Richard A. Dysart; Robert Clary; Rene Auberjonois; Peter Donat;*
*Alan Oppenheimer; Katherine Helmond; Joanna Cook Moore; Stephen Elliott.*

I was still at Universal, and they had a project called *The Hindenburg* that was not going along very well in the scripting stage. They said, "It's not going very well, so would you be interested in it?" Anybody that was alive back then remembers that terrible, terrible crash. I was caught up by the whole mystery of what that might have been about, what it cost in human lives, and, very frankly, about the romance of flying on one of those big dirigibles—the idea of getting on one of those big airships and taking two and a half days to fly from New Jersey to Frankfurt. They had those big lounges and if it were a nice day they'd have the windows open. They might be flying at one thousand feet above the ground and hear a train whistle down below. They could hear dogs bark, see buoys on the ocean, and they served marvelous food and had lovely small but high-quality accommodations, and I just got caught up with the romance of that.

My biggest problem was could I make it work, could we make the blimp real. As a matter of fact, before I accepted the assignment I had a meeting with Al Whitlock, who was a matte painting specialist at Universal. I said, "Al, can we do this? Can we show that giant aircraft outside the hangar in Frankfurt? Can we get her up in the air? Can we fly it across the ocean? Can we take it around by New York? Can we bring it into its hangar in New Jersey? Can we do that successfully?" And he said, "Yeah," and he started to talk about how we could do it with a miniature and this, that, and the other. Then I went back and said I would do it, but I wanted to clear it with him.

Some of the final explosion looked like it was dangerous to the actors, but it really wasn't. We had only one where it might have been chancy, and that was when the ship burned. We had men up in the nose cone and we had that covered with about thirteen cameras because it was one of those fire scenes that if we hadn't gotten in one take, there would be no second take. Stuntmen acted as crewmembers and they were well protected with the clothes that they had on. We spent a whole day just planning, timing, and doing dry runs without setting anything off to be sure that the timing was going to be right before we ever shot it.

It's really the director's responsibility for whatever happens in a scene, I think. You have to rehearse an action scene that has any kind of danger to it very carefully. You have to rehearse it and rehearse it, time and time and time again, to be sure that everybody on the set understands exactly how it's going to go. In the end, the director has to take responsibility for that.

Anyway, on *The Hindenburg* nobody got hurt. We lost a couple of cameras but we got great footage.

# Star Trek, The Motion Picture (1979)

*William Shatner; Leonard Nimoy; DeForest Kelley; James Doohan; George Takei; Majel Barrett; Walter Koenig; Nichelle Nichols; Persis Khambatta; Stephen Collins; Grace Lee Whitney; Mark Lenard; Billy Van Zandt; Roger Aaron Brown; Gary Faga.*

After I finished *Audrey Rose* with Anthony Hopkins and Marsha Mason, I got a call from Michael Eisner at Paramount asking if I would be interested in doing a feature of *Star Trek*. I had never gotten caught up in the TV series so I didn't know too much about it, but I knew of its popularity. But what intrigued me about it was that I had done two science-fiction films before: *The Day the Earth Stood Still* and *Andromeda Strain*. They were both earthbound, and I thought maybe it was time I got up in the heavens, and that's what hooked me into going into it.

I went in and talked to them and said, "Frankly, I'll have to see some of the episodes because I'm not familiar with the series." They got ten or twelve of what they considered to be some of their best episodes and I ran them over a period of a couple of weeks. I thought five or six were excellent, a couple okay, and a couple I thought were pretty bad. But I was hooked by the idea of doing something up in the skies and I took it on.

It was not one of my happiest experiences. Working with Bill Shatner and Leonard Nimoy and all the other cast members was fine. We got along wonderfully well. They were a great gang. But we were rewriting the script all the way through. When we finally started to shoot, for contractual reasons we only had the first draft. We were rewriting until the very last day of shooting and that's never a very successful way of doing it. We kept rewriting and there were so many tugs and pulls between Gene Roddenberry, the producer, and my own views of it. And the actors had strong views about certain aspects of the thing so it was almost kind of a pulling back and forth in a tug to finally get this thing done. That is just not a good way to make a movie.

## His Parting Words

Since I've started directing I've always been looking for that perfect story and that perfect script. If I am to be remembered at all as a director I would hope it is for my taste in films. There might be some critics who won't agree with that. But I've tried to be somewhat choosy in what I've done and tried not to do anything that one would call really out-and-out distasteful or objectionable.

# Director Filmography

*The Magnificent Ambersons* (1942, uncredited)
*Curse of the Cat People* (1944)
*Mademoiselle Fifi* (1944)
*The Body Snatcher* (1945)
*A Game of Death* (1945)
*Criminal Court* (1946)
*Born to Kill* (1947)
*Mystery in Mexico* (1948)
*Blood on the Moon* (1948)
*The Set-Up* (1949)
*Two Flags West* (1950)
*Three Secrets* (1950)
*The House on Telegraph Hill* (1951)

*The Day the Earth Stood Still* (1951)
*Something for the Birds* (1952)
*The Captive City* (1952)
*So Big* (1953)
*Destination Gobi* (1953)
*The Desert Rats* (1953)
*Executive Suite* (1954)
*Tribute to a Bad Man* (1956)
*Somebody Up There Likes Me* (1956)
*Helen of Troy* (1956)
*Until They Sail* (1957)
*This Could Be the Night* (1957)
*I Want to Live!* (1958)
*Run Silent, Run Deep* (1958)
*Odds Against Tomorrow* (1959)
*West Side Story* (1961)
*Two for the Seesaw* (1962)
*The Haunting* (1963)
*The Sound of Music* (1965)
*The Sand Pebbles* (1966)
*Star!* (1968)
*The Andromeda Strain* (1971)
*Two People* (1973)
*The Hindenburg* (1975)
*Audrey Rose* (1977)
*Star Trek: The Motion Picture* (1979)
*Rooftops* (1989)

# Awards

**Academy Awards, USA**
Irving G. Thalberg Memorial Award, 1967
*The Sand Pebbles,* Best Picture, 1967 (nominated)
*The Sound of Music,* Best Director, 1966

*The Sound of Music,* Best Picture, 1966
*West Side Story,* Best Director (with Jerome Robbins), 1962
*West Side Story,* Best Picture, 1962
*I Want to Live!,* Best Director (nominated), 1959
*Citizen Kane,* Best Film Editing (nominated), 1942

**American Cinema Editors, USA**
Filmmaker of the Year Award, 1967

**American Film Institute**
Life Achievement Award, 1998

**American Society of Cinematographers, USA**
Board of Governors Award, 1997

**Broadcast Film Critics Association Awards**
Lifetime Achievement Award, 1998

**Directors Guild of America**
D.W. Griffith Award, 1988
DGA Award, Outstanding Directorial Achievement in a Motion Picture
    for *The Sound of Music,* 1966
DGA Award, Outstanding Directorial Achievement in a Motion Picture
    for *West Side Story* (with Jerome Robbins), 1962

**Golden Globes, USA**
*The Sand Pebbles,* Best Motion Picture Director (nominated), 1966
*The Sound of Music,* Best Motion Picture Director (nominated), 1965

**Istanbul International Film Festival**
Lifetime Achievement Award, 1996

**Temecula Valley International Film Festival**
Lifetime Achievement Award, 1996

# The Films of Ron Howard

Ron Howard was born March 1, 1954, in Duncan, Oklahoma, to an acting family. At the age of eighteen months he appeared in his first film, although his first real part was at the age of four. Soon a regular on *Playhouse 90*, he was eventually cast as Opie on *The Andy Griffith Show* and later moved from being a child in Mayberry to playing America's teenager as Richie Cunningham in *Happy Days*. Ron's parents wanted his life to be as normal as possible—he attended public schools and at age fifteen took nine months off to play a basketball season. The transition from child actor to adult actor is always difficult, but for Ron the real transition was from child actor to adult director.

He had some roles as an adult actor, such as in the 1976 film *The Shootist*, starring John Wayne, for which he received a Golden Globe nomination. But his dream, and certainly his focus from that point on, was directing. He began shooting Super-8 films as a young teenager and after high school spent two years in a film program at the University of Southern California. Eventually he left USC, thinking that he could learn more from practical experience. He struck a deal with Roger Corman to finance a couple of films that Ron wrote, directed, and starred in. Both films were successful.

Married since 1975 to his high school sweetheart, Cheryl, Ron is living his dream of telling stories as one of Hollywood's top directors.

> *He's just unflappable. I mean he honestly is. I've seen Ron get angry at something not being done right, but never to the point that it stops work, you know. He doesn't throw temper tantrums. Never that I've seen. He doesn't scream at anybody, he doesn't yell at anybody. It all runs pretty well because he's done his homework. And at those times when intangible things come up he doesn't let it faze him.*
>
> Tom Hanks—Actor

# The Conversation

I definitely grew up in the business. My father, Rance Howard, is still working. He's a character actor. My mother, Jean, who is now acting, gave up the business when I was born. She and my father had met at the University of Oklahoma. They were introduced by Dennis Weaver in the drama department. They wound up meeting again in New York. Very romantic.

One of the most precious things that I have is an old photo of the two of them. They were on a bus tour doing productions of *Snow White* and *Cinderella*. They only had four dwarves so my dad would occasionally get on his knees and put a beard on and be another dwarf. They all played a bunch of parts. They fell in love on that trip and got married. They stripped all the sequins off of Cinderella's dress and that's the dress that my mom used for her wedding. It's kind of a romantic, show business story.

I have no memory whatsoever of my first movie role, *Frontier Woman*, although I remember seeing the film. I was about eighteen months old. My dad was actually in the Air Force at the time, and I think he sort of had to go AWOL or he managed to disappear for a couple of weeks so he could play the bad guy in this grade C Western called *Frontier Woman*. I do remember seeing it and seeing my father getting shot and dying on screen. And it was one of those things where he's shot with an arrow or something, but then miraculously falls forward instead of being hurled backward, breaking the banister and tumbling down. Really classic cornball Western serial stuff. Apparently at one point they needed an infant to cry.

I don't remember any of this, but the story goes that I was on the set with my mom. They gave me a little Indian tomahawk with a feather on it to play with and apparently I was pretty happy with that. They rolled the cameras and yanked the tomahawk away from me and I started crying. Then they cut and gave me the tomahawk back. And that was my debut.

Later I did act in this film called *The Journey* starring Yul Brenner and Deborah Kerr. I really do remember a lot of working on that film. I had just turned four but I remember a lot about it. My dad had played a part in it as well and that was one of the reasons my parents agreed to let me be in it. They had some reservations about having a child actor in the family. My brother Clint was not born yet. The idea was that we would all get a chance to go to Europe together and have our way paid and so we did it.

I remember it was a film about the Hungarian revolution and I thought it was a blast. There were all these Soviet tanks in the film. I was climbing all over them and hanging around with these bigger-than-life characters including Yul Brenner, who I remember as being fun and buoyant and fascinating. So it was a very positive experience for me.

When the film was finished we moved back to New York. My father had toured with Henry Fonda in *Mr. Roberts*, but his real bread-and-butter work was in live TV, and all of that was moving out of New York. This was in 1958, and the television Western and detective shows were being produced in Hollywood. So that's where we moved. Like the Oakies a couple of decades before us, we loaded up the car. We kind of rumbled across the United States, stopping in the Midwest and visiting the farm where my dad grew up, and also the small town where Mom grew up. We went on across the Painted Desert, past the Petrified Forest, and to Hollywood, California, where we got an apartment.

I started working because I had some experience and my dad got me an agent. I think the first job that I got was the *Red Skelton Show*. I was a kid in a "Freddy the Freeloader" sketch. By this time I was four and a half years old. I also did three *Playhouse 90*s that year. I did a couple more of the Red Skelton sketches. I also started doing shows like *The Twilight Zone*, *Dobie Gillis*, and *Dennis the Menace*.

My parents were extremely vigilant in terms of the supervision that they provided. There were a couple of things that they were concerned about. One of them was that kids working in an adult environment were sort of doted on and played with but then were expected to turn right around on a dime and be able to perform because that's the way it is on a set. What my dad would observe watching other kids working is that the crew would wind them up and goof around with them, and then they'd start working and the kid would keep goofing around. Then everybody would be shaking his or her head saying, "Brad can't concentrate." My dad thought this was really unfair. So early on he tried to remind everybody that I was a kid and I needed to be treated like a kid. Dad was protective in that way—in a really nice and constructive way.

When I got on *The Andy Griffith Show*, my father went to Andy and said he noticed that they were writing the character of Opie the way they always write kids in situation comedies. They were going for a joke, which is great, but all the jokes seem to be at the father's expense. It's always like the kid is the smartest one in the family and he's sort of a little wise guy. He told Andy that was funny, but wouldn't it be interesting if Andy really was the dad, really was the grown-up, and if Opie really was the son, and was respectful, and couldn't they find humor in a more everyday, regular kind of relationship. Andy loved this idea and it became one of the tenets of the show, and he's often given my dad credit for making that suggestion.

I think it was significant because it also gave me as an actor the chance to really work from a very honest and organic place. The great thing about the Opie character, for a young actor trying to learn how to be in the business, was that the comedy did come out of character and it was really about an honest feeling and a legitimate sort of reaction. So I was able to draw from myself and through my dad learn the fundamentals of method acting, understanding how you connect with the logic of the scene, but at the same time I had to learn about jokes. Early on, very early on, I remember being allowed to contribute, to participate. That's the way the environment was on *The Andy Griffith Show*. It was amazing. Imagine being a little kid and being able to sit in on these sessions where everybody would read the script. Basically I learned to read by reading scripts. We'd do these readings and then all the actors were allowed to talk about the scenes and their characters, and I was included in that.

Once in a while, even at six, seven years old, I could say, "I don't think a kid would say it that way." Usually they wouldn't take my ideas. As a matter of fact, I remember the first moment that they accepted one of my ideas. During a rehearsal I was running in through the door from the courthouse. I stop and I'm supposed to say something. In rehearsal I raised my hand and said to Bob Sweeney, the director, "You know, I'm not sure a kid my age would say it that way." "Well, how would he say it?" Bob asked. I changed it around a little bit and he said, "Great, say it that way." I remember sort of standing there just beaming. And Andy said, "Well, what are you waiting for?" I said, "That's the first suggestion of mine that you ever took." And I remember Andy saying, "Well, that was the first suggestion that was any damn good. Now let's go back and do the scene." Early on I realized just how amazing and fortunate it was for me to be around that and to be able to be part of it.

The whole world remembers me, at least in America, as Opie. In Europe people tend to be more aware of *Happy Days*. I hosted *Saturday Night Live* about fourteen years ago and in a sketch Eddie Murphy dubbed me Opie

Cunningham. I get a lot of that, too. But I don't have any regrets. If I felt that my history on *The Andy Griffith Show* or *Happy Days* was somehow creating limitations for me, then I might have some regrets, but I don't. And look, I owe everything to those characters and to those shows. So it's clearly worked out for the best.

> *Ron Howard on the transition from child star to adolescent actor:*
> *You're fourteen or fifteen, and they can hire an eighteen-year-old and not have the child-labor law restrictions, and so they do. Just at the point when you're feeling confused and vulnerable, you're being rejected.*

*Happy Days* was a more complicated learning experience. At that point I was nineteen and really on my own. My parents might come by and watch an episode being filmed or something like that, but I wasn't dependent upon them the way I had been as a child. *Happy Days* was really a growing up experience for me. I learned so much about so many things. I learned a lot about a different style of comedy from Jerry Paris, a brilliant, great comedy director. And Garry Marshall was just the best boss anyone could ever have. He was and is an extraordinary writer and producer and a great leader. But I also learned about the business and that it was a numbers game. It was about succeeding.

I began *Happy Days* as the lead of the show. As it evolved, Henry Winkler emerged in the Fonzie character and really took over the show in a lot of ways. I understood it intellectually because Henry was doing extraordinary things with the character. But it was also very painful for me. It was painful to see the way the network responded, the way their focus shifted from me, as the lead of the show, to Henry playing Fonzie, this new phenomenon. It was something that I had never experienced before and I had to come to terms with it.

Fortunately, because Henry and I were and remain great friends and the cast was close and Gary Marshall, Tom Miller, and Ed Milkis were great producers, I didn't feel the pressure at work. But I felt it from the network and the studio and the media. It was an important test to just understand that, well, this is the entertainment *business* and it is about getting the best ratings or about getting an audience to show up for a movie or whatever, and you have to be ambitious and aware of these things.

Back when I was working on *The Andy Griffith Show,* there were a couple of things going on in my life. My father had written a play called *Look*

*Down on the Hudson,* and he was staging it and directing it at an Equity-waiver house in Los Angeles. I remember watching him direct the actors, build the sets, and get the costumes together, and I'd watch them rehearsing endlessly and I'd go to performances. It was a very funny show and it was fascinating to see that.

## The Directing Bug Bites

At that same time, Bob Sweeney was directing *The Andy Griffith Show.* He was fantastic because he had been an actor. Everybody loved Bob. He'd been an actor. Later Bob moved on and started producing and directing shows on his own and was replaced by Lee Phillips, who started as an actor and had become a director. So I was sort of beginning to make this connection between acting and directing. There was something about the directing job that just looked great to me.

I'll tell you what it was. The whole environment on the set of *The Andy Griffith Show* was enjoyable. There was just a lot of laughter. But it wasn't just with the actors. It was also the crew. I used to spend a lot of time hanging around with the crew, looking through the camera, turning the wheels, operating the boom mike, making it go in and out. The crew would get a kick out of showing me what they did. So it didn't take me long to realize that the director was the person who got to hang out and play with everybody. And that was the job. That was the gig. So I thought that looked pretty good to me.

From an early age I said I wanted to direct. There's an interview that I did right after appearing in the movie *The Courtship of Eddie's Father* where they asked me what I wanted to do when I grew up. I said I wanted to be an actor, producer, director, and cameraman. So I was really fascinated by the whole thing at an early age.

I made *Deed of Derring-Do* in 8MM for a Kodak teenage filmmakers contest. I didn't have time to make an entire film because I was acting in a TV series with Henry Fonda at that time called *The Smith Family.* But I was writing a lot of short stories and I wanted to enter a film in this contest. They had a category called the one-reeler. The idea was that you had to expose a complete roll of film—that was three minutes and twenty-four seconds. But you couldn't get it developed. You had to mail it directly to the judges and they would develop it and then whatever you had they'd evaluate. Most people chose animation but I chose to do a live-action fantasy.

I used the back lot of the studio where we were filming, a place where they used to do a lot of old Gene Autry Westerns and things like that. I cast my brother, my father, and my then girlfriend, now wife, Cheryl. It was sort of this Twilight Zone thing about a little kid who wanders into a ghost town dressed in contemporary clothes who looks up and sees this desperado and all of a sudden, POW! He's got his own Western garb on. Guns, tin star, the whole thing, and suddenly he's the sheriff.

Then he looks over and sees this doorway and, POW! there's this saloon girl, played by Cheryl. Once he blows away the bad guy he walks over there to claim the saloon girl, and BOOM! she's gone. He looks over and the dead desperado is just a tumbleweed traveling by and then suddenly he's back in his regular clothes.

I timed out everything. As I recall, it was like thirty-seven shots. I storyboarded it, timed each shot, and rehearsed it with everybody. I had brought three cassettes in case we needed to do it again but we got it in the first pass. I mailed it in and I came in second. I'll never forget getting the word that I'd won. I even won a cash prize of about seventy-five bucks. Just before we started shooting, my brother Clint, who's been in a lot of my films since then, was clever and held out for 50 percent of the profits. I remember him saying, "Hey, I'm a professional and I don't know what to tell you, but I didn't realize there was a cash prize here and if you get something you gotta' cut me in." So, under duress, I had to cut him and he got half of the seventy-five bucks.

My goal had always been to try to direct a feature film while I was still in my teens so by the time I was twenty, twenty-one I was really desperate (*laughs*). The reason I laugh so hard is because now I realize just how absurd the whole thing was. But at that time I felt like everybody was giving me these patronizing pats on the head when I would talk about directing. Nobody was taking the idea seriously, even though I was making a lot of films on my own on the weekends and doing a lot of writing.

*Happy Days* had become the number one show and still I wasn't getting any feature offers even though just two years before I had been in *American Graffitti* and a couple of other features. Then I got this script from producer Roger Corman. I knew that Roger was the one person in the industry who had a record of giving first-time filmmakers a shot, like Coppola, Scorsese, Bogdonavich, and Jonathan Demme. Later he did it for Joe Dante, Jim Cameron, and myself. The script he sent me was called *Eat My Dust,* and God, I thought it was just terrible. But all of a sudden a light went on in my head and I thought, the network's not going to let me do a TV movie and no studio will let me do a feature. So I'm going to take this script that my dad and I wrote, and I'm going to see if I can parlay acting in *Eat My Dust* into directing something for Roger Corman. I sort of made that my mission.

I remember my agent at the time wanted to go with me to meet with Roger but I wouldn't let him. I knew that all he cared about was my getting the acting job and me getting as much money as possible. But I wasn't concerned about the money. What I really wanted was a chance to direct. I told Roger I didn't care much for *Eat My Dust* but that I would do it if he would help finance this script that my dad and I had written.

He read the script, he looked at my films, and we had another meeting. At the meeting he said, "Look, the film that you and your father have written is a good project, it's a worthy project, but it's not as commercial as I'd like it to be. It's really just a character slice-of-life and I like to do action films and genre pictures, but this is good writing. If you'll act in *Eat My Dust* I won't guarantee that you'll get to direct, but you and your father can write an outline for a movie and I'll pay you fifteen hundred dollars. And if I like the outline you can write the script and I'll pay you Writers' Guild minimum for that. And if I like the script and I want to make it, I'll let you direct it, provided you're in it. And," he said, "if none of that works," and this was the real hook for me, "I'll give you a chance to direct second unit on another film. You'd direct the car crashes and the fights and things like that." Well, it wasn't great but it was the closest thing I'd ever had to a professional directing opportunity. So I did *Eat My Dust* and it was a hit. On the theater-or-drive-in-near-you circuit it was very successful. And I got the chance to direct *Grand Theft Auto*.

The way that *Grand Theft Auto* evolved was kind of typical of Roger. I would say it was the easiest green light I've ever had for a movie. I kept going in and pitching various stories to Roger, every genre you can imagine. Science fiction, detective noir-ish pieces, comedy—everything. I just pitched my heart out. He'd always say the stories were very entertaining and that he enjoyed it when actors come in and told stories. But he never bought any of those stories.

> I'd gone down to the set and Ron was up on a Chapman crane telling Wilford Brimley what to do and checking to see if Don Ameche was all right. And I said, "My Lord, this kid's a director. That kid's okay. Yeah, he's made his goal. He's gonna' be all right."
>
> Rance Howard—Actor (and Ron's father)

# Grand Theft Auto (1977)

*Ron Howard; Nancy Morgan; Elizabeth Rogers; Barry Cahill;*
*Rance Howard; Paul Linke; Marion Ross; Don Steele; Peter Isacksen;*
*Clint Howard; James Ritz; Hoke Howell; Lew Brown; Ken Lerner; Jack Perkins.*

Finally, after pitching my heart out with about fifteen different ideas, Roger finally said, "Ron, when we were testing titles for *Eat My Dust*, there was another title that came in a very close second. It was *Grand Theft Auto*." He said that if my father and I could concoct a story that we could call *Grand Theft Auto*—a car crash comedy—he'd let us make that picture.

My dad and I kicked the idea around for a while and after we came up with a story line I called Roger and told him the idea over the phone. He okayed it, and within a month we were in preproduction on the movie and it turned out to be a great experience. We started filming the day after my twenty-third birthday, March 2, 1977, and it was a dream come true.

Up until that time I had been talking and talking and talking about directing to just anyone who would listen, just bugging and pestering people, and there I was on the first day of filming and I was failing. Part of what you have to do on that kind of schedule and budget is get your day's work done. By lunchtime I'd only managed to make five or six shots. By big studio feature standards that's okay, but with a Roger Corman film you're expected to make somewhere between twenty and thirty shots a day. I thought, "Oh my God, here I've been shooting my mouth off about this forever and I'm going to get canned at lunchtime on the first day."

Roger turned out to be very supportive and we made it through the day. Gary Graver, the cinematographer, kind of came to my rescue. We made it through that day and by the second or third day I just felt so comfortable with the job. One day I ended up doing eighty-eight setups with car crashes and stuff and we wrapped the film on schedule. At the wrap party I was dancing with my wife Cheryl, who worked as a production assistant as well as the caterer, and I remember leaning in and saying, "My god, I actually enjoyed directing this movie more than I imagined I would." And she said, "I could see it, I could see it." I never really looked back. In my heart from that moment on I was a director and nothing else.

On a return to investment basis I'm sure I'll never equal what we did on *Grand Theft Auto*. It cost us six hundred thousand dollars to make and it grossed fifteen million or so here and then went on to network and cable sales and all that. And it even got decent reviews. I don't quite know how that happened. But it did. It opened a lot of doors for me.

## NBC is His Training Ground

The time when I was making television movies for NBC was invaluable. There was an executive there, a woman named Deanne Barkley, who was one of the first real powerful women in network programming. She believed in the idea of actors directing. She was a big supporter of Michael Landon directing and some others, and she saw *Grand Theft Auto*. She wanted to make entertaining TV movies and allowed me to direct without having to appear in the films. She also introduced me to my partner in Imagine Films, Brian Grazer, who was then a young TV producer.

What was really valuable about the TV movie business was that it fit with my *Happy Days* schedule and gave me a great creative outlet and a lot of discipline because, among other things, I executive-produced these films and I was on the hook for any overages. That was great discipline. And sometimes we would go over budget and I'd go into my own pocket and hope that I could sell the rerun rights and syndication rights and get my money back.

I began to understand the whole thing as a financial undertaking as well as an artistic one. I learned a lot about working within the system. My studio was NBC and they were the people that I had to try to work with and had to sell my ideas to. It was crucial because three years later, when I had a chance to make my first studio feature, I was absolutely terrified. But when it came to actually making the film and being on the set and doing the work I was absolutely comfortable. I was in good shape. I'd been making these movies on a tight schedule and taking a lot of responsibility. I wasn't daunted by the daily process. I was staging the scenes, executing them, getting a day's work done. It was great.

## Night Shift (1982)

*Henry Winkler; Michael Keaton; Shelley Long; Gina Hecht; Pat Corley; Bobby Di Cicco; Nita Talbot; Basil Hoffman; Tim Rossovich; Clint Howard; Joe Spinell; Cheryl Carter; Becky Gonzalez; Corki Corman; Ildiko Jaid.*

Brian Grazer and I were the two youngest guys on the lot with offices. We were proud of ourselves because by God, we had offices. We weren't doing a hell of a lot, but enough to somehow warrant having a little overhead and having a place at the studio. Brian came to me with this idea that he based loosely on a real incident. There had been a couple of guys arrested for running a prostitution ring out of a New York City morgue. He thought it was a hilarious idea. I thought it was a real good comedy idea and, more importantly, not what people would expect from me.

We worked on a script with Lowell Ganza and Babaloo Mandel, who were *Happy Days* veterans. I think that Brian had a real uphill battle getting me approved as the director. It really forced him to hang in there with me. But, somehow, lo and behold, we got it through. I think that Alan Ladd, Jr., who was running the company, called George Lucas and asked George if I could handle it. I think George vouched for me. I've never really gotten confirmation of that but I got a sense of that along the way.

In *Night Shift* I got to direct Henry Winkler. By then we were almost like brothers. So that was wonderful. Shelley Long, extremely talented woman, was in it. And we got to introduce Michael Keaton to the movie world. Michael was explosively funny, but the studio was very terrified. They were unnerved by Michael's performance at first, because they were looking at the dailies and at that time Michael was just this raw talent and the dailies were very erratic. They were sort of all over the place. But I had total confidence in what we were getting because I believed in the script, plus the benefit of Michael's imagination and his improvisational genius.

Sure, the dailies were a little rough, but I knew that within there resided a really good performance and it was just a matter of editing. For a while it even looked like they might stop the movie, try to recast, can the whole thing and fire Michael. But I just kept saying, "Come on, guys, relax." I cut together a couple of scenes and showed them how good Michael could be once he was edited and they backed off and supported him, and the movie wound up being a very successful comedy.

*Night Shift* was fascinating for me on a lot of levels. One was the nudity. We had a lot of nudity in that movie. It was interesting to see that you actually could become rather blasé about beautiful women with no tops on. I'd find myself rushing up to a beautiful girl with not much on at all and giving her important direction without even a glance down. Once I actually had to go up and threaten to fire a girl with no top on because she wasn't doing something that I thought she needed to be doing.

*Night Shift* was great because the material was good and Michael and Henry had such good chemistry between them. On the last day of filming I remember sitting there for a minute with Brian. We weren't formally partners then but we'd become good friends while getting this movie made. We were sitting there with a glass of champagne and just saying, "Well, we got our first studio movie made and this is what it feels like." Every once in a while in our relationship he and I stop and just sort of say let's keep track of this and let's remember this moment. And that was definitely one of the special moments.

# Splash (1984)

*Tom Hanks; Daryl Hannah; Eugene Levy; John Candy; Dody Goodman; Shecky Greene; Richard B. Shull; Bobby Di Cicco; Howard Morris; Tony DiBenedetto; Patrick Cronin; Charles Walker; David Knell; Jeff Doucette; Royce D. Applegate.*

*Splash* really cemented my relationship with Brian Grazer. It also cemented my career as a mainstream Hollywood director, somebody who'd be on one of those lists that the studio executives claim don't exist. *Splash* was a project that Brian had started developing even before *Night Shift* but hadn't been able to get off the ground. We developed the screenplay and it looked like we were going to make the movie. Then all of a sudden, out of nowhere, there was this article in *Variety* about a film called *Mermaid* that Ray Stark was producing and Herbert Ross was directing. It was supposed to star Warren Beatty with Jessica Lange as the mermaid. It rocked the people at the Ladd Company where *Splash* was set to be produced and eventually they said, "we're sorry, we're going to pass. We're not going to make the movie."

At that point, much to Brian's credit, he would not give up. And even when I was kind of getting a little wobbly about it myself he doggedly set up meetings at every single studio. And he kept trying to go to agents and get big name actors to commit, and no one would because everyone was frightened of this other project. Finally our last stop was Disney. Now, this was still the era when Disney was making movies like *Tron* and *Gus*, the one about the field-goal kicking donkey. So they were not considered to be a major player at that point at all. But we went in and pitched the project to them. I said to the executives, "Look, they might be getting ready to make this other movie, but we're younger and hungrier. If there's one thing I can guarantee you, our movie will be out first if that means I have to live in the trailer and edit around the clock. So if you believe in the script don't think you're going to get trumped by the other project because they simply will not go as fast as I will. I've got nothing to lose."

They believed us. They believed in me and committed to the movie. Ray Stark tried to buy the movie off and did everything he could to try to submarine our project but couldn't. We became the first Disney film under the Touchstone banner. And the film was a great success. I talked earlier about moments in our partnership where Brian and I stopped and smelled the roses. Well, one of them was the night that *Splash* opened. We got in a limousine with our wives and drove around visiting all the theaters and there were lines at every single one of them. The day before I had signed to direct *Cocoon* and Brian had Dan Ackroyd and Chevy Chase commit to make *Spies Like Us* for Warner Bros. So we really felt like we had arrived. It was another great night.

The casting of *Splash* was interesting. Daryl Hannah was somebody that Brian wanted to cast from the beginning. She'd been in *Blade Runner* and she was very interesting and effective in that film. Tom Hanks was cast first. He had not really done a feature yet—I think he had a small part in one—but he had been in the TV series *Bosom Buddies* for a couple years, and he had done a great guest shot on *Happy Days* after I had left.

My assistant then and now, Louisa Velis, has a great casting eye and kept saying, "This guy, Tom Hanks, take a look at him. He's just great. He's funny. He's charming. You've got to meet him." And so finally we did bring him in and were really thinking of him for the role of the brother. We had sort of hoped to get John Travolta or Michael Keaton to play the part that Hanks finally played. By the way, both Travolta and Keaton turned it down. Then we went through a whole list of people before bringing Tom back for an audition. He was just great. He was fresh from doing the TV series and nothing makes an actor sharper than being the lead in a TV show. He nailed his audition.

Then we had to do a film test with Daryl Hannah and Tom was going to do it with her. I'll never forget this. I told Tom, "You're in, so I'm not going to do coverage on you." I told him he wasn't being tested so he should just relax. I thought that he might be so nervous thinking he was on the hook that it might in some way sort of throw Daryl off. Tom Hanks walks in there and it's like he's already a veteran of ten films. He's so cool. He's so calm. He's fully prepared. He is very giving to Daryl Hannah. From that moment on I just thought he was an extraordinary talent and just an exceptional person. He couldn't have been that relaxed, but whatever he was doing he was able to put himself in a place where he just showed no nerves whatsoever, and their chemistry was great from that moment on. It was a great test for Daryl and she got the job.

The lobster scene in the restaurant is one that I'm particularly proud of. I didn't write it or even conceive of it. But here's why I'm proud of it. Daryl Hannah didn't want to do it. Daryl was, and I think still is, a devout and militant vegetarian. And when she got to the moment of having to actually eat these lobsters she didn't want to do it. I asked the prop guys to make lobsters out of the stuff that you make fortune cookies out of but that didn't work. It didn't look right. It was too hard. You couldn't really bite into it. I didn't know what to do. I wasn't sure we were going to be able to film this scene and it was really an issue of principle to Daryl. I can respect that. I went back to the kitchen, pacing around, and I picked up a real lobster. I felt the shell, then bit into it, and found you could actually break through the shell and it wouldn't hurt you. What could we stuff this with?

We went ahead and started shooting the reaction shots of all the patrons to vamp for time. The prop guy went out and got hearts of palm and baked potato and jammed it into real lobster shells. And I said to Daryl, "This is going to work. Watch this now. Look what's inside. No tricks!" And I bit into one. And I said, "See, it doesn't hurt at all. And I'm not eating any meat because look what's inside."

She wasn't sure she could do it. But there in the kitchen of that restaurant she tentatively bit into one and found that she could do it even though she still found the whole notion very upsetting. But we got several takes of her doing it. She was a real trooper and she cried after the takes because she was crying for the lobsters, you know. But she knew it was a great scene and it was important and she wanted to come through for me. We got just enough on film to be able to build that scene. I'll never forget we pulled that one off somehow.

One of the great and exciting aspects of making *Splash* was all the underwater work. I really learned why filmmaking was going to be an important career for me. I was always afraid of the ocean and afraid of the idea of scuba diving. I didn't even like swimming in the ocean. There was just something about it that disturbed me. But I had to dive in order to direct these underwater scenes. Every once and a while I'd get a little panicky but I'd get through it. By the end of filming I was relaxed and comfortable diving. It was like I'd overcome some neurotic fear and it turned out to be one of the great twenty-day periods of my life.

# Cocoon (1985)

*Don Ameche; Wilford Brimley; Hume Cronyn; Brian Dennehy; Jack Gilford;*
*Steve Guttenberg; Maureen Stapleton; Jessica Tandy; Gwen Verdon; Herta Ware;*
*Tahnee Welch; Barret Oliver; Linda Harrison; Tyrone Power, Jr.; Clint Howard.*

I think getting the *Cocoon* job had everything to do with *Splash*. To this day I'm not sure whether Richard Zanuck had seen *Splash* or not, but somehow I got the offer for *Cocoon* and it was extraordinary. I didn't love the script but I loved the idea.

Cheryl and I had written a spec script that we came very close to selling a couple of times and it was about senior citizens. One of the central concepts or premises of the piece was that you never get out of high school. Your attitudes and the way you behave don't change as you get older. Your body changes, you gain some wisdom maybe, but fundamental emotional reactions remain very much the same.

I asked Cheryl to read *Cocoon* because she has a degree in psychology and had done a lot of work in the field of geriatrics. That's one of the reasons we developed the theory for the script she and I had worked on. We began applying that point of view to this science-fiction story, *Cocoon*, and suddenly it seemed to open up a lot more in terms of the character development. I told my ideas to Richard and Lilly Zanuck and David Brown and they seemed to like them. We immediately went to work on a pretty substantial rewrite and kept reworking it right through the rehearsal period. We put together this great cast and I was very proud of the film. I may be proudest of that movie of anything that I've ever done.

*Cocoon* is not an overtly commercial idea. Yes, it's got this fantasy concept but it was a balance of real human drama, terrific performances, comedy, and science fiction that I felt was very tricky. I felt the script prior to making the movie was complicated and difficult and the direction was kind of hard because of the large cast. As it turned out the lead actors all had very, very different styles of working. Wilford Brimley, for example, is a brilliant improvisational actor, but subscribes to no film technique at all. As a matter of fact he sort of militantly refuses to embrace anything remotely like film technique because he thinks it makes his performance phony and false. But he's an inspired actor, particularly when given a chance to improvise.

Don Ameche, on the other hand, is really old school. Hit the marks, say the lines that have been written, and go home. Trust the director and do the day's work. Hume Cronyn, a writer himself with a stage background, is highly disciplined. Jack Gilford was an old song and dance man. Everybody had a very different approach. Yet it was important to find cohesiveness. As a young director it was a real challenge. I was so thrilled with the way the performances worked and that the film was popular and successful. I got my first Director's Guild nomination for that movie. I was very proud of the way it all worked.

I think I was more intimidated by the fact that I was working for Richard Zanuck and David Brown than by the relationship I had with the actors. Of course, I was respectful of the actors. My last television movie was a film that starred Bette Davis. It was called *Skyward*, and Bette Davis was formidable. She liked the role and the job but resented the hell out of the fact that this director was so young. I really had to win her over. She was difficult. She kept referring to me as Mr. Howard. I remember speaking with her on the phone before I had met her in person. I said, "Miss Davis, please call me Ron." And she said, "No, I'll call you Mr. Howard until I decide whether I like you or not." And then she hung up. I was having sleepless nights worrying about how I was going to handle Bette Davis.

My dad was the one who gave me a good piece of advice. He said, "You know, I've been around a lot of actors, a lot of big stars. All the best actors share one thing. They want to be good and they want to believe the director is there, supporting them and creating an environment where they can be good." So at one point I was directing Bette and she said, "Oh no, no, no, that won't work at all." She said it really loud so the crew could hear. And I said, "Well, Miss Davis, just try it." And she said, "Okay, I'll try it, I'll try it. I'm the director's kid and I'll try anything, but I don't think this is going to work."

She tried it, got half way through the rehearsal, and said, "You're right, you're absolutely right. Very good direction." And she did it the way I had suggested. The scene seemed to work and we went through the day. That evening I remember saying to her, "Well, Miss Davis, you're wrapped for the day. I'll see you tomorrow at nine." And she said, "Okay, Ron, see you tomorrow." She literally patted me on the ass and went off to her limousine and went home. And from then on we got along much better. I think having that experience under my belt, and also having acted with Henry Fonda and John Wayne, I felt pretty comfortable directing the likes of Hume Cronyn, Jessica Tandy, Don Ameche, and the rest of that great, great cast.

I learned an awful lot about two things that were important on *Cocoon*. I was always intimidated by special effects. I understood the power of special effects but I'm not a techy, you know. I started having these meetings with the special effects team from Industrial Light & Magic, George Lucas' company, and I found that I was dead wrong. These people are in fact very creative individuals. All you had to do was talk to them like actors, talk to them like creative collaborators, and they could do extraordinary things. So I learned a great lesson there.

In the editing of *Cocoon* I found I had overshot the film in trying to explore these characters and we wound up with a tight first cut that was over three hours. I remember that the producers were really concerned about that. They liked the film but it was too long. Over a two-week period of time, Daniel Hanley and Mike Hill, the editors that I work with (they won the Academy Award for *Apollo 13*), just kept working on it. We just kept combing through the movie. Because of the ensemble nature of that story some aspects and elements were almost modular and we did a kind of re-shaping of the story to facilitate some. Not only did we shorten it, but also we were able to bring a lot of points into focus.

I learned that you really could make over a film in postproduction. George Lucas is fond of saying that the editing room is where you actually make the movie. Everything else is gathering raw material. I think that the postproduction period on *Cocoon* was where that became very clear to me.

# Gung Ho (1986)

*Michael Keaton; Gedde Watanabe; George Wendt; Mimi Rogers; John Turturro;
Sô Yamamura; Sab Shimono; Rick Overton; Clint Howard; Jihmi Kennedy;
Michelle Johnson; Rodney Kageyama; Rance Howard; Patti Yasutake; Jerry Tondo.*

I developed *Gung Ho* with Lowell Ganz and Babaloo Mandel. It was sort of a tricky script and we never really ironed out all of the problems. There were some fundamental weaknesses in the script but there were great, great funny sequences. In my mind Michael Keaton was always my ace in the hole. The studio wanted Bill Murray or Eddie Murphy. We certainly tried to cast those guys and that would have been fine in my book. But to me the role was always written for Michael Keaton. Once Murray and Murphy had either passed or weren't available I very quickly sold the studio on the idea of doing it with Michael Keaton, who was fresh off the success of *Mr. Mom*.

One of the central locations for *Gung Ho* was an auto manufacturing plant. None of the American companies would allow us to film. The script was about the Japanese coming in and taking over the auto industry in a way, and politically it wasn't going to work. So we went to Buenos Aires and found a plant that was manufacturing cars, only about fifty a week or so. We went down there with a suitcase full of dollars and managed to get the approval to film in this plant. At the last minute we had to pony up more money and it was really a rough go. The studio almost pulled us out of there because they would not make any under-the-table payments whatsoever. Everything had to be completely aboveboard. Some of the people involved in the automobile plant were looking for cash payments. For a while it looked like we would just never find a place to shoot this movie. But we did and it was a neat experience.

Buenos Aires is a great city but we had to make it as American as possible. The American banking system had loaned a lot of money to that country and they were calling in a bunch of these loans and refinancing them. So there was a lot of animosity towards the United States and particularly the U.S. banking system at that point.

One of the things we were warned about was one scene where we wanted to put the American flag up in the background. The folks in Buenos Aires, who were being nothing but cooperative, said, "You know, we don't think you're going to have any problems filming here as an American company, but if you put up that American flag we're a little worried about our workers and how they're going to respond." They advised against it so we didn't do it. We always felt that just under the surface there was some tension there and we were glad to wrap it up and get home.

I felt that the point we were trying to make was that the world was getting smaller and it was inevitable that we learn to work together and to learn to accept the differences in the cultures and find a common ground and build on that. That was really at the center of the story. One of the criticisms that really frustrated me the most was that people felt we weren't authentic in our depiction of the Japanese and the Japanese executives. A few years ago I remember bumping into a guy who does a lot of business in Japan. He said, "You know, whenever I hire a new employee who's going to be dealing with Japanese executives or buyers, the first thing I do is sit them down and make them watch *Gung Ho*." I've had several of those conversations with people over the years and it always makes me feel kind of vindicated.

Certainly I think we made some mistakes along the way. I think it's an uneven movie, but I think it's a movie that certainly had its heart in the right place. And it's very funny. One of my favorite scenes is the drunken scene between Michael Keaton and Danny Wantanabe. A lot of it was improvised but also a lot of it was writers Ganz and Mandel at their funniest. There's nothing better than Ganz and Mandel writing two strong funny characters one-on-one like that.

# Willow (1988)

*Val Kilmer; Joanne Whalley-Kilmer; Warwick Davis; Jean Marsh; Patricia Hayes; Billy Barty; Pat Roach; Gavan O'Herlihy; David Steinberg; Phil Fondacaro; Tony Cox; Robert Gillibrand; Mark Northover; Kevin Pollack; Rick Overton.*

*Willow* represents a one-of-a-kind experience in my career. I think I learned more in making *Willow* than any film I've ever worked on, and in some ways it was a frustrating experience. I really wanted to work with

George Lucas. I had acted for him in *American Graffiti* and we had remained friendly and he had been very supportive of me as a director. He called me one day and said, "Would you like to make a fantasy film?" Cheryl was pregnant with our fourth child and I thought, "My god, my kids are at the perfect age for them to appreciate my making a fantasy film."

George didn't have a story at that point but he told me what he wanted to do. He suggested we just commit to making a movie together and he agreed to finance it himself. I called back a couple of days later and said, "Let's go." Along with Bob Dolman, we devised *Willow* together. It was a great, great creative collaboration. Exciting as hell. But about halfway through the process I realized something. I realized that for the first time I was trying to make someone else's movie. Oh, I was throwing in my two cents and collaborating, but I was really trying to get into George Lucas' head because I trusted his taste, his instincts, his sense of what this movie ought to be better than I trusted my own.

For me that became the exercise. I never really articulated it but it was nerve-wracking. Here George was financing this very expensive movie on his own. I was a neophyte at that point in the genre. *Cocoon* had won the Academy Award for special effects but it was child's play compared to what we were doing in *Willow*. It was a really arduous task for me, but I learned so much working with George and I was fairly happy with the movie when all was said and done. But I told myself when it was over that if I could avoid it I was going to try to stay out of that situation in the future. I was going to make movies and rely upon my point of view. Certainly collaborate with people, but I wasn't going to commit to a film until I thought I understood what there was about it that I could identify with.

## Kids Can Motivate You to Make a Movie

When we went to Buenos Aires to shoot *Gung Ho*, my oldest daughter, Brice, was about four and my twin daughters, Jocelyn and Page, were seven months old. It was about a seventeen- or eighteen-hour flight. We packed up and went, and I counted twenty-five pieces of luggage and twenty-five carry-on items. I had to enlist the aid of all the actors, the crew, anybody who was on the plane to please carry something through because we were only allowed two carry-ons each. It was a nightmare. Brice projectile-vomited on me forty-five minutes into the flight. The twins wouldn't sleep at the same time.

When we landed I was absolutely exhausted. I'm pulling all this luggage off and I thought, "Oh my God, I've become a pack mule. My life has changed. I'm completely transformed. When did this happen? It's parenthood! It's parenthood!" I made some notes in my diary about it. When I got home I was working with Lowell and Babaloo and was sharing the story with them. Before you know it, we started swapping stories and decided that we just had to do a movie about being a parent, about how much it changes you in ways that you simply could never imagine and no one could ever explain to you.

> *I think the thing that's really extraordinary about him is he has this wonderful clarity of vision. He has an ability to go above the piece and look down at it and be very clear about the whole process.*
>
> Mary Steenburgen—Actress

# Parenthood (1989)

Steve Martin; Mary Steenburgen; Dianne Wiest; Jason Robards;
Rick Moranis; Tom Hulce; Martha Plimpton; Keanu Reeves;
Harley Jane Kozak; Dennis Dugan; Joaquin Phoenix; Eileen Ryan;
Helen Shaw; Jasen Fisher; Paul Linke; Rance Howard; Clint Howard.

It's one of those projects that evolved over a period of many, many years and many, many script drafts. At one point we almost gave up on the project. And then in one of the drafts it just crystallized. And from that point on it became one of the best scripts that I'd ever been involved with or ever have been involved with. Actors wanted to be involved with it. It was a joyous experience. You always say that when the experience is sort of too easy. You've got to worry about it because there's probably something wrong with the movie or people aren't trying hard enough. Well, the *Parenthood* experience disproves that theory because it simply was a pleasure. Really, the creative process was a joy, shooting was great, editing just wonderful and when it got reviewed it was a hit. It was just a blessed project. I guess it's nice every once in a while to get one of those.

   *Parenthood* is without a doubt my most personal film to date. But I think that Lowell and Babaloo would say the same thing and so would Brian Grazer, the producer. We all brought a lot of ourselves to the project. In the film a lot of Steve Martin's anxiety comes from the desire to do well, to be a great dad, and not quite knowing how. That's something I certainly could relate to. But a lot of the specifics had been things Lowell and Babaloo had been through.

Steve Martin was the first superstar at the sort of height of his or her career that I'd worked with as a director. Don Ameche had been a superstar, but wasn't when we did *Cocoon*. Bette Davis had been a superstar, but she wasn't when I did the TV movie with her. But here was Steve Martin, just one of the top stars in the industry. I was very, very nervous about what it was going to be like. Steve made it so easy and brought a lot to it. Steve is an inspired writer in his own right so he did nothing but help us at every turn. The entire cast was a pleasure but Steve really set the tone. In his mind it was an ensemble piece and he was part of the ensemble and he really helped create that environment.

## Never Work With Kids Or Animals

I got very frustrated working with the kids in *Parenthood*, particularly in some of the party scenes. We did a bunch of Little League scenes and a bunch of party scenes and I remember calling up Lowell and Bob at one point and saying, "God, I feel like a camp counselor." It was like one big birthday party that would never end. Sort of like being in the Twilight Zone. Working with kid actors is hard. These were good kids and they were trying hard. But it's not the same as working with adults. You can't go up and just talk to a kid actor about something in conceptual terms. And different kids work in different ways. I'm always glad when those scenes are done. But the wonderful thing about working with kids is that when something clicks it can be so truthful and so fascinating.

The one thing that I try to do for child actors is to try to make it a learning experience. I think that all too often directors are under pressure to get results. And I'm not saying I'm perfect at this and that I don't at times just rely on some kind of trick to get that result on film. But if I can I really try to make it an experience where a child is one step closer to actually understanding what the whole storytelling process is about and what acting is all about.

## Backdraft (1991)

*Kurt Russell; William Baldwin; Robert De Niro; Donald Sutherland;*
*Jennifer Jason Leigh; Scott Glenn; Rebecca De Mornay; Jason Gedrick;*
*J.T. Walsh; Anthony Mockus, Sr.; Cedric Young; Juan Ramirez;*
*Kevin Casey; Jack McGee; Mark Wheeler; Clint Howard.*

*Backdraft* was challenging on a lot of levels and very satisfying because of the overall degree of difficulty of making the movie. I became involved in

*Backdraft* because I was fascinated by the idea of trying to deal with fire as a kind of a monster, as a kind of a character. I remember Jennifer Jason Leigh saying, "God, I wish I could play the fire." It was written so vividly in the script and it was one of the great attractions of the movie.

I had always wanted to deal with a brother relationship in a film. I've got a very close relationship with my brother Clint, who's five years younger, and, particularly at that time, the relationship was a pretty complicated one. I tried to take this slick, commercial idea and live up to its entertainment potential, but at the same time infuse it with a kind of relationship story that would somehow hold water. It was a bit of a tap dance. Some would say more successful than others would, but when the film was all done I was proud of it and very happy with the way the fire scenes had worked, also.

## The Fire Got Hot!

The fire scenes in *Backdraft* were a really unique challenge. I didn't know how in the hell we were going to shoot them. In the beginning I thought it would be primarily special effects and also computer-generated imagery, which was just coming into its own. But when we ran tests we found the computer-generated images were not up to snuff. It just didn't look real. Our special effects team began experimenting with real fire. They learned how to control it, how to change its color, how to make it travel, what we could do with various camera speeds. Then they tried filming it upside down burning against the ceiling versus blowing it with mortars, planning where the actors would be in relation to the fire. It was a really interesting process.

We actually started filming before we ran all the tests, without knowing everything that we could do. It was the most frightened I've ever been in a movie because we came so close to having some serious accidents. One time I cued a mortar at the wrong time and almost burned Kurt Russell. Another time some barrels blew up that weren't supposed to and at the wrong time. Thankfully, no one was around. One of the actual firefighters, who was also acting in the movie, had his eyebrows singed off and when he went home his wife flipped out. She said, "You've been ten years in the department and you've never been hurt. Now you damn near get burned on that stupid movie. What's going on?"

We were consciously pushing the envelope but trying desperately not to get anyone hurt. The day we said wrap and we were done with the fire I said, "That's it, there is no sequel." I was relieved but very proud in terms of what we were able to pull off in terms of the physical effects.

## The Characters Come First

Since I began as an actor I'm always interested in what the characters are doing. That's always the most important thing to me. What I tried to do with *Backdraft* and later with *Apollo 13* was to draw the audience into the environment as an experience. One of the ways is to set up characters that are credible and human enough that they help draw you into the story. So instead of one-dimensional movie characters surrounded by a lot of effects I really try to come up with characters that ring true. Then you throw them into this swirl of special effects and then you as an audience member feel, oh my God, it really is happening and this is what it must feel like to be in a fire or in a spacecraft.

I don't quite know when it happened but I was embraced by the A list members of the creative community. Maybe it was after *Cocoon*. It might have been that early. Certainly *Parenthood* helped. But somewhere along the line I began to realize that the world's best actors were willing to work with me.

The day that I was able to cast Robert De Niro for *Backdraft* was a major thrill for me. We were meeting at this restaurant and we talked for a while, then he had to go to the restroom. All of a sudden some people came up and started talking to me about *The Andy Griffith Show* and *Happy Days*. They're tourists or something and I'm trying to be polite and then De Niro comes back. Their backs are to him so they never really see that Robert De Niro is there. But they're kind of going on about Opie and Richie and stuff like when I killed the bird on *The Andy Griffith Show* and how it made them cry. And I'm sitting there thinking, "Oh God, I'm losing it. De Niro's never going to work with Opie." Bob's standing there listening and grinning. I think to myself, "I'm dead in the water. I'm screwed right here." Finally the people leave and De Niro jokes around about it. Then he talked about my having been an actor. Not long after that he worked for Penny Marshall—Laverne—so obviously he's not prejudiced about TV actors.

## Far and Away (1992)

*Tom Cruise; Nicole Kidman; Thomas Gibson; Robert Prosky;*
*Barbara Babcock; Cyril Cusack; Eileen Pollock; Colm Meaney; Douglas Gillison;*
*Michelle Johnson; Wayne Grace; Niall Toibin; Barry McGovern; Gary Lee Davis;*
*Jared Harris; Rance Howard; Clint Howard.*

I had gone to a Chieftains concert. They're an Irish group that tours the world and plays great Irish music. This was in 1980 or 1981. Their music absolutely transported me. They sang one song about a couple who were separated because one of them went to America, then they got back together and they were lost again. Just sort of a sad Irish song. But I found it very moving and very romantic. And at that point I started thinking about the whole immigrant experience and my own family's history. They're not entirely Irish, but there's an Irish element there that I'm well aware of.

I began concocting a story, not based on my family particularly, but the idea of portraying the immigrant experience in a very romantic way. I never intended it to be an epic or David Lean sort of experience. I really thought of it as more of a romantic comedy like It Happened One Night. But I always intended for the climax to be the land race. I had three ancestors who had been in the Oklahoma land race, a couple of great grandfathers and a great uncle, and I thought it would make a great climax to our film. I worked on the script with Bob Dolman, the guy who had written Willow. As a matter of fact, we were working on Far and Away before Willow. We had been nursing this thing along for years and finally got a good script that Universal really went for.

Lo and behold, I was able to cast Tom Cruise and Nicole Kidman in the lead roles. This was before they were married. I knew that they were together but they wound up getting married before we started shooting, so it was kind of a honeymoon project for them. But it was the one project I had dreamed of making for many years and it was a great experience.

It was very important to Nicole to maintain her own identity and Tom was protective of that, and while they shared the same dressing room I was careful to make sure I wasn't directing Nicole through Tom or some kind of idiot thing like that. I have a lot of respect for Nicole and she was really at the top of my list before I knew they were a couple. A lot of people don't believe that. When the movie came out they thought I was just making that up so it wouldn't seem that nepotism played a role in Nicole getting that part. But in fact I had seen her in a couple of Australian films and really could not think of anybody better to play Shannon. So it was really wonderful when the two of them wanted to do the movie.

Cruise is a great professional but with him it's more than just professionalism, it's passion. And it's a kind of film wisdom. Now, Tom is a bright guy but he's not an intellectual, nor is he a genius. He's kind of a blue collar, regular guy. Certain athletes, for example, basketball players, have good court sense. Certain players have a gift for knowing how to win. Well, I think Tom has this kind of a sense about movies. I think that's why he's in so many hits all the time. He puts himself in movies that he would love to see and he also has got great movie taste.

If I have any regret whatsoever about *Far and Away* it's that I feel a little bit robbed. The experience was just damned perfect right up to the moment we released the movie and the critics absolutely nailed us. And it was so disheartening because suddenly this thing that had been kind of a magical two-year filmmaking experience, a realization of a dream, a film that I was very proud of, all of a sudden was hit hard by the critics.

I felt it sort of deflated the momentum of the movie and colored people's perception of the film. I'm constantly getting journalists and other people coming up to me to this day and saying, "Gee, you know I didn't see *Far and Away* when it came out but I saw it on tape or TV, or whatever, six months ago. I really enjoyed that film. It was terrific." Comments like that make me feel good but in a bittersweet way because I really felt a little robbed when it came out.

There was one moment that was really extraordinary in making *Far and Away*. At dawn we wanted to shoot the beginning of the Oklahoma land race. The first time we did it we had no actors in it, just stunt people. My father, who played a part in the film, came up to me and said that he'd like to ride in the shot. And I told him that the stunt guys really don't want any actors in there. He said, "Well, let me just say this, I'm a good rider." So I said, "I know you're a good rider, and the stunt guys know you're a good rider." He said, "Well, let me tell you that I had three relatives who rode in this race. I heard about it all through my childhood and now, almost exactly a hundred years later, my son is directing a movie about it. I'd really appreciate it if you'd let me ride in the scene. But it's up to you." And he turned and started to walk away. And just like in a movie scene I said, "Okay Dad, get your horse and you can be in it." And he was.

At the moment the race began we had thirteen cameras set up and we had about seven hundred people on horses, in wagons, and on foot. I was sitting up on this camera crane and we were getting ready to roll and it was one of those times where I looked down and I saw everybody in absolutely authentic attire and gear and I thought, "Oh my God, isn't this an amazing experience? This is as close as I will ever come to stepping into a time machine and going back because this is what it was like. This is pretty much what it had to have been." I sort of jarred myself out of that, called action, and watched these men and women take off. It was just one of the most awesome spectacles. I almost cried just watching the scene. It was an incredible experience.

# The Paper (1994)

*Michael Keaton; Robert Duvall; Glenn Close; Marisa Tomei; Randy Quaid;*
*Jason Robards; Jason Alexander; Spalding Gray; Catherine O'Hara; Lynne Thigpen;*
*Jack Kehoe; Roma Maffia; Clint Howard; Geoffrey Owens; Amelia Campbell.*

David Koepp is a great screenwriter and his brother Steven is a newspaperman and now one of the editors of *Time* magazine, so the script for *The Paper* was very authentic from the get go. I heard that they were writing the project and asked to read it. I think a week or so after they finished writing it I had committed to making it. I just fell in love with the script. I have always been fascinated by journalism. I was a high school journalist. And I always thought that if I didn't stay in this business I'd either be a coach or a newspaper person. I had no idea how broad the appeal there would be but I knew I was fascinated by it.

The research was a blast. I went and hung around, mostly at the *Daily News* but also the *New York Post*. I had my own little reporter's notebook and was constantly jotting down phrases, terms, and behaviors that looked interesting to me. I just had the greatest time researching that movie. I had the chance to work with Michael Keaton again, too. He's a brilliant guy and we are good friends and every time I work with Michael it's a joy. I have a lot of laughs and I'm excited about directing him in scenes and it's just a good relationship and I hope we get to keep working together.

Glenn Close is one of my favorite actors. Her role was originally written for a man. It was my idea to make the character a woman and Glenn actually accepted the role even before it was rewritten. I told her to just imagine the character with some other name. We didn't change very much dialogue and that was kind of the fun of it for her. Glenn is just a very gutsy, courageous performer and that is her greatest attribute. Certainly she's talented and gifted and she can sing and do comedy. But I think the thing that you must salute about Glenn Close is her guts, her willingness to play extreme characters. She gives everything of herself and holds nothing back and still can be truthful, entertaining and delivers a great performance.

*. . . and then to come up with this crazy KC 135 idea, which was shooting in a zero G airplane, not to mention the fact he had to*

*convince me to go up in this stupid plane. I mean, that was a big
job in itself.*

Kevin Bacon—Actor

# Apollo 13 (1995)

*Tom Hanks; Bill Paxton; Kevin Bacon; Gary Sinise; Ed Harris;
Kathleen Quinlan; Mary Kate Schellhardt; Emily Ann Lloyd;
Miko Hughes; Max Elliott Slade; Jean Speegle Howard; Tracy Reiner;
David Andrews; Michele Little; Chris Ellis; Clint Howard.*

My attitude about *Apollo 13* changed from the time I committed to making
it to when we actually began filming it, and I'll explain why. In the beginning I approached it the same way I approached *Backdraft*—wow, this is a
great cinematic challenge. I can use today's technology to really allow the
audience to feel what it must be like to be in a spacecraft. That'll be interesting. I don't know how we'll do it, but that's a great challenge. It will be
interesting to salute the space program.

But then, as I started doing the research, particularly one day when I actually went to the mission control room and met with a bunch of the mission control room veterans, I started to understand what the experience was
like, not only for the astronauts but also for the people on the ground. I
began to understand that it was life or death to them in a very, very personal way. Not like a kind of a war situation, it was much more like a sort
of a battlefield medical unit. The mission controllers had a huge personal
investment in not losing this patient. I began to understand the whole
movie in much more personal and heroic terms. The astronauts were obviously heroic, but on a broader level I began to understand the sort of in-
tensity of the teamwork and the general heroism of the whole rescue. That's
really what made the space program great. And the reason so much was accomplished was because this group of individuals made it totally personal.
For them it was everything. I understood that it was a rare kind of government undertaking. Not just the Apollo 13 mission, but the whole era. So I
really wanted to try to present that spirit in addition to telling the story of
the Apollo 13 mission.

I remember telling Brian Grazer that I didn't know how we were going
to do the weightlessness. But remember, we didn't know how we were

going to do the fires in *Backdraft* either and we figured that one out, so we would come up with something.

Tom Hanks came on board. He loved the space program. Loved it as a child, knew everything about this story. He knew more about the space program and the story of Apollo 13 when we went into the development process than I did. I had to try to play catch up with him but I never really did catch up. He became a crucial collaborator in making the movie.

I said to Tom, "Hey, we're going to do the weightlessness and it's going to be great." He said, "How are we going to do it?" I said, "I don't know yet." I did my song and dance and he trusted me. I kept thinking about doing it underwater or maybe on wires. I knew about this plane that NASA had that created weightlessness, but I didn't know how it really worked or how practical it was.

I had this meeting with Steven Spielberg. He had no formal involvement with the project but he was a good friend of Tom's and had a keen interest in the space program. He asked me how I was going to do the weightlessness scenes. I told him we were looking at everything. He said he'd either do it underwater or try to get on that NASA plane. I told him I didn't know if we could get on that plane. He said, "You'll figure out how to do it," and that was that.

Walking back from Steven's office I became resolved to face the bureaucracy and see if we could get that plane. I walked back to our offices and said, "We've talked about getting NASA to cooperate with us but we haven't initiated any talks, so let's get serious and find out whether we can do it." I think everybody thought I was nuts. But lo and behold at the end of the day, we did it. We got a test run. We proved to NASA that we weren't a bunch of flakes and that we would honor their rules and that we could be productive. Then they committed to us.

Kevin Bacon did not like the idea of the plane but he was game if I could prove to him that it was safe. He went up on the first trial flight, as did Bill Paxton, Tom Hanks, myself, Todd Hallowell, the executive producer and second unit director, and Gary Sinise, who was playing Ken Mattingly. Gary didn't have to go at all but just wanted to see what it was like. When it was over we knew we could do it. Even Kevin, who still wasn't thrilled about it, thought it was safe.

Then we sunk all this money into sets that would fit inside this aircraft. We had to design special lights that were run on a fiber optic lighting system because everything had to be so compressed. It was a lot of design work that went into making it possible for us to work inside this aircraft.

Again, nobody really believed that we were going to necessarily be able to pull this off physically.

We all went down there again and before I arrived they had run another test flight. This time Tom got sick. He didn't throw up but he was really miserable. Here was Tom Hanks, Mr. Go-Go, leading the charge, loving everything about making this movie, willing to go through any degree of discomfort just to get this right and be authentic. I looked him in the eye and he was unnerved. He was scared. He said, "Man, I don't know if I can do this."

I'm telling you, when that sickness hits you up there you're frozen. In fact, a couple of our crew members who had been cleared physically and done everything they needed to do got so sick they couldn't carry on. It turned out Tom had not taken the air sickness medication on that particular flight as he had for the test flight. I said, "Let's all take the medication and then let's see how we do. Let's take it a flight at a time." I calmed everybody down. Calmed Tom down. We went up and had a great first flight. We got progressively better and better at it. Then the plane went down. It had a crack in one of the turbo props and we lost our window to complete our filming because they had to repair the plane and by the time it was repaired a scientific group was going to be using the aircraft and they had priority.

I then went back to the studio, showed them all this footage, and told them we had to go back once we finished principal photography and do more. I sold them on the idea. Kevin Bacon was less than thrilled to go back because he thought he was over that hump. But when he saw the footage he realized how important it was to the film. We eventually went back with an even more ambitious set of shots and the actors just did some great stuff and it ended up being an experience of a lifetime.

There was no precedent for *Apollo 13* being a commercial movie. *The Right Stuff* was a wonderful film but it did not succeed at the box office at all. I was aware of that. Still, this was a very different kind of story and it innately has good dramatic form. I was depending on that. When people would tell me that everyone knew the outcome, my standard glib comeback was everybody knows the outcome of a Clint Eastwood movie too, but if it's good, it's good. And I thought this was a good story.

I knew for sure that we were okay when I saw a really comprehensive documentary that was produced on the mission. They didn't spend a lot of money on models but they had computer-generated models and they just carefully explained the mission. I watched it, but more importantly my kids watched it with me and they were riveted. We actually became emotional watching it.

I remember going to work the next day and Hanks asked me if I had watched the documentary. I told him I had. He joked and said, "You've got your work cut out for you if you're going to beat that documentary." I kept going back to the documentary at low points when I had doubts. I kept telling myself, if we can just show it. That's what I wrote on my script. Just show it. It's powerful. If we bring it to life in the theater we can be powerful. It is a fascinating story. And you know what? Every account that I ever read, every version that I'd heard repeated to me by somebody who was involved was always riveting, time and time again. I found myself engrossed in the story. So, I trusted that and tried to make the story as suspenseful as it could be.

One of the things that I did with the help of the writers was to try to shape this thing like an adventure story. Let's say you're going down the river. You say, we're coming to the section where the hippos can flip us over and God knows what could happen, the crocs could get us. You lay it out and then you experience the scene of making it by the hippos and the crocs and then you say whew, made it through that, now we've got the waterfall. And then you talk about dealing with the waterfall. I knew this was what we had to do with our film to make people understand. The more I kept learning about the details of the mission, the stuff that hadn't necessarily been reported in the newscasts, the more terrifying the mission became for me and the more extraordinary their success became. I depended on bringing to light those details and shaped it in a way that people could follow each mini-crisis within the greater crisis.

## Ransom (1996)

*Mel Gibson; Rene Russo; Brawley Nolte; Gary Sinise; Delroy Lindo; Lili Taylor; Liev Schreiber; Donnie Wahlberg; Evan Handler; Nancy Ticotin; Michael Gaston; Kevin Neil McCready; Paul Guilfoyle; Allen Bernstein; José Zúñiga.*

I really didn't know that I was doing a remake of an earlier 1956 film until about four weeks or so before we started shooting. I'd always told myself that in principal I wouldn't want to do a remake of anything. But I'm very glad I made *Ransom*. It was an interesting, creative, and rewarding experience in a lot of ways but I probably would have passed on it had I known in the beginning that it was a remake. So now I have learned that there is validity in taking a strong idea and just exploring it further from another perspective. That you're not doing the original any dishonor but instead have an opportunity to make something that feels original and alive for you at this moment.

## To Improvise or Not to Improvise, That Is the Question

I allowed all the actors a lot of input, as I am inclined to do. It doesn't mean that I like shooting a lot of improvisation, although I'm willing to do that at times if it seems right. I always open it up for the actors and I always try to create an environment not unlike the one that we had on *The Andy Griffith Show*. It was an environment where actors were encouraged to participate, to challenge, and at a certain point step back and let the powers that be determine what is actually going to get filmed that day. That's very much what I try to do now. So, yeah, I was certainly trying to take advantage of the creativity of Mel Gibson, Rene Russo, Gary Sinise, and Lili Taylor and writer Richard Price. It's very stimulating when you do that. It's a lot of fun.

*Ransom* wound up being logistically complicated. In the beginning I went into the project thinking it was going to be pretty simple and pretty straightforward. There were a lot of rewrites and yes, the schedule was delayed because of the weather. And we had to rethink our whole production plan when Mel had his appendicitis. But it was never for one moment a project in crisis.

We were doing rewrites but it was never out of desperation, it was never sort of, oh my god, we've just uncovered a horrible fundamental weakness! What the hell are we going to do? It was always well, we've got this strong central base to work from and now how do we protect that and let's get creatively greedy about this thing. Let's make sure that we're not only delivering the suspense goods but that we're also taking advantage of the emotional and psychological potential of this piece. And that's how I felt we could differentiate it to some extent from other thrillers. So yeah, we went through a lot of rewrites but it was always about embellishment and it was always about building on what we had.

We really covered some new emotional territory in *Ransom*. When I say "we" I am referring to Mel Gibson, Rene Russo, and myself in particular. Mel kept characterizing it as a descent into hell. We shot all the scenes from the time their son is kidnapped to when they feel that they've lost their son for good, along with the final resolution of the movie, in sequence. So day in and day out it was this emotional grind with no days off for Mel or Rene and every day a deeper, darker moment to try to bring to life.

There's a scene toward the end of the film where they believe that their son has been shot. They've heard a gunshot over the phone and they think that this is it and both of them finally let go. They'd been holding back that deep grief throughout shooting until this scene. We all agreed that this was the place to let it go. They were both brilliant and powerful. In the midst of this fairly slick and urgent and fast-paced thriller was some really strong acting.

## He Looks Into the Mirror and What Does He See?

I'm not a comic or a big personality and I can't stand in front of an audience with a microphone and entertain them for two hours. To me that's the purest kind of entertainment. But nothing means more to me than working on a film, then sitting there feeling an audience responding emotionally, being involved by a film that I've directed. Professionally it is really a great thrill. Extraordinary, in fact. So, I definitely want to entertain.

As a storyteller I'm trying to broaden my own understanding of what actually is entertaining and what kinds of stories can be entertaining that aren't necessarily the genre films that you immediately associate with high entertainment. That's one of the reasons why I'm so proud of *Cocoon*. It's a very difficult movie to label. You could say fantasy but it's not clearly a genre picture and it was very difficult to market for that reason. So I'm always pushing myself to find that which is compelling and entertaining and presenting it to an audience and have them feel that they've been transported and entertained, but differently and hopefully better than the other eight genre films they've already seen that year.

I hope my films are different in some way.

## Does He Have a Dream Project?

I don't have any sort of dream project but at the same time I feel tremendous frustration in that I know that I'll never get to tell all the stories that I'd like to tell. It's endless. There are some things I haven't done yet, like a Western, for example. I would enjoy that if I could find the right story. I also have yet to do a film in the spirit of *Lilies of the Field* or *Tender Mercies*. Just a sort of small, simple, character-driven film with no bells and whistles, no high concepts, no special effects. I'm always looking for that. But I really don't choose types of films, I just stumble across stories and characters, and when I do then I just accept or apply whatever genre or style or tone seems appropriate.

One of the things I keep doing as a director is to gain enough experience with enough different styles, enough different tones, that I don't have to be intimidated by the issue of style. I can apply the appropriate genre or tone or rules to whatever character or idea that I fall in love with or have confidence that I'm capable of. I try to apply my process to a story and maximize its potential for the audience. That's what I'm always trying to do.

## His Thoughts on the Film Industry

I think that the film industry today is very healthy, with a few reservations. I think that for filmgoers it's a great time. It's a great time because there's much more experimentation going on. That experimentation is generally not being offered by the studio system and that's my great regret, that's my reservation. I wish that the studios were a little bolder about that kind of thing. But they're not. A lot of that is dictated by the economics of their visions.

Studios are driven by hits. It's a little like the record business. For years it was referred to as a hit-driven business. Put out a lot of records and if you have two or three hits your company is strong. Studios are that way now. They really don't want to roll film on a movie that they don't believe has a solid chance of being a huge mainstream hit and they leave the other kinds of stories to independent and smaller distributors.

Generally, I think there are more films being made, more opportunities for diverse film directors with varying sensibilities to get their movies made. I think that's great. Over all, I'm upbeat. I would just like to see the studios take more creative risks and find a way to be satisfied with some modest successes as well as the blockbuster hits. I think they need to get away from the blockbuster mentality.

## His Parting Words

I hope that people who enjoy movies will think that a film of mine is worth giving a chance to, that it stands an above-average chance of being good, involving, and worthy of their 90 to 120 minutes—or sometimes more

NOTE: Since this interview, Ron Howard has completed *EDtv* starring Matthew Mc-Conaughey, Jenna Elfman, Ellen DeGeneres, Woody Harrelson, Martin Landau, Sally Kirkland, Rob Reiner, Dennis Hopper, Elizabeth Hurley, and Todd Krainin. He is scheduled to shoot *How the Grinch Stole Christmas* with Jim Carrey in the year 2000.

(*laughs*). I hope that reaches a point where they don't have to characterize my films. I hope they can just say, "Oh, Ron Howard directed it? That's probably worth checking out." To me, that would be very satisfying.

# Director Filmography

*Deed of Derring-Do* (1969)
*Grand Theft Auto* (1977)
*Cotton Candy* (1978, TV)
*Skyward* (1980, TV)
*Through the Magic Pyramid* (1981, TV)
*Night Shift* (1982)
*Splash* (1984)
*Cocoon* (1985)
*Gung Ho* (1986)
*Willow* (1988)
*Parenthood* (1989)
*Backdraft* (1991)
*Far and Away* (1992)
*The Paper* (1994)
*Apollo 13* (1995)
*Ransom* (1996)
*Edtv* (1999)

# Awards

**Directors Guild of America**
*Apollo 13*, Outstanding Directorial Achievement, 1996

**Emmy Awards**

*From the Earth to the Moon,* Outstanding Miniseries (shared with Tom Hanks, Brian Grazer, Michael Bostick, Tony To, John P. Melfi, and Graham Yost), 1998

*Through the Magic Pyramid,* Outstanding Childrens Program (nominated), 1981

**Golden Globes, USA**

*Apollo 13,* Best Director (nominated), 1996

*Happy Days,* Best TV Actor—Musical/Comedy (nominated), 1978

*The Shootist,* Best Motion Picture Actor in a Supporting role (nominated), 1977

# The Films of Sydney Pollack

Sydney Pollack was born on July 1, 1934, in Lafayette, Indiana. Pollack originally set out to be an actor and then became an acting teacher, working alongside the legendary acting coach, Sandy Meisner. His own acting credits include *Tootsie*, which he also directed, Robert Zemeckis' *Death Becomes Her*, and Woody Allen's *Husbands and Wives*. His directing career began with many hours of episodic television. Then in 1965 he began his feature film–directing career with *The Slender Thread*, starring Sidney Poitier, Telly Savalas, and Anne Bancroft.

Of the eighteen films Sydney Pollack has directed (through 1998), eight have appeared in *Variety*'s list of "All Time Rental Champs." His films have received forty-six Academy Award nominations, including four for Best Picture. Pollack himself has been nominated three times. His film *Out of Africa* won seven Oscars including Best Picture, Best Director for Pollack, and Best Screenplay. He won the New York Film Critics Award for his 1982 film *Tootsie*. He's also won the Golden Globe, the National Society of Film Critics' Award, the NATO Director of the Year Award and prizes at the Brussels, Belgrade, San Sabastián, Moscow, and Taormina Film Festivals.

In 1985 he formed Mirage Productions. Under that banner he has produced the films *Presumed Innocent*, *The Fabulous Baker Boys*, *White Palace*, *Major League*, and 1992's summer hit *Dead Again*.

To say that Sydney Pollack has been a major force in the motion picture industry would be an understatement.

> *Sydney is that rare director. You don't identify him with just one kind of film. He can do a western. He has. He can do an urban thing like Tootsie. He has. Or The Electric Horseman or Jeremiah Johnson.*

*He has what I call an omni-talent. It's 360 degrees. He can do all types of films and he does them well.*

Cliff Robertson—Actor

# The Conversation

When I was in school in South Bend, Indiana, maybe the fifth grade or sixth grade, I remember a man who worked for the school system coming around who put on plays. I remember him being very amusing. We were gonna make up a play and put it on, and he made each one of us get up and act out something. I remember being absolutely terrified and forcing myself to sort of dive into doing this the way you would dive into the deep end of a pool or something. I also remember the exhilaration I felt from forcing myself to do it, and I think that's sort of my first memory of acting. I remember that as being my discovery of the excitement of what it was like to go into another world other than the real world that I lived in.

I don't remember when I first began to think about it seriously. The idea of constantly being able to shift back and forth between the real world and something that was totally in your imagination became increasingly appealing to me. I kept it very secret for a while. I talked about becoming a doctor or a dentist. My father was a pharmacist and he always wanted me to be a dentist, so I sort of went through the motions of preparing to go to college. Then at the last minute, on an impulse, I decided to study acting from the time that I graduated high school until the time that, I was certain, I would be drafted into the military. I was able to convince my father on the basis of that that we wouldn't have to try to scrape together money to pay for my college. If he gave me two years and let me do whatever I wanted, when I did go to college I could go on the GI Bill. He said okay, and so I went off to New York to go to acting school and that was the beginning.

I don't recall having access to art of any kind. I certainly wasn't a writer. It never occurred to me to be a director. That seemed like you had to know too much. But acting was something that I toyed with in grade school and high school. I would do these plays and I enjoyed it enormously. I didn't have any illusions about myself. I mean, I never thought that I was going to be a movie star or anything like that. I knew what my physical limitations were and that I would be a kind of character actor. I thought, what a wonderful way to make a living. You get paid for it and get to research and become another character, living in some rarified strange existence for an hour or two a day in the theater. I had no aspirations toward film at all and certainly no aspirations to be a director.

I went to New York on spec, if you will. I had a fixed sum of money and a couple of pairs of clothes and a bag that I had packed, and I checked into a YMCA. Now, a young man by the name of Jimmy Sullivan lived down the street from me in Indiana and he had gone to the Pasadena Playhouse. He was quite a bit older than I was and I kind of looked up to him. He came home one summer and he told me not to go to the Pasadena Playhouse. He suggested the Neighborhood Playhouse in New York City. So I took his word for it and it turned out to be an extraordinary school. I didn't realize it at the time. I was seventeen years old and studying dance with Martha Graham and then two hours a day with Sandy Meisner in the acting department. I was studying fencing and I was studying mime. I was studying with the great, great teachers of the theater world and the dance world. It was a very intensive two-year course. As soon as I got out I began to get very small parts on television. In those days you did the shows live—they were just beginning to integrate film into it. So I was making a living. Not a great living, but I was making a kind of minor living doing small roles on live television shows.

Then I was asked by Sandy Meisner to come back as a teacher at the school. I had no aspiration to be a teacher, but I was so in awe of this man that I did it for the opportunity to keep observing him. So I had two careers going simultaneously. I taught most of the time and then when I would get a job they would let me off to act. I did a series of television shows. I did a lot of summer stock for a period of, let's say, four years or five years and I did two very small parts in Broadway shows. One was with Catherine Cornell and Tyrone Power. It was also Christopher Plummer's first show in America. And that was the extent, really, of my acting career.

Through the teaching I began to get jobs as a coach. Some director would get a new actor, or somebody from the school would get a job in a summer stock show, and they might hire me to coach them. Now, this is a very delicate job, because coaching means you have to not cross the director. It's very difficult to coach an actor in a performance and be an adjunct to the director and not an enemy of the director at the same time. I was kind of walking on eggshells a bit. Then I was hired by John

Frankenheimer to coach on a *Playhouse 90* back in 1959. It was the first television appearance of Ingrid Bergman, who was a very big star then. She was appearing in *The Turn of the Screw*, a Henry James piece. In that piece the principals are these two children, and John hired me to coach the kids. I had to work very carefully with John but not be at odds with him. John was the director and I was really trying to understand what John wanted from the children, and then I would go off and work with them.

John and I worked very well together. When he got the feature film *The Young Savages,* with Burt Lancaster and Shelley Winters and Telly Savalas, he hired me to come to California and coach two or three young adolescents who were playing juvenile delinquents. I was able to work without treading on John's toes. But the key to this was Burt Lancaster, who was at the peak of his stardom. I was afraid of him but so was everybody. We were all very intimidated by him. He called me "kid" all the time. He would see me talking to these young boys and he would say, "Hey kid, what did you just say to them?" I would just turn beet red. I didn't know what to say. But he was always saying, "Hey, New York acting coach, come here and tell us what you said to those kids." He wasn't really trying to embarrass me but he was curious. Burt was an extraordinary guy and he was curious about everything.

I began to talk to him a bit about what I was doing with the young actors, and then he and I would begin to talk about the picture in general. When the film ended and I was ready to go back to New York and rejoin my family, Burt's secretary called and asked if I would come over to his office at Columbia Pictures, which was on Gower Street in those days. Burt sat me down and said, "Listen, you should be a director." I had never thought about being a director. I didn't particularly want to be a director, to be honest with you. But Burt Lancaster said I should be a director. He said I should be telling people what to do, not having people tell me what to do. So he picked up a phone and he called Lou Wasserman, one of the most powerful men in the business, although I didn't know who Lou Wasserman was at the time. I thought he was just a wealthy friend of Burt's. Burt called him up and he said, "Listen, Lou, I'm here with a young man. His name is Sydney Pollack and I think he's a director. I haven't seen him direct anything but I've got a feeling about him. Anyway, he can't be any worse than a lot of those bums that you've got working for you now."

So I went out to meet Mr. Wasserman, who asked me what I had directed. And I said, "Nothing." "Well," he said, "Burt thinks you could be a director. Can you move out here to California?" I said, "Yeah, sure I can move out here," trusting that I could convince my wife. He asked me how much I needed to live on, and like a dope I said seventy-five dollars a week, so he agreed to give me seventy-five dollars a week for six months. He said, "You move out here and you can work at Universal Studios and observe. I'll put you under the wing of a producer out there who will let you watch and we'll see what happens."

I met a very, very lovely man named Dick Irving who produced a lot of television. It was kind of meat-and-potatoes series television. I went there every day on my little Vespa motor scooter. I watched and learned for three or four months. Then one of their series (*Shotgun Slade*) was canceled, but they still had four or five shows left to make. It was a half-hour western and I just did a terrible job with it. I didn't know anything about the camera. I didn't know anything about the mechanics of film. I didn't know what the hell I was doing, but I made the show somehow and they pasted it together. But I became intrigued from directing that show and I thought, "Wait a minute, this is kind of interesting. I could really learn this." Somehow the second show was better and I was off and running. I went on to direct episodes of *Ben Casey, The Alfred Hitchcock Hour,* and *The Fugitive.*

By the sixties almost all television was filmed. The tape era was over, with the exception of soap operas. I was doing fifteen or twenty shows a year for four years. It was a wonderful film school because I had to deal with all kinds of shows and all kinds of situations with actors who hadn't had a chance to rehearse. I had to deal with sets that I hadn't seen before, with dramas, comedies, animals, outdoors, indoors. It was really a thorough school. By the time I had directed my first feature film I had done maybe sixty or seventy television shows, all on film. In the sixties there was still a lot of anthology drama, where you'd have a brand new cast and an original screenplay and an original drama to do for a full hour. I did a lot of those.

## A Slight Detour as We Discuss His Recent Acting Assignments

I've never acted of my own volition since I gave up acting. I didn't act for twenty years. I was directing *Tootsie* and Dustin Hoffman, who is a very precise kind of method actor, kept worrying about why he put on the dress and kept asking, "Where are the machine guns?" He was referring to *Some Like It Hot,* in which Jack Lemmon and Tony Curtis put on dresses to avoid being killed by the gangsters. They had a reason to put on dresses but we didn't have any such reason in *Tootsie.* The only thing we had was that his agent said to him, "You're never going to work again if you don't put the dress on." Dustin worried about this. Dabney Coleman was originally set to play Dustin's agent. Dustin said to me, "If Dabney Coleman says I'm never going to work again, I won't put on the dress. Dabney Coleman is a peer of mine; he's a colleague of mine. He's not a director. But if you say it I would do it." Well, I didn't take him seriously. I just ignored him.

Pretty soon I started getting telephone calls from my agent, Mike Ovitz, who was also Dustin's agent. Michael would say to me, "Listen, Dustin really wants you to play this part." I said, "Michael, I'm not gonna play this part. I haven't acted in twenty years and I've got too much to do. This is too difficult a picture and I don't want to stop and put a costume and makeup on. I just won't be able to do it." He said, "Okay, but I'm telling you, Dustin's serious." Then I started to get flowers every other day with a card that said, "Please be my agent. Love, Dorothy." It was Dustin who was sending me these flowers. Finally it got to be such a campaign that I agreed because Dustin was adamant about it.

That's how I began my second acting career. I wasn't intending to do any more acting. I think the scenes are funny when I watch them, but I didn't enjoy doing it. First of all, it had been so long since I had acted, and I had been so much in the habit of directing, that the only time I could really act was in individual shots where I wasn't watching Dustin. Any time there was a two-shot of us I was very aware of what he was doing. I didn't even want to look away because I was afraid I would miss what he was doing and I was always thinking about what I would say to him afterwards. It was very hard for me to concentrate as the character unless I was in a single-shot where I was the only one acting. So I wouldn't say that I had a good time doing it, but it came off okay.

Over the years I got asked to do some more acting roles. Often I was doing a favor for a friend. Robert Altman asked me to do him a favor in *The Player*. Blake Edwards was originally going to play the part but something happened and Blake couldn't do it. Altman is a good friend so I did *The Player*. Robert Zemeckis asked me to do this one scene with Meryl in *Death Becomes Her*. I sort of enjoyed that. Then Woody Allen asked me to be in *Husbands and Wives*, so that's the extent of my acting career.* I often get requests to act. I just got a request to do *Chicago Hope*, the television show, but I don't have the time. But when I have the time it's kind of enjoyable as long as I'm not directing.

---

* Since this interview, Sydney Pollack has appeared in Stanley Kubrick's *Eyes Wide Shut*.

# The Slender Thread (1965)

*Sidney Poitier; Anne Bancroft; Telly Savalas; Steven Hill; Edward Asner;*
*Indus Arthur; Paul Newlan; Dabney Coleman; H. M. Wynant; Robert F. Hoy;*
*Greg Jarvis; Jason Wingreen; Marjorie Nelson; Steven Marlo; Thomas Hill.*

I was beginning to make a reputation in television—I had begun to be nominated for Emmys—and in those days the film world looked toward television for its directors. I was a part of a second wave of directors. The first wave that came from television was John Frankenheimer, Sidney Lumet, Arthur Penn, and George Roy Hill. Up until that time the film community was dominated by great film directors from the thirties and forties. I was a part of a second wave of directors who came from filmed television. It was Robert Altman, Richard Donner, Mark Rydell, and myself and other people that had done TV film.

Toward the end of the period that I was doing television, I began to get offers to do films. Occasionally I would get an offer to do a film, and for a combination of reasons either they didn't come to fruition or they were films I didn't want to do. *The Slender Thread* seemed like the right one at the right time. It was the right size, it was closer to the kind of television work I had done, and I think that one of the reasons I got it is because of Elizabeth Ashley. Elizabeth Ashley had been a student of mine when I taught at the Neighborhood Playhouse and I think she brought my name up to the people at Paramount.

The entire cast was wonderful to work with. I had Sidney Poitier and Anne Bancroft. They had both recently won Academy Awards. They did a magnificent job in the picture. I don't feel that I did a particularly good job, however. It was my first film and I'm very uncomfortable now when I watch parts of it, just in terms of the way it's directed. I was a novice and I directed it a lot like a television show. I think you have to take Dramamine to watch it. It's full of zooms and swish pans. I was trying too hard, I think.

Part of the mistake I made with *The Slender Thread* was not allowing for the differences that exist between film and television. In television you are always fighting for the viewers' attention because they watch in a lighted room, more often than not, with more than one person and all sorts of distractions, and you're gearing up for a climax and every six or seven minutes there's a commercial break. A one-hour television play used to be in five acts, so you'd go for six or seven minutes at a time and you'd have to reach a big climax. Then there would be the bum-ba-bum-bum, and then fade out and you go to a commercial. It's a contest for attention. I had no sense of letting the momentum of the piece develop by itself. That picture is just one big bold piece of drama after another, and I was just working too hard at it. I mean, I'm very fond of the picture, I think there are a lot of lovely things in it, mostly to the credit of the actors and the writer. I had a lot of other good actors in it, too. Better actors than I deserved at the time.

I had a wonderful old cameraman named Loyal Griggs, who was George Stevens' cameraman on *Shane*. Loyal was getting on by then and I was just a young kid. I had so much enthusiasm. I kept running up mountains and wanting to put cameras there and he was just bored with me and he would say, "Oh, give the kid what he wants." I just remember arguing in a good-natured way with him about everything. I was trying too hard. I was shooting everything from low angles or high angles or between two cracks in a door. I mean, I would do anything except let the camera sit and let the characters live in the environment of the film. That took a couple of films for me to learn.

## This Property is Condemned (*1966*)

*Natalie Wood; Robert Redford; Charles Bronson; Kate Reid; Mary Badham;*
*Alan Baxter; Robert Blake; Dabney Coleman; John Harding; Ray Hemphill;*
*Brett Pearson; Jon Provost; Bob Random; Quintin Sondergaard; Mike Steen.*

I believe that *This Property is Condemned* came to me because of the work of my agent, a wonderful man named Joe Schoenfeld who was also Natalie Wood's agent. Natalie Wood was a big star in 1965 and got to choose her own stars, co-stars, and directors. She chose Redford and Redford and I happened to be good friends, and I'm sure Redford put in a good word for me. But it was Natalie that I had to audition for.

Joe Schoenfeld took one of the television shows that I had done with Shelley Winters and Marty Balsam, and that had won an award at the Monaco Television Festival, and showed it to Natalie. She asked to meet me, so I had to go and audition. I remember being absolutely petrified because not only was she a huge star, but I had this monster crush on her from watching her in *Rebel Without A Cause*. I thought, "What am I going to do? How am I gonna audition as a director? Say action? Cut? What am I gonna say?" I remember going to her house and sitting and chatting with her about the script and what its weaknesses and strengths were, and what we thought needed to be done with it. She gave her okay, and that really was how I got the job. It was, of course, the first of a series of films I eventually did with Redford.

The film was a difficult adaptation because the Tennessee Williams piece that it came from was a very short one-act play that was really just the two kids on the railroad track. That got used as a framing device and everything in between was invented for the film. By the way, I believe the film was originally to star Elizabeth Taylor, and John Huston was its original director. John Frankenheimer was on that picture for a short time. I think I was the fourth, fifth, or sixth director hired.

I worked with James Wong Howe, who was a great, great cameraman. I learned an enormous amount watching him work. He did things nobody else was doing, really, at that particular time in terms of the way he lit and the way he used the lens. You know, the reason that the most interesting photographs of poverty are black and white, whether they're Walker Evans or whoever, is that it's very difficult in color not to have it be beautiful. Even when it's ugly it assumes a certain beauty in color. James Wong Howe worked very, very hard with the production designer to achieve the look we got.

The other great thing that happened on that film is that I met a great production designer, Stephen B. Grimes, who I kept with me as long as he lived. He died rather tragically right after *Out of Africa*, which was the last film he did for me. He often worked with John Huston and often with David Lean. I got him because John Huston was originally on the picture and he remained on after I came on. Stephen Grimes and James Wong Howe did some extraordinary things to try to take the color out of the color, if you will. They sprayed the trees with a kind of creosote, a kind of semi-transparent brownish liquid, to take some of the color out. We burnt tires that gave off a terrible, awful black smoke and a residue. The residents there hated us, but the black smoke kind of drifted in and out of the scenes and filtered everything down. These things are not necessary today. You can do it technically, digitally, computer-wise, whatever. But in 1965 this was a kind of bold technique that James Wong Howe did.

It was a great experience because it was the first time I got to work with Wong Howe, Robert Redford, and Stephen Grimes, who really became a close colleague of mine. I worked with him on every film I could after that.

I thought that *This Property is Condemned* was a good film. I think particularly Redford and Natalie were wonderful in the film. It's the kind of film we would call a B picture, but it had an enormous amount of success, particularly in France. There are things about it I would do differently, of course, but I think it's a nice film. I don't think it's a great film. I think it's a nice film.

# The Scalphunters (1968)

*Burt Lancaster; Shelley Winters; Telly Savalas; Ossie Davis; Dabney Coleman; Paul Picerni; Dan Vadis; Armando Silvestre; Nick Cravat; Tony Epper; Chuck Roberson.*

*The Scalphunters* is the third time Burt Lancaster came into my life. In 1963, before I ever directed a feature film, I was under contract and doing well at Universal in my television career. I got a call from Burt Lancaster to go to Italy and observe Luchino Visconti dubbing *The Leopard* because they had not used live sound. Burt was going to have to post-synchronize his entire role in English and he wanted me to help him do it, because Visconti spoke very little English at the time, and I was too dumb to realize what a great opportunity this was. I mean, I knew who Visconti was but I didn't know who he was the way I know who he is now.

I went to Rome for a month and observed and talked with Visconti about what he was doing, then came back to New York and worked with Burt. That was the second time Burt came into my life. Then in 1966 Burt called me again. He had read a book called *Castle Keep* which he and I loved but he couldn't get anybody to hire me to direct it because I was considered a guy who did straight drama and *Castle Keep* was a big action film. I really wanted to do an action picture and Burt had this comedy western called *The Scalphunters* that was an original idea. He got United Artists to agree to hire me to direct it which was a pretty brave thing on his part because I hadn't done any action. I'd never done a single big exterior movie of any kind.

We all went and made this comedy western. It's actually a pretty good film. It's a very old-fashioned movie but it's fun. It's got a lot of energy and humor in it. When we had finished about four weeks of shooting, Burt sent Martin Ransahoff, who was producing *Castle Keep,* some footage as a sort of audition—some of the fight scenes and scenes where the horses stampede and go crazy—and then Marty Ransohoff agreed to hire me to direct *Castle Keep.*

Westerns have a peculiar place in American film history and in the imagination of most filmgoers. Westerns were kind of the simplest, most basic morality plays, and as such were actually universal. The appeal of a western transcends languages, transcends countries. There's not a country in the world where they don't like westerns. Unfortunately, they're not popular here now. But for years they were a kind of staple. And you know, you weren't really a director, I don't think, until you directed a western. I don't know why that is. I guess it's because it's the most simple and primitive form of movie in a certain kind of way, but you can make it as complex as you want. The form is usually quite simple. It's usually the build to the gunfight at the OK Corral, or wherever it's going to be. The equivalent of the gunfight, in my case, was a fight between two men. But it's the same thing. It's building and building and building and building and building all the time.

*Scalphunters* was an all-outdoor picture. I learned to take advantage of the light in a way that I had never learned before. You learned about space and classic composition. It was all shot in Mexico, and it was a wonderful, exciting time for me to shut out the real world and my real life and go away to a strange country and just live in the world of the film for the duration of that movie.

# Castle Keep (1969)

*Burt Lancaster; Michael Conrad; Bruce Dern; Bisera; Caterina Boratto; Elisabeth Tessier; Anne Marie Moskovenko; Marja Allanen; Eya Tuli; Elizabeth Darius; Karen Blanguernon; Marie Danube; Jean-Pierre Aumont; Tony Bill; Peter Falk; Al Freeman, Jr.; Astrid Heeren; Patrick O'Neal; James Patterson; Scott Wilson.*

*Castle Keep* was a film that was made a little bit before its time and before my ability to grasp its complexities. It was a surrealistic war film, a strange thing for Americans to make. I don't think Americans are particularly gifted at surrealism. That's a European phenomenon or art form. It was the first of the American films like that. I'm talking about films like *Catch 22* and *Slaughterhouse Five* and those films. Later, in '69, '70, and '71, there were more of those films made.

We shot the film in Yugoslavia for economic reasons. Most of it was shot outside of a city that was not far from Belgrade. We built a castle there out of Styrofoam. We sort of made a kind of dream version of a chateau with mixtures of towers and turrets and things. It was half Walt Disney and half not because the whole film was a kind of dream. I loved working on it and I loved the material from William Eastlake's book. It was a very difficult screenplay to do.

We built a huge moat in front of the castle that was reinforced with concrete because tanks were going to drive into this moat. But the morning that I came out to do the tank sequence the moat was frozen solid. All these people got out there with picks and picked at this thing. Then we got a big heater that blew hot air to keep the water warmer than the air at night so it wouldn't freeze again. When I went out the next morning to film the sequence, I couldn't see the castle for the steam rising from the water. In one of the later sequences we burned the castle down accidentally, shooting explosions. The Styrofoam caught on fire and it burned to a crisp in thirty seconds. It was a million-dollar set. So it was a bad-luck plagued film. We had terrible problems making it, but it's a film I've always liked very, very much.

## They Shoot Horses, Don't They? (1969)
*Jane Fonda; Michael Sarrazin; Susannah York; Gig Young; Red Buttons;*
*Bonnie Bedelia; Michael Conrad; Bruce Dern; Al Lewis; Robert Fields; Severn Darden;*
*Allyn Ann McLerie; Madge Kennedy; Jacquelyn Hyde; Felice Orlandi.*

*They Shoot Horses, Don't They?* made a big change in terms of international attention, if you will. The films I had made up until *They Shoot Horses, Don't They?* were moderately successful. They weren't big hits but they weren't flops. The actors acquitted themselves well. The films got decent reviews and they made some money. But *They Shoot Horses, Don't They?* achieved a kind of critical success that was a first for me. It got a lot of Academy Award nominations and got a lot of attention in Europe. It was a strange film because it was a film that many people had owned the rights to, from Charlie Chaplin on. Many, many people owned the rights to it and wanted to make it at odd times. But the problem had been that somebody owned the European rights and somebody else owned the American rights. In any case, it finally got resolved, and I hired a writer who really had never made a film before.

I was not the first director on the film. The first director was a man by the name of James Poe, who wrote the first screenplay, and this was to be his first film as a director. He was dismissed early on for whatever reasons, and I was brought in and set about to do my own screenplay with writer Bob Thompson—Red Thompson, as we call him—who did a beautiful job. He wrote six or seven pages a day and he'd meet me and we'd boil them down to about four pages.

It was a very difficult film because, if you think about it for a moment, it is a director's nightmare. First of all it is a film in which people do the same thing for two hours. The same thing over and over and over, representing days, of course, but for a full two-hour movie, it is in the same place. There's nowhere to go. But worst of all they have to get more fatigued as they go on. So instead of being able to pace it so that it gets faster and faster toward the end, it has to get slower and slower. You say well, okay, I can't show a new activity, I can't show a new location, I can't introduce new characters, and I have to make it slower and slower and slower. How the hell are you going to get anybody anyone to sit there for two hours and watch this? So it was a very difficult challenge from that point of view, to keep you interested in it without resorting to building a glass floor and shooting up through it.

I learned to roller skate, and I got a small sky-diving camera that had only fifty feet of film in it, and Panavision made me a very special 50-millimeter lens that was made out of aluminum that was anamorphic* and lightweight. I finally was able to roller skate and gun-sight it. I couldn't hold it to my eye, but I could hold it and gun-sight it. I could skate backwards and I could skate forward and I used it quite a bit in the derby sequences. I had an extraordinary cinematographer on that film named Phil Lathrop, who had done a gorgeous film called *Point Blank* with John Borman. We did some amazing stuff, for the time in which it was made. You have to understand that cameras were not lightweight then and we didn't have the fast film they have today. To photograph those derbies we had to make a contraption that weighed a ton that had to be pushed by four guys to photograph those sequences. It was quite a job.

It was the first film that Jane Fonda did that was taken seriously. She had just come off of *Barbarella* and films like that. It was her first real deeply serious performance, and she got an Academy Award nomination for it. She was great, as was Gig Young, Bonnie Bedelia, and Bruce Dern. I worked with them like I work with all actors. It's very, very difficult to try to explain publicly what is really a very private process. Directing actors is as varied as the actors and the roles they are playing. There isn't any one thing that you always do or one thing that you never do. It changes with every actor. To try to explain what the process is has always been elusive to me. I don't know how to explain it. You try to tailor what you do to the particular needs of the actor and the particular needs of the script and the story.

I've never had a film in which every actor came to work every day whether they were needed or not. It was very difficult to say, "We're gonna shoot this scene and Jane isn't in that scene so she has today off." She never knew whether she was going to be in the scene or not, because if I was shooting over here in a corner and I turned around, she might be dancing over here in the background. So everybody came to work every day. It was the only film I've ever made that I went in straight continuity. I went from the first scene to the last scene and I shot everything in sequence. The lines

---

* Wide lens.

got worn off of the floor. The set got ratty and signs got old and torn down. The actors began to look worse and worse because what we did is we reversed the process. We started with makeup and we gradually took the makeup off rather than the reverse. And because I had to have 360 degrees to shoot, I couldn't use floor lighting units. I couldn't light into the actor's eyes, so as a result the lighting was up high and made big deep shadows. That worked in our favor—it made the actors look tired. It was a very interesting film from a technical point of view. I enjoyed making it.

# Jeremiah Johnson (1972)

*Robert Redford; Will Geer; Delle Bolton; Josh Albee;*
*Joaquín Martínez; Allyn Ann McLerie; Stefan Gierasch; Richard Angarola;*
*Paul Benedict; Charles Tyner; Jack Colvin; Matt Clark.*

*Jeremiah Johnson* is almost a silent movie. If you were to add up all of the dialogue in that film, it amounts to about ten or twelve pages. It's a movie in which nobody can talk to anybody. First of all, he marries an American Indian who can't talk to him. She can't talk to him, he can't talk to her, and the child is mute so nobody can talk to anybody. It was all sort of visual. It was a strange movie because I think the dailies were probably the most boring dailies in the world to watch because nobody said anything and nobody seemed to do much of anything. This guy was just wandering around in the wilderness. But it was a film that I had a really deep affinity for. I love the soulfulness of it and I loved that character. It's the classic fable of the man who tried to escape society and went up into another civilization and then that old society followed him up the mountain and said you can't get away from us.

Robert Redford is quite unique. For me he was the quintessential American, in a way—the kind of American that I like to think of America as. Not the conventional American. He has a darker color inside that appealed to me enormously. I like the contrast between the beige, conventionally handsome, WASPY, blue-eyed blonde American and the complex personality and intellect that he has. Those two things together made him rather special to me. I like doing love stories and I think that the love stories are often about, I won't say exactly the same character, but pretty damn close. It's usually the same guy in a different place. Sometimes he's in Africa, sometimes he's in the West, but he's usually the same person in a different incarnation and often as Redford.

# The Way We Were (1973)

*Barbra Streisand; Robert Redford; Bradford Dillman; Lois Chiles;*
*Patrick O'Neal; Viveca Lindfors; Murray Hamilton; Herb Edelman; Diana Ewing;*
*Sally Kirkland; Marcia Mae Jones; Don Keefer; George Gaynes; Eric Boles.*

*The Way We Were* was a brand new project that came to me from Ray Stark, who had produced *This Property Is Condemned*. Arthur Laurents had written a short novella treatment and I was given that to read, and then I met with Barbra Streisand. I wanted Redford very badly, and so did Barbra, but Redford really didn't want to do it. It took me months of hard work to talk Redford into doing that part. I didn't think I could make the picture work without him. For the very reason that he didn't want to do it, I felt I had to have him. He didn't want to do it because he felt that the role was too representational. The role was a weak, pretty man with nothing else going on inside. And it was precisely because there was a danger of that happening that I felt I needed Redford rather than another pretty boy, blonde, blue-eyed leading man.

It was essential to have someone who had a streak of tragedy, complexity, and darkness in them. The hard work on that script was to try to give some credence and value to what clearly is the less sympathetic point of view, which was his point of view. Everyone identifies with her as the passionate, committed doer and, in fact, in the long run she is more right than he is. But I didn't feel I would have a movie if it were that simple. I think Redford brought an enormous amount to that movie.

Barbra was great in the film. I loved working with her and I've been sorry that we haven't been able to find anything to do since then. We've always wanted to work together again. The two of them together were really quite wonderful, but it took me three or four months to talk him into doing it. I yelled at him, begged him, cajoled him, sat night after night drinking wine, talking, screaming, and, finally, I think I had just worn him down one day. He finally just, in a very depressed way, said, "Ah, okay, I'll do it."

I remember bumping into an executive while I was making the film, who said to me, "You're making a movie where Barbra Streisand plays a Jewish communist and she doesn't sing? What in the hell are you doing?" Nobody knew that it would become the cliché love story of the sixties. I think it tapped into something very universal about Prince Charming, about falling in love with someone that you feel you're never gonna get, that runs deep in every culture. It's the immigrant and the American. It has very rock-solid basic storytelling elements from fairy tales on. And it was blessed with two rather extraordinary people. I don't think anybody else could have done that movie other than Barbra and Redford.

## How Does He Choose His Projects?

I try to choose projects the same way I decorate an office or how I decide what to wear in the morning. I can't help it. I mean, it's the same. I choose what I like, and how do you explain what you like? It's very hard. If I were to try to analyze it, I'm sure it has something to do with trying to imagine living with the people over a year's time, which is what it takes to do a film. I read a lot of material that keeps my attention for two hours and when I finish I ask myself, "Would I go see this film that asks me to give up two hours of my life? Would I want to hang out with these people? Would I want to have them to dinner? Would I want to be their friend?" I don't literally say that, but, unconsciously, that's what I'm saying when I'm reading. Do I really care about this? Because I'm gonna have to care about it for a year.

## The Yakuza (1975)

*Robert Mitchum; Ken Takakura; Brian Keith; Herb Edelman;*
*Richard Jordan; Keiko Kishi; Eiji Okada; James Shigeta; Kyosuke Mashida;*
*Christina Kokubo; Eiji Go; Lee Chirillo; M. Hisaka; William Ross; Akiyama.*

I had never done anything like *The Yakuza*, which was a kind of a clear, straightforward exploitation/action picture. I became very, very interested in the whole culture-clash part of it. It was the combination of an American and a Japanese and the two ways in which they look at honor, love, and commitment. What made them have something in common, in a curious way, was that they looked at those areas in the same way, and I got hung up on that somewhat. I kept thinking of that poem, "The woods are lovely, dark, and deep, But I have promises to keep, And miles to go before I sleep, And miles to go before I sleep." It was a poem that sort of expressed the spine of that film to me.

And the idea of filming in Japan, working with a Japanese crew, and getting a look at the visual approach interested me. You know, it's an extraordinarily visual culture anyway. The Zen garden, the sense of calligraphy, the haiku poetry. Everything about that culture is visually oriented—the way the food is served, the way it's set on a plate, even, the ceremonies associ-ated with it. So I was very interested in seeing what it would be like and what I could learn from doing it.

I got to work again with Steven Grimes, this marvelous, marvelous de-signer, who did a beautiful job with the film. I also worked with a magnif-icent Japanese cinematographer named Kozo Okazaki. He didn't speak a word of English and I don't speak any Japanese and we were an amazing pair. He had a gray-scale card that had eight values from white to black, and I had a gray card that had eight values from white to black. He would walk up and point to the actor's cheek and he would go [gestures], and I would go [gestures] and point to the eye, and he would go [gestures], and I'd go [gestures], and that's kind of how we lit everything. He did it like he was painting a picture. He would start in the upper left-hand corner of the frame and go across. They didn't have any large lighting units the way we do in American studios. Everything was lit with very small units, but hun-dreds of them. Usually there were little light bulbs inside of tin cans which were painted black on the outside and they were tin on the inside and there would just be a little light bulb inside and that would be it. And the studios all had dirt floors because they were used to making costume dramas. It was an extraordinary experience. I enjoyed making the film very much.

I loved working with Robert Mitchum. Mitchum is a real professional who has no pretensions at all about what he does. I think the idea of act-ing for a living is a little embarrassing to him in some way, although he un-derstands what art is as well as anybody in the world; he sort of disowns any pretension to it. That's why he makes statements like, "I'm an actress, I'm a movie actress," or he'll say, "I show up, hit my mark and go home. Well, how do you get a good performance? Pay me." He'll make statements like that. The fact is he was a real professional and he had a lot of emotion. He was an incredible raconteur. He tells stories that go on forever that are mesmerizing, and he's been all over the world. He's one of those characters who wanders in and out of places that nobody's ever been and always comes back with a great story.

His head and my head were always bleeding from hitting the roof. We were always in areas that were too small. We were in a small hotel in Kyoto in Japan that was built for smaller people and I was always banging into the eaves on the roof and so was Mitchum. He was bigger than I am and he had a hell of a time trying to sit down, because you have to sit cross-legged on the floor for all these meals and everything, and it was hilarious to watch him go through this. But he was great to work with.

# Three Days of the Condor (1975)

*Robert Redford; Faye Dunaway; Cliff Robertson; Max von Sydow; John Houseman;*
*Addison Powell; Walter McGinn; Tina Chen; Michael Kane; Don McHenry;*
*Michael B. Miller; Jess Osuna; Dino Narizzano; Helen Stenbure; Patrick Gorman.*

Redford and I were already working on another film when someone sent him *Three Days of the Condor*. It wasn't the script that we shot, but it had certain story elements in it already. He sent this script to me and I agreed to do it. I then brought in the writer that I worked with all the time, David Rayfiel, and he started rewriting it. It was made from a book called *Six Days of the Condor* that was really about heroin smuggling. We tried to make it a little bit more about where we thought things were going at that time with the CIA.

It was a tough picture to shoot. We got into the seasonal problems again. We had to take all the leaves off of the trees on Sixty-third Street because we were doing a picture that was going to take over four months of shooting but the film's action happened in three days. So we had to look exactly the same for a four-month period. I found that when we tried to tighten this film up and really keep the tension in it, I could only get three days out of it, so *Six Days of the Condor* in the book became *Three Days of the Condor*.

I think there's some great writing in that film and I think one of the things that makes it a little bit unusual as a thriller is that the level of the writing is a cut above most thrillers. It's very literary and very poetic. It is a kind of writing that Redford is particularly good at. There are a lot of actors that read those words and can't say them. Some of that dialogue is very literary—it doesn't sound like it belongs in the middle of a thriller set in New York City.

You never know when you're making a film whether it's gonna be popular or not. I tend to be a worrier. My friends would say that's an understatement, but I don't ever expect anything to be popular. I never know whether it's going to work. Once you get inside of it and you start working on it, it always feels like it's not as good as it ought to be. You feel like you're doing certain things wrong. You worry about it. I mean, I've been afraid on every film that I've ever done and worried about whether it will be successful or not. So, yes, during the making of *Condor*, I worried about whether or not it was going to work or be popular.

There was an incident that I think was funny. Mr. Helms, who was a famous CIA guy, wanted to come and watch. He came to this scene we were shooting with Cliff Robertson and Redford and he sat in a chair on the set. We actually have some photographs of him there. He was giggling and he was, like, having a great time sitting there watching this scene in which a CIA operative, Cliff Robertson, is kidnapped by Redford, who knows that he's being lied to by his boss. And Helms was sitting there on the set just grinning from ear to ear saying, "Great, sounds great."

# Bobby Deerfield (1977)

*Al Pacino; Marthe Keller; Anny Duperey; Walter McGinn;*
*Romolo Valli; Stephen Meldegg; Jaime Sánchez; Norm Nielsen; Mickey Knox;*
*Dorothy James; Guido Alberti; Gérard Hernandez; Aurora Maris.*

*Bobby Deerfield* was a film that originally I spoke with Paul Newman about before I made *Three Days of the Condor.* It was a film that was written for Newman by a wonderful writer named Alvin Sargent, who I've often worked with. I almost did that picture with Newman just before *Condor.* I decided not to and went off and did *Three Days of the Condor.* When *Condor* was over I came back and dug out *Bobby Deerfield* and decided I wanted to make it, but then Paul decided he didn't want to make it. So I went through a whole series of people in my mind and ended up wanting to do it with Al Pacino.

It's a film that was not successful here at all. In fact, I don't think it was successful anywhere. But oddly enough it's a film that I'm personally very fond of. I think Al gave an extraordinary performance and the girl, Marthe Keller, I thought was brilliant. I was particularly attached to what the film was about, this love story in which a man was cut off from his own roots and wasn't really a solid person until he reestablished his own connection with those roots. It just had an appeal to me and I loved it. I liked making it and I loved the film when it was done. But I was obviously wrong in terms of being out of step with what audiences wanted.

When you make films, it's very hard for you to know what people are going to want, so you can't really think about that. You have to think about what you like and sometimes you're right and sometimes you're wrong. The only way you can make a film is to make it for yourself and hope that if you like it, somebody else will like it too. Often you're right and often you're wrong.

# The Electric Horseman (1979)

*Robert Redford; Jane Fonda; Valerie Perrine; Willie Nelson; John Saxon;*
*Nicolas Coster; Allan Arbus; Wilford Brimley; Will Hare; Basil Hoffman;*
*Timothy Scott; James Sikking; James Kline; Frank Speiser; Quinn K. Redeker.*

*Electric Horseman* had been around the business for a while and I think everyone had read it and it wasn't being made. It was stagnating somewhere. In the meantime, Redford and I had decided to make another film called *A Place to Come To,* which was a Robert Penn Warren book that we both loved and wanted very much to make. But we struggled and struggled and struggled and it seemed finally to be too much story to try to tell in too short a time, because it was a biography. It was the arc of a whole life and very difficult to pack into two and a half hours. I had hired a crew and had a start date and realized that we couldn't do it, so we desperately started looking around to find something we could substitute and keep everyone who we had signed on working.

We had thought about *The Electric Horseman,* so we took it and started from scratch and rewrote it. After we had about forty pages I went to Jane Fonda and I said, "Jane, I don't have a whole script, I don't know the ending, and we have to start shooting in a few weeks. Will you do this?" And Jane said okay. Since we didn't have a finished script halfway through shooting, she was asking questions like, "Am I gonna end up with him? Are we going to be together? What's gonna happen here?" We took a break at Christmas and I came home and finished the script so we could go back and finish shooting. It was literally one of those movies where I was able to stay about one day ahead of shooting.

You get to see another aspect of Redford in this film. You see more of the comedy. He's a great comedian and very rarely gets a chance to do that. One of the things I'm gonna regret, if we don't get a chance, is not doing a full-out comedy with Redford. We always joke about it. We always say we've got to do a comedy together because we do spend a lot of time laughing when we're not shooting, but we always end up doing these serious dramas. *Electric Horseman* was kind of lightweight and funny.

> *I think Sydney helps you prepare for the role by giving you a lot of*
> *confidence—the confidence to experiment and the confidence to work*

*things out on your feet. He knows how to make suggestions feel as though they are yours. Of course, that's a great gift.*

*Paul Newman—Actor*

# Absence of Malice (1981)

*Paul Newman; Sally Field; Bob Balaban; Melinda Dillon; Luther Adler; Barry Primus; Josef Sommer; John Harkins; Don Hood; Wilford Brimley; Arnie Ross; Anna Marie Napoles; Shelley Spurlock; Shawn McAllister; Joe Petrullo.*

By the time I made *Absence of Malice* I was beginning to feel that I was making films of modest success. *The Way We Were* was a big hit, *Jeremiah Johnson* was, in its own way, a big hit, and *They Shoot Horses, Don't They?* was a big critical success. But for some reason I didn't feel like I had hit a home-run yet, whatever that was. I was beginning to feel that I had reached a level and that would be the level that I would stay at. I wasn't unhappy about it. It was a good life and a good way to work. But I've never been completely content with what I'm doing or where I am in my career. If you ask me would I do something different or would I change something, I could look at every one of my films and say, "Yeah, if you'd give me the chance to do it over." And I felt that way pretty much about my career up to that point.

I think it was a terrific performance by Paul Newman. It was a performance that was very internal. There was a lot of thinking in that performance and you could see it. You could see him thinking and I think you saw him at the height of his career. I think that was a particularly wonderful performance that he gave in that film. It was extremely economical and it was full of reality and a kind of truth and it had its own very focused and quiet passion.

He was a delight to work with. He was the most professional guy and always prepared. He was conscientious because he had directed himself. He knew the responsibility and he knew how much time was worth and so he was always prepared and always on time and always extremely professional. It's the only film I've ever made where I was a week ahead of schedule and a million dollars under budget—*under budget!* I don't know what accounts for that because it wasn't that easy a film to make. Some of it was on the water and we were outdoors a lot and in big sets. But it just clicked and it went along beautifully.

# Tootsie (1982)

*Dustin Hoffman; Jessica Lange; Teri Garr; Dabney Coleman; Charles Durning;
Bill Murray; Sydney Pollack; George Gaynes; Geena Davis; Doris Belack;
Ellen Foley; Peter Gatto; Lynne Thigpen; Ronald L. Schwary; Debra Mooney.*

I often hear that I was an odd good choice to make *Tootsie* since I'm associated more with straight drama, but the fact is that I had made comedy
before. I was just never considered a comedy director. But there's a lot of
comedy in *The Electric Horseman*. There is a lot of comedy in *The Scalphunters*. It's true that people associated me more with, let's say, *The Way We
Were* or *Jeremiah Johnson,* since those pictures were more popular. But I had
made some comedy before *Tootsie*. I had never made something that
broadly comical.

Dustin Hoffman, I think, originated the project, and I think there were
a couple of other directors on that picture as well. I wasn't the first director
on it, but the others never got the film made and they never got a script
they were happy with. They never got the picture off the ground. When it
first came to me I had a tough time seeing myself doing it. I didn't like it.
It was in a different form when it first came to me, and I just didn't think I
was the right director for it. I couldn't find anything that made me personally interested in it. It seemed to me to be too much of one joke over and
over and over when I first looked at it. But I had a very persistent agent and
a very persistent man who ran the studio at that time, Frank Price of Columbia Pictures. Every time I would say no they would wait a week or so
and they would ask me again. Then finally my agent, Michael Ovitz, said,
"Look, why don't you work with Dustin and Larry Gelbart, the writer, for a
week, and if at the end of the week you still don't want to do it, then fine.
But at least you'll give yourself a chance to get into it," and of course that
was the trap and the trick.

As soon as I started to work on it I asked myself that same old question:
do I want to get up every morning of my life and spend my day with these
people? What's going to happen that's going to keep me interested for a year
with a guy dressed up like a woman? I mean, if you do that once or twice
or three times, then how do you do it the fourth time or the fifth time? This
was what I was worried about at the beginning. But working that week with
Dustin and Larry, we were able to come up with an approach that made me
feel like it could be a little more than a silly comedy. It could be a comedy

but it could also be about something else. It could have an idea that is centered that would prevent it from being the same joke over and over. And so I committed to do it and that's precisely what we worked on.

It was a very difficult film to make. I mean, comedy is the most difficult form there is in many ways. There's nothing worse than a joke that doesn't work. Drama has a wide variety of working. It can work here, it can work here, or it can work here. Comedy either works or it doesn't work. If it doesn't work, it's deadly. So it's very, very difficult to find precisely the right tone for a comedy and still keep it believable.

I think some of the arguments that I had with Dustin were well publicized. Even though they were creative arguments they were arguments just the same. We did a certain amount of fighting on that film but a lot less than what was reported. But we still disagreed sometimes about what was funny or what wasn't or what a particular scene should or should not be about. We worked very well together once we got the arguments out of the way. The arguments usually were in the morning. We'd come in the morning, talk about a scene, maybe argue, maybe not argue, and then forget the arguments and go ahead and make the picture.

> *I had heard that Sydney thought I was a very good actress, but he didn't know if I was sexy enough. I hadn't known that was an enormous part of Karen Blixen's character, but it was in a way. It was a love story. Anyway, to make a long story short, I went to my audition wearing something very low-cut. Cheap, but it worked.*
>
> Meryl Streep—Actress

# Out of Africa (1985)

*Meryl Streep; Robert Redford; Klaus Maria Brandauer; Michael Kitchen; Joseph Thiaka; Stephen Kinyanjui; Michael Gough; Suzanna Hamilton; Rachel Kempson; Graham Crowden; Leslie Phillips; Shane Rimmer; Mohammed Umar; Donal McCann; Kenneth Mason.*

I had made *Absence of Malice* with Kurt Luedtke. Kurt was a brand new screenwriter at the time and *Malice* was his first film and Kurt and I worked a long time together before the film got set up. Frank Price at Columbia, the same man who made *Tootsie*, said to Kurt, "I'd like you to write something else, what would you like to write about?" Kurt said, "I'd like to do *Out of*

*Africa.*" Frank laughed and said, "You and eight million other people." Columbia had owned the project for years and many directors had tried to make it and many writers had tried to write it. There were tons of scripts over there. At one time Nicholas Roeg had a production of it all set up with Julie Christie and Ryan O'Neal. But then for whatever reasons the film never got made. Kurt, who hadn't known of any of the history, had a kind of blissful naiveté about it and said, "Well, I think I'm going to try it." So Frank paid him to try it. Kurt went off and I went off and made *Tootsie.*

At the end of that period, Frank Price and Kurt sent me the script of *Out of Africa.* I did the exact same thing with *Out of Africa* that I had done with *Absence of Malice.* I read it and I was sort of intrigued but I felt it needed work. I didn't want to commit to it but I made a private deal with Kurt that I would work with him on it if he would agree to work with me on it. We spent one year doing two more drafts together and then I agreed to do it. Kurt did a beautiful job and we got some help on it later from David Rayfiel. It was a beautiful screenplay and of course it was an opportunity for me to work again with wonderful people: Redford, Meryl Streep, and Klaus Maria Brandauer.

*Out of Africa* was extremely difficult to make. I mean, Africa is not a country that is accustomed to big American film companies. The rules and the regulations were absurd. The red tape was bizarre and they didn't trust us. We had to pay customs duty on film that was coming in and going right back out. We kept saying, "Wait a minute, you don't understand. We're bringing the film in but we're taking it right out." "No, it doesn't matter; you have to pay customs duty," they would tell us. They didn't like us. They didn't want us there and they were extremely suspicious. I think we doubled tourism after the film came out. Then they fell over themselves because it really gave a terrific infusion to their economy. They had no idea it was going to do that, and at the time we were there, they made it very, very difficult for us. We received no government cooperation or any local cooperation.

There was a man named John Sutton who was a hunter and a guide there without whom we couldn't have made the film. He built roads for us. He built landing fields for us. He catered food for us. He set up these safaris for us because we had to do a lot of the film under canvas, camping out. Trying to get somewhere in that country is impossible. Now, having said all that, it's the most beautiful country in the world. I mean, it's extraordinary and it's the most magical place in the world, but it's very tough to make a film there. So many times I am blessed and cursed—blessed by the opportunity to go to a wonderful, exotic, foreign place and be there and live there, but cursed by the fact that I have to make a film there. So oftentimes I see the best and the worst side of it at the same time. The frustrations of trying to do business in a place that you're not familiar with, while at the same time trying to enjoy the beauty is frustration. What I really want to do is go back to Africa when I'm not making a film and enjoy what was so extraordinary about it.

It was tough for me from the point of view of just dealing with the animals. Tough from the point of view that it was the time span. Tough from the point of view of trying to make a picture in which there is very little narrative drive. It's essentially a character study. It's episodic. It's essentially a look at the life of a woman of great wisdom and courage, but there's very little conventional narrative drive. So for all those reasons it was a very difficult film.

I always say that working with Meryl Streep risks being boring because she's such a perfect person to work with that there's not a lot you can say. She's a gift. That's all I can tell you. She's the most extraordinary actress, lovely to work with, not difficult, no tantrums, no idiosyncrasies, no silly ego problems, never, ever, and ever! She's always willing to give up an extra hour of time and is always perfectly prepared. I can't say enough about her. On the other hand, it's hard to not sound boring when you talk about her. You just sort of gush over her. I was sorry that Meryl didn't win an Oscar because I thought she deserved it. But I was pleased that we won so many.

# Havana (1990)

*Robert Redford; Lena Olin; Alan Arkin; Tomas Milian; Daniel Davis; Tony Plana; Betsy Brantley; Lise Cutter; Richard Farnsworth; Mark Rydell; Vasek Simek; Fred Asparagus; Richard Portnow; Dion Anderson; Carmine Caridi.*

I was very sorry that *Havana* didn't work better than it did. I think it's one of the best performances Redford's ever given in a film. I think it's a really marvelous performance and very touching. A kind of a slightly over-the-hill, handsome guy, who knows he's beginning to lose it, and falls in love with someone he doesn't feel he totally deserves and knows it, and has to live with that. I was really surprised that it didn't reach more people, but it didn't. As I say, that's the way it goes. In the end you make films for yourself. It sounds egocentric, but it's the only way you can work, because if you could honestly figure out what people want and there was a way of doing that, then we would all just be billionaires and just make nothing but hit pictures. Nobody does. Nobody knows what people want. So the only alternative you have is to say "There have to be other people out there like me. If I love this, somebody else is going to love it," and sometimes you're right and sometimes you're wrong. I was wrong with *Havana*. If it came to me today, I would make it again.

We shot it in the Dominican Republic. I wanted to shoot it in Havana but our federal government was petrified that I might spend some money in Havana and that Mr. Castro would bomb us or something. It cost American stockholders an extra two million dollars to send us to the Dominican Republic rather than to go to Havana and shoot it in Havana where it took place. But we weren't allowed to shoot in Havana because it's against the law.

The Dominican Republic is a very poor country. It's a country where the line of demarcation between the poor and the rich is extraordinary. I really found it rather sad to be there. You see very, very rich people in compounds and then you see this poor, desolate area. This picture was difficult for another reason. We were trying to make *Havana* in a country that really wasn't Cuba and a city that wasn't Havana at all. We were trying to work under really horrible conditions—no proper air conditioning and it was stiflingly hot. We were in a tin makeshift warehouse because there were no stages, so we had to build our sets in this unbearably hot place that had no sound-proofing. It was technically difficult, let me put it that way. It's not a country that's easy for that kind of filmmaking. We probably should have made it somewhere else where it was a bit easier. In the end the film didn't work because people were not interested in it for whatever reasons. But boy, was it difficult from a technical point of view.

# The Firm (1993)

*Tom Cruise; Jeanne Tripplehorn; Gene Hackman; Hal Holbrook; Terry Kinney; Wilford Brimley; Ed Harris; Holly Hunter; David Strathairn; Gary Busey; Steven Hill; Tobin Bell; Barbara Garrick; Jerry Hardin; Paul Calderon.*

*The Firm* is a film that I had difficulty accepting at first. I didn't want to make it, initially. I had a lot of trouble trying to visualize it as a film. It was an immensely popular book and it was an enjoyable book to read, but I had difficulty when I read it trying to figure out how I could make it work as a film. I didn't think I could make it work as a film if I did the book literally, and so I had to make some changes, which some people have disagreed with but I felt I had to make them—changes in the characters and changes particularly in the way the film ended. I didn't have difficulty reading the book with the ending but I had difficulty trying to visualize the ending as a film.

Tom Cruise is a delight to work with. He's just a lovely young man who's full of enthusiasm. He's like a sponge. He wants to learn and he works really hard. Again, he was, thankfully for me, just completely professional. I think Cruise is developing and developing and is a terrific actor in addition to being a popular star, and he's going to get better and better and better. Gene Hackman . . . what can you say about Hackman? Hackman is a genius, he's great. He's one of those actors that has had an extraordinary career, and you're always mesmerized when you watch him act. I am anyway. I loved Jeanne Tripplehorn. She was great. She had a tougher job than people think. She had to play a role in which she was youthful enough to be absolutely believable to Tom Cruise and mature enough to be absolutely acceptable to Gene Hackman and that's a big spread in age. And I thought it worked very well.

> *The fact of his being an actor, I think, has an influence on the way he directs. But, again, good directors don't direct everyone the same way. They know what buttons to push, what cords to pull for different actors. I have enormous respect for him as an actor and as a director and writer.*
>
> Harrison Ford—Actor

# Sabrina (1995)

*Harrison Ford; Julia Ormond; Greg Kinnear; Nancy Marchand; John Wood; Richard Crenna; Angie Dickinson; Lauren Holly; Dana Ivey; Miriam Colon; Elizabeth Franz; Fanny Ardant; Valérie Lemercier; Patrick Bruel; Becky Ann Baker.*

I don't like to talk about films before they're out. I'm doing a remake for the first time, which may be the dumbest thing I've ever done and it may not be. I wanted to work with Harrison Ford and that's finally what it came down to. Again, it's a film that I said no to several times and then Harrison called me personally and I couldn't say no to him. I think he's marvelous,

---

NOTE: This interview was conducted after the filming of *Sabrina*. Pollack was editing the film at the time.

particularly in love stories. I like to do love stories and that's the other reason I guess I agreed to do it. Good love stories are harder and harder to find. The climate is not a climate that's conducive to love stories right now.

Most of the movies I've done—all of them, really—have been love stories of one kind or another. So the combination of the fact that it was an opportunity to do a love story and it was an opportunity to work with Harrison made it interesting. But I just sort of jumped in and I don't know whether it'll work or not. I'll have to see what happens, I don't want to say too much about it because it's not finished yet.

## It Is a Long Time Between Films

It takes a long time, sometimes, between films to find something that you really can fall in love with enough to, as I say, get up every morning and want to be with those people. And so in between-time I have a small company called Mirage and we've produced quite a few films since I've started the company. These are films that I don't direct like *The Fabulous Baker Boys*, *Searching for Bobby Fischer,* and *Sense and Sensibility,* a Jane Austen novel scripted by Emma Thompson and starring Hugh Grant, Emma Thompson, Kate Winslet, and Alan Rickman. It's a nice way to be busy until I fall in love with another script.

## Has the Industry Changed?

I guess the thing that saddens me most in terms of then and now is that the economics of the business have changed somewhat. Every single studio is now owned by a large conglomerate. Conglomerates are usually large publicly-held businesses that are required to issue quarterly reports. As a result, the film industry is being forced to perform like the conglomerate's other products, whatever they might be. The large body of intermediate films has moved into television now. It's much easier in Hollywood to make a $60 million film than it is to make a $15 million film. A company is just not interested in the profit they're gonna end up making with most $10, $12, $15 million films. Everybody's looking now for the $200 million-grossing movie. It's designed for two hours of entertainment and then it can be disposed of and never thought of again. Now, I don't say that you shouldn't make films for entertainment. That, of course, is what you make them for. But right now it feels to me like the economic pressures have made it really impossible to speculate the way you could at one time.

Marketing costs have become astronomical. So that even if you spend $10 million, which is cheap today, you still have to spend $12 million opening it. And that's become a deterrent to a lot of experimental movie making, out-of-the-mainstream movie making, personal movie making, special movie making, which produced some of our best films at one time. I feel like that's one of the more depressing changes.

## Working with Actors?

You know, I think the fact that I've been an actor, and that I spent so much time teaching acting when I started out, and so much time trying to understand the psychology of actors, that lets me feel comfortable, let's put it that way, with the actors. And so I suppose that's been a help in terms of a rapport that can happen, that I can speak to them as somebody who's been there or who's at least been in that arena. As I said before, that's not a requirement at all. That's only a lucky break for me. It helps me in a certain way.

## His Favorite Films

Trying to talk about films that are favorites is a little like your fingers and toes. It's very hard to say. You have sentimental favorites and I suppose they are like your fingers and toes or your children, the least popular ones are the favorites. You don't worry about a film that's a big hit, but you worry, you feel bad about the ones that you like that aren't. And so in many ways you sometimes feel a distorted fondness or affection for a film that's a failure. I've never made a film that I didn't want to make and I've never made a film that in some way hasn't become a part of me while I made it, so I don't feel a dislike for any of the films. I'm sometimes embarrassed when I see an old film of mine. I see a particular kind of heavy-handedness or a little bit of amateurishness or something that I might say, "Gee, I wish I could do that scene again," or, "I wish I could do this a different way." But I was true to myself at the time and so I don't apologize for them in any way.

## Where Does He Go from Here?

As far as the future is concerned, really what I would love to do, and I don't know that I'll ever get a real opportunity, is to make a small film. I'm tired of making expensive movies where every second is costing thousands and thousands of dollars and where if the film doesn't gross hundreds of millions of dollars it's a failure. I've never had that opportunity except in the days when films didn't cost that much. I would make films like everybody else, but there wasn't so much attention paid to them. Today, every time you go out there everybody knows about it, everybody knows what it costs. The releasing business is a jungle. There are so many films competing in a limited marketplace, and so much money being spent on the promotion, that it doesn't feel as good as it used to feel. There was a time when you felt that everybody had a shot and each film had a chance of finding its own audience.

So I'd love to get an opportunity to make a less expensive film, a smaller film, and see what that's like. Maybe I'll hate it, but maybe not.

# Director Filmography

*The Slender Thread* (1965)
*This Property Is Condemned* (1966)
*The Scalphunters* (1968)
*They Shoot Horses, Don't They?* (1969)
*Castle Keep* (1969)
*Jeremiah Johnson* (1972)
*The Way We Were* (1973)
*The Yakuza* (1975)
*Three Days of the Condor* (1975)
*Bobby Deerfield* (1977)
*The Electric Horseman* (1979)
*Absence of Malice* (1981)
*Tootsie* (1982)
*Out of Africa* (1985)
*Havana* (1990)
*The Firm* (1993)
*Sabrina* (1995)
*Random Hearts* (1999)

---

NOTE: Since this interview was completed, Pollack has directed *Random Hearts*, starring Harrison Ford; Kristin Scott Thomas; Richard Jenkins; Charles Dutton; Bonnie Hunt; Dylan Baker; Dennis Haysbert; Lynne Thigpen; Susanna Thompson; Peter Coyote; Todd Malta; Paul Guilfoyle; Bill Cobbs; Tal Carawan, Jr.; and Vincent De Paul.

# Awards

### Academy Awards, USA
*Out of Africa*, Best Director, 1985
*Out of Africa*, Best Picture, 1985
*Tootsie*, Best Director (nominated), 1982
*Tootsie*, Best Picture (shared with Dick Richards, nominated), 1982
*They Shoot Horses, Don't They?*, Best Director (nominated), 1969

### Berlin International Film Festival
Berlinale Camera Award, 1986

### Bodil Festival
*Tootsie*, Best American Film, 1982

### British Academy Awards
*Sliding Doors*, Best British Film (shared with Philippa Braithwaite, William Horberg, and Peter Horwitt, nominated), 1998
*Tootsie*, Best Direction (nominated), 1982
*Tootsie*, Best Film (shared with Dick Richards, nominated), 1982

### Golden Globes, USA
*Out of Africa*, Best Director—Motion Picture (nominated), 1985
*Tootsie*, Best Director—Motion Picture (nominated), 1982
*They Shoot Horses, Don't They?* Best Director—Motion Picture (nominated), 1969

### New York Film Critics Circle Award
*Tootsie*, Best Director, 1982

### ShoWest Convention, USA
Producer of the Year, 1983

# The Films Of James Cameron

**B**orn in Kapuskasing, Ontario, Canada, James Cameron grew up in Niagara Falls. He moved to Brea, California, in 1971, where he studied physics at Fullerton College while working as a machinist and, later, a truck driver. Setting his sights on a career in film, Cameron quit his trucking job in 1978 and raised money from a consortium of dentists in Tustin, California, to produce a short film in 35mm. He served as producer, director, co-writer, editor, and miniature builder, cinematographer, and special effects supervisor.

His work on the short film led to a position at Roger Corman's New World Pictures in 1980 on *Battle Beyond the Stars*. In the frenzied world of low-budget guerrilla filmmaking, Cameron found a home on the production where he could wear many hats again: miniature builder, model unit DP, and matte painter. Most importantly, he became the art director of the picture's main unit and found the energy of the set exhilarating.

James Cameron has been called one of the most innovative producers, writers, and directors working in Hollywood today. He is willing to take chances, even against the greatest of odds, to create new and exciting visual motion-picture entertainment. He has many critics on many levels, but that does not seem to bother or deter him—or his loyal audiences, who demonstrate their support for his work at the box office. In Hollywood, that is where it counts.

> *I think that Cameron is a very intense person. He's very intense with his writing. He's very serious with his directing. He knows about every single thing. If it is makeup, if it is visual effects, special effects, stunts, stunt coordinating, himself holding the camera. So he's just so involved. It's really extraordinary to work with a per-*

*son like that and to see that firsthand, and to also be a close friend and to know the other side of Jim Cameron.*

*Arnold Schwarzenegger—Actor*

# The Conversation

As early as I can remember, I loved film. I was fascinated by the imagination, the creativity of film from as early as I can remember. I think there's a transition point where you say, "I'd like to try that."

I certainly remember making super-eight films in high school—playing around with animation, pixel animation, and doing kind of documentary films about the city that I lived in. Things like that. Nothing terribly profound. I think I turned them in as geography class term papers in the eleventh grade.

As a teenager there was an inherent curiosity about how shots were done, how cameras worked, how a zoom lens worked. I was quite a techno-nerd and president of the science club in my high school. I was fascinated by the nuts-and-bolts aspect of filmmaking very much. I was also interested in writing and interested in art, so there was a very nice convergence of all those things.

I'm not sure it was all terribly clear to me how much sense filmmaking really made to me until later. I remember that in high school I was in the theater arts department and writing and producing plays and working with neophyte actors. So there was a definite sense of wanting to tell stories, of wanting to fulfill what I call that narrative drive, the drive to try to tell a story, which I think is psychologically inherent in some people. Like when you're sitting around a campfire, there's always one guy who thinks he can get everybody else to laugh or whatever. That's the earliest thing I can remember.

When I went to college I actually studied physics. I thought, "Oh, I'll be a scientist, I'll do something important." I kind of turned away from filmmaking. I probably thought I couldn't get there from here. Other people, sort of deities, make films. I don't get to be one of them, so, realistically, I'll be something else. So I actually clipped my own wings before the fact. It wasn't until years later that I thought the hell with it. Film is what I should be doing. So I threw out all those other grand schemes for what I thought my life should be somewhere around the age of twenty-four. I said, okay,

I'm going to be a filmmaker. I'm going to take a run at this with everything I have. Not holding back. Not trying to keep a job and do a little on the side or whatever, but just all guns blazing.

Then some friends came to me and said they had some money lined up to make a little film. They wanted to know if I had any ideas. They sort of had put the cart before the horse and had fallen into a situation where they had some funding from a tax shelter group and they had no film. I said, "Oh, baby, did you make the right phone call." I immediately took over their project and quit the job I had as a truck driver. And the next day I literally woke up, yawned and stretched, and said, "Now I'm a filmmaker." It was pretty much that rapid a transition.

I think it was two years before I actually made any real money at it. I had to go through a number of entry-level jobs in low budget, independent films as a model builder and as an art director. I employed my art skills to sort of wedge myself deeper and deeper into the filmmaking system. It was pretty much the light bulb flashing on one day saying I need to be doing this.

I'm not really sure why I started writing scripts. I think there was some desire to tell a story and screenwriting seemed like an interesting thing. I had done a little bit in high school. I had written some scripts for films that I never got the money to make, so I was fascinated by the form, fascinated by the idea of writing a movie. I don't think I even knew what a director was at that point. I mean, I knew that there was this guy, Stanley Kubrick, and he made these films, but I don't think I really understood what a director really was or what they did.

I was very unsophisticated, you know, although some of the fictional ideas I was playing around with were fairly sophisticated. Some of them I would be happy to go make a film about today. A lot of my early thinking was good thinking and I still harvest a lot of those concepts. But in terms of knowing how the film system worked, I was a total outsider. I'm not even sure there was literature available at that time. There weren't a lot of "how to" books on filmmaking at that point and I didn't have access to a film school. Later, a few months after I decided to be a filmmaker, it occurred to me that there was this place called USC where they taught people how to be filmmakers. So I would drive down there a couple of times a week and sit in the library all day and just read books on filmmaking. I'd read all the back issues of *American Cinematographer*.

I'd photocopy thesis papers on how optical printing worked and how front screen projection worked and all the nuts-and-bolts, high-tech areas of filmmaking. At that time there was no computer image creation. It was all photochemistry and optics. I read that, I absorbed that, and learned how to do it, and essentially gave myself a high-tech filmmaking education for the cost of the xeroxing.

I certainly didn't get all the benefits of a film-school education. I still didn't know how a film was made. I had to make one and kind of invent all the positions. You do this, and I'll do that, and pretty soon we had invented all the various positions that were necessary.

The most invaluable training that I got was the next stage, which was working on a real movie. That was working for Roger Corman. I didn't care if it was the bottom of the heap in terms of film budgets and so on. That was absolutely invaluable crash training—nearly crash-and-burn training because people burn out very, very rapidly in that low budget, independent area. But then, of course, certain people do manage to live through it, survive, and learn what they need to know, and go on.

## Working on *Battle Beyond the Stars*

Roger Corman has been invaluable in starting a number of careers. I didn't get to deal directly with Roger. His organization had grown to a point where there was a layer in between him and people at the production level. I was actually hired by the head of visual effects on a movie called *Battle Beyond the Stars*. I think it was the first time Roger actually had a head of visual effects.

On one of the few times I actually got to meet with Roger in person I remember pitching him the idea of doing front screen projection so that we could do some cool imagery like they did on *2001: A Space Odyssey*. I told him it could be done dirt-cheap. I knew exactly how much it was going to cost and I showed him a little budget. He said, "Okay, fine, you're now the head of front screen projection." So I made up a little plaque that said "Process Projection Department." I put it on the door of an empty office. I didn't even ask if I could use the office. And anybody who wanted to talk to me about front screen projection had to go there. So immediately I had created this niche that didn't exist at three o'clock in the afternoon the day before. And everybody was kind of scratching his or her heads going, "What the hell's this? Now we have a front projection department?" They started getting check requests and they just kind of like stamped them. And pretty soon I hired a few people. It was like this tumor growing on the inside of the production. They didn't know how to classify it, so they just let it go.

Then they fired the art director because he wasn't prepared; he wasn't ready for shooting. So I said, "Oh, I'll do that." So I became the art director on the film. I turned over my front screen projection duties to my assistant and became the production designer. Then I was really working around the clock.

My work on *Beyond the Stars* was comprised of production design and art direction, and then in postproduction it evolved into heading up a visual effects camera unit. I did that for three months. Subsequent to that we actually took Roger's facility and used it as a service company to service other film productions and do visual effects. So we kept the place alive and we did it long enough for Roger to start up another picture. So we held the core group together. When we started the next picture, once again I was the production designer. I also had my hand in visual effects. What I pretty much had decided at this point was that I should be directing because I looked at some of the losers that Roger had directing movies for him and I thought I could do better than those guys.

## His First Directing Job

So I had already made that cognitive leap that production design was not where I should be. I should be directing. So I asked Roger if I could make that leap on *Galaxy of Terror* as second unit director. At first he said no. He needed me to do production design. Then they got into hot water halfway through shooting and started dropping too many scenes and getting behind schedule. So Roger asked how I was doing on production design. I told him I could turn it all over to my assistant and tried to convince him that he needed me to do second unit directing. He agreed. I actually ended up doing dialogue scenes with some of the cast to pull up the slack. And this was the first time I had ever worked with actors and real scenes and it was fun. The actors liked me and I liked them. I realized there was a whole other dimension to this job that hadn't really occurred to me. It's not just about creating images. It's about creating emotions. This is so intuitively obvious to anyone who started on the other end of filmmaking, maybe coming from writing or coming from acting—not necessarily intuitively obvious to the president of the science club in high school. I had to come full circle.

So I had all these high-faluting ideas going into this big second unit director gig on *Galaxy of Terror.* The very first thing they had me do was film an insert of a severed arm that's being eaten by maggots. Of course, they don't use maggots. They use mealworms and they cover them with slime, methylcellulose actually, so they look kind of slimy and horrible. We put them all over the arm, put the lights on and rolled the camera, and waited for the worms to do their thing, and they didn't do anything. They just kind of sat there. They looked completely inert. So I thought, well, what would happen if we put a little electrical current through these worms? Maybe they'd jump around a little more.

So we get all ready to do the shot and two guys I knew who were producers had come up behind me to watch me work because they had heard I was doing some directing. I rolled the camera and when I said "Action," what they saw was two hundred mealworms all come to life. When I said "Cut," they stopped moving. This must have been tremendously impressive to two low-budget horror-movie producers. I'm sure they ratcheted up in their mind that if I could get a performance out of worms, I probably could work very well with actors. So they hired me that day to direct a low budget horror film which was called *Piranha II*.

## Piranha II: The Spawning (1981)

*Tracy Berg; Captain Kidd Brewer, Jr.; Phil Colby; Dorothy Cunningham; Carole Davis; Gaetano Del Grande; Paul Drummond; Ancile Gloudon; Leslie Graves; Connie Lynn Hadden; Lance Henriksen; Paul Issa; Lee Krug; Hildy Magnasun; Jan Eisner Mannon; Steve Marachuk; Tricia O'Neil; Jim Pair; Ricky G. Paull; Anne Pollack; Johnny Ralston; Sally Ricca; Ted Richert; Arnie Ross.*

Unfortunately, I didn't get along very well with the producer, whose ideas were pretty bogus. I wound up only directing about seven or eight days of that shoot before we had irreconcilable creative differences and they fired me down in Jamaica where we were shooting.

*Piranha II* was my first official directing gig. But when people ask me what my first film was, I say *Terminator* because I wrote and directed it and I didn't get fired. *Piranha II*, which preceded that, was the first time I got a paycheck as a director, but I got fired after a few days. So it's hard for me to claim that film in any reasonable way.

But the experience of working with the actors was wonderful. I realized I could do it.

I came back to Los Angeles after *Piranha II* and I had worked up through the system and was now a director. But I had been chopped off at the knees on that picture and now I didn't know where I was. Was I still an art director? Should I go back to that? Or should I stay on the course of directing? I couldn't get a phone call returned from anybody. I literally was further removed from my goals as a filmmaker at that point than I was previously. Because previously I had potential. Now, I was just a loser.

# The Terminator (1984)

*Arnold Schwarzenegger; Michael Biehn; Linda Hamilton; Paul Winfield;*
*Lance Henriksen; Rich Rossovich; Bess Motta; Earl Boen; Dick Miller; Shawn Schepps;*
*Bruce M. Kerner; Franco Columbu; Bill Paxton; Brad Rearden; Brian Thompson.*

I finally realized that the only way I was going to get my career jump-started was if I created my own project and then held on to it tenaciously, like an abalone, until somebody would put up the money for it. So I conceived a project that had the imagery that I could create cost-effectively with my experience in visual effects. It had some of that imagery but not so much that the budget was proportionately large, because I knew no one would trust me with a large budget.

So my target was to write a script that could be done non-union, independent, maybe in the three to four million-dollar range, inclusive of the visual effects. And I think I actually hit that window pretty well, because the below the line on the first *Terminator* film was about $4.5 million. With Arnold Schwarzenegger's salary and various other above the line considerations, since there were several production entities involved, it actually cost on the books $6.4 million.

But still, that was pretty cost-effective filming. So I thought, how could I do visual effects, how can I create visual effects? Visual effects generally are used to create some sense of wonder, some sense of otherness, futuristic, outer space, creatures, fantasy—all that sort of thing. I thought, how can I introduce that otherness, that element of wonder, into a low-budget environment that can be shot on the street, very conventionally, very guerrilla film making.

So, I thought, fine. It's present day. It's Los Angeles. It's the back streets of L.A. So, what happens next? Maybe it can come from space. It can come from the future. From a narrative standpoint, it starts to limit your options. It starts to lay out a certain way based on those givens. So I had a given— a contemporary environment that was determined by budget. No big movie stars, so maybe the main characters can be kind of young. What element could I personally bring to it that another filmmaker might not, which of course was visual effects.

So then I came up with this idea of a futuristic hit man that comes back to try to change the present, and one thing led to another, and pretty soon I had the *Terminator*. It really was reverse-engineered to fit in the box of what I thought I could do as a first film.

It was hard to make *The Terminator*. It was tough. We had to drop scenes and we went through all the low-budget nightmares. Although, I think we had a sense, as we watched dailies, that something pretty cool was happening. And I think my sense of just how cool came from the fact that nobody called me up and gave me any trouble about the dailies. So I thought that was a pretty good sign. I don't think any of us went into the movie thinking it wouldn't be a hit. Before we started shooting I had invested two years of my life in *The Terminator*, just waiting and living at sustenance level, storyboarding the picture, turning it every which way in my mind, taking out the scenes I didn't need. It represented pretty much the best that I could do and I don't think it ever occurred to me that it wouldn't be a good film. I don't think I necessarily could have predicted that it would be a cult hit that would have an enduring value in the way that it has. That would have been impossible to predict in the same way that the success of *Titanic* was impossible to predict.

Sometimes there's just an alchemy that happens between the movie and the audience that is impossible to quantify. Because I worked just as hard on *The Abyss* and the alchemy didn't happen. I think *The Abyss* was just a better quality film from a filmmaking standpoint, but that perfect elusive equation never happened.

## The Casting of Arnold

*The Terminator* was a film that came out of nowhere in terms of the Hollywood mainstream. It just came whistling in out of the dark as far as Hollywood was concerned. Nobody connected with the film was anybody. We were all newcomers, except for Arnold, of course. But Arnold was being reinvented in a new way that no one expected to work and yet it worked so well. So he flashed onto the scene now as a viable entity beyond just standing around in a loincloth swinging a sword.

Arnold was never really slated to be in the picture. Mike Medevoy at Orion suggested Arnold play Michael Biehn's character, Reese. I don't think there's anybody that would think that was a great idea. At that point in his career, doing twenty-five pages of expository dialogue, and talking really fast, and painting this picture of a future world that we didn't have the budget to actually visually create was not going to be Arnold's strong suit, you know. He's evolved tremendously as an actor and I would throw him any dialogue now and feel confident that he could do it and make it play. But at that time I certainly didn't think he was the right guy to play that character.

So anyway, the phone call with Medevoy went like this—and I am not making this up. He asked if I was sitting down. Then he said he had the perfect casting for *Terminator*: O.J. Simpson as the Terminator and Arnold Schwarzenegger as Reese, and I'm thinking, that that is the dumbest idea I've ever heard in my life. But I couldn't say that. I just thought it was idiotic. I put O.J. Simpson out of my mind but I thought Arnold Schwarzenegger was pretty cool. I thought he was just a cool guy. I thought I would like to go and have lunch with Conan just to shake his hand. Not that I thought it would go anywhere.

So I'm having lunch with Arnold and I found him to be just this wonderful, amazing, captivating human being, which of course we all know now. We understand his charisma. But the whole time we were talking about this script I'm thinking he sucks for the role of Reese, but he'd make a great Terminator. I'm looking at the angles, the brow, the look, and everything. He's a human bulldozer. He's a panzer tank. He is the Terminator. He is the guy that I imagined that I never quite found the face for.

He talked about the script. He talked about the scenes. He loved the scenes. And every scene he quoted was a Terminator scene, but he never said anything about playing Reese. He was just enthusiastic about the piece and willing to tackle it. And if it meant learning twenty-five pages of expository dialogue, so be it. That's how he thinks.

The line "I'll be back" was right in the script. I remember when I wrote it. I thought it would be funny. I didn't think it would become the signature line of the film, but it was intended in the writing to work the way that it did, which is that the audience knows that the character means more than I'm going out for a hamburger and I'll be right back. I knew that the audience would be on the inside of the line that they would get it, and they would be tingling with anticipation to see what the Terminator would do next.

I never changed a line for Arnold. I never changed anything, but there was something that he brought to that line that made it so vivid and allowed the audience's imagination to work ahead of time in that way, in anticipating what would happen next, you know. It gave that moment a really nice turbo boost and made it memorable.

Casting Arnold in the role of the Terminator was a very lucky stroke for us and for him, too, quite frankly. So I think from the standpoint of the Hollywood mainstream, they got up one morning and opened the trades and went, "What the hell is this movie that's number one this weekend?" And by the way, it was number one the next weekend and the weekend after that. It dominated the Thanksgiving weekend against a couple of big pictures, like *Dune,* for example, and *2010,* which were big studio pictures. Actually, *2010* was a big studio picture and *Dune* was a high-end independent film. But these were big megabuck movies and *Terminator* just steam- rolled over them. And it had been done by these nonentities.

## Suddenly He's a Hot Property

So, all of a sudden, we were hot properties. After *Terminator* every agent was trying to get me to go to lunch. All of a sudden they want to know who I am and why I have the number one movie four weeks in a row and they never heard of me. I did some of those lunches because I was curious. I knew nothing about the agency world. That was interesting for about a week.

The inevitable question was, what am I going to do next? But I had actually already sown those seeds because in the interval between *Piranha II* and when *The Terminator* actually started shooting, there was a period where the film was set to go but then got postponed for six months, and during that period I had written the second *Rambo*. It was called *Rambo*, which everybody now calls *Rambo II*, which was actually *Rambo: First Blood Part II*.

> *Making movies is like being in a war. Every day's a battle. You're fighting the budget or the schedule or just the elements. Jim pushes himself harder than anyone he's ever pushed as far as the cast and crew. But in return he expects a hundred and one percent from everyone on that set.*
>
> Bill Paxton—Actor

## Aliens (1986)

*Sigourney Weaver; Carrie Henn; Michael Biehn; Paul Reiser; Lance Henriksen; Bill Paxton; William Hope; Jenette Goldstein; Al Matthews; Mark Rolston; Ricco Ross; Colette Hiller; Daniel Kash; Cynthia Scott; Tip Tipping.*

I had also written this other thing called *Alien II*. I wrote it for David Goddard, Walter Hill, and Gordon Carroll with the proviso that they make a best effort to allow me to direct it. They said, "Sure kid, no problem." But I'm sure if *Terminator* hadn't been a hit, there wouldn't have been a snowball's hope in hell of me directing that film. But I had written a good chunk, maybe the first two-thirds of the screenplay, for what became *Aliens* before I did *The Terminator*. And they loved it. It was a damned good thing I didn't finish the script because they probably would have been in production before I finished *Terminator*.

But Walter Hill actually took the high road. The others were ready to fire me and hang me up by my heels because I hadn't gotten the script done because I had to go off and direct *Terminator*. Walter called and said he was going to wait until I finished *Terminator* because he really liked what I was doing with the script. And I thought, that's great. The guy's standing up for something. So I'm always thankful to Walter for that.

So the second I finished *Terminator* I went back to work on *Aliens*. I slammed the door to my little apartment in Tarzana and didn't answer any calls. *Terminator* came out the end of October and I remember writing over the Christmas holidays into early 1985 and delivering the script in January. Man, I was a real hard charger in those days.

So now everybody started taking me to lunch and saying, "Kid, kid, kid, trust me. Don't make this *Alien II* thing. It's a losing proposition. It's a no win for you. If it's good, it'll be good because Ridley Scott did such a good first film. And if it's bad, it'll be totally your fault." My response was, "Yeah, but I really like it. I think it'll be cool. Can't I just do it?"

I was very unsophisticated from the standpoint of strategizing a career. I've always kind of been that way. I just go where ideas excite me. And I could just see that movie in my head at that point. I had to make it. Then there were some little issues like the fact that no one had made a deal with Sigourney Weaver and I had written the script about a character named Ripley that only she could play. Little things like that. But all that stuff got solved and I was making *Aliens* next. I didn't have to play the development game and read a bunch of scripts. I was already on a trajectory and just continued on that trajectory.

*Aliens* was very well received. We got seven Academy Award nominations. Sigourney Weaver got nominated for Best Actress. You can correct me if I'm wrong, but I believe that's the first time that an actor has been nominated for best actor or actress in a hard-core genre picture like a horror or a science-fiction film that I can think of.

I love science fiction. I don't see why it should be limited by this genre box that it's put into. I don't see why you can't make an A quality movie for a grown-up sensibility that happens to be about a science fiction subject. There was a period where science fiction was ghetto-ized to be thought of as juvenile. It was kid's stuff. People are finally realizing that we live in a science fiction world. We live in a world that has been transformed in the last fifteen years by microchips, and we are living in a world that no one could have imagined fifteen years ago, and we've just adapted to it. So maybe our tolerance for that kind of imaginative thinking has increased quite a bit and been absorbed into the mainstream, and maybe that was happening around the time that *Aliens* came out.

We didn't see it as camp. We took it very seriously. I think the reason that subsequent *Alien* films haven't done as well is because they didn't invest in the reality of it. When Ridley Scott made his film, he took it totally seriously. He wanted to make that place real. He wanted to put the audience in it and have them live there for two of the longest hours of their lives.

That was pretty much my same goal in *Aliens*, except that I added the additional goal of turbo-charging, to create an adrenaline rush that comes from not just fear but also from exhilaration, by putting in the action elements as well as the suspense.

All of a sudden, as opposed to having a sophomore slump, the second picture was even more successful than the first picture. So that went a long way toward cementing my career as a filmmaker and Gail Herd's career as a producer.

The furthest I could ever have imagined when I started into film making is that I would make a big Hollywood science-fiction film that would be seen around the world and be a big hit, that people would line up around the block to see. That was the furthest I could have ever imagined. That was the end goal. Well, I had accomplished that with *Aliens*. I hadn't thought any further than that because I didn't think I'd ever get there. The films that inspired me to be a filmmaker in the first place were films like *2001, Close Encounters of the Third Kind*—films like that. Visually imaginative science fiction epic films. Well, I had done that. So what next? Do it again? I don't think that way.

> *He is known for being tough. He's someone who does things that no-body else would ever, ever, ever do in the movies. You can't imagine the movie business without Jim Cameron.*
>
> Jamie Lee Curtis—Actress

## Is He Tough To Work With?

I think anybody that's ever read any article about me knows that I'm completely dictatorial and never give the actors any leeway whatsoever. (*Laughs.*)

Those articles are a lot of crap. First of all, actors don't respond to that. Even if it were the way I wanted it to be on the set, which it is not, it would not work. It just wouldn't work. You wouldn't get good performances. You have to be in an eye-level partnership with your actors. And that's with every actor, not just the stars. Anybody that's got a moment in your film, no matter how fleeting, is just as important as anybody else in the film. I think of it as a series of fleeting moments. The stars have more of those moments so they have that same amount of responsibility more often. But if you're on my movie for one day, you have equal responsibility for that day. Because I think the film's effect on the audience is like a chain, and the chain is only as good as the weakest link. And if the weakest link is some person that doesn't give a great performance, they'll stand out and weaken the film. So I work with everybody equally.

# The Abyss (1989)

*Ed Harris; Mary Elizabeth Mastrantonio; Michael Biehn;
Leo Burmester; Todd Graff; John Bedford Lloyd; J.C. Quinn; Kimberly Scott;
Captain Kidd Brewer, Jr.; George Robert Klek; Christopher Murphy; Adam Nelson;
Dick Warlock; Jimmie Ray Weeks; J. Kenneth Campbell.*

I had to look around for what was interesting to me as a filmmaker. *The Abyss* was actually a concept that I had in high school. I wanted to play with ideas that were more emotional and philosophical and less about action shots. I think that probably accounts for *The Abyss's* middling performance, business-wise. It wasn't a bomb, but it didn't make a lot of money. I think that people wanted it to be more of that adrenaline thing. They wanted more of the suspense, and the jolts, and the thrills and spills. It was never intended to be that, you know. But does that mean you don't make a film as a filmmaker? I think you have to explore new territory.

In the *Abyss*, I was exploring new territory and you know what? The audience didn't rally behind the flag. But I was exploring new territory in *True Lies*, playing around in comedy, and the audience responded. And I was exploring really new territory in *Titanic*, and they really rallied behind the flag, so I think that in the abstract sense it's important always to keep moving into some new region, keep it fresh, keep people off balance. The second you start cookie-cutting your own stuff, I think, is when you're going to get hosed.

On *The Abyss*, one of the goals was to really put the audience underwater. Of course, I don't believe you can put an audience anywhere that you haven't put your character. The audience's doorway into the experience is always through the character or group of characters. So if the audience doesn't recognizably see the people that they know in that underwater environment, then they're there just watching some Jacques Cousteau special from a distance. So I knew I had to put my actors in the water and under-water and I had to see them.

Now, anyone familiar with scuba equipment knows you put this mask on your face and put this thing in your mouth and your face is all distorted and you can't talk and you don't even look like yourself. Scuba was not the answer. And actors communicate so much of what they're feeling emotion-ally through the timber of their voice and their vocal performance. They needed to be able to talk. Now we're talking about helmets. Most actors don't know how to scuba dive, let alone dive in a helmet. First we had to design the helmet. Then we had to teach the actors how to use it, and teaching them how to use it had to go beyond two hours of familiarization. They had to be safe in those helmets. To be safe you had to put a safety diver with them in case they got into trouble. They have to know what to do. They have to know how to equalize their ears so they can descend. They have to know how to get out of it. How to hold their breath. How to ascend to the surface while exhaling so they don't embolize and rupture their lungs. So we trained the actors.

Now we're all down there underwater and we're doing scenes. Ed Harris has his script laminated in plastic so he can read the dialogue before each take. We literally had an underwater stage for the first time. We could talk to each other and do production dialogue, and most of the dialogue that seemed to be underwater in the film was actually recorded underwater. There was a little looping, but not much. And it was great for me. I wore a helmet also and I could talk to the actors. I think it revolutionized under-water filming.

The actors responded to this in varying degrees. Most of them thought it was an adventure and they really enjoyed it, up to a point. When it got to be long, long hours underwater, it got to be fatiguing, physically fatigu-ing. I think that got to be a bit much, especially for Ed Harris. Ed had a harder job than anybody else because he had to also act in a water-filled helmet, which is a whole different deal. He had contact lenses in his eyes so his eyes could focus in the water, and his helmet was filled with water and he had to hold his breath and act. So he had a whole other level of stress to contend with as an actor.

It was a good film to have done. It wasn't always a good film to be doing. But it was a good film to have done, because you make a film like *The Abyss* with all the technical and emotional challenges and you come out the end of it and you say, you know what? I feel like I just climbed Mount Everest. So every mountain after you've climbed Mount Everest looks easier. Or maybe the downside of that is you convince yourself that you can do more, you know, which could be a mistake. You might wind up doing a movie like *Titanic*, which was certainly more than *The Abyss*.

# Terminator 2: Judgment Day (1991)

*Arnold Schwarzenegger; Linda Hamilton; Edward Furlong; Robert Patrick; Earl Boen; Joe Morton; S. Epatha Merkerson; Castulo Guerra; Danny Cooksey; Jenette Goldstein; Xander Berkeley; Leslie Hamilton Gearren; Ken Gibbel; Robert Winley; Shane Wilder.*

I think it's always flattering when someone asks you to make a film based on a world that you have created. It gave me an opportunity to explore my original characters further. They put on no creative constraints whatsoever. They said, "If you can sell it to Arnold, you can do it." It was my world, my characters, so it was an opportunity to expand the imagery and do more.

But there's certainly a challenge with every sequel in that you have to satisfy the needs of the built-in audience while expanding to a new audience, and for that new audience you cannot assume they know anything about the original film. You can't afford to be repetitious but you have to convey enough information about what happened the first time so the new audience can enjoy the second one. The biggest thing, and this applies to any sequel and was certainly true of *Terminator 2*, is that you have to balance two opposite factors and those factors are familiarity and surprise. The audience must have their need for contact with the familiar satisfied, and yet it can't be so familiar that it's boring or feels like a retread. There must be surprises. But surprises can cut either way. They can be negative surprises like, "Oh, I didn't expect that and I really don't like it." Or, "Oh, I didn't expect that, but now that I see it, it really fits very well with everything else and I should have expected it." The best surprises are the ones where the audience says, "I should have known they were going to do that." But yet, they never think of it. So there's real art to writing a sequel.

I'd done a few sequels at that point—*Piranha II, First Blood II, Aliens II*. I did a lot of movies with "twos" after them. I tried to get rid of the twos as much as I could in the titles but they're still twos. But clearly the trick there is to give the audience what they think they want and then give them that much more.

A lot of the "that much more" came from the creation of the T-1000 character. The technology was advancing to the point where those things became possible at exactly the point where they called me up and said, "Would you like to do *Terminator II*?" The irony of course, and not too many people know this, is that the T-1000, the liquid metal man, was my original idea for the Terminator eight or nine years earlier, but we had no way of doing it. That's the image that I had in my head. The Terminator was that liquid-metal guy. But we couldn't figure out how to do that so we switched it to the other story. So that liquid-metal guy got resurrected and became the nemesis of the second picture.

In my mind it was all part of that same universe right from the beginning and maybe that's the key to why people found it to be organic or consistent in some way.

# True Lies (1994)

*Arnold Schwarzenegger; Jamie Lee Curtis; Tom Arnold; Bill Paxton; Tia Carrere;*
*Art Malik; Eliza Dushku; Grant Heslov; Charlton Heston; Marshall Manesh;*
*James Allen; Dieter Rauter; Jane Morris; Katsy Chappell; Crystina Wyler.*

The reason that I made *True Lies* goes back to a very particular moment. I was sitting at Arnold's restaurant in Santa Monica having a bowl of oatmeal and we were just talking. He asked me what I wanted to do next. I told him I had a number of ideas. I asked him what he wanted to do next. He said he had just seen this little film that he thought would make a good movie and a good character for him. And I thought to myself, I've never heard Arnold talk about a project from the standpoint of the character. I wanted to hug him and thought, he's an actor now. Because now he wants to do a movie because of the character and not because of the action sequences or how much money it could make and all of that stuff.

When I saw the film (*La Totale*, French, 1992) I thought it was going to need a lot of work. The character was kind of this Wally Cox little nerdy guy. I had to think for a minute to see what Arnold liked about the guy. What he liked about it was the juxtaposition of the fact that on the one hand he was this James Bond character who was involved in all this really complex international espionage, and on the other hand he was a homebody. I know Arnold is a family man and that appealed to him. That juxtaposition—those two worlds. Because those are Arnold's worlds, where he goes out and the world at large knows him as this big hero who saves the

---

NOTE: *True Lies* was the first film to cost more than $100 million.

world, and on the other hand he has to go home like anyone else and argue with his wife over who should deal with the gardening problems.

I knew how to write this guy. What appealed to me about it was the same thing that had appealed to Arnold—it was the opportunity to do a fun character. So when I think back about *True Lies*, I don't think about a scene with Harrier jets and the fact that they blew up all this stuff. I think of the scene where Arnold's character thinks Jamie Lee Curtis' character is having an affair and he's looking at her and she's like, the peas are falling off her fork and she's trying not to lie. The eye-contact stuff. To me that was what was fun about that film and that's what attracted us to it originally.

For me the real fun of *True Lies* as a filmmaker is the juxtaposition of scales. You've got the very small scale of the domestic environment and then you've got the opposite end of the spectrum where you've got the vast scale—marines and a huge air strike and firing Maverick missiles at a convoy of terrorists who have nuclear weapons in the back of a truck. We jokingly called the film a domestic epic.

Obviously the ending had to be spectacular. It had to be as big as we could make it. We mixed real military jets with mock-ups and we used digital composites and so on. From a safety standpoint, I think it was done extremely safely, especially for the actors. Some of the second unit photographers who were flying around in a Lear jet chasing the Harrier jet may have been a little less safe. But none of the actors were ever exposed to those environments.

Arnold was sitting in a mock up of a Harrier jet up on a big hydraulic six-axis motion base, sitting on top of a building in downtown Miami. It was very well thought out, very well engineered. So the trick was to make it look dangerous without having it be dangerous.

There's a great scene where Arnold's wife gets plucked out of the limo just as the limo goes off and hits the drink at a hundred miles an hour. When Jamie Curtis saw her stunt double, Donna Keagan, hanging from the helicopter doing that stunt, and saw what a great time Donna was having, Jamie then demanded to do her shot from the real helicopter. We had planned doing it on a stage in front of a green screen. So I said, "Okay, if she wants to hang from a helicopter, then I'll shoot it." So Jamie got into a body harness. I got into a body harness. They strapped me to the skid of the helicopter. They hung her from a safety cable under the helicopter and we took off over a bridge at eighty miles an hour. So there's a shot in the film of her screaming and dangling from the helicopter where you see the landscape going by. That's a hundred percent real. That's Jamie hanging from the helicopter.

And speaking of Jamie, she was my first choice for the role. I wrote the character with her in mind. I only knew her in passing. When Katherine Bigalow and I were married, Katherine was just finishing *Blue Steel,* starring Jamie. I just really thought Jamie was a cool person. She was my fantasy casting for the role of Helen Tasker.

Now the problem was Arnold didn't see Jamie in that part. He didn't know her. He has no specific negative; he just didn't see her in the part. So I was encouraged by the Arnold camp to explore every other possibility. So I saw a lot of other actresses and there were a lot of good ones. But I had already spoken to Jamie to make sure she was available, so she was kind of standing by wondering what was going on. I would show Arnold tapes and so on.

Now, I feel comfortable telling this story because ultimately it makes Arnold look great, because this is how big a guy he is. As I said, he did not see Jamie in the role. He just didn't get it. And he was very honest about it. He had nothing personal against her; had never met her. Just didn't see her in the character for whatever reason—I never did understand why. After I explored all the other options I called Arnold up and I asked him to come over. We had some lunch and I said, "How much do you trust me?" He says, "Jim, I trust you completely." I said, "Yeah, yeah, how much do you really trust me?" He said, "Completely." I said, "Then it's Jamie." And there was like a split second where you could see he thought about how I'm Arnold Schwarzenegger and I said that I didn't want this, and so forth. Then he said, "Fine." He wasn't doing back handsprings for joy; he just went, "Fine." And from the day he met her, he thought she was spectacular and he really enjoyed working with her and they got along great.

Now jump to the end of the picture. When Jamie signed on, her agent had asked for her name above the title. But Arnold gets that solely and no one else can invade that space. It's just one of those agent game things. But I told Jamie that when the movie was completed, we'd ask Arnold. If he says, no, it's no. They agreed to that. So the movie's all done and it's time for me to call up Arnold and ask him about Jamie's credit. I get him on the phone and he says she was such a Great Spirit, she contributed so much to this movie; she should go above the title. Now, I think it takes a big guy to do that. Because most people in Hollywood wouldn't.

*He's constantly willing to re-evaluate in light of new information, and he keeps his eye on the integrated whole of what he's trying to create.*
*Rae Sanchini—Producer*

# Titanic (1997)

*Leonardo DiCaprio; Kate Winslet; Billy Zane; Kathy Bates; Frances Fisher;*
*Gloria Stuart; Bill Paxton; Bernard Hill; David Warner; Victor Garber; Jonathan*
*Hyde; Suzy Amis; Lewis Abernathy; Nicholas Cascone; Dr. Anatoly M. Sagalevitch.*

For me, *Titanic* started with history, and from history I extracted the story that I thought best told that history. Now this is not necessarily obvious, especially to history buffs. There have been twelve or thirteen films made about *Titanic* that seem to be much more historically accurate, in the sense that they only have historically known things in the content of the film as opposed to grafting in fictional elements. My feeling was, yes, they're fine films, but they don't involve me. The liberties that would have to be taken with historical fact to involve me in the kind of passionate story I wanted to tell would be too offensive from a historical standpoint, because it didn't really happen to those people. It may have happened to somebody who died, but we don't know about it.

So I thought, let's tell a story that might have happened that does not in any way violate historical fact. We won't do something that could not have happened, that was mutually exclusive of what was reported. Let's do the story of somebody that *could* have been on the ship and died and we never heard their story. In the process we're going to learn a lot of history, but we're going to have the added bonus of a real subjective sense that you are really there, because you now have a focus for your emotions and your fears and your hopes and all those things that involve an audience in the story, that takes you through that screen barrier and puts you into history as opposed to watching it from the outside.

So I considered that to be a valid approach. Some people disagree. That's fine. I think a lot more people have learned the history of *Titanic* from the historical fiction in my film than from the true docu-dramas that have gone before. One could debate that endlessly. But it certainly started with research, research, and more research. And I was completely anal about detail. I would not put anything in the screenplay if it could not have happened. For example, they make love in the back of a car. That car was

---

NOTE: While editing *Titanic*, Cameron supposedly had a razor blade taped to the side of the editing computer, and written underneath were the instructions: "Use only if film sucks!"

there. A thirty-five horsepower, 1911 touring car was in Hold Number Two. It belonged to William E. Carter, and it was insured for $3,500 that he recovered later because he survived.

I know all these things. Now, the audience doesn't know those things. They just see them go into the hold and there's the car. That car's still there—it's still down in the hold. In fact, we tried to get a look at it with our R.O.V. camera, but the R.O.V. was too bulky to get into the little tiny opening that's left in that hatch.

Everything we did had to have a basis in fact. When you get into the scenes of the officers and the captain and how the ship hit the iceberg and all the things that happened and how it broke up and sank, I wanted it to be able to stand up in court. I wanted it to be the definitive forensic analysis of the *Titanic* disaster. We really went the extra mile in research and had endless debates over metal stress and cracking and how the ship broke apart, none of which I think is what made the film successful. The film is successful because it works at an emotional level in many ways, and at several different levels, and in many ways for many different people. One can talk about that endlessly and certainly it's all been said, pro and con.

At the point that I had the script done I didn't have a clue as to how we were going to film it. Instinctively, in writing it, I tried to incorporate as much of what was visually powerful about the *Titanic*, the ship, as I could. I pretty much guaranteed that we were going to have to figure out how to build those spaces and show them. In other words, I was literally hanging myself up by the thumbs in the writing process—and knowing that I was doing it—because I wanted to see it. I wanted to see the grand staircase. I wanted to see the grand dining salon. I wanted to see the ship in its glory. I didn't want it to be some cheesy section of a set. They did that in the television mini-series for about $15 million, less than a tenth of what we did the feature version for. But it didn't have the richness, it didn't have the opulence, it didn't have the visual reality.

Not only that, but we had to create all this opulence, and then sink it. So, all of these sets had to be built on big steel structures that could be moved up and down while in the water. And where was the water? Well, a tank. Well, where's the tank? Well, we'll have to build that, too. It just became this amazing process of figuring out how to do this imagery. But the way everybody approached it, the imagery was sacrosanct. Our attitude was, we're going to bend heaven and earth to make it happen. We'll go to Poland and build the ship and take it out to sea in the Baltic. I'm not saying we were ever going to take a real *Titanic* out and sink it, but we were going to build a large portion of the ship in a shipyard in Gdansk and mount it on a container ship and steam it around and then bring it back. But eventually we decided to consolidate everything that we were going to do all in one place to optimize our resources, and that's when we decided, well, we're going to have to build a studio, because there's no one place in the world that existed at that point that allowed us to do everything. So now we're building a studio.

We got the green light in June 1996 for a film that was going to be out the following July. So you've got a twelve-month window to essentially make the movie and deliver it, so that they have time to make the release prints. And in that time we had to build a studio which ultimately comprised five sound stages, including two that are among the largest in the world, build the largest outdoor filming tank in the world. Then build the set, which is going to be in the Guinness book for the largest set ever built. Then shoot the movie. Then do all the visual effects. And get it all done in twelve months.

It was a pretty risky proposition going in. I was very up front about it. I said, "Look, I can't guarantee we'll get this thing done." Yes, it's very desirable coming out in July. I'd had my biggest success prior to that with *Terminator II* opening on a July 3 and 4 weekend. We'll plow through this going full steam ahead, doing whatever we can to try to hit that date, but we should look at it in March and see where we are. But when we got to that point of review in March, nobody would back off their position. Everybody started to posture. It's like a blowfish that puffs up to scare its enemies away. Everybody was puffed up trying to scare the enemies away and they weren't being very realistic, because in March we were really screwed up. We were a month behind schedule. The visual effects were at least two months behind schedule. It was impossible to hit the July date but nobody dealt with that until it was too late and then we all looked like idiots.

But in my mind, July had always been a risky proposition and not the most important consideration. The most important consideration is doing the best possible film. Then they left the decision up to me so I'd look like the bad guy. So I finally called them and told them that we should release the film at Christmas. And everybody was like, "It's Cameron's fault!" So I told them, "Okay, fine, I'm the bad guy, but here's what we should do or we're going to hurt ourselves and we're going to spend too much money and the film's going to get a bad release and nobody's going to win." All because the interest is $3.5 million to hold the film for an extra four and half, five months. It was an incremental cost compared to what they were risking—two hundred million dollars.

Then it turned out to be beautiful because we were able to position the film properly with the press. We got to take it to some film festivals. We got to screen it in England. We got to build some international goodwill on the picture. The press has a short attention span. We managed to outlast their attention when it came to all the negative stories, to the point that when the film finally came out, all the bad things they were saying about us were so old hat you couldn't print that as a headline anymore. Pretty soon there was nothing left to say about the movie except what was in the film itself. I'd love to take credit for that strategy but it was more of an instinct play. The best way out of this was to wait them out. Wait out all the negatives. Position all the positives. Get the film just right and come out at Christmas. It worked.

The film went through various DEFCON stages, the lowest being DEFCON One. We had a budget going in of $150 million, plus the cost of the new studio facility in Mexico. So Fox had to risk at that point $130 million for a costume drama that was going to be three hours long. And they knew that going in. I told them it was going to be a three-hour movie. If they didn't want to make a three-hour movie, then don't make the movie. That was a given. I've got letters that I sent them with the script drafts. I've looked back at them and chuckled. It's all there. They knew about it ahead of time if they took the time to read the fine print. They knew it was a costume drama, they knew everybody died in the end, and they knew it was a three-hour movie.

Every film I've ever worked on has gone through stages. Like, oh, what's it about? That's really cool. Yeah, we'd really like to make that. Oh, gee, it's going to cost a lot of money! Oh shit, things are going really wrong! Oh my god, oh my god, oh my god, this is horrible, this is horrible, this is horrible! Oh wait, this is great, this is great! Oh, we've made a lot of money!

It goes through this unbelievable wave. And then the wave repeats when you start on the next project. On *Titanic* the amplitude was just that much greater. Actually, it wasn't. The amplitude wasn't quite as high at the start and it got a lot deeper at the bottom of the trough and it got a lot higher later.

So the studio's on the hook for $130 million. In their minds they could think *Titanic* wouldn't be as successful as *True Lies,* but they've got the relationship with me and we can make more films, so it's kind of justified. Then the film starts to cost more money. So in their minds they're going into this marginally profitable enterprise and all of a sudden this film's costing so much money that they believe they cannot make a profit. So they start coming to me and saying, "You've got to take out this, this, this, and this. You decide, but you've got to take something out and we recommend things." They'd give me ten pages of recommendations. And I'd go through it and I'd say if we take that out, take this out, and take that out, you'll ruin the whole thing.

They'd already built the studio in Mexico. They already had built the sets and the ship. So, you're there. You've spent the dough. Now you're going to wreck it by not filming what you've built. The logic to me was not great. I tried to express this in very polite terms and they were very polite back. Pretty soon it wasn't very polite. It got to be pretty strained. I told them that we should just not cut all of this stuff out. We can take out some things, give some things to second unit, and we'll try to shorten the number of days. We'll try to shave it as much as we can, but I've got to try to protect the underlying investment of this thing even if you don't have the courage to protect your own investment at this point.

## How Much Money Was He Willing to Give Up?

To begin with, I gave up half my salary just to get the film green-lighted, just to get them into the ring. The reason for that was there was a certain amount they wanted to spend and we were a certain number of million dollars over that. So I agreed they could take it out of my salary. I still had my back-end points* and still had part of my salary.

So now I'm into the film and things are even worse. So I told them to take the rest of my salary. It certainly showed that I completely believed in the film because if I ever made a dime from the film it would be on the back end. And what I felt I was demonstrating to them was that I had not gotten them into this situation intentionally; that I was willing to take responsibility for it. That it was just happening to all of us. And yes, maybe some of the things could have been prevented. But you know what, my producer John Landau and I, we're pretty smart guys and we've done some pretty big films and we couldn't have predicted a lot of the things that went wrong.

So at a certain point you say maybe we just shouldn't have made the film at all. But if we were going to make it, some of these things were probably inevitable and they were not easily foreseen. And I welcome anybody from outside who thinks they're a big shot producer to come in and go through that process and not make some of the same mistakes. At least that's how I felt at that time.

---

* Profit participation.

By now we're at Christmas and we're about two-thirds of the way through the shooting. Now a whole bunch of hidden costs have come out that hit like an artillery barrage day after day, boom, boom, boom! All of a sudden, in the space of like a two-week period, the budget jumped up like $20 million or the cost of the film had jumped $20 million. It was going up faster than I was shooting. It's impossible. It's just nuts. Things were basically really bad.

I had a meeting with the powers that be at Fox. Fox was the point studio. Paramount was just kind of along for the ride. Fox were crying the blues. "We can't make any money off this movie," they said. "Now it's not a question of how much are we going to make or not make, it's a question of how much are we going to lose," they said. So I said, "All right, that's really embarrassing to me. Why don't you take all my back-end points, too?" That way, you know that I basically worked for three years for nothing. That's the best I can do. But what I'm not willing to do is work for three years whether you pay me or not and do a bad movie. So those are your choices.

Then they did something interesting which has haunted them ever since. At this point they put no value in the profits because they didn't think there were going to be profits. They put zero value on that. So they said, "Sure, sure, kid, you can give us your points; you can do whatever you want because there aren't going to be any profits anyway." But they wanted more than that. They wanted more cuts. They wanted visual effects taken out and they wanted a lot of other stuff. So at a mid-management level somebody got the bright idea not to write up a contract or a letter formalizing that. So legally they never accepted my offer to give up my points.

Now cut, and it's a year later. The film is the highest-grossing film in the history of motion pictures. Don't they feel a little stupid? Now they owe me an enormous amount of money. And only because they were trying to strategize for that little extra something. Let that be a lesson to us all. They stepped over a bar of gold bullion to pick up a penny. I was pretty innocent in all this because I still was motoring along wearing the hair shirt and flagellating myself, thinking I'm working for free.

Now they had a filmmaker that had the bit in his teeth. I had nothing to gain and everything to lose by making a bad film. I had nothing to lose by going to war with them over the quality of the film and nothing to gain by compromising. Just a little word of advice to anyone who wants to be a studio executive. Never put a filmmaker in that situation.

There's a famous quote that says, "When you take away everything a man has, you make him free." So I became very dangerous to the studio at that point, and it's just the strangest thing in the history of films that it actually worked out.

There was something about making the film the way it was supposed to be that ultimately was the magic formula. It was the magic formula for getting all the money back. All the things that they knew and all the things that I knew from previous experience could not have solved the problems we had. We were in unexplored territory. We were trying a magic spell that had never been tried before. And it worked. So kids, don't try this at home. I don't care if the guys at Fox ever see this because they know it's true. And by the way, none of this produced any great animosity. We're still ready to go make another movie tomorrow. We were always gentlemanly about the whole situation. Ultimately all we had left was to do it right.

## What Does the Future Hold?

I'm at a crossroads in the sense that I now have a lot of possibilities. With *Titanic*, I've proven I can viably do a drama. *Titanic* is a drama. It's a movie with a kind of grown-up value system. A lot has been made about it being a movie that fourteen-year-old girls see fifty-seven times. But that's not why it made a lot of money. And the exit demographics did not reflect that. Yes, there was a high repetition rate among fourteen-year-old girls, but there were eight-year-old boys and twenty-year-old men and fifty-year-old couples. The film demonstrates that as a filmmaker, I'm viable doing things besides the genre stuff that people mostly knew me for previously. So now with a great deal of choices comes a great deal of indecision. Not that I'm really indecisive, it's just that making *Titanic* was three years of putting my private life on hold. So right now I'm just having a lot of fun spending time with my daughter and relaxing and thinking about new horizons.

## How Would He Like to Be Remembered?

Ultimately, filmmakers are remembered for their films. The private stuff is irrelevant. It's what made it up on the screen. So I never want to put anything in a film that I'm going to have to feel a little cringe about later. And so far, I haven't. So far I feel pretty good about the stuff that's made it up on the screen. Maybe not some of the stuff that's on the editing room floor, but the stuff that made it into the final cut.

# Director Filmography

*Piranha II: The Spawning* (1981)
*The Terminator* (1984)
*Aliens* (1986)
*The Abyss* (1989)
*Terminator 2: Judgement Day* (1991)
*True Lies* (1994)
*T2 3-D: Battle across Time* (1996)
*Titanic* (1997)

# Awards

**Academy Awards, USA**
*Titanic,* Best Director, 1998
*Titanic,* Best Picture (shared with Jon Landau), 1998
*Titanic,* Best Film Editing (shared with Conrad Buff & Richard A. Harris), 1998

**Academy of Science Fiction, Horror & Fantasy Films, USA**
President's Award, 1998

**American Cinema Editors, USA**
*Titanic,* Eddie Award/Best Edited Feature Film, (shared with Conrad Buff & Richard A. Harris), 1998

**British Academy Awards**
*Titanic,* Best Editing (nominated, shared with Conrad Buff & Richard A. Harris), 1998
*Titanic,* David Lean Award for Direction (nominated), 1998

**Broadcast Film Critics Association Awards**
*Titanic*, Best Director, 1998

**Chicago Film Critics Association Awards**
*Titanic*, Best Director (nominated), 1998

**Directors Guild of America, USA**
*Titanic*, Outstanding Directorial Achievement in Motion Pictures, 1998

**Golden Globes, USA**
*Titanic*, Best Director—Motion Picture, 1998
*Titanic*, Best Screenplay—Motion Picture (nominated), 1998

**Golden Laurel Awards**
*Titanic*, Motion Picture Producer of the Year (shared with Jon Landau), 1998

**Golden Satellite Awards**
*Titanic*, Best Director of a Motion Picture, 1998
*Titanic*, Best Motion Picture—Drama (shared with Jon Landau), 1998
*Titanic*, Best Motion Picture Film Editing (shared with Richard A. Harris & Conrad Buff), 1998
*Titanic*, Best Motion Picture Screenplay—Original (nominated), 1998

**Razzie Awards**
*Rambo: First Blood Part II*, Worst Screenplay, 1986

**ShowWest Convention, USA**
Producer of the Year, 1995

**Writers Guild of America, USA**
*Titanic*, Best Screenplay Written Directly for the Screen (nominated), 1998

# The Films of Spike Lee

Spike Lee has established himself as one of Hollywood's most important and influential filmmakers. In 1986, his debut film, the independently produced comedy *She's Gotta Have It*, earned him the Prix de Jeunesse Award at the Cannes Film festival and set him at the forefront of the Black Wave in American cinema.

*School Daze*, his second feature, was not only highly profitable, but also helped launch the careers of several young black actors. Spike's timely 1989 film, *Do The Right Thing*, garnered an Academy Award nomination for best original screenplay and Best Director award from the Los Angeles Film Critics Association. Lee's *Mo' Better Blues*, *Jungle Fever, Crooklyn,* and *Clockers* were also critical successes.

Shelton Jackson Lee was born on March 20, 1957 in Atlanta, Georgia, and raised in Brooklyn. He returned to Atlanta to attend Morehouse College. After graduation, he returned to Brooklyn to continue his education at New York University's Tisch School of the Arts in Manhattan, where he received his Master of Fine Arts Degree in film production. Lee then founded 40 Acres and a Mule Filmworks based in the Fort Greene section of Brooklyn, where he has resided since childhood. Spike also created a record label, 40 Acres and A Mule Music Works, and a retail company, Spike's Joint East, in Brooklyn.

In addition to his achievements in feature films, Spike Lee has produced and directed numerous music videos for such diverse artists as Miles Davis, Chaka Khan, Tracy Chapman, Anita Baker, Public Enemy, Bruce Hornsby, and Michael Jackson. His other music videos include work for the late Phyliss Hyman, Naughty by Nature, and Arrested Development.

Lee's commercial television work began in 1988 with his Nike Air Jordan campaign. Collaborating with basketball great Michael Jordan on seven commercials, Lee resurrected his popular character, Mars Blackman, from *She's Gotta Have It.*

Spike is also involved in documentaries and sports programs; he directed a documentary for HBO entitled *4 Little Girls: Bombing of the 16th Street Baptist Church in Birmingham, Alabama.* He received an Emmy Award for his piece on Georgetown's John Thompson for HBO/Real Sports. Additionally, Spike has authored six books on the making of his films; the fifth book, *Five For Five,* served as a pictorial reflection of his first five features.

Spike Lee is talented, opinionated, and determined.

*Personal Quote*
*Making films has got to be one of the hardest endeavors known to humankind. Straight up and down, film work is hard shit.*

# The Conversation

I was the first of six children. I was born in Atlanta and my mother was from Atlanta. She went to Spellman College in Atlanta. My father went to Morehouse College, which is across the street from Spellman. But my father, Bill Lee, was a jazz musician, and jazz musicians want to get to mecca, where the music was happening, so we moved to New York.

My nickname, Spike, was given to me by my mother, who has since passed. She died when I was a sophomore in college. She said I was a tough baby. The nickname stuck. My real name is Shelton Jackson Lee. Shelton is my mother's maiden name.

I think because I was the oldest, I felt, whether it was right or wrong, that more responsibility was on me to be strong for my siblings, so in retrospect I don't think I really grieved as much as I should have when my mother died. I couldn't do that. My sister said that when she and my brother wrote the first draft of *Crooklyn,* it was only after we finished that film that it was like the final catharsis, because she'd never been able to really let go of our mother's passing.

I was in college before I ever thought of making films. A lot of filmmakers talk about their careers and they say they saw a movie when they were six years old and knew they wanted to make films. Whether that's true or not, I can't say, but it was very late for me. Like all kids I went to movies growing up. We lived in this neighborhood called Cobble Hill. The theater was called the Leto and it was on Court Street in Brooklyn. And every Saturday we'd go to the matinees, act crazy and throw stuff at the screen and try not to get thrown out. But it never occurred to me that people actually made movies and that kind of stuff. You just went to the theater and had a good time.

I got my Bachelor of Arts from Morehouse. I graduated in 1979, and I was a mass communications major. But Morehouse didn't have that major, so I took my major, actually, across the street at Clarke College, which is now Clarke University—Clarke Atlanta University. Mass communications was print journalism, TV, radio, and film. But their film department was kind of small. It only had facilities for super-8. So it wasn't until my sophomore year that I knew for sure that I wanted to be a filmmaker. Upon graduation, I knew I did not have the necessary skills, so I had to learn them. I applied to the top three film schools—USC, UCLA, and NYU. Unfortunately for me, to get into USC or UCLA you had to get an astronomical score on the GREs. But luckily, to get into NYU all you had to do was submit a creative portfolio, so I got into NYU.

NYU had a three-year program. Intensive. For three years that's all you do, make films. My thesis film was a film called *Joe's Bed-Stuy Barbershop: We Cut Heads*. It's about a barbershop that also fronts as a numbers joint, and I was fortunate enough to win one of the student academy awards that year. And being young and dumb and naive, I thought because of this award that all the studios would call me up and within a year I would be directing films in Hollywood. That was not the reality. I finished school in 1982, and the climate for African-American directors was not the same as today. Not that the doors are now wide open, but it's more receptive today. Back when I began you had Michael Shultz, the only African-American director working, and Eddie Murphy and Richard Pryor. They were there, but that was about it.

For three years I was working part time at this place called First Run Features, which is a small independent distribution company. I worked in the shipping department. I cleaned films, stored them, ran errands. It was a great, great job. The office was right in the same building as the Bleeker Street Cinema. It was a good job to have.

# She's Gotta Have It (1986)

*Tracy Camilla Johns; Tommy Redmond Hicks; John Canada Terrell; Spike Lee; Raye Dowell; Joie Lee; S. Epatha Merkerson; Bill Lee; Cheryl Burr; Aaron Dugger; Stephanie Covington; Renata Cobbs; Cheryl Singleton; Monty Ross; Lewis Jordan.*

In the summer of 1984, I tried to make a film called *Messenger*. The money fell through and it was a disaster. Later that winter I wrote *She's Gotta Have It*. We got a ten-thousand-dollar grant from the Jerome Foundation to start and we shot the film in twelve days in July 1985. Ironically, back when I was trying to do *Messenger*, I had gotten a grant from the American Film Institute for twenty-five thousand dollars. So when *Messenger* fell apart, I thought I could transfer the AFI grant money to *She's Gotta Have It*. But AFI said hell no. We gave you the money for *Messenger,* not *She's Gotta Have It,* so you can't have the grant. I was mad at AFI for a long time. That was a long time ago.

It's funny, you know. I don't really remember my first day on the set as a director. I have been very fortunate and blessed. In my first decade as a filmmaker, I've been able to do ten films—a film a year, as it works out. And so much of this stuff is blended together, or I've just completely blanked it out of my mind, or I've just forgotten, but I cannot tell you much about those twelve days shooting *She's Gotta Have It*.

I do remember the reason I wore so many hats in *She's Gotta Have It*. It was fiscally sound because we had no money. If we had a budget, I don't think I would have acted in that film. But I would have edited it.

It was because of that film that I got involved with Nike. The character I played in the film was named Mars Blackman. In the film Mars wears Air Jordan's. In fact, even when Mars is making love to Noli, he refuses to take his Air Jordan's off. He's the biggest Michael Jordan fan in the world. Two gentlemen, Jim Riswold and Bill Davenport, in Nike's advertising agency had seen *She's Gotta Have It*. They went to Nike; they went to Michael Jordan. It was their idea to put Mars Blackman together with Michael Jordan and we went on to make it a very successful campaign. We did it for six years and it built the brand and built Nike and Air Jordan's too.

I was very happy with *She's Gotta Have It*, but of all the ten films that I've done, for me that's the most difficult one to watch because some of the acting bothers me and I take full blame. Anytime there's a bad actor in a film, it's the director's fault. Either they weren't directing, or they cast the wrong people. In this case, I think it really was my inexperience as a director. I think it's safe to say that most directors who come out of film school are terrified of actors and really haven't had the experience working with actors so they tend to be more technically inclined. You hide behind the camera. Instead of dealing with the actors they work with the other aspects that go into filmmaking.

By the way, my father did the music score for *Sara*, which was the student film before *Joe's Bed-Stuy*. Then he did the music for *Joe's*, *She's Gotta Have It*, *School Daze*, *Do the Right Thing*, and *Mo' Better*. He's a great musician.

I'm often asked how I got to work with so many talented actors early on in my career. I think the talent has always been out there, but there wasn't always a vehicle for it. Look at the cast for *School Daze*. Tisha Campbell, Larry Fishburne, Samuel Jackson, Bill Nunn, Giancarlo Esposito, Ossie Davis, Joe Seneca, who recently died, Jasmine Guy, and Dean Hardison. They are all very talented people. Originally I had Vanessa Williams in the Tisha Campbell role, but she had some issues so I didn't go with her. Looking back at what we've done in ten years it's been most gratifying to see the shots we've given people in front and behind the camera. And remember, that was Jasmine Guy's first film, Martin Lawrence's first film, and Queen Latifa's first film. You can go on and on with people, people we were able to find. Talented people.

# School Daze (1988)

*Laurence Fishburne; Giancarlo Esposito; Tisha Campbell; Kyme; Joe Seneca;*
*Ellen Holly; Art Evans; Ossie Davis; Bill Nunn; James Bond, III; Branford Marsalis;*
*Kadeem Hardison; Eric Payne; Spike Lee; Anthony Thompkins; Erik Dellums;*
*Jasmine Guy; Samuel L. Jackson; Joie Lee; Kasi Lemmons; Gregg Burge.*

*School Daze* for me was my four years at an African-American institution jam-packed into a homecoming weekend, and I wanted to look at some of the issues that keep African-Americans from being a more unified people, these issues really being superficial stuff based on skin complexion. Whether you're light-skinned or dark-skinned. Whether you've got, quote, "good hair," or, quote, "bad hair," which is nappy. Whether you're in a fraternity or not, what class you come from, and so on. We wanted to use a college campus as a microcosm of an African-American community as a whole.

I think one of the biggest misconceptions white America has about African-Americans is that we're a monolithic group. That we all think alike, dress alike, live alike, and, you know, go all the way down the line.

I think that *School Daze* was true as you looked at how life was at a predominantly African-American institution.

# Do the Right Thing (1989)

*Danny Aiello; Ossie Davis; Ruby Dee; Richard Edson; Giancarlo Esposito;
Spike Lee; Bill Nunn; John Turturro; Paul Benjamin; Frankie Faison;
Robin Harris; Joie Lee; Miguel Sandoval; Rick Aiello; John Savage;
Samuel L. Jackson; Rosie Perez; Martin Lawrence.*

The idea for *Do the Right Thing* came from several places. Number one, just living here in New York and seeing the racial animosity and the tension, which was fanned by Mayor Ed Koch, who seemed to enjoy playing the races against each other. One incident stood out: the Howard Beach incident, where three black men were driving home from work. Their car gets a flat tire. They go into New World Pizzeria in the Howard Beach section of Queens, New York, which is predominantly an Italian-American neighborhood. They get chased out of the pizzeria by a gang of bat-wielding Italian-American youths.

When I was growing up I remember seeing the TV show *One Step Beyond* or *Twilight Zone* or something like that. It was about this scientist doing a study where they said after the temperature hits ninety-five degrees the murder rate goes up. And the scientist is looking at the thermometer throughout the show and sure enough it goes up, and he gets murdered himself. I grew up in New York, and I can tell you that after a certain point heat does have an effect on human nature, particularly in New York.

So I got this idea to show one block in Bed-Stuyvesant on the hottest day of summer, with different ethnic groups, which reflects the city as a whole, and see what happens. That's basically how that film came about.

I think it was a true document of racism at the time. You have to realize this film came out before what happened in Los Angeles with Rodney King, that and the whole Korean-American, African-American thing. So in a lot of ways we had a crystal ball working for us on that film. I think that it was a true exploration of a subject that we all know exists, but tends to get swept under the rug. The film presented a frank discussion of the subject matter and it made a lot of people uncomfortable. That's why people like Joe Kline, David Denby, and people like that said that *Do The Right Thing* incited black youths to come out of the theaters and start riots all across this country. And of course there's the myth that black people in the summertime are prone to riot. Some of the reactions to that film were ridiculous. I remember Jack Matthews criticizing Tom Pollack, who at the time was running MCA Pictures, for being socially irresponsible for releasing a film like that and suggesting they release it in the fall when it wasn't so hot. And David Denby saying things like, "Just hope to God that this film doesn't open up in your neighborhood."

*Personal Quote*
*I put my own life, my own experiences into my films. I think any artist, whether a painter or a novelist, does that, you know. Everything is not going to be all fiction. So, there's Spike Lee in everything I do.*

I think that Hollywood, if it really tries, can do honest portrayals of African-Americans and other minorities, but I think they actually don't want to or don't really care. But no matter how they're getting around it, more and more this country is getting less white. We're becoming a multicultural nation, so they'll get it now or get it later, hopefully.

On *Do The Right Thing* we originally had tried to get Robert DeNiro to play Sal, the owner of the pizzeria, but I forget why he said he couldn't do it. But we were very happy that Danny Aiello accepted the role, because I think we needed someone who wasn't a great big star to overshadow everybody else. Danny got an Academy Award nomination for his portrayal of Sal.

Danny had a definite idea of how he wanted to play that role. Danny was fighting extra hard for Sal not to be a racist. He wanted Sal to be the most lovable, as he said, pizzeria owner in the world. So we had several discussions about that character. He was worried that I was going to portray Sal as a one-note racist. That was not my intent at all. But this was the first time we worked together and I don't think the trust was there at first.

We had this scene at the end where the characters of Ray and Buggin' Out come in and they're demanding that Sal put up some black people on the wall of fame. And Danny is supposed to say the word "nigger." But Danny would not say the word. He looked at me like, come on, I ain't gonna say that word. I told him that no one would think that's Danny Aiello saying that word. It's his character, Sal, saying it. Then I told him that he had probably used that word anyway. Maybe it was ten years ago, but don't tell me you've never used the word "nigger" before. He still refused to say it. So we said okay, we're going to shoot anyway. So I pulled Giancarlo Esposito over to the side. He was playing the role of Buggin' Out. The next shot was to be a close up of Danny behind the counter, so I told Giancarlo to really give it to him, really let him have it. So we rolled the camera and Giancarlo started calling him a fat bastard. He called him a stupid ass spaghetti bender. A greasy Italian. Whatever he could think of. And then something just clicked in Danny's mind. And what you see in the movie is that same scene with Danny yelling, "I will kill you, nigger!" It was like, all this invective just started to vomit out of his mouth. And I thought to myself, where did that come from? I thought he said he never used the word. Anyway, we needed a lot of prompting from Giancarlo offscreen to get that take and that's the one we used in the film.

That film made money. It only cost $6 million to make and took in something like $30 million. It was on the ten best list. It didn't have too much success with the Academy, though. It only got two nominations. Myself for best original screenplay, and Danny for Best Supporting Actor. Best Film that year was *Driving Miss Daisy*.

Now, here you've got *Do The Right Thing* on the one hand, and *Driving Miss Daisy* on the other. Look at Morgan Freeman's role. That's the one that white America and the Academy was comfortable with. Subservient black man. Of course he got a nomination, of course it's the Best Film of the year.

I think that's when I finally woke up. Up to that point the Academy and that kind of stuff was important to me. But not after that. You really cannot let any group have so much power over you that you make their validation. What it says is unless you get an Academy Award, or this, or that, your work has no value. It's not deemed necessary. *Driving Miss Daisy* as best film of the year? Not hardly. And *Ordinary People* won over *Raging Bull*. Who are the people voting, anyway?

*She's Gotta Have It* was done independently, raising money ourselves, but the next five, six films were all mega pick-up deals. I had a deal at Universal. At Universal, we did *Do the Right Thing, Mo' Better, Jungle Fever. Malcolm X* had to go to Warner Bros. We came back and did *Crooklyn* and *Clockers* at Universal. That's where most of the films were done.

# Mo' Better Blues (1990)

*Denzel Washington; Wesley Snipes; Samuel L. Jackson;*
*Giancarlo Esposito; Rubén Blades; Tracy Camilla Johns; Bill Lee; Joie Lee;*
*Spike Lee; Branford Marsalis; Joe Seneca; John Canada Terrell; John Turturro;*
*Nicholas Turturro; Mamie Louise Anderson; Raye Dowell; Angela Hall;*
*Robin Harris; Abbey Lincoln; Coati Mundi; Charles Q. Murphy; Bill Nunn;*
*Deon Richmond; Scot Anthony Robinson; Leonard Thomas; Jeff 'Tain' Watts;*
*Steve White; Cynda Williams; Dick Anthony Williams; Terrence Williams.*

*Mo' Better* really just comes from being the son of a great jazz musician and growing up around music, and at the same time being a sports fan. That's why I made that film. I've always been intrigued by athletes, world class athletes, athletes who play professional sports. Most of these guys, whatever sport they're doing, they've been working at since an early age. Every day, every waking moment has been aimed towards this one goal of reaching this level.

I've always been interested in what happens to these guys or women, who have this one goal in life, and then they get a knee injury, or a pitcher blows his arm out. Their life is over, and they're only twenty-five. What do you do the rest of your life? We just applied that to music.

Denzel's character, Bleek, has been taking trumpet lessons since he was four years old. His whole life is totally devoted to music. Because of an accident, him getting beat up and getting his mouth messed up, he can no longer play the trumpet. That was the first time I got to work with Wesley and Denzel. Wesley was supposed to be in *Do the Right Thing* but he got a bigger role. He did *Wildcats* with Goldie Hawn, but we were glad he was able to do *Mo' Better*. I think that was the film that put Wesley over. People were surprised. Oh, Denzel's going to kill Wesley. I think Wesley surprised Denzel somewhat. Wesley really stood up to Denzel, and that's what we needed for the film to work, this competition between the two.

I was much impressed with Wesley during the shooting of *Mo' Better*. I said, "I'm going to write the next film for you." He said, "All right." I don't think he actually believed me. *Jungle Fever* again came out of an incident here in New York. It was the murder of Yousef Hawkins, an African-American man who stumbled into a crowd of Italian-Americans looking for this guy. The killer pulled out a gun and shot him in cold blood. That was a big deal in the city here. There's always been this strange, somewhat violent relationship between African-Americans and Italian-Americans. We somewhat explored it in *Do the Right Thing*. Just look at what Martin Scorsese's done in his films. So there has been this love/hate thing.

*Personal Quote*

*You know, I work kind of funny. I put everything into it. I put everything under the umbrella of filmmaking. I don't try to put stuff in separate departments. I produce, I write, I direct, and sometimes act, and for me, it all goes under the theme of filmmaker. I enjoy it all. But the hardest thing for me to do is to act in a film. It's just so physically draining.*

# Jungle Fever (1991)

*Wesley Snipes; Annabella Sciorra; Spike Lee; Ossie Davis; Ruby Dee; Samuel L. Jackson; Lonette McKee; John Turturro; Frank Vincent; Anthony Quinn; Halle Berry; Tyra Ferrell; Veronica Webb; Veronica Timbers; David Dundara; Nicholas Turturro.*

Of all the films I've done, I think probably the one that has been misinterpreted most is *Jungle Fever*. People see the film and they think Spike Lee is against interracial relationships. The film wasn't saying that at all. This film was just examining the relationship between two people who came together for what could be the wrong reasons. I think the people who misinterpreted the film just looked at the relationship between Wesley's character and Annabella Sciorra's character and failed to see the story in between. There was another book in there between John Caterra and Todd Farrell.

Wesley, Flipper, and Angie came together because of sexual mythology. That was the sole reason for it. But is that how you build a relationship? Is that a base for it? Because you think all black men have ten-foot long penises and are superhuman sexual studs? Or because you believe deep down in your heart that white women are the epitome of beauty? Those are the reasons why those two got together.

The war council scene is an interesting story. For those who are into doing research on films, they should look at the script and then see what actually ended up in the film itself. I knew from the beginning that I could not write that scene, so the script was just a blueprint, an outline of what I really wanted. I felt all I had to do was get the right actors, turn the cameras on, and they would be there all day, talking about what black men had and had not done to them. It took a whole day to shoot that scene with two cameras. I couldn't write that stuff. We just turned the cameras on.

The story of drugs in that film was partially personal. My father, who was a jazz musician, had been involved with heroin. But even more important than that, my number one priority, beyond the interracial love story, was showing how crack is destroying the African-American family in this country. For me that was the heart of the story. We just used that black/white interracial thing as a hook to get people interested in the film. The tragedy in the film is not that Flipper and Angie can't get it together, but that a father, played by Ossie Davis, would shoot his own son.

Sam Jackson played "Gator." That's the role, I think, that really propelled Sam. Even more so than *Pulp Fiction* did. I had used Sam before in *School*

*Daze, Do the Right Thing*, and *Mo' Better*, but what he did with "Gator" was phenomenal. The Cannes Film Festival created that award for Sam for his portrayal of "Gator."

Here's an interesting side note to the making of *Jungle Fever*. We were shooting in Bensonhurst and we received a bomb threat. I had to shut down production for three or four hours while the New York City bomb squad came and checked it out. The next day I was on the cover of the *Daily News* and the caption read, "Cops Protect Spike Lee."

*Personal Quote*

*I've never really thought of myself as a spokesperson for thirty-five million African-Americans. All my views have been solely my views, and I think that there are African-American people who agree with me, but we also have African-Americans who don't agree. It is a fallacy that all of my critics are white.*

# Malcolm X (1992)

*Denzel Washington; Angela Bassett; Albert Hall; Al Freeman, Jr.;*
*Delroy Lindo; Spike Lee; Theresa Randle; Kate Vernon; Lonette McKee;*
*Tommy Hollis; James McDaniel; Earnest Thomas; Jean LaMarre;*
*O. L. Duke; Larry McCoy; Joe Seneca; Giancarlo Esposito*

I would say that all of my films are a labor of love, but a lot was riding on *Malcolm X* and Denzel and I knew that. During the making of the film we repeatedly joked that we both had our tickets to leave the country if it didn't work out. We would slip out under the cover of dark if things didn't turn out well. For the most part if a film turns out bad it's not a crime, but African-Americans were reminding Denzel and me every day not to mess up the story of Malcolm X. But that was good pressure to have because Malcolm meant so much to everybody. We all understood that and we knew that going in.

Denzel was attached to the project before I was. He was originally hired by Norman Jewison, who was going to direct. Denzel had played Malcolm X Off Broadway. So he was in the equation before I was. When I read about Norman Jewison directing this film for Warner Bros., that's when I began to campaign that maybe this guy's not the right choice, maybe you need an African-American filmmaker with talent. The producer of this film, who had been trying to make this film for twenty some

years, asked me to stop going to the press. He and I sat down and had a
talk. I told him why I thought I should direct it. He had another meeting
with Norman Jewison and Norman, to his credit, bowed out. He did not
have to do that because he had the job. It was his.

Denzel had a good start by playing Malcolm in that Off Broadway play a
couple of years earlier and he's also a great actor. There were many times
me and the crew would have to pinch ourselves because we thought we saw
the reincarnation of Malcolm. Malcolm's spirit was definitely going through
Denzel when we shot this film. And it's evident when you see the film now.

Anytime you do a film about somebody who has lived on this earth it
becomes difficult. People would tell you they knew the guy and he didn't
hold his fork like that. A lot of stuff like that. I think as a filmmaker what
you have to do is try to get the spirit of that individual, the essence of that
individual. You're not trying to do a xerox copy of that person. That person
has lived, and you get an actor to try to play that person honestly. It's something that Oliver Stone has had more problems with than I have because
he's done more bio pictures. And you always have people coming out of the
woodwork and saying this is not true, that is not true. But you're dealing
with the medium of film and you have to condense stuff, you have to add
characters, you have to take away characters. Some stuff is fabricated but it
helps tell the story. At the same time you still have to be as truthful as possible, so it's really like walking a tightrope.

The biggest problem was the money. Our original budget was $32 mil-
lion and Warner Bros. said no. So we shot the film for $28 million. We had
$21 million from Warner Bros. In a bad business move they sold the for-
eign rights to Largo Entertainment for $8 million. *Malcolm* made $8 million
in Japan alone, so it was a bad deal on the part of Warner's.

So everybody knew going in we weren't going to have the budget, but
they were willing to commit to making the film knowing I didn't have all
the money. It's like saying you're half pregnant. Marvin Worth had been trying to make this film for over twenty years and who knows, if we didn't try
to do this right now at this moment, it might be another twenty more. So
we took the leap. Began shooting in September, and lo and behold, at end
of the year, around December, we ran out of money, and that's when Warner
Bros. let the bond company take over. It's something they shouldn't have
done, but they felt this was giving them leverage because they did not want
the film released at the length that it was, and when I refused to cut it they
said, "Okay, it's in the bond company's hands." So before Christmas they
sent registered letters to all the editors and everybody still on the postpro-

duction payroll and told them they were fired. So we had no more money coming in. That's when I had to make the call to people like Bill Cosby, the Artist Formerly Known as Prince, Janet Jackson, Tracy Chapman, Magic Johnson, Michael Jordan, Miss Winfrey, and a woman named Peggy Cooper Caperson. That's how we got the money to keep this going, until Warner Bros. found God and decided to start funding us again.

Shooting *Malcolm X* was a wonderful experience. We went to Egypt and saw the Sphinx and the pyramids. We shot scenes in the Sahara Desert and we even convinced the Saudi government, the highest Islamic court, to allow us to bring cameras into the holy city of Mecca during hajj, something that had never been done before in the history of civilization. Movie cameras during hajj!

And going to Soweto, to be there after Mandela was released from prison, and to have Mandela make a cameo appearance in the film—it was all a joy.

# Crooklyn (1994)

*Alfre Woodard; Delroy Lindo; David Patrick Kelly;*
*Zelda Harris; Carlton Williams; Harif Rashed; Tse-Mach Washington;*
*Christopher Knowings; José Zúñiga; Isaiah Washington; Ivelka Reyes;*
*Spike Lee; N. Jeremi Duru; Frances Foster; Norman Matlock; Joie Lee.*

I'd say a substantial part of *Crooklyn* is autobiographical. My sister and my brother had this story so I agreed to read it. I was really surprised at how good it was. I wanted to help them make it, but it had to be rewritten, fleshed out, and they agreed to that. The script was an answer for my sister's need to finally let go of the past of our mother's death. She is that ten-year-old girl in the film who grows up in a male dominated household in Brooklyn during the early seventies.

*Crooklyn* is a film that's really loved by people who grew up in New York and who are my age or older, because those games the kids played in the film brought back so many memories. Stellies, stoop ball, double dutch, hot piece and butter, kick the can, and all of that stuff. And in shooting this film, we had to teach these kids these games because they had no idea whatsoever. I mean, they could have been from Mars. They had no idea what these games were. It was really sad, because the young kids don't know. Today kids sit in front of the TV and do this computer shit. So the games that kids used to play in the streets of New York City are gone forever, I'm afraid.

I had a lot of kids in that film and the biggest challenge working with child actors is trying not to kill them (*laughs*). Trying not to grab them by their skinny necks and choke them to death. That is the biggest challenge (*laughs*). There is nothing worse than a child actor. We really tried to stay away from children who were actors, who had agents and stage mothers and stuff like that. So we went to public schools to cast a lot of them and they were all good.

I think anyone who considers himself or herself to be a good actor should have a range. You can be a great actor who does one thing well, but what's interesting is when you compete with people who can do a whole lot of things, who play opposite ends of the spectrum, and then you can make the comparison. Look what Delroy Lindo did with the character of Weston Arch in *Malcolm X* and then look at what he did as a father in *Crooklyn*.

We had to cast Crooklyn early because we knew we had to let people's hair grow to get Afros. Nothing looks worse in the world than Afro wigs. And anybody who wants to know what I'm talking about, go see *The Inkwell*. You just have to have people grow their hair because Afro wigs can't stand up under scrutiny. It just drags the whole movie down.

# Clockers (1995)

*Harvey Keitel; John Turturro; Delroy Lindo; Mekhi Phifer; Isaiah Washington; Keith David; Peewee Love; Regina Taylor; Thomas Jefferson Byrd; Sticky Fingaz; Fredro Starr; E. O. Nolasco; Lawrence B. Adisa; Hassan Johnson; Frances Foster.*

I was quoted as saying that gun control and black-on-black crime are two great unsolved issues facing African-Americans and that's what motivated me to make *Clockers*.

A lot of times I get hit with these quotes, and I don't know if I said them, or where I said them, or in what context I said them. But anybody with a conscience would have to feel concern at the alarming rate that young African-American males were killing each other. At the same time, we were dealing with this phenomenon of the hip-hop, gangster, shoot 'em up, rap movies which were the scourge at the time. All the studios were making films like that. John Singleton's *Boys in the Hood*, a great film, was the first one of that kind. I don't even think he knew that the success of that film would open up this whole genre of film. And it seemed to me at the time that this was the only type of film being made about African-Americans. It was so limited. It was only showing one aspect of our lives.

This culture was really being glorified with the gangster rap and the drugs and the guns, and I was hesitant at first to do this film because of those reasons. I didn't want to be number twenty on the list. Martin Scorsese was originally supposed to direct the film. Richard Price was writing the script for him and Robert DeNiro was going to play the Harvey Keitel role. You would have to ask Marty why he changed his mind and decided he wanted to do *Casino* instead. So I was asked to come in and Marty stayed on as executive producer. But my approach was to try to tell the story through the eyes of Strike, the nineteen-year-old crack dealer. In the novel, Richard Price alternated chapters between Rocko Kline and Strike, but in the script he was writing, with De Niro as the star, it was all about Rocko Kline. So we had to change that focus. We also wanted for this film to show some hope at the end because so many of the films I mentioned before were just too bleak. You would leave the theater resigned to the fact that it looks like every African-American kid in the country is not going be able to get past his or her eighteenth birthday. That's just the law. I don't believe that. And so we just tried to turn all these things against each other.

"Clockers" is a term for a low-rung drug dealer, someone who's out there actually selling goods. He's like a soldier. They're out there on those benches on the streets, twenty-four hours a day. You know when you go to a job, you punch a clock? Well, they say they're clocking dollars, so that's how the term came about.

We really wanted to grab the audience by the throat right away. So often Hollywood films that depict violence and gunplay are made lighter. But we really wanted to show what a bullet does to a human body. In doing research for this film, I was hanging out with the crime scene unit here in New York City. That's the homicide unit. They're the ones who show up at every homicide in the city and have to take the pictures and all that kind of stuff.

Visitors who come to visit the crime scene unit are always shown the family album book. The lovely family album book. And that book consists of some of the worst homicide photos you ever wanted to see in your life. We created the least grizzly photos we could. The photos we used were all created by us. Those were not real homicide photos during the opening credit sequence.

In the end I was very pleased with the film. But even though this film was like an antithesis of those types of films I spoke of earlier, the audience still perceived *Clockers* as a hip-hop, rap, drug movie.

# Girl 6 (1996)

*Theresa Randle; Isaiah Washington; Spike Lee; Jenifer Lewis;*
*Debi Mazar; Peter Berg; Michael Imperioli; Dina Pearlman;*
*Maggie Rush; Desi Moreno; Kristen Wilson; K Funk; Debra Wilson;*
*Naomi Campbell; Gretchen Mol; Quentin Tarantino; Richard Belzer;*
*Madonna; John Turturro; Ron Silver; Joie Lee; Halle Berry.*

*Girl 6* in a lot of ways was a return to what we did with the first one, *She's Gotta Have It.* The film was about the empowerment of women, or the supposed empowerment of women, and the decisions that they make and the ramifications of those decisions. The story is about an actress—you never know her name—who, until the end, is struggling here in New York. And like most struggling actors, if things aren't happening here, they think it's happening out in L.A. But she needs to finance that trip. She needs a car and she needs money. So in order to finance this sojourn out to la-la land—Hollywood—she starts working at a phone sex operation. After a while she gets hooked on the work and forgets why she even took the job in the first place. It was only to get money so she could move on and she comes to that realization just before it's too late.

As for the sex in this film, look at *Girl 6* and then compare it to *She's Gotta Have It.* There's no sex scene in *Girl 6.* Everything is verbal. It's people talking on the phone. Whereas in *She's Gotta Have It,* it was visual. So for me it was interesting to do something where there's just people talking about fantasies. And I have no idea why critics gave me flak about Theresa Randle, who played the lead character, baring her breasts in one scene. I mean, that's light compared to what actually happens in this industry. So I don't know what the big deal was.

My problem with critics is that they seem more involved with who they think Spike Lee is than what my films are all about. They seem more involved with the persona or their perception of what Spike Lee is rather than the actual work. That somewhat detracts from the real appreciation of the work. People get caught up on the other stuff and don't really focus on what they're paid to be doing which is looking at the work. I'm reading a review and they're talking about Reggie Miller and me at a Knick's game! It has nothing to do with what the movie was about.

# Get on the Bus (1996)

*Richard Belzer; De'aundre Bonds; André Braugher; Thomas Jefferson Byrd; Gabriel Casseus; Albert Hall; Hill Harper; Harry J. Lennix; Bernie Mac; Wendell Pierce; Roger Guenveur Smith; Isaiah Washington; Steve White; Ossie Davis; Charles Dutton.*

Two producers, Bill Borden and Barry Rosenbush, came up with the initial idea for this film. They knew it might be difficult for them to do this film alone so they contacted the great casting director, Ruben Cannon, who had been looking to make *Get on the Bus*. In 1996 he wanted to transition into production, into producing films.

So, Ruben Cannon called me and told me about *Get on the Bus* and I agreed to do it. Bill Borden told me that Columbia Pictures was going to finance the film. At the time the project was budgeted at $2.4 million. I just felt that if we were going to keep with the spirit of the march, Ruben and I should be able to raise a measly $2.4 million rather than let Columbia, or some other studio, finance it outright. So that's what we did. And it was a good business deal because we were able to sell the film to Columbia for a profit. They bought it for $3.6 million. That's why we were able to pay back investors their entire investment plus interest before the film opened.

Everybody worked for scale on that film. People were committed to the project. We shot it in eighteen days, which is how we kept it on budget. You also have to call in a lot of favors, but to do that it has to be a project that inspires people and makes them want to commit and not take their normal fee.

It was very challenging to me as a director. I had to photograph this bus, this confined space, so it would not be monotonous and not lull the audience to sleep. Because of the small space, we decided to shoot it on a Super 16 and we also shot with two cameras. Two 35mm cameras would not have been able to fit in that bus.

I think it's a very good film and at the same time, very disappointing that the audience did not respond like we thought they would. That could have been for a number of reasons. I think there was a market for the film but I also believe there was a perception out there that this was a documentary and people thought they'd be getting a history lesson. And a lot of people had a problem with the issues, you know. But we still believe we made a great piece of work and it will stand the test of time. The low box office response does not effect how I feel about this film or what I believe we accomplished by doing it.

*Personal Quote*
   I don't think I'm all that private. I just don't really speak until I have something to say.

*Branford Marsalis on Spike Lee*
   The most that Spike ever tells an actor is, "Here's the script. Ready? Action!" And it used to be very funny for me to watch the seasoned veterans say, "Well Spike, what is your vision?" and Spike says, "I paid you good money to act. That's my vision. Now act. Action!"

## Spike on Actors

What I'm looking for in actors is people who have ability, talent, and who can improvise. People who aren't scared of taking chances, who are open minded, and don't want to do the same thing they've been doing in their last ten roles. People with versatility and flexibility, and, most of all, people who don't look like they're acting.

## On Directors Who Act as Well as Direct

It doesn't help my directing to be an actor, because I don't really think I'm an actor. They're a lot of people that would agree with that (*laughs*). It was a total accident that I was in *She's Gotta Have It*. I was very surprised and pleased at how people reacted to the character of Morris Blackman. Because of that I've done similar roles but never something big enough that would detract from what I can do behind the camera. And of the ten films I've done, *Get on the Bus* was the first one I wasn't in. There really wasn't any room in that film, which was fine with me. I don't have to be in everything I direct.

## What Drives Him?

Well, I just love what I do. I love what I do. I've been blessed. Not everyone gets to do what makes them happiest. Ninety-nine percent of the people in the world go to their graves having worked at a job they hated all their lives. That's not the case for me.

## On the State of the Industry

I think movies cost too much. So much is riding on these films that people are scared to make interesting movies. So everybody's looking for that big blockbuster, and a lot of those movies suck. They're terrible.

## On Opportunities for Minority Filmmakers

The landscape right now is much better than it was when I was in film school. It really was two films that turned everything around: Robert Townsend's *Hollywood Shuffle* and my first one, *She's Gotta Have It*.

And right now the struggle is for African-American directors to get films made dealing with other aspects of our culture. To get films that cost as much as everybody else's and get the same amount of money spent on them. Right now there are no African-American executives who are in jobs in a studio who can green-light a picture. Very few people in marketing departments or booking departments, so we need much greater representation in the studios.

## If Not a Filmmaker, Then What?

I don't know. I really never thought about that. Growing up I wanted to be an athlete, but that didn't work out. Not that I was pursing it. I'm really a pragmatic person so I don't really think like that—what if, what if. What would have happened if I had been born a woman? Why even waste time thinking about something like that? What if you weren't a filmmaker, what would I be doing? I don't know. I'm a filmmaker so I really can't answer a question like that.

## Spike's Parting Words

Any artist wants to be remembered by their work. That's all we can do. I think what has happened in the country and this society is that the people doing the evaluating are judging people who have only done one album, one novel, one movie, and one play. That's crazy. How are you going to intelligently evaluate someone who's only done one thing? You can only evaluate an artist when that artist has developed a body of work.

---

NOTE: In 1998, after this interview was completed, Spike released his twelfth feature film, *He Got Game*, the story of a basketball player's father who must try to convince him to go to a college so he can get a shorter prison sentence. The film starred Denzel Washington, Ray Allen, Milla Jovovich, John Turturro, Lonette McKee, and Ned Beatty, with special appearances by basketball stars Charles Barkley, Michael Jordan, Reggie Miller, Shaquille O'Neal, and John Thompson.

In summer 1999, Spike released *Summer of Sam*, his take on the "Son of Sam" murders in New York City in the summer of 1977. Written and directed by Spike Lee, the film stars Adrien Brody, Jennifer Esposito, Roger Howarth, Anthony LaPaglia, John Leguizamo, Patti LuPone, Idina Menzel, Bebe Neuwirth, Michael Rispoli, John Savage, and Mira Sorvino.

At the end of the day, what is your body of work? So that's always been my goal, trying to build a body of work.

# Director Filmography

*Joe's Bed-Stuy Barbershop: We Cut Heads* (1983)
*She's Gotta Have It* (1986)
*School Daze* (1988)
*Do the Right Thing* (1989)
*Mo' Better Blues* (1990)
*Jungle Fever* (1991)
*Malcolm X* (1992)
*Crooklyn* (1994)
*Lumière and Company* (1995)
*Clockers* (1995)
*Girl 6* (1996)
*Get on the Bus* (1996)
*4 Little Girls* (1997, documentary)
*Subway Stories: Tales from the Underground* (1997, TV)
*He Got Game* (1998)
*Summer of Sam* (1999)

# Awards

**Academy Awards, USA**
   *4 Little Girls*, Best Documentary, Features (nominated, shared with Samuel D. Pollard), 1998
   *Do the Right Thing*, Best Writing, Screenplay Written Directly for the Screen (nominated), 1990

### Berlin International Film Festival
*Get on the Bus*, Special Mention, 1997

### Broadcast Film Critics Association Awards
*4 Little Girls*, Best Foreign-Language Film, 1998

### Emmy Awards
*4 Little Girls*, Outstanding Non-Fiction Special (nominated, shared with Samuel D. Pollard, Daphne McWilliams, Jacqueline Glover, and Sheila Nevins), 1998

### Golden Globes, USA
*Do the Right Thing*, Best Director—Motion Picture (nominated), 1990
*Do the Right Thing*, Best Screenplay—Motion Picture (nominated), 1990

### Golden Satellite Awards
*4 Little Girls*, Best Documentary Film (nominated, shared with Samuel D. Pollard), 1998

### Independent Sprit Awards
*She's Gotta Have It*, Best First Feature, 1987

### Locarno International Film Festival
*Joe's Bed-Stuy Barbershop*, Best First Film, 1983

### Los Angeles Film Critics Association Awards
*Do the Right Thing*, Best Director, 1989
*She's Gotta Have It*, New Generation Award, 1986

### Venice Film Festival
*Clockers*, Golden Lion (nominated), 1995

# The Films of Richard Donner

Richard Donner was born in New York in 1930. He began his career in front of the camera as an actor for producer/director Martin Ritt in a television production of *Of Human Bondage*. Ritt cautiously suggested that Donner had a limited career as an actor, so Donner turned to the production side of the business as Ritt's assistant, which led to a successful career as a director of television commercials. This work eventually led him to Los Angeles and the commercial production unit of Desilu Studios.

Eventually he began directing such TV programs as *The Twilight Zone*, *The Fugitive*, *The Man From U.N.C.L.E.*, and *Kojack*.

His feature film career began with *Salt & Pepper* in 1968. The film starred Sammy Davis, Jr. and Peter Lawford, but was not very successful, so Donner returned to directing television episodes. It was not until 1976, when he directed *The Omen* starring Gregory Peck, that his feature film career began to take off.

Richard Donner bounces into a room like a tornado and you find yourself instantly liking him. It has been said that his movie sets are like big parties, yet Donner never loses sight of what he wants and he goes after it with a vengeance, making him one of the most popular and successful feature film directors working today.

> *The majority of directors today storyboard everything. They have it all laid out. Donner has it in his mind, so he can literally put an entire scene together, visually, in detail. That takes years and years and years to develop that kind of skill. He literally makes the movie in his mind and I found that to be a pleasure. It's almost a vacation working with him.*
>
> Sylvester Stallone—Actor

# The Conversation

My first job as an actor was when I was about fifteen years old. It was in a little theater group in upstate New York called Providence Town Players and it was run by a wonderful New York Shakespearean actor named Reginald Gooding. I started parking cars there and then eventually got on stage. I think it was *Applesauce,* or one of those traditional summer New York State Theater Group plays. Whatever a repertoire company would play. It was *Mustard* or *Applesauce*, something like that.

I started working in live television and the show I was on was shut down for a summer hiatus. I was an assistant director, a floor manager. I was desperate for a job. A dear friend of mine said they had a friend whose father, a young man of thirty-four, was a producer and director of documentaries and commercials and industrial films. He had a heart attack at thirty-four and he was looking for an assistant. It turned out his name was George Blake and he was nominated for an Academy Award for a documentary he wrote, directed, edited, and produced when he was twenty-four. A very beautiful story about Nicholas Gaffney, an opera singer who learned to sing in a concentration camp. In any event, I went to work for George, driving him around.

Remember, up until then I had been working in live television. In live television the actors were taught to concede to the equipment because it was live. You had to work to the cameras so that the cameras would be mobile enough to meet you when you got into the next set or next set-up. It was interesting but I really felt it must have been very inhibiting to the actors.

And then I got to be George Blake's assistant. It was the first time I had ever seen film shot. George would do a set-up and then he would put the camera on the other side. And I thought how could they do that? How was it working? I began to realize that the mechanics of film conceded to the acting. It was an actor's platform, much like theater. I realized this is what I wanted to do so I learned it. I stayed with George for almost five years. In those five years I did everything. I drove him, I was a cameraman for a while, and we did our own sound. I also edited.

One day he gave me the opportunity to direct my first commercial. It was with General Claire Chenault and it was for Camel cigarettes, which eventually killed him. He died of lung cancer, I believe. That was my first shot at directing and I knew that's where it was for me from that day on.

The tragedy was, George Blake, one of the most talented men I've ever met, died of a heart attack at thirty-eight. I was somewhat lost. I didn't know what to do. A big piece of my life was gone. But I stayed on with his company and I continued to direct. I even started my own little commercial company. Eventually, Marty Ransohoff, who owned Filmways, a commercial company in New York, asked me to come to California to direct commercials for him. I thought it was a great opportunity to come out, pay my way, and get back into acting. I wanted to both act and direct. So I came out and just kept working in the commercial production business. I ended up under contract to Desilu Studios who had a commercial division.

Among the other things that I did there was the show openings of *The Lucy Show* as well as the commercials, which were for Westinghouse and featured Betty Furness as the spokeswoman. Some of those commercials would feature Lucy, Desi, and Bill Frawley and Vivian Vance, and Betty Furness. It was really tough to get the four of them on the set and to get them all working at the same time.

## Fun and Games with Steve McQueen

In any event, there was a producer by the name of Eddie Adamson visiting the head of the commercial division, a wonderful man named Lee Savich. Adamson came over to me and said, "Listen, if you can work with those four, do you think you can work with Steve McQueen?" I said, "Hey, we were actors together, we studied together, and we rode motorcycles together." He said, "Great, I want you to direct the *Wanted Dead or Alive* show." I was thrilled. This was the opportunity I was waiting for.

So Mr. Adamson took me over to meet Steve McQueen. Steve and I greeted each other as friends and he asked what I was doing there. "Well, I'm the director of your next show," I told him. And there was this kind of deathly silence. And then he told me that was great. I walked away but I thought he seemed a little cold. Mr. Adamson told me not to worry, that Steve was like that.

I got home that night and Ed Adamson called me and told me that Steve didn't want me directing. "You're an actor and you direct commercials and he doesn't think you're right for the show," he said. I thanked him for giving me a shot at the job. Then he told me that he was going to work on Steve and that I would direct the show. Eddie kept his word and Steve did eventually accept me.

In the old days the most difficult shows to shoot were westerns because you had maybe three, four days at the most to shoot a half-hour show. So I planned and blocked the episode out in my mind six ways to Sunday. I did the first set-up and they called Steve out and I explained the blocking of the scene to him. He said, "Nope." I said, "What do you mean, nope!" He told me that the way I had it blocked he would never leave his back exposed like that. I said, "OK, where would you be?" And he said, "You're the director, you figure it out," and he walked away. It went like that all morning.

We finally wrapped on Friday and we still weren't done. I went home and I knew it was over. I picked up the phone Sunday morning and called McQueen and said, "Steve I'm sorry, I thought this was going to work but it's not and I know you want me to quit, so I'm going to quit." He said, "What do you mean, you're going to quit? Nobody quits my show." I said, "Well, we've got a problem." He said, "Yeah, we've got a problem but nobody quits my show." I suggested we talk. He agreed and told me to be at his house at 7:15.

At 7:10 I was sitting in his driveway. At 7:15 I rang the doorbell. He and a whole bunch of guys from the show and some people I knew were there drinking wine and having a few laughs. Steve was very cold to me. He wouldn't communicate. Gradually, I had a few glasses of wine with everybody else and I started to loosen up. Finally at about one o'clock in the morning, a little drunk but feeling wonderful, McQueen came over to me and said, "Hey man, I'm sorry. Let's take a shot at it tomorrow. You're too loaded to drive so you'll sleep here." I went to sleep on his couch.

The next morning I drove in with him in his racing Jaguar. We did two days work in one day. We had broken the barriers in the silliest way. Not actor to director, but as just old buddies and him accepting what I was going to do as a director. And I stayed on with him for six or seven shows. But it started my career in television.

## From Television to His First Feature Film

## X-15 (1961)

*Charles Bronson; Brad Dexter; Ed Fleming; David McLean;*
*Mary Tyler Moore; Patricia Owens; James Stewart; Ralph Taeger.*

Normally, if you did a half-hour western, you were stuck in westerns. I managed to stay very versatile and do all the shows from *Route 66* to *Get*

*Smart* to *Gilligan's Island* to *Naked City.* It helped me tremendously later when I got into features. I was fortunate to do all these various TV shows. I was never characterized as only a certain type of director. I did well with them. I was very happy doing television. I was preparing myself in a strange way for the day that I would direct a feature film. And one day a feature did come along.

A feature film producer had seen one of my Steve McQueen or Loretta Young shows and liked what he saw. They were doing a movie called *X-15* starring Charles Bronson and Mary Tyler Moore and wondered if I'd be interested in directing the second unit, specifically the aerial work, because they liked the way I directed action. I read the script and thought it was fantastic and said yes and they hired me. About three weeks later I get a call telling me the director had quit the project and would I like to direct the whole picture. I immediately accepted.

We did the whole picture in about fifteen or twenty days. When the time came for the second unit stuff the producer told me there was no money left. So I went to Edwards Air Force Base where I had become friendly with some pilots and aerial photographers and I shot the second unit myself and put the picture together and I was very proud of it.

The day after the picture opened I went back to directing television.

# Salt and Pepper (1968)

*Sammy Davis, Jr.; Peter Lawford; Michael Bates; Ilona Rodgers;*
*John Le Mesurier; Graham Stark; Ernest Clark; Jeanne Roland;*
*Robert Dorning; Robertson Hare; Geoffrey Lumsden; William Mervyn;*
*Llewellyn Rees; Mark Singleton; Michael Trubshawe.*

Then one day I was working on the series *Wild, Wild West.* I had redone the pilot and the producers asked me to come around and do some more scenes with Sammy Davis and Peter Lawford. The three of us became very friendly and they suggested we find a feature we could all do together. We came up with an idea called *Salt and Pepper* and went off to England to shoot it.

I had a wonderful time but it was a little rough because Sammy and Peter were a little undisciplined at the time and I didn't have the strength and control of actors that I really needed. Besides, they were the producers and had hired me. Everything that I had allowed them to indulge themselves in I knew I would cut out of the finished film, and I did, but they fired me for it. The picture was released and was successful enough and they did a sequel, brought Jerry Lewis in to direct.

Then I went right back to television again!

# Lola (1969)

*Susan George; Charles Bronson; Orson Bean; Honor Blackman; Michael Craig; Paul Ford; Jack Hawkins; Trevor Howard; Lionel Jeffries; Kay Medford; Robert Morley; Peggy Aitchison; Tony Arpino; Eric Barker; Erik Chitty; Sheila D'Union; Judith Furse; Maria Garton; Cathy Jose; Anthony Kemp; Sue Lloyd; Barney Martin; Ruth Masters; Nina Monique.*

During this time Charlie Bronson called. I had worked with him on *X-15* and we were friends. He told me he had been offered a picture in London called *Twinkie*, which eventually was released as *Lola*. He was going to play a thirty-eight-year-old writer who meets a sixteen-year-old girl, who he falls in love with, marries, and brings her back to the United States, and then everything goes wrong. He thought my sense of humor would be good for the picture.

I read it and I loved it and we had a wonderful time doing it. We shot a good picture, but I really wasn't ready for features. It came out and I went right back to television. That was the story of my life.

Then one day a wonderful agent named Ed Rosen called me on a Friday and said he had just read a script that every studio in town had turned down. Warner Bros. had it and they were going to put it in turnaround that following Monday, which means they're going to give it up. Ed thought there was something wonderful about the script and wanted me to read it. It was called *The Anti-Christ*. Well, let me tell you, I couldn't put it down.

# The Omen (1976)

*Gregory Peck; Lee Remick; David Warner; Billie Whitelaw; Harvey Stephens; Patrick Troughton; Martin Benson; Robert Rietty; Tommy Duggan; John Stride; Anthony Nicholls; Holly Palance; Roy Boyd; Freda Dowie; Sheila Raynor.*

I was going to dinner one night at Ian McShane's house and Alan Ladd, Jr. and Patty Ladd were also there. Alan was head of Fox at that time and we'd been friends for years. As a matter of fact he had been my agent. I told him about this script and asked him to read it, which he did while taking his kids to summer camp that weekend.

He called me at midnight on Sunday and said he liked it a lot, but there were some problems with it. He thought it was very heavy-handed, but was a very interesting story. I told him that we should treat it not as a demonic genre film but as a suspense thriller with the characters being victims of circumstances. He agreed and we had a deal. The next day I had to call the producers who owned it. I introduced myself and I told them I had just sold their movie to Fox. They hung up on me and called Fox right away and Alan Ladd confirmed it.

One of the producers went out of his way to try to take me off the picture. This is the beauty of Hollywood. I sold their picture and then one of them tried to take me off the picture. And Alan Ladd, God love him, said, "Dick Donner brought me the script and I won't make it without him." That started my life. I was finally ready. I knew I wasn't going back to television. We renamed it *The Omen*. We were lucky enough to get Gregory Peck and Lee Remick, which validated the story. Overnight Dick Donner became a success. It only took about twelve years.

With *The Omen* I felt I was ready for features and I really learned that I had to surround myself with the best people. Up to then I really kind of left it up to the producers to hire the cameramen, the editors, and I found I wasn't working with the best people. We were shooting in England and I did a little research on my own. As a result I was lucky to get Gil Taylor to be my cinematographer and Stuart Baird as my editor. Having these two wonderful professionals with me made all the difference in the world.

By the way, we did that entire picture, believe it or not, with Peck's and Remick's salary and shooting in England and Jerusalem and Italy, for $2.2 million. I'm very proud of that.

There were a lot of things we had to improvise. For example, I had a scene where Lee is on a balcony in her home and her son, who is supposed to be from hell, intentionally or inadvertently knocks her off. I planned this great shot. I was going to put her on a crane right in front of the camera and bring her all the way down to the floor so you feel her falling all in one shot. Totally controlled and safe, but a very dramatic shot. So I sent the special effects man out to her house to measure her for the body harness. But the guy called me from her house to tell me she wouldn't do it. I got her on the phone and said, "Look Lee; you've got to have this on to be safe on the rig." She said, "You do it. I'm an actress, not a stunt person. This is my career and my face and my life and I'm not going to jeopardize it for any film."

I realized she was right. Accidents happen no matter how safe you make it. But we had to shoot this the next day. We had to improvise. One of the stunt men came over to me and said he had a crazy idea. A few other people had some ideas and out of it evolved a great scene. Here is what we did.

There's a goldfish bowl that she has set on this balustrade and her arm hits it and she gets knocked over. We shot that falling to the floor with a high-speed camera, I shot the goldfish bowl falling away from us shattering all over the floor. Then we took that floor and we put it on a wall. We took plastic and cut it out like water and pinned it and took fake dead sardines and pinned them to the wall. Now here we had the floor actually in an upright position. Lee Remick was standing upright on a flat dolly. We shot in slow motion and she came away from the camera on the dolly with the floor behind her. She turned, the dolly turned, and she smashed into the floor. Actually, she was standing up the whole time and it was totally safe. But because you saw the fishbowl fall first and hit the floor it registered what it was and everybody totally believed it. So out of a desperate situation, a solution evolved and we created a shot that people talk about all the time.

We opened on June 6, which is the sixth month on the sixth day, in 1976. And every sign in the theaters when you came out said, you've just seen this on 666. I was in awe of what happened. In any event that was *The Omen* and I never looked back.

> *I think what makes Dick a unique director are two things: his desire*
> *to enable his co-workers to do their best, and a real innocence about*
> *the story, so that he can really look at it from an audience's point of*
> *view and say, "Tell me the story."*
>
> Christopher Reeve—Actor

# Superman (1978)

*Marlon Brando; Gene Hackman; Christopher Reeve; Ned Beatty;*
*Jackie Cooper; Glenn Ford; Trevor Howard; Margot Kidder; Valerie Perrine;*
*Maria Schell; Terence Stamp; Phyllis Thaxter; Susannah York;*
*Marc McClure; Jeff East; Sarah Douglas; Harry Andrews.*

Interestingly enough, when *The Omen* came out I was like the new kid on the block. I had been here for many, many years and had done a lot of work, but nobody remembered that. All of a sudden they were treating me like the new fruit of the month, if you will. Everybody was after me! But I was getting the same kind of genre films offered to me.

One day my phone rang and a man said he was Alexander Salkind and asked if I knew who he was. I said, "No." He said he had produced many films and one of them was *The Three Musketeers*. I said, "Oh, I know who you are. You did *Three* and *Four Musketeers*." There had been a big problem because they had shot *Three Musketeers* but then edited it into two movies. The actors sued them and there was a tremendous outcry in the Screen Actors Guild. You had to declare when you were making a movie whether or not you were making one or two. That was all because of the Salkinds.

He asked if I knew who Superman was. I said of course. He said he was producing it and his director was no longer on the picture and he'd like me to do it and was sending me the script. He said he was going to pay me a lot of money. I said, "Really!" He said he was doing two pictures and would pay me a million dollars. A million dollars! That was a license plate! That was like somebody using the expression all the tea in China!

Before I hung up there was a knock on the door and the script was there. It was five hundred pages. Two complete screenplays! I read it and it was not very good and I certainly couldn't shoot five hundred pages. I called them back and said I didn't think the script was very good and I thought it needed a lot of work. Will you give me that opportunity? They said, no, no! We've got to shoot that script. So I turned them down. Then they called back and agreed I could bring a writer on, which I did, and we rewrote the screenplay.

I think I had about eleven weeks to prepare both movies. Their preparation up to that point was horrible. They had told me everything was prepared and all ready to go. They showed me their preparation for the flying scenes. The actor would run and jump in one cut and in the next cut he was literally on a board, which was underneath his costume, and they had him on wires. Then they would cut and drop him down. I said, "Hey, fellas, this is the eighties and this is Superman and this picture's not going to work unless he really flies." We really did have to start from scratch.

We developed a flying unit and in that flying unit was a piece of machinery that revolutionized the industry. You put the actor on an arm or a pole so you wouldn't see where it was coming out. You could roll the actor anyway you want it. You could roll the camera counterwise. You could zoom in and zoom out and the backgrounds went with you at all times. But it was in its infancy and the Salkinds wouldn't give us the money to develop the equipment. I went to Warner Bros., who was the distributor, and they advanced us twenty-five thousand dollars to make this machinery work. It took us about six months before the day we all sat in dailies and we saw Superman fly for the first time. It brought tears to everyone's eyes because he was really flying. We had perfected it.

## More Tricks of the Trade

There's a shot in *Superman* that everyone always asks about. Superman flies in and lands on Lois Lane's balcony. He talks to Lois. And then in one shot, from over her shoulder, he flies away into the distance. Lois hears a knock at her door and she walks into her apartment and opens the door and there's Clark Kent. But you just saw Superman leave. There's no way we could have taken an actor off that rig, change his costume, change his hair, and put him outside that set to walk in the door in fourteen seconds. It would take more like an hour. But I wanted to do that shot in one fluid move.

Here is what we did. We photographed a ledge of her apartment with the entire city of Metropolis in the background. We started with Superman by himself and he turns and says goodbye to Lois and he flies away on wires off into the distance and then we cut. Six months later we now have this piece of film and we're on the set of Lois' apartment. Instead of Superman we put a front projection screen up. We projected Superman's image past her—she's live—onto the screen. What we're photographing is an image of him flying, of him standing there. He says goodbye and turns and he flies away and she's looking at a screen. Then she turns into the living room and Christopher Reeve as Clark Kent is standing at her door. So when you put the film together you see him fly away and fourteen seconds later walk in the door. And every film school, every cinematographer wants to know how we did that. It's like Lee Remick's fall in *The Omen*.

When I came on *Superman*, Marlon Brando and Gene Hackman had already been signed. The Salkind's paid a lot of money to have them in the picture. They had even given them stop dates, which meant they had to finish by a certain date before they even knew they were going to make the movie. So I had this terrible responsibility. I had to get rid of Brando and Gene Hackman within a certain amount of days.

## Lose the Mustache, Gene

Gene Hackman had a mustache and I was just starting to grow a mustache myself. We talked a little bit about Lex Luther and who he was and I asked if he would consider shaving his head or wear one of those bald caps. He said, "I'm not going to shave my head and I'm not going to wear one of those bald caps. They're terrible." Even though I agreed that bald caps were uncomfortable, everyone knew that Lex Luther was bald. I asked if he would at least take off the mustache. He said, no, he liked his mustache. But, I said, "Gene, everybody knows Lex Luther is bald and he has no mustache!" And he said that was my problem.

So I went back to England and continued shooting other pieces of the film and I got a call that Gene had arrived and he was in makeup. I called up there and asked the makeup man, Stewart Freeborn, if Gene still had his mustache. Sure enough, he did. I had already shaved mine off. I told Freeborn to come down to my office and put the best fake moustache on me he had ever done. When he was finished I walked up to the makeup room and greeted Gene. I told him I had worked out the hair thing and he only needed to wear the bald cap in one scene. He said that was fine. Then I told him the moustache had to go. He didn't want to do it. I told him that if he would take his off I would take mine off. He looked at me for a while, then agreed, but only if we both did it then and there. I said OK and instructed Stewart to shave Gene's mustache off.

Stewart used an electric razor and shaved him clean. Then Gene wanted mine to come off. I stayed right where I was and just peeled the fake mustache off. Gene just stared at me. I saw the sides of his neck start to throb and I knew I was dead. It took about thirty seconds and he broke out laughing. It started a great relationship and a great friendship and it worked. It was one of those moments that can never be repeated and I've loved Gene ever since and I've never grown a mustache since.

## Brando is Brando!

I had never met Brando. So I called Francis Coppola, who had directed him in *The Godfather*, and asked him what he could tell me about him. Francis said that Marlon was a genius with an incredible gift of gab and that I'd be awestruck listening to him. But really listen when he talks, because he always hangs himself, so just listen.

So I went to Brando's house and he turned out to be the most gracious icon I've ever met in my life. We sat down and talked for hours. We talked about everything except *Superman*. I could have gone for days. At one point he was telling a story about children. He thought children were quite amazing. He said he told his son a fairy tale recently about a fox that jumped over a wall and around a log. His son said, "No, Dad, the fox jumped over the log and went around the wall." He went on and on.

Finally he said, "You're not here to listen to all these stories, you're here to talk about my wardrobe, right? Well here's what I have in mind. I think I'd like to play it like a bagel."

A bagel? We were all thunderstruck! Then he said, "I don't really mean a bagel. What I mean is, I come from another planet, right? How do you know what people look like up there? They could look like bagels. Because I'm sending my son to Earth to save his life, I am going to make him into the image of a human. But I can still be a bagel." He went on and on and on about it.

Finally he asked us what we thought. I said that earlier he told us a story about the fable he was telling his son about the fox that jumped over the wall and went around the log and his son said, no, the fox jumped over the log and around the wall. Children know these things, I told him. Then I told him that Jor-El, the father of Superman, had been around since 1936. There wasn't a child from four years of age to my age that didn't know what Jor-El looked like. He looks like you the way you are now. He smiled and said, "I really hung myself talking too much, didn't I?" He laughed and asked to see his costume. I showed him and that was the end of it. He was just delightful. It was great. There are really some wonderful Brando stories.

## Inside Moves (1980)

*John Savage; David Morse; Diana Scarwid; Amy Wright; Tony Burton;*
*Bill Henderson; Steve Kahan; Jack O'Leary; Bert Remsen; Harold Russell;*
*Pepe Serna; Harold Sylvester; Arnold Williams; George Brenlin; Gerri Dean.*

Shortly after I did *The Omen*, a literary agent gave me a book called *Inside Moves*. It was a wonderful story but I really didn't know how to beat the book. It had major problems in transposing it into a motion picture. I spent some time on it with a few writers and we never got a handle on it. Then *Superman* came along and I went away for well over a year to work on that.

When I came back I was given a screenplay to read. I said, "God, this is *Inside Moves* but it's brilliantly written." The original book had a lot to do with Vietnam and I thought it was wrong and I couldn't touch that area at that time. This screenplay totally stayed away from it. It had become a true story of love and friendship and relationships between men and it was brilliant. It had a great sense of humor and it had great meaning for me. Two young writers, Valerie Curtin and Barry Levinson, wrote it. I called them and told them I had fallen in love with their screenplay and I wanted to make it and they were thrilled. But I couldn't get any studio to make it even though I had completed two very successful films. The studios felt it was a dark and depressing film. I tried to convince them it was anything but. It was a film of great hope and tremendous emotional highs but I couldn't convince anybody.

I was working on another screenplay with two young producers named Bob Goodwin and Mark Tanz and I gave them this screenplay by Curtin and Levinson. They both loved it and wanted to make it right away. Mark raised the money out of Canada and we went out and made *Inside Moves*. At one point I almost had Dustin Hoffman play the role that John Savage played. But Dustin felt it was too close to the character of Ratso in *Midnight Cowboy*. So we didn't get Dustin but John Savage came into my life and he was just brilliant in the part.

David Morse was an unknown that we found in New York. We also had Diana Scarwid who got an Academy Award nomination for the picture and Amy Wright. I had an incredible ensemble. And then on top of that I got three wonderful actors to play the characters that sat around the card table. I got Harold Russell, Burt Remsen, and Bill Henderson, a jazz singer. These three wonderful cronies sat around this card table and introduced life to John Savage.

We took on the subject of a man who attempts suicide and comes out of it handicapped. Through this relationship with these three guys he finds the beauty of life, he finds the beauty of love, he finds the beauty of friendship. They teach him that there is no such thing as being handicapped. Because of the experiences they've experienced in their lives they are much stronger and richer. It became a story of love and friendship and giving and caring in its gentlest form. Most people do not want to go to the movies and see a depressing film. I think people thought that's what they were going to see, but it was just the opposite. It was about a very up relationship among five people who all were handicapped in some way. It was a very eclectic group who were handicapped physically or emotionally who found that life really has its glory and its beauty. It was simply and purely an allegory.

The picture is one of the most dearest to my heart. It was critically acknowledged. I should get that kind of critique on every film I do. But because it was a film about the handicapped and probably sold and marketed improperly, it didn't do well. It became a great cult film on video. To me it's one of my greatest, dearest films.

## How Does he Choose his Material?

In this business everyone has a different way of choosing the material they want to do. In my case it's either something I developed from scratch and I fall in love or it's something I've read. And if it's something I read and I want to see it and I shoot it in my mind, that's the decision for me to make it. I want to see that picture the way I saw it, not the way someone else does. That's the way I pick a picture. I become deathly afraid that if I don't take it it's going to be made and it's not going to be made the way I want to see it and I'm always going to be upset with myself. It's that simple.

# The Goonies (1985)

*Sean Astin; Josh Brolin; Jeff Cohen; Corey Feldman; Kerri Green; Martha Plimpton; Jonathan Ke Quan; John Matuszak; Robert Davi; Joe Pantoliano; Anne Ramsey; Lupe Ontiveros; Mary Ellen Trainor; Keith Walker; Curtis Hanson.*

*The Goonies* came along in my life by way of Steven Spielberg. We'd been friends for many, many years and he called me and said he had this wonderful script and he had a young writer by the name of Chris Columbus on it. Chris, of course, has gone on to become one of the better directors in the business. I read the script and couldn't stop laughing. I fell madly in love with it. It was with kids. There's nothing in the world better for a director than to work with young, raw talent, because they're yours and they're fresh and they're clean. There are no affectations. You have this wonderful opportunity to kind of pull the best out of these fresh, young minds.

We ended up with this wonderful group of children and we improvised at lot. We went out and shot this picture and I think I had the best time I've ever had in my life, or one of the best times. With rare exception, every picture is one of the best times in my life. We're the luckiest people in the world to be doing what we're doing. One of Steven's quotes is, "It's like having the world's largest erector set." It's true. It's one of the great toys that we've been given. We're blessed.

But every morning I had these seven or eight children there. If you hugged one and not the others, they were depressed all day because you were being a favorite to one. If you yelled at one, they all cried, they all got upset. It was just an incredible education for me. We had this wonderful experience. We bonded.

Near the last week of the shoot, the children were very strange. Here we had shot for ten weeks and there was this wonderful homogenous family with a lot of love, but this last week was very strange. They were very alienated toward me. I thought, well, I don't know much about children, I guess, because I thought I really knew these kids inside and out by now. We had a wrap party and at the party where I expected hugs, I got these cold hand-shakes. I was very disillusioned.

I had just bought a little house in Hawaii and I decided I was going to take a week or two off before I went into the editing. So I flew over to Hawaii. One day my neighbor came over and asked if I'd be kind enough to drive her into town. She said her car was broken. I offered her the use of my Jeep but she said she didn't know how to shift. So I drove her into town, which was supposed to be a fifteen-minute trip, but she had to do this and that and before you knew it two and a half hours had gone by and the sun was going down. It was getting late and I was really getting angry.

Finally, I took her home, put the car in the garage, and I walked through my house to the beach because it's glass on both sides. The television set was on but I didn't remember leaving it on. Anyway, I walked around to the beach. As I walked I saw the oldest boy from the picture, Josh Brolin, coming up the walk with a surfboard. I thought, what the hell is he doing here? He said hello and reminded me that his mother had promised to take him to Hawaii. He kept looking behind me so I turned around and there was the entire cast from *Goonies*. I mean the entire cast. Spielberg had flown them all over as a surprise for me. He told them that if anybody tipped it and I found out about the sur-prise, the trip would be off. So that week of total alienation at the end of the picture was the best acting those kids ever did because they never gave it away.

The deal was they could only stay two hours and then they were going to fly to another island and have a vacation. But I was so thrilled to have them there we bought out the supermarket and we had a great barbecue and they stayed the night. It was one of the greatest put-ons of my life. I called Spielberg and said, "Watch your back, pal." He's still waiting.

*The Goonies* was a wonderful experience. It was just pure, wonderful fun. I could do anything I wanted to do as a director. Just total freedom and con-stant laughter. To do a movie like that with those great kids and to be able to look back on it is just one of the great experiences of my life.

# Ladyhawke (1985)

*Matthew Broderick; Rutger Hauer; Michelle Pfeiffer; Leo McKern; John Wood;*
*Ken Hutchison; Alfred Molina; Giancarlo Prete; Loris Loddi; Alessandro Serra;*
*Charles Borromel; Massimo Sarchielli; Nicolina Papetti; Russell Kase; Don Hudson.*

After *Goonies* I didn't know what I was going to do next. There was a young female producer by the name of Lauren Schuler who had a property called

*Ladyhawke,* and she kept calling and sending it over. I just wasn't in the mood to read at the time but this woman kept nailing me. I had to go to Florida on a trip so I took the script with me and started reading it on the plane and I couldn't put it down.

The story is about cursed lovers. He is a man by day and a wolf by night. She is a lady by night and a hawk by day. And so as the sun rises and sets there's that infinitesimal moment where they can almost touch as lovers. There's a passage where the writer has very brilliantly expressed this impossible love. As I read it, tears came to my eyes and a stewardess who was standing there asked if something were wrong. I told her there wasn't and asked her to read that page. She did and she started to cry.

That did it. I got to New York and called this lady producer and told her I was very interested in her property. It took us about two years to develop the screenplay properly and to get a cast. We tried to shoot it in Czechoslovakia but it was still under Communist control and had too many restrictions so we finally ended up in Italy. In the interim I did a picture called *The Toy* with Jackie Gleason and Richard Pryor. But we kept preparing *Ladyhawke.*

During that time this lady producer became a really good friend of mine, a real buddy. She was married but whenever we would travel, she would ring my room or I would ring hers and we'd go for walks. We became really good friends.

Oh, here's a wonderful little anecdote about Michelle Pfeiffer. I was in Europe and we were casting. A lot of actresses were put on tape back here and the tapes would be sent to us and we'd view them over there. One of the tapes was an audition for Michelle Pfeiffer. She was startling to look at on screen and quite good in the reading. At the very end she said, "I don't know if I can be a hawk but I sure can be . . ." and the tape cuts to a birdcage with a little budgie in it and she says, ". . . at least a little bird if I can't be a hawk in your life." Automatically we fell in love with her and she got the part.

Now, back to my lady producer, Lauren. We shot in Italy, which is the most romantic country in the world. During the shoot, my good friend the producer separated from her husband. The weekend that it happened she came into the office and I knew she had gone to see her husband. I asked her how her weekend had gone. She said her marriage was off and tears came to her eyes. I'd always seen her as this hard-nosed, tough lady producer—my buddy. But all of a sudden I saw her as this wonderful, vulnerable woman. I couldn't believe what I was looking at. I had fallen in love with my friend. I eventually married my friend. We've been married eight years, going together eleven. So *Ladyhawke* is the most beautiful love story in the world as far as I'm concerned because it's my love story.

It is a film that has became a tremendous cult film on video. It did well at the box office, but not great. It was wonderful to make. It took me to Italy and became my favorite—our favorite—country. I was very fortunate.

> *I've work on a number of films with Dick, and you don't do that for no reason. And sometimes the scripts won't be there yet, but it doesn't matter because I like working with Dick. And you know they'll get there, and you know he's going to make a really good film.*
>
> Mel Gibson—Actor

# Lethal Weapon (1987)

*Mel Gibson; Danny Glover; Gary Busey; Mitch Ryan; Tom Atkins; Darlene Love; Traci Wolfe; Jackie Swanson; Damon Hines; Ebonie Smith; Bill Kalmenson; Lycia Naff; Patrick Cameron; Don Gordon; Jimmie F. Skaggs.*

Mike Ovitz, an agent, gave *Lethal Weapon* to me. I love Mike very much. He's a genius. He called one day and told me that Warner Bros. had the script and a producer by the name of Joel Silver was attached to it. He said a young writer fresh out of USC had written it and it had great potential. I read it that night and then gave it to Lauren to read. I had never done an action film like this, but this one seemed to have a great deal of meaning beyond the action stuff. It had this wonderful character by the name of Riggs who was very dimensional. He went from being suicidal to having a great desire to live. I decided I wanted to make it.

Casting the picture was very difficult because I had to cast with a combination in mind for the roles of Riggs and Murtaugh. Marion Daugherty is a casting director at Warner Bros. From her loins have come all the great young casting people in the world, but she's still the greatest, the grand dame of casting. She suggested we meet Mel Gibson, who she thought was going to be a big star. We sent the script to him in Australia and he liked it very much. He was coming over to the States and we decided to meet.

It was Marion who also suggested Danny Glover. She had cast him in Spielberg's *The Color Purple* and thought he was a wonderful actor. But I said, he's black! And then I realized how intolerant I was. I had always considered myself very tolerant and liberal. But because it wasn't typed on the page black or white, I automatically thought white. I felt so ashamed that I characterized him that way. And so we sent it to Danny who was doing a play in Chicago. He responded favorably so I asked him if he could fly in.

We held a reading of the script at my house with Mel and Danny and the script came to life like I'd never seen a script come to life before. The relationship between the two of them came to life. Their rapport and their sense of humor were just wonderful and brilliant. Their sense of improvisation was just great.

Because it was an action film it was a difficult picture to shoot. It was tiring, it was night, there was chases and explosions and busses hitting cars in the middle of Hollywood Boulevard at five in the morning. Once again I surrounded myself with the best stunt people in the world, the best special effects people, and to everyone's credit they all helped me make that film. The cast and crew were like a family and everybody contributed.

The most pivotal scene in the movie for me was an attempted suicide by Martin Riggs. He's lost his wife in an accident and he's just disillusioned with life. He sits in his trailer and in a moment of depression takes his police weapon and contemplates suicide. It was a difficult scene for all of us. We tried it once and it didn't work. Mel wasn't up to it and nothing was happening. So I suggested we wait until Mel felt the time was right. We always carried his trailer with us on the back of a truck. And every once in a while I would go to Mel and ask, "Are you up to it?" And he'd always say no.

Then, very late one night, we were on the studio backlot and almost ready to wrap when Mel suggested we try the scene. We had rehearsed and shot it once so everybody knew exactly what to do. It was lit and set up in a matter of moments. The only other people in the trailer besides Mel was myself on camera pulling focus for the camera operator. I wanted Mel to feel the isolation of what he was doing without a crew around. He started the scene. I just let him go and he started to improvise and the scene started to happen. As the scene developed, the operator and I found ourselves crying, trying to cover our sobs so we wouldn't disturb Mel.

There was no way of saying cut. The scene never really ended. I finally had to break it by running in and hugging him and taking the gun out of his hand. We all looked at each other and thought we were going to cry but we all broke into laughter instead. When I saw that scene on film I knew what Mel Gibson was going to be and what he was made of. He was dynamic. It may have only been an action film but that moment totally made that film above all others.

# Scrooged (1988)

*Bill Murray; Karen Allen; John Forsythe; John Glover;*
*Bob Goldthwait; David Johansen; Carol Kane; Robert Mitchum;*
*Nicholas Phillips; Michael J. Pollard; Alfre Woodard; Mabel King;*
*John Murray; Jamie Farr; Robert Goulet.*

*Scrooged* was a screenplay submitted to me by Paramount that had been written by two geniuses, Michael O'Donoghue, who unfortunately passed away very early in life, and Mitch Glazer. Remember what I said earlier. I do a movie when I read something and I want to see it so badly I must do it because if I don't somebody else will and it won't be the way I wanted it.

Bill Murray is one of the great crazies that will ever come into your life. He delivers a phenomenal character and a wonderful performance in *Scrooged*. I had Glazer and O'Donoghue around all the time so when we got into improvisation they were there to fill it in and work it out.

## Just a Bit of Personal Philosophy

You know, it's hard when you talk about a movie you've made. When you're making it you get so emotionally involved. That year of your life is dedicated strictly and only to that film. That movie is your life, even to the exclusion of your wife and family.

People ask me how I approach the making of one of my movies. It's very simple. You develop a screenplay and prepare a movie in pre-production. And that's like dating somebody and building the foreplay, if you will, and building the relationship. Then one day you start to shoot the film. And that to me is like making love. That's eight, ten, eleven weeks of making love every day and sometimes it's good, sometimes it's not. Then one day it's over.

Then you have anywhere from ten to sixteen, eighteen weeks of editing, and I call that the period of the development of the child. You put the whole picture together and you're developing. Then one day in the laboratory your baby's born. It comes out and you look at it and now it's no longer yours. It's all over. It's all gone. The people you loved and were involved with for a year are all gone on to other projects. Your baby's been taken away from you. You hope the people who are taking it away are going to educate it properly, market it properly, and send it out into the world properly. At that point it's out of your control and everything is gone. Hopefully that year of your life has been well spent and productive and fulfilling. But it's gone. So in its simplest form that is filmmaking.

When we talk about *Scrooged* I remember many wonderful moments and a lot of rough moments, like there are in any film. I can't talk about the bad moments because I don't like to re-create them. They're gone. It's best you forget them. You go on and remember the fun ones, the good ones. It doesn't contaminate the memory. You remember the bliss, not the pain. There was great bliss in that film.

I had great character actors in that film from Buster Poindexter* to Carol Kane to Bob Goldthwait. They were insane human beings who got inside their characters better than I or anybody else could have written them. They improvised and came up with magical, insane moments. I remember many times I would laugh out loud on the set and ruin takes. Yes, there were rough moments and there were bad moments. But if we have the ability to control our own minds it's better to go through life remembering the good things, not the bad.

# Radio Flyer (1992)

*Lorraine Bracco; John Heard; Adam Baldwin; Elijah Wood;*
*Joseph Mazzello; Ben Johnson; Sean Baca; Robert Munic; Garette Ratliff Henson;*
*Thomas Ian Nicholas; Noah Verduzco; Isaac Ocampo; Kaylan Romero;*
*Abraham Verduzco; T. J. Evans.*

*Radio Flyer* was a departure from the films I was making but it wasn't a departure from the films I had made. As far as I was concerned, *Inside Moves* and *Radio Flyer* shared a great parallel. You can always find the beauty behind the ugliness and you can always find joy behind pain. *Radio Flyer* was a very emotionally difficult film for everyone to make except for the two children, who were wonderful actors. You never really allow them to know the dark side. They were acting, they were having fun, and they were playing a game.

But for David Evans who wrote it, Lauren who produced it, myself, and the adult cast it was a great burden. It was an important picture to make because child abuse was something that had just started to come out of the

---

* Credited in *Scrooged* as David Johansen

shadows. We were warned beforehand it would be a very difficult picture for the general public to accept. Like *Inside Moves* and its handicapped theme, people might shy away.

The picture intentionally had a very ambiguous ending. People would come to me afterwards and say, "Gosh, did the picture end this way?" I'd say, "What way?" They thought the child didn't really have that brother. That it was really about him. And I'd tell them that was exactly right. Other people told me their wives saw it totally different. I'd asked them "How?" They'd tell me and I'd say they're right. I tried to force the audience into a sense of subjectivity at the end so everybody would relate on the level they would.

We would hold screenings and then have a conversation with a little group of twelve people at the end. And invariably there wasn't one night that we had a screening that somebody in that group of twelve didn't say it happened to them. It was cathartic. I wanted that picture to go out like that. It was probably one of the major mistakes I made in my life because I really find that audiences don't like to be given that opportunity. They want the answers given to them. Maybe if I had re-evaluated it and given it a positive answer, or a negative, but given an answer to people, the picture would have had more success in theaters. It wouldn't have been the picture I set out to make or the picture that David Evans wrote.

*Radio Flyer* has became a tremendous cult film on video. Everybody still talks about it. People always tell me *Radio Flyer* was an emotionally charged moment for them.

# Maverick (1994)

*Mel Gibson; Jodie Foster; James Garner; Graham Greene; Alfred Molina; James Coburn; Dub Taylor; Geoffrey Lewis; Paul Smith; Dan Hedaya; Dennis Fimple; Denver Pyle; Clint Black; Max Perlich; Art LaFleur.*

I said earlier how I met Mel and loved working with him. I guess I never really said this before but he is one of the most talented human beings I've ever met in my life. He's talented as an actor and as a director. He called me one day and said he wanted to see me. It was a Sunday. He came over and he hemmed and hawed and he ate most of my breakfast and my wife's breakfast. Then he said, "Listen, can I leave this screenplay with you?" I asked him if he wanted me to critique it or star in it. He told me he wanted me to direct it. That script was *Maverick*.

He had watched *Maverick,* the series, as a kid and always loved it. He went to Warner Bros. with his own money and bought it away from them. Then, again with his own money, he hired William Goldman, one of the great screenwriters of our time, to do an original screenplay and then he had the good taste to come to me with it. When I read it I just loved it. I had always wanted to do a western so of course I told him I'd do it.

We had wanted James Garner to appear in a cameo role as kind of homage and respect to him. We sent the script to his agent. Jim thought it was wonderful but didn't want to play a small part. The agent asked who was going to play the other character of the father. I told him it hadn't been set yet. He told us that Garner would love to play it. I thought he was kidding. Not to play *Maverick* but to play his father! And you don't even know it's his father until the end of the movie. So Garner came aboard.

Then somebody suggested Jodie Foster. I said, "Come on, Jodie's not going to do this. This is an outright romp and a bizarre, witty character in a western. She's not going to do it!" But we sent it to her anyway. To everyone's surprise she called and said she was dying to play the part. She said, "I'm yours. I'm putting myself in your hands because I've never played this kind of character before."

We needed a Commodore and who better than that big crazy guy who puffs those big cigars, Jimmy Coburn. I always wanted to work with him. I used to kid Jim Garner when I was a young TV director because I never got hired to do *Maverick.* He always claimed he had nothing to do with it. Same thing with Coburn. I'd never worked with him either and here I had this great opportunity.

We also had Doug McClure. It was his last picture. Doug later died of lung cancer. But he had his last glory in *Maverick* and he was a delight. We surrounded ourselves with every great western TV actor we could possibly get. There wasn't one we asked that turned us down.

*Maverick* was a delightful experience. It was a day on the beach. It was the most wonderful experience of my life with the exception of meeting that wonderful producer, my wife. Jodie hasn't stop talking about it. She and Mel were like two peas in a pod. The funniest couple of kids I've ever met in my life. That was *Maverick.* It turned out to be a big success. A sequel, you ask? It's up to Mel. He owns it.

---

NOTE: This interview was conducted just before filming began on *Assassins.* Since that time Donner has also completed *Conspiracy Theory* and *Lethal Weapon 4,* both starring Mel Gibson.

# Assassins (1995)

*Sylvester Stallone; Antonio Banderas; Julianne Moore;*
*Anatoli Davydov; Muse Watson; Steve Kahan;*
*Kelly Rowan; Reed Diamond; Kai Wulff; Kerry Skaisky;*
*James Douglas Haskins; Stephen Liska; John Harms;*
*Edward J. Rosen; Christina Orchid.*

The next project I'm going to do is *Assassins* starring Sylvester Stallone and Antonio Banderas. I think it's a little bit of a departure. It's more a thriller than an action piece. I've looked at a lot of Stallone's work. I'm kind of excited about him doing this. It's not your normal Stallone film. It's more of a thriller. He never takes his shirt off, he never hits anybody, but he plays a very strong character and very vulnerable at times. Antonio plays a heavy who idolizes the Stallone character but is totally in competition with him. It's a wonderful, delightful piece. For me it's very unusual. I think we can deliver a different Stallone to the audience and I'm looking forward to it.

## His Thoughts on the Industry

I haven't lived through the changes in the studio system per se. By the time I was working in the system it wasn't the producers who really had the control, it was the directors. In the old days I guess it was the producers who ran the show along with the studio executives, and the stars were all under contract and people would do five or six movies a year. I've been very fortunate that every relationship I've had with a studio so far, especially Warner Bros., has been that they really respect the process and I've learned to respect their process. As I've said, you finish a movie and it's your baby and you turn your baby over to someone and hope they educate it properly. The studio trusts me with picture making and I trust them to know how to sell and deliver their end of it.

When I was starting there were no universities teaching cinema except maybe Northwestern. Now almost every university has communications, theater arts, or cinema courses. It's very exciting, but it's a little scary. You have to keep looking over your shoulder because you know the young ones behind you are going to knock you out pretty soon. But I love to encourage newcomers because I like to watch and learn from them and maybe I can keep myself going for a while.

## Editing Films

The editing process is the most painful and the most rewarding part of making a film. You've prepared your picture, you've made your picture, and now you have to put it together. When you've shot a scene in a movie you know in your mind how it's suppose to fit in. After you shoot it you turn your dailies over to your film editor. If you have the right kind of relationship with your editor you can practically talk in shorthand. But now you have this editor who's seeing it through his eyes. Sometimes you are happily surprised with the results, sometimes dreadfully surprised, but it begins another amalgamation of two people's minds constantly challenging each other.

Then you finally get this picture up on its feet and you look at it for the first time and you want to quit the business. You know you've made the biggest dog that ever happened. You know you've wasted a year of your life, that you've spent all the studio's money and you've failed miserably and you want to cut and change everything. That's where the editor comes in and calms you down and helps you find a perspective and helps you find your values again and you go back through it and think well, maybe it is working. The editor is a very large part of it. Greatest love/hate relationship that ever happened.

## On Actors

Actors are so very fragile because each moment they are up on that screen you are playing with their lives and they know it. You must give them all the attention you give an adult or a baby. At times it's everything from love to discipline. But if they like me it's because I felt and still feel that same fear, that same timidity and indecision that they go through. I try to comfort them in the gentlest, nicest way and give them all the freedom to try something new. A lot of them improvise. I guess it's my respect of acting. It comes back to me.

## On Producers

My wife Lauren is the perfect example of what a producer really means to me. The title of producer is a misnomer in today's films. Films have credits for producers, executive producers, associate producers, co-producers, and a lot of them mean nothing. It might mean they were an agent and they represent the actor who's the star. Then there are producers who really make the movie happen, who bring you into the project. They do nothing more than support you. They carry you through the process of screenwriting, of casting. They're great hand-holders.

More important is a good producer who will allocate the authority to let you go out and make the movie and protect you from everything on the outside that would disturb the process of directing. If they're not good, you have to do it yourself. The reason I produce my own films is to protect myself from producers, with the exception of Lauren or Joel Silver. But up until now I produced to protect myself because I've experienced producers who know nothing, who are there for the ride, and who try to impose themselves.

But there are good ones. There are some bright young kids coming along who are becoming wonderful producers. There is a new breed of producers. Unfortunately, there are still the other ones.

> *He's amazing because the minute that he steps on to the set he demands attention. Dick is very demanding of energy, he's a man that is phenomenal himself, and he wants that in front of the camera all the time.*
>
> Lauren Shuler-Donner—Producer

## What Does the Future Hold for Dick Donner?

I have no idea what my future holds. As far as the industry goes, I hope I keep going until they have to beat me off with a stick or wheel me off the set. I would like to slow down a little, but I already know my next film after *Assassins* and the one after that. When I'm not working, I'm a bastard to live with. I've been one of those blessed to be in the motion picture industry and blessed to be successful and I just want to live with my blessing as long as I can.

My parting words are I hope that twenty-five years from now you'll come back and we can do this interview again about what I've done in the last twenty-five years.

# Director Filmography

Episodic television (1958–1959)
*X-15* (1961)
Episodic television (1962–1966)
*Salt and Pepper* (1968)
Episodic television (1968)
*Lola* (1969)
Episodic television (1971–1975)
*The Omen* (1976)
*Superman* (1978)
*Superman II* (1980)
*Inside Moves* (1980)
*The Toy* (1982)
*Ladyhawke* (1985)
*The Goonies* (1985)
*Lethal Weapon* (1987)
*Scrooged* (1988)
*Tales from the Crypt* (1989, TV)
*Lethal Weapon 2* (1989)
*Lethal Weapon 3* (1992)
*Radio Flyer* (1992)
*Maverick* (1994)
*Assassins* (1995)
*Conspiracy Theory* (1997)
*Lethal Weapon 4* (1998)

# Awards

**Academy of Science Fiction, Horror and Fantasy Films, USA, Saturn Award**

*Superman*, Best Director (nominated), 1979

# The Films of Norman Jewison

**N**orman Frederick Jewison was born on July 21, 1926, in Toronto, Ontario, Canada. He made his professional debut on the stage at the age of five. He began staging and performing both dramas and musical comedies at Malvern Collegiate Institute. Shortly thereafter, he left for World War II service with the Royal Canadian Navy. Upon his return in 1946, he enrolled at the University of Toronto's Victor College, where he earned a bachelor's degree in general arts in 1950.

While driving a cab for a living, Jewison found occasional work as an actor on the stage and in radio for the Canadian Broadcasting Corporation. After a two-year work/study program with the BBC in London, he returned to Canada and wrote, directed, and produced for the CBC some of Canada's most popular musicals, dramas, comedy-variety shows, and specials for a period of seven years.

In 1958 Jewison accepted an invitation from CBS in New York to direct the memorable series *Your Hit Parade*. He followed that with *The Andy Williams Show*, two *Harry Belafonte* specials, *The Fabulous Fifties*, Danny Kaye's television debut, *The Broadway of Lerner and Lowe*, and the award-winning Judy Garland specials. His film debut as a director came with the 1963 comedy *Forty Pounds of Trouble*, starring Tony Curtis.

Jewison has been a vibrant force in the motion picture industry for over three decades and has been personally nominated for seven Academy Awards, as well as three best director awards by the Directors Guild of America and a number of international film awards.

In November 1986, Jewison established the Canadian Center for Advanced Film Studies (CCAFS), akin to the American Film Institute in the United States.

*Norman makes movies about people under human conditions, be-
cause this is what he's connected to. This is what he cares about. He
is compelled to tell these human stories. That is who he is.*

Goldie Hawn—*Actress*

# The Conversation

As a small child I grew up with two maiden aunts because my parents were
very busy running a store. My elder aunt was a schoolteacher. She taught
me to read at a very, very early age, four or five, I think. I had to memorize
Psalms out of the Bible and I ended up reading *McCalley's History of England*
when I was about six years old. She stimulated an imagination in me
through poetry and through images.

I think by the fact that I was alone a lot I could create imaginary characters and friends whom I lived with. I remember sitting at the dinner table
with my parents and all of the sudden I would fall over dead. I would top-
ple right off the chair onto the floor. And if you were a stranger in the house
I guess you found that rather alarming. But my family didn't pay any attention to me. They used to step over me if I continued to lie there dead for a
moment or slowly dying. And then I would get up and continue eating.

I was always performing. And then my mother decided that I should re-
cite poetry at the age of five. So I had to memorize Robert Service, you
know, "A bunch of the boys were whooping it up in the Malamute Saloon;
The kid that handles the music-box was hitting a jag-time tune . . . When
out of the night, which was fifty below, and into the din and glare, There
stumbled a miner fresh from the creeks, dog-dirty, and loaded for bear."
Coming from a five-year old, Robert Service was quite different. And I used
to have little comedy ones, too. So I was performing quite early in my life
and I guess I've always been an actor. And then the acting turned into direction during my college days. It was kind of a natural evolution. Although
there were times when I was a cab driver and working for a living, but there
was always the dream that some day I could be an actor.

My interest began around 1950, when I was driving a cab in Toronto, and
television at that time was starting to exert its influence on people's lives. In
Canada there was no television. We were picking it up from transmitters in

Buffalo. And television, indeed, was in its infancy in America. I was told that the BBC in England was far superior because they had been broadcasting in the forties and that they were much further advanced in television programming. So I got on a boat and went to England. I started out as an actor and a writer. But I did meet with Bernie Braden who was doing a show for the BBC. He was kind enough to allow me to write a little bit and be a stand-in. So I learned a lot about live television way back in 1950, 1951.

I was in London for two years. In 1952, I got a telegram from the CBC in Canada, the Canadian Broadcasting Company, that they were going to start a television service. They brought Pat Weaver up from New York for advice, and I was lucky enough to get into a training program in Toronto. At that time I was still an actor and working in theater at night doing various plays and shows, but I got into this training program, so when the CBC went on the air I was a floor director. Television, at that time, had captured my imagination. I thought it was the greatest medium of communication ever devised by man and it was going to change the world. It was going to be a medium of expression through which we could reach audiences far greater than we ever could in the theater. I had no idea of film at that time.

Movies to me were magical and something I went to Saturday afternoon and paid ten cents and saw two features, cartoons, and a serial. But television captured my imagination. And similar to a lot of people in the theater and radio, we moved into television. There were no film people. I never met anyone who worked in film. As a matter of fact, there was a kind of antagonism between the film industry and television because the television industry began to grow rapidly and the film industry became terrified that they were going to lose their audience to people sitting at home watching the box. So that's how I got into it.

Gradually I was allowed to direct. I started out with a puppet show—a very satirical, sophisticated show where we could attack political systems and the network for which we worked. It was all live television until the sixties, when they discovered videotape. I stayed in Canada for the next six years and worked my way up to a producer/director. I finally ended up doing late night comedy shows and a lot of music. I was trained musically. I had been given piano lessons by this spinster aunt that I had who had a great influence on my life, and being a schoolteacher she decided I should be equipped. I was enrolled in the Royal Academy of Arts and Music in Toronto. I went to grade six or seven in classical piano and this gave me the background of music that I've been able to use in television and film. I can read a score and I can cut and edit live television from a score that they put in front of me in the booth, so I could work very closely with the singers and choreographers and conductors. So that was a great help to me.

## CBS Television Calls and New York Beckons

I moved from CBC in Canada in 1958. I was invited to New York to breathe some life into *Your Hit Parade*. It was Dorothy Collins and Snooky Lanson. That was my first live television show in New York. But the work I'd been doing in Canada must have impressed the people at CBS because I was one of the first directors to work against white instead of black velour. In those days everyone worked against black, but I worked against solid white so you had distance—no end in sight—and it added a very elegant look to some of my shows. They saw these kinescopes in New York. William Morris called Larry Auerbach, an agent. So it was Larry Auerbach who talked me into coming down to New York and meeting with William Paley and all those people who ran CBS in those days.

We were all classified in those days. I was doing musicals and I was doing variety. I went from the *Hit Parade* to *The Andy Williams Show*. It was a summer show. That's where Andy kind of became a star. Then I moved from there to *Night With Belafonte*, which was the first black show, so to speak, on American television. We were live and we shot it in a theater at 72nd and Broadway somewhere. We had an integrated cast of singers and dancers and we lost twenty-six stations before we were off the air. Those were in the south and they were so deeply segregated at that time that the idea of a black show on American television was something they couldn't handle. But I think that first Belafonte show did win some Emmys and it was a big influence on my life because I got involved with the civil rights movement and with Belafonte and the struggle for black performers on American television.

I then went on to cast people on the *Hit Parade*. I remember I cast a young man who was black who had recorded a song called "All in the Game" (Brook Benton). I just picked the record as being one of the top records and the young man who recorded the record turned out to be black. I got him before Ed Sullivan got him and I thought I was doing the right thing. The sponsor of the show at that time was Lucky Strike, which was a southern company from Carolina. I was called on the carpet on Madison Avenue and they said there had never been a black performer on the *Hit Parade* in the last four years, either on radio or television. And I said, "Well, there's going to be one now. I cannot face this performer or his agent or his manager and tell them he cannot be on the show because you run a segregated television program." I said, "You can tell them." But I warned them if *The New York*

*Times* hears about it, or the press hears about it, I think you'll be doing a great disservice to your country. They said, "Are you trying to blackmail us?" I said, "No, I'm not." I went to the program director of CBS and he stood behind me and so from that point on the *Hit Parade* became an integrated television show and we booked Ella Fitzgerald and Cab Calloway and a whole lot of other black performers. So a lot was going on at that time in America which affected me emotionally and affected my work.

## Meeting and Working with Judy Garland

In my mind, Judy Garland was a legend. I had seen her perform at the Palladium Theater in London, where she sat on the edge of the stage and said, after two hours of performing, "You haven't heard nothin' yet," and sang "Somewhere over the Rainbow." I realized at that time that Judy's career had taken a dive and I wanted to remember her as she was. So when Freddy Fields and David Bergman, who represented her, came to me because I was the young New York maven for television specials, and asked me to do Judy Garland I said, "I really think Judy should be left as a legend." They said, "You don't understand, she's in great form and we have a possibility of selling an hour show to CBS and we really want you to meet with her."

I went over to Haddonfield, New Jersey, or someplace, on a rainy Saturday night, and there was Judy and six thousand people. She was totally brilliant. I went backstage to meet her, and when I walked in she said, "Oh gosh, can you give me just a minute? I have to make one phone call." She picked up the phone and she called the White House. And she asked for President Kennedy. All of the sudden I realized the president was on the phone. She sang (*sings*) "Somewhere over the rainbow, da dee da." Then she said "Happy birthday, Mr. President," and she hung up. Then she turned to me and she said, "Now, what about this show?" I was just blown away.

Judy was like quicksilver. You had to capture the moment. She was such a brilliant performer that I decided I had to commit myself to this one glorious moment that she would appear on live television for the first time. Then I was informed I had to get two guests to appear with her or CBS wouldn't go with the show because they didn't think Judy was a big enough star at that time in her career. I was given a list of ten names. I got two of them. I went for the top one, Frank Sinatra. I called him and said, "You'd be doing Judy a great favor." He said he'd do it. Then I said, "Would you bring Dean?" He laughed and said, "Sure, kid." The show was a great success. Kay Thompson and I and Gary Smith, the production designer, did the show in Burbank on the West Coast. The last seventeen minutes of that show is the most brilliant stuff, brilliant performance, I think that's ever been captured on Kinescope. It was just Judy alone on a ramp with lights, and I had five cameras, and, of course, it was all live. But it was an exciting evening. It was really one of those programs that stunned the country and phone calls started to come in. Judy again became an enormous star. It won a lot of awards.

## Tony Curtis to the Rescue

During the rehearsals on the final day, when Judy and Sinatra and Dean were not there, Tony Curtis, who was quite an important film star at that time, walked up to me and said, "I've watched your shows over the last few years and I want to know if you'd be interested in doing a movie." I said, "I don't know how to make a movie. I'm a television director of television shows." He said, "But that's what all the directors said who had moved from live television into film," because the film directors at that time were all getting older and we were all younger. There were no film schools. We were coming in from another medium. We'd used the cameras and we were our own editors and we discovered the zoom lens and we knew how to direct and stage and how to move the camera, so I guess we were the new wave in the American film scene. But I must say I approached it with great trepidation. I didn't know anything about making a movie.

> *When you are a part of one of his movies, there is a certain tradition and there is a certain standard to which you've got to come up, and it's expected. I think it's all unspoken. But that's certainly part of the nature of it. I was surprised to find a very genial, very warm, very receptive human being behind his classic movies.*
>
> *Craig T. Nelson—Actor*

## Forty Pounds of Trouble (1963)

*Tony Curtis; Suzanne Pleshette; Sharon Farrell; Stubby Kaye;
Kevin McCarthy; Howard Morris; Edward Andrews; Jim Bannon;
Nicky Blair; Eduardo Ciannelli; Paul Comi; Gerald Gordon; Steve Gravers;
Hallene Hill; Charles Horvath; Jack La Rue; Syl Lamont; Tito Memminger;
Mary Murphy; Gregg Palmer; Ford Rainey; Tom Reese; Ruth Robinson.*

Tony Curtis, who had implicit faith and confidence in me, took me on the set the first day by the hand and said, "Ladies and gentlemen, this is our director, young Norman Jewison. He looks like a paperboy, but don't worry about him. He knows what he's doing." The picture was *Forty Pounds of Trouble*. I hired Suzanne Pleshette, Stubby Kaye, and Phil Silvers. I brought in a lot of people from New York and made my first film for Universal. Three-quarters of the way through the film, the head of Universal at that time, Ed Mull, came to me and said, "You're good, kid. We like what you're doing. We've got another picture for you when you finish this one, with Doris Day." So, that's how my career got started in film. It was by pure chance and I owe Tony Curtis a great deal. All my life I've been looking for the one great role so I can put him in one of my movies. I haven't found it yet. I'd like to find another *Sweet Smell of Success* for him. He's a wonderful actor.

# The Thrill of It All (1963)
*Doris Day; James Garner; Arlene Francis; Edward Andrews; Reginald Owen;*
*ZaSu Pitts; Elliott Reid; Carl Reiner; John Alderman; William Bramley;*
*Pamela Curran; Robert Gallagher; Alex Gerry; Maurice Gosfield;*
*Paul Hartman; Kym Karath; Bernie Kopell; Lucy Landau; Hedley Mattingly;*
*Burt Mustin; Brian Nash; Anne Newman; Alice Pearce; Hayden Rorke.*

# Send Me No Flowers (1964)
*Doris Day; Rock Hudson; Tony Randall; Paul Lynde; Hal March;*
*Edward Andrews; Patricia Barry; Clint Walker; Clive Clerk;*
*Dave Willock; Aline Towne; Helene Winston; Christine Nelson.*

In those Universal days there was *Forty Pounds of Trouble*, and then there was *Send Me No Flowers* with Doris Day, Rock Hudson, and Tony Randall, and then there was *The Thrill Of It All* with Doris Day and James Garner. That was his first big starring role. But in those days, you were contracted. I was contracted to the studio and I didn't quite understand that. I didn't know very much about film. So when I made this deal with Tony Curtis to direct the film, I was signing with Universal for seven years and couldn't work for anyone else without their approval. The next four films were comedies because they thought that I had a gift for comedy and I had the experience of working with Doris Day.

Doris Day was America's sweetheart. She was an enormous star, but she didn't think that she was very attractive. There were all these cameramen who were being fired and there were a lot of problems because Doris didn't like herself, in a way, I guess. I'll never forget our first meeting. I said, "You know, if you are worried about what you are going to look like, you should really do it yourself. You should get the lighting the way you want, and don't let them influence you in any way. And if you're worried about the direction, where the film is going, you should direct it yourself." She looked at me and said, "What are you doing?" I said, "I'm just telling you the truth. I don't think you should be worried about those things. I think you should be worrying about your performance. It's up to us to make you look beautiful, to make you look glamorous, and to make you as exciting and thrilling on the screen as we possibly can. That's our job. That's my job." She said, "You mean you don't want me to look at the rushes." I said, "Why? But if you want to check up," I said, "hey, pass the dice, I'm out of here." So it was very interesting. She never looked at a foot of rushes for the first time. We had no problems and I had a great relationship with Doris. I had a lot of fun doing those pictures. I got to meet Carl Reiner and work with him on a screenplay. So those four films at Universal were very important to me, but I was anxious to get out of being typecast as a comedy director and I felt I was doing films that were very commercial. Everybody was happy. Everybody went to the seashore at the end of the picture. Everything turned out great. And I was part of that commercial Hollywood type of film that was taking place in the early sixties.

I was getting a little depressed and decided that maybe I would be better off going back to television where I could deal with more interesting subjects and perhaps make some sort of comment on society and the life which we lead and so on. I just wanted to move on to more serious subject matter. And so I managed to get out of my contract because they didn't send me an option letter. I didn't say anything. I just sat at home. I waited two weeks, then sent a letter saying I decided to move on.

## The Cincinnati Kid (1965)

*Steve McQueen; Edward G. Robinson; Ann-Margret; Karl Malden;*
*Tuesday Weld; Joan Blondell; Rip Torn; Jack Weston; Cab Calloway; Jeff Corey;*
*Theodore Marcuse; Milton Selzer; Karl Swenson; Émile Genest; Ron Soble.*

The thing that really kind of saved me emotionally at that point in my career was the film called *The Cincinnati Kid*, with Steve McQueen, Edward G. Robinson, and Joan Blondell. It was a powerful story adapted from a book. Sam Peckinpah had started to shoot the film and he was shooting it in black

and white. Now, why he was shooting in black and white I could never figure out, because in the card game the hearts and diamonds are red and the
spades and clubs are black. I mean, how are you going to tell the difference
if you are in grayscale? That I couldn't understand. I had never shot a film
in black and white and had no desire to. For me, color is emotional. Colors have been used by painters for centuries. There are very few painters
who paint in black and white. In the theater I used color.

Two weeks into the picture Sam Peckinpah was fired by producer Marty
Ransohof. My agents came to me and said, "They're inquiring whether you
would take over the film." I said I would never replace another director.
They said, "It's not a matter of replacing him. He's gone. If you don't do it
they'll move on to someone else." I read the original book and the screenplay and then I met with Chuck Eastman and Terry Southern and brought
them in and started to rewrite the screenplay. They closed the picture down
for two weeks to give me a chance to rewrite. They allowed me to recast. I
brought in Tuesday Weld, Jack Weston, Cab Calloway. Karl Malden was already hired. I started shooting three weeks later.

I wanted to shoot in color so therefore they couldn't use anything that
Sam had shot. It was an interesting experience. I asked Steve McQueen not
to look at the rushes. Again, I was concerned about creative control over the
project. I felt that was important for the director and it's difficult if the star
is going to look at the rushes every day. I also thought in those days that it
affected their performances. I started to change my mind after that film.
*Cincinnati Kid* also brought me together with Hal Ashby, a young editor who
had been working with Bob Swank and William Wilder as an assistant.

*The Cincinnati Kid* is a very interesting film. I mean, to make a film about a
card game is not easy. It's not the most exciting, action-filled image. But as I
kept telling Steve and Edward G. Robinson, this was a struggle for power between them, between the king and the young challenger, and the weapons are
cards. So what you are really trying to do is gut the other person. A card game
has everything to do with winning and losing and so it becomes very dramatic.

So we were locked in a room at MGM for about a month with a lot of
beeswax smoke and I got to know people like Edward G. Robinson very
well. I came to admire him and respect him and we became very close. *The
Cincinnati Kid* was a great experience. It was the first film that I felt that I
was the filmmaker. I was involved with the writing, I was involved with the
casting, and it was my film, in a way.

I remember Marty Ransohoff saying to me, "I demand that you bring the
company back from New Orleans and cease and desist shooting scenes that

are not in the screenplay." I said, "If I come back from New Orleans I'm going home. I'm off this picture. You've got to let the director create and make the film within his own boundaries, and I promise you I'll bring this picture in on budget," because that's what they were worried about. That's all they were worried about. All the studios are ever worried about is their investment and their responsibility as shareholders. I know that. I'm not a spoon-fed idealist, for God sake. I'm a very responsible Canadian Methodist. Why would I not understand that? I understand the responsibilities that I have. But I also must have the artistic freedom to express and to tell the story the way I see it. And if someone is not going to allow me to do that or if someone wants that final cut, then I'm out.

I remember that at the end of *The Cincinnati Kid*, I had third cut to third public preview, which I really fought for, because I was being advised by the older directors like George Stevens that that power was important in Hollywood. If the director was to have any power he had to have final cut. He had to control the film and not the studio. Because if the studio has final cut they can change your colors, change your story, cut it to ribbons, and that's not what you set out to do. So I realized that creative control is more important to me than money. So what I have always offered to do is make less money, but please give me total artistic control. And that was the first film I had it on, and that's why it's my ugly duckling. It's one of my favorite films from the standpoint that there is a lot of me in the picture. So that's *The Cincinnati Kid*.

## The Russians Are Coming! The Russians Are Coming! (1966)

*Carl Reiner; Eva Marie Saint; Alan Arkin; Brian Keith; Jonathan Winters; Paul Ford; Theodore Bikel; Tessie O'Shea; John Phillip Law; Ben Blue; Andrea Dromm; Sheldon Collins; Guy Raymond; Cliff Norton; Richard Schaal.*

When I finished *The Cincinnati Kid*, the studios and Hollywood, the critics and the audience saw that I had moved out of just being a comedy director and had moved into a dramatic form. I then met up with the Mirisch people. The Mirisch Corporation produced films for United Artists. I had read a book called *The Off-Islanders*. It was about a Russian submarine running aground off Cape Cod. I turned to an expatriate American who was living on the island of Jersey, William Rhodes, who had written *Guess Who's Coming to Dinner* and *Mad, Mad World*. I thought *Mad, Mad World* was one of the strongest scripts I had ever read. I don't think it's the greatest picture, but I love the script because it was about greed. And greed is a fundamental part of human nature. With *Off-Islanders* I felt I could make a political statement of communism versus capitalism without using either of those two words, because I felt it was a very human story. It was at a time when paranoia had swept the county, people were being persecuted for their leftist ideas, where there was a communist behind every rock. Khrushchev was banging his shoe at the United Nations, and I was trying to make a film called *The Russians are Coming! The Russians are Coming!* So it wasn't easy.

At one point the Mirisch Corporation said, "How are you going to get a submarine?" The American navy had turned us down. They didn't want to be involved, because they said this was a film being made by some sort of Canadian pinko. The Canadians offered me a submarine, but the American government wouldn't allow it within twelve miles of the coast. The Russians offered me a submarine, but of course that was out of the question. At one point I was trying to hire Russian actors to play the Russians.

When William Rhodes and I finished the script, Harold Mirisch sent me to New York to meet with Arthur Crimm. I told Crimm that he had to give me another $150 thousand because I had to build the submarine. The moment that he heard the U.S. navy didn't want to cooperate and that there was a lot of interference in making the film because of the political climate he immediately embraced it and said, "Norman, you go make your picture and you build your submarine." We built this enormous submarine. Robert Boyle, the production designer, built this incredible thing out of Styrofoam, with four big ninety-horsepower motors underneath. And we literally sailed this into a harbor. We got a conning tower from Twentieth Century Fox, and we got some guns. You can get guns anywhere in America. We put all the proper equipment on it.

I was lucky enough to get Alan Arkin to play the lead. I put Alan together with a Russian-speaking translator at the UN in New York. So Alan speaks Russian in the film with a Georgian accent, because this guy from the UN was from Russian Georgia. When the film was finally shown in Russia it was incredible because they all thought Alan was a Russian actor. His Russian was that good. I hired all of the other characters with Russian-speaking actors. It was a big shock, I think, to the audience to see a film about Russians and Americans at a time when the Cold War was at its height. It was a plea for détente. It was a plea for co-existence. It was about the absurdity of international conflict at a time when that reasoning or that voice was not really being heard. It had a tremendous impact on the world audience.

## He Couldn't Get the Print Back

When it was shown in Washington, an admiral came up to me and said, "That's an extraordinary film. How did you get the air force to cooperate and give you two jets?" I said, "It's because they knew I wasn't getting any cooperation from the navy, sir." Which was true. It was shown to all the ambassadors. The guest of honor that night was Vice President Hubert Humphrey. Arthur Crimm was there. He loved it. He knew it was important. Although it was a comedy it was a satire. Then the most extraordinary thing happened. The Russian ambassador asked if the film could be sent to the Russian embassy. When he saw the film he sent it to the Russian ambassador in the UK. He sent it to the Russian ambassador in Paris and he sent it to Moscow. And it was screened six times in the Kremlin. We couldn't get the print back.

About a week before the film opened in New York I got this strange call to come to Moscow. The head of United Artists in Europe was in Moscow and had seen the picture and had heard the waves coming from the Kremlin. I went to London. Somebody from the Russian embassy showed up at my suite. They took my Canadian passport and came back six hours later with a visa. I got on a flight and flew to Moscow. I went to the Soviet Film Workers' theater, that is as big as Radio City Music Hall. The place was jammed. The film started with a Russian interpreter on a microphone playing all the parts. At one point the Russians sail into town and threaten all the American citizens and there's a standoff and they're all looking down all these guns at each other. And all you can see are rifle barrels, and nobody knows what do to. Then the child falls from the belfry and everyone runs to save the child. The Russians are instrumental in saving the child too. And of course, at the end of movie the town protects the submarine as it sails away.

When they don't like something in Russia they make a noise. And when the confrontation started, I thought, "Oh, no, they'll think they're going to be the villains again." And then, at the end of the picture they started this rhythmic clapping. And I realized the power of film from this social political sense, that perhaps life does imitate art, or perhaps art imitates life, that maybe there's a chance here. From that point on, I realized the Russians didn't want war. It was a matter of two people being filled with such propaganda and ideology that the truth was disregarded.

## Immigration Problems

When I got on a plane three days later to go to New York, the Americans had bombed Haiphong Harbor and so there was even more estrangement. When I went through Customs and Immigration into America, the guy looked at my passport and said, "What were you doing in Russia?" I told him I had been invited over for a screening of a film. He said, "You're a resident alien." I said, "Yes sir; here's my green card." He said, "Well, you're unacceptable." I said, "That's a terrible word to use, unacceptable. What are you talking about? My family's in Los Angeles. I've got my green card and my passport." He said, "Well, you don't have a re-entry permit and you have no right to be behind the iron curtain." I said, "I'm not an American citizen. I'm not traveling under an American passport. I didn't know that. The Canadian government said I could go. I'm sorry." He said, "Well, you're unacceptable." He wouldn't let me back into America.

I was sitting there by myself at two o'clock in the morning. So I rapped on the glass and I said, "Is the supervisor here?" He said, "I don't care what you do. You can get the next plane back to Moscow or go to Montreal." So I thought, I'll do what they did in the picture. I said, "I want to make a phone call to Washington. I want to talk with the Vice President of the United States and I'm going to talk to him and then you're going to talk to him." He said, "You don't have the number." I said, "Yeah, I do have the number. I want to call Hubert Humphrey and I'm going to talk to him and then you're going to talk to him. Because he saw this film three weeks ago and I'm trying to explain to you that I was invited to show this film and I'm sure the Vice President can explain to you the problem." So the guy backed down and said, "Okay, you can get on a plane and go to L.A., but you have to report to Immigration Monday morning." So for the next five, six years I was kind of persona non grata with the forces in Washington, including Hoover's FBI, and I was in the black book and had great problems moving in and out of the country. But it shows you how far we've come since that film.

The casting on that film was strange. I remember meeting with Jack Lemmon, because I wanted him to play the writer who was married to Eva Marie Saint. Jack turned me down. So I turned to my old friend Carl Reiner, who is a writer and an actor. He was delighted to play the role. He loved the screenplay. He was brilliant at improvising. Alan Arkin was on Broadway in a Mike Nichols play. United Artists was fussy about hiring him because nobody knew him and they wanted a star. I did a screen test, as a matter of fact, with Alan Arkin playing a Russian in disguise. I said, "You're here with the ballet and you work for the NVKD and let's do an interview." I borrowed a set from Sidney Lumet from a film he was shooting. I did this interview and showed it to the people at United Artists. So they finally, but reluctantly, agreed to let him play the role. God, he's brilliant, you know. One of the most brilliant actors I had ever worked with.

Then I got Jonathan Winters, who is off this planet. Jonathan was every character you can imagine on that film. He would move from being a sculptor to being a forest ranger to a policeman to a fireman. You never knew what he was doing. At one point he began carving a piece of wood because he was trying to give up drinking. So we bought him some carving tools. Whenever you wanted to find Jonathan you just followed the trail of shavings. He had carved a perfect egg. It had taken him about six weeks but from this great big chunk of wood here was this egg. It was the strangest group of people and we were all isolated in this tiny little town called Fort Bragg.

We used to show the dailies in the town cinema. You couldn't keep anybody out so I just invited the whole town in. They came with their kids and their dogs. They showed up every day around five o'clock to see the rushes of *The Russians Are Coming*, and, of course, they were all part of the film. So really it was a delightful, bizarre experience, but we finally finished it. It was a great joy.

> *Those were the days when times were somewhat tumultuous in the culture, in racial terms and in class terms. Norman was then very sensitive to the times. Norman has always been very sensitive to such questions, not just in America, in his own country as well.*
>
> Sidney Poitier—Actor

# In the Heat of the Night (1967)
*Sidney Poitier; Rod Steiger; Warren Oates; Lee Grant; Larry Gates; James Patterson; William Schallert; Beah Richards; Peter Whitney; Kermit Murdock; Larry D. Mann; Matt Clark; Arthur Malet; Fred Stewart; Quentin Dean.*

After *The Russians Are Coming*, since I was involved with Mirish Corporation at this time, I had signed a deal with United Artists, and Freddie Zinnerman, Billy Wilder, and William Wyler all told me that if you worked with United Artist and Arthur Crimm, you always had artistic freedom. And these were the people that gave me final cut. That to me was a great vote of confidence. I was devoted to that company for that, for allowing me to do that. *In the Heat of the Night* came from a tiny little novella about a black detective on the Pasadena police force. I read the project and said to Walter Mirish, "I'd love to do this film." And he said they were not going to shoot on location because they didn't have enough money.

It was a very low budget film because of the nature of the piece. You had a black actor in the lead and it was highly controversial at that time.

America was totally segregated in 1966. I had to make this film. I just had to make it. I convinced Walter Mirish that if they allowed me to shoot on location I would make the film for what it was budgeted for if it had been shot on the backlot in Los Angeles. I had Sidney Poitier, who had made a film before that called *Lilies of the Field*. I decided that Rod Steiger would be the right casting. He was in Italy so I sent him the script and talked to him on the phone. He agreed to play the part of Sheriff Gillespie. So I had Poitier and Steiger. I knew it was going to be fireworks because they were both very strong actors. I got Haskel Wexler as the cameraman.

We went to a small town in southern Illinois called Sparta, near the Missouri border, quite close to the upper reaches of the Missouri River. And that was because at that period of time Sidney said he wouldn't go south of the Mason Dixon Line because at that time there was a tremendous amount of violence in America and the civil rights struggle was reaching its peak of confrontation. That was the year I met Bobby Kennedy at Sun Valley. Our families were skiing together. I told him I was going to make this film and I told him the storyline. He said [*doing an imitation of Kennedy*], "It's very important, Norman, you make this film. The timing is right. I promise you everything is timing in life, in politics, and in art. You must make this film this year." He sent me a lot of literature, books and interviews with young people in the southern states.

When I was a kid in the navy I hitchhiked through the segregated south at the age of seventeen and as a Canadian coming into the southern United States I experienced for the first time discrimination in a way I had never seen it. I was shocked by it and couldn't understand it. There were black soldiers, airmen, and sailors in World War II, and I couldn't understand if you were asked to die for your country why you didn't have the right to use the same urinal or sit at the same soda fountain. I felt it was total hypocrisy. But I never forgot it and I drew upon a lot of those experiences when I made the film.

The film was made for $2.5 million. We couldn't even afford a crane. We did a lot of hand-held shots. I helped put a lot of weight on Mr. Steiger. Poor Rod would finish dinner and then I would come in at about eight or nine, after finishing the rushes, and say, "Hey, Rod, what did you eat? Come on, sit down and join us. Bring another piece of pecan pie for Mr. Steiger." And Rod started to get big. I wanted him to look like Bull Conner. I wanted him to look like the typical southern, small-town, red-neck sheriff that you saw on the news broadcasts. We did manage to talk Sidney into going to Tennessee for the cotton-picking sequence. That was the night there was a lot of pickup trucks and red-necks around and guys banging on doors. I called Sidney in his room and told him I had got a gun under my pillow.

It was a difficult time in America. Again, when the film came out, Bobby Kennedy was right, the timing was right. It was the strangest thing. When *In the Heat of the Night* won the New York Critic's Award I was invited to fly to New York to accept the award. And who presented the award but Bobby Kennedy, who was then a senator from New York. He presented the award and whispered in my ear, "I told you the timing was right, Norman." The film did have a tremendous impact on America and throughout the world. It was really the first film where a black man slapped a white man back. It meant a lot to a lot of people that that kind of film could be made in America, which shows the freedom not only of the artist, but the courage that was exhibited throughout the years by the film industry. I believe the film industry has made some highly controversial films. Of all the films I've made it probably had the greatest impact on the audience. It went on to win a number of Academy Awards. It won every award—best picture, best actor, best writer, best editor, best cameraman—and unfortunately not best director. I think they were asking me to wait. It was a film that I guess will always be one of the most important ones.

# The Thomas Crown Affair (1968)

*Steve McQueen; Faye Dunaway; Paul Burke; Jack Weston; Biff McGuire; Addison Powell; Astrid Heeren; Gordon Pinsent; Yaphet Kotto; Sidney Armus; Richard Bull; Peg Shirley; Patrick Horgan; Carol Corbett; Tom Rosqui.*

As you know, Steve McQueen was not the easiest guy to work with. I used to call him Spanky McFarland and Peck's bad boy. Steve was always looking for a father. He never had a father. I couldn't be his father. I explained that to him. "I'm your older brother. I'm your older brother who went to college. You're happy when you're taking apart an automobile engine. I'm going to look out for you. I'm going to take care of you." He accepted that.

We had a very close relationship, but, man, if you were the slightest bit indecisive or if he saw you worried about something he could bore in and he was relentless. He wanted to play the role very, very badly. I didn't really want him to start with because Steve McQueen had never worn a necktie in a film. I saw Thomas Crown as being very elegant, a graduate of Dartmouth. It was a big jump for Steve to play a very sophisticated character and in *The Thomas Crown Affair*, it's style over content. That's what it is. It's all style.

The script was only eighty pages long. And I must say Haskel Wexler's cinematography and the editing and Michel Legrand's music really gave the film a wonderful aura of sophistication. In Europe the film was far more successful than it was in America, for some reason. We also used multiple screen technique in the film. It was quite a jump for me, stylistically.

Steve was always a challenge. There was one day when I was trying to get a sunset shot and I wanted him and Faye Dunaway in silhouette. And we had to shoot at the magic hour just as the sun was setting. Just as I was ready to shoot I said, "Where is Steve?" There he was down in his dune buggy doing wheelies on the seashore, because, as you know, he loved to punish machines. That's what gave him his excitement. Anyway, he came back late. The light had gone. So I said, "Well, it's a wrap. Let's forget it." He said, "What's the matter?" I said, "What do you mean, what's the matter?" I said, "When I needed you, you weren't here." Then I saw a feather on the ground. I picked up a feather and I stuck it in his hat. He had a sweatband. I said, "You want to wear the feather? You can be the chief." I went and got in my car and left. I guess he never forgot that.

When the picture was finished I got on a plane to go home. Just before the plane took off, this stewardess came on. She said, "Are you Mr. Jewison?" I said yes. She said, "I have something for you," and she gave me a box. I opened up the box and it was a sweatband with a feather on it that Steve McQueen had sent me. Unfortunately we lost him at an early age. I think he died when he was only fifty-three or four. The last few days that I saw him before his death was very sad because there was nothing anyone could do.

# Fiddler on the Roof (1971)

*Topol; Norma Crane; Leonard Frey; Molly Picon; Paul Mann;*
*Rosalind Harris; Michele Marsh; Neva Small; Paul Michael Glaser; Ray Lovelock;*
*Elaine Edwards; Candy Bonstein; Shimen Rushkin; Zvee Scooler.*

There is an interesting story about *Fiddler on the Roof*. I got a phone call from Arthur Crimm, the head of United Artists, asking me if I would come to New York for a meeting and not tell my agent and not speak to anyone about it, that it was a highly confidential meeting. I didn't know what they were talking about. I went to New York and there was Arthur Crimm, Bob Benjamin, and Arnold and David Picker. I said, "What's this all about?" They said, "What would you say if we were to ask you if you wanted to direct *Fiddler on the Roof*?" And I thought oh, my God. Like most people they think I'm Jewish and I would understand the Jewish religion and the implications of this film, which of course was all about tradition. I didn't know what to say. I walked over to a window and I looked down on 7th Avenue. Then I turned and I looked at them. They are all waiting. I said, "What would you say if I told you I was a goy?" And I watched the shock of three of them. Their faces just fell. Norman Jewison is a goy? I watched them fall. And Arthur Crimm said, "Why do you think we asked you to do the film? We don't want a 7th Avenue Yiddish production." So that's how smart he was. He covered himself.

For the next six months I not only studied the Jewish religion, of which I knew a lot about because I'd been called Jew-boy all my life, but I spent a lot of time in Israel. I went to Hungary and Rumania where there were still little Jewish communities on the Russian borders. I talked them into making the film in Yugoslavia. I wanted to shoot it in a little town in Rumania near the Russian border, but at that time they couldn't get insurance. Political insurance. The Russians, of course, didn't want the film made because even though it was Czarist Russia in 1910, it showed anti-Semitism on the part of the Cossacks. I ended up in Yugoslavia and shot in Zagreb and all these little villages, which are now caught up in the Bosnian War. I spent the next two years of my life on *Fiddler*.

It was a three-hour film. One of the last big films. John Williams did all the music and he came to London and it was at a period of my life where I was disenchanted and very unhappy. The Vietnam War was at its peak, and Nixon was President, Reagan was governor. The investigations politically into my life had brought me to the point where I was disillusioned with the American dream and I decided to move all of my family to Europe. For the next nine years I headquartered in London. I had a place in the mountains in Switzerland and I made my next group of films in Yugoslavia and Germany and England and Israel.

# Jesus Christ Superstar (1973)

*Ted Neeley; Carl Anderson; Yvonne Elliman; Barry Dennen; Bob Bingham;*
*Larry Marshall; Josh Mostel; Kurt Yaghjian; Paul Thomas; Pi Douglass;*
*Robert Lu Pone; Jonathan Wynne; Thommie Walsh; Richard Molinare; David Devir.*

*Jesus Christ Superstar* I made in Israel for $3.5 million. No one knew how the film could be made because it was just two phonograph records. I wrote the screenplay with an English writer by the name of Melvyn Bragg. It's hard to describe because there is no dialog. I treated it as an opera. Melvyn, who now heads up the arts television program in England for Thames, he and I just wandered through Israel with earphones and Walkman and literally dreamed up the idea.

It was a film that had a tremendous impact on the audience. When you deal with the New Testament, or the full Testament, you're going to get into trouble. Even though, in my opinion, *Jesus Christ Superstar* is an opera about the good, the bad, and the beautiful, and it's very loosely based on the New Testament, it did have tremendous impact on certain religious communities. The observatory in Rome, the Vatican, sent over some people to London when I first screened the film. They were just overwhelmed with it. They said it was the greatest painting since the Last Supper. So I knew that we were going to get the support of the Catholic Church. I wasn't prepared for the attack from the Jewish community. I felt secure because I had made *Fiddler on the Roof*, and I made this film in Israel with the cooperation of Golda Meir. I had used Israeli crews and I didn't think I was making a highly controversial film and I certainly didn't think I was making a film that was anti-Semitic. Why would I? With the name Jewison, why would I make an anti-Semitic film? But it was attacked quite vociferously in America. So Andrew Lloyd Webber and Tim Rice and a lot of people came under attack. The film went on to win all kinds of international awards and probably is the most popular film I ever made. Certainly it's been the most rewarding because it was made for so little money and it was the first film which I participated in the gross of the film. In a way I think *Superstar* gave me the opportunity to put an opera on film where there was nothing but the camera and music and our imagination. I'm very proud of the film from that aspect.

# Rollerball (1975)

*James Caan; John Houseman; Maud Adams; John Beck; Moses Gunn;*
*Pamela Hensley; Barbara Trentham; John Normington; Shane Rimmer; Burt Kwouk;*
*Nancy Bleier; Richard Le Parmentier; Robert Ito; Sir Ralph Richardson.*

*Rollerball* was my chance to do a political statement. Living in Europe and looking back at America I was terrified with the power of multi-national, multi-global corporations. I realized the General Foods Corporation had a bigger gross output than Belgium. I realized that Exxon, General Motors, United Airlines, to name a few, were getting more important than the government. The chairman of General Motors is far more important than a senator from Michigan. When the Arab boycott came along, President Carter asked the heads of all the oil companies to come to Washington to be assured that the American fleet would have enough oil and that the American air force would have enough oil and gas. They looked at him and said, "But Mr. President, we are the Arab boycott." Huge multi-nationals, most of them American companies, pump all of the oil that's pumped in the Middle East.

These companies were far more important than the individual because they not only controlled the market, they also supplied the goods. And if they controlled television and the appetite, that was the next big fall. I wanted to fight the company store. What *Rollerball* is about is the individual against the corporate world. So I said it was the only film I made about the future, and I said in the not too distant future there would be no wars. There will be no poverty. There will be no government. There will be no political system. But there will be Rollerball.

*Rollerball* was just so totally bizarre a concept. During the Olympics that were held in Munich, they built an indoor bicycle track. So we got the man who built that track to build us a track on which we could put roller skaters and motor bikes at tremendous speeds to play this totally bizarre and violent game. It's the only film I really dealt with where I was dealing with the subject of violence and the subject of violence for the entertainment of the masses, which I think is a totally obscene thought. What I was trying to recreate was Circus Maximus that took place in Rome over two and a half thousand years ago. Man, as a society, seems to have this need to participate in a violent experience. I watched what was happening to my beloved NHL. I realized that the demands of the American television network called for more violence and more blood on the ice. When you get blood on the ice thousands of people stand up and they feel like they've been fed. That frightened me.

What *Rollerball* is about is not just a corporate society that has taken over control of the world—we have transportation, we have food, we have energy, there are no political systems—but it's about violence for the entertainment of the masses to fill that gap of warfare. So it's a very bizarre film. The best review was by Red Smith of *The New York Times,* the celebrated sports writer. He knew what the film was about. Most audiences in America saw the film and said, "Gee, where can we play the game? Can I get the franchise for this?" They thought it was a film of violence that I was making to entertain people. Whereas the European audiences understood the film totally, and as a result the film became a cult film in Europe and was probably one of the most important films I ever made as far as the British and Scandinavians were concerned.

I chose James Caan for the part simply because I felt he was the greatest jock I had ever met. His testosterone level was much higher than most other actors. He was a rodeo rider. He was fearless. He loved physical contact. He made a film called *Brian's Song* where he played a celebrated football hero. I thought he was quite brilliant. I met with James and he agreed to do the film and off we went. My biggest problem was trying to stop him from being hurt because he insisted on doing a lot of stunts himself. But I explained to him that his character, Jonathan E., was an individual fighting against the system. That this was indeed a highly dramatic, powerful role. We got along well. I just think it was the right casting. Just like Sir Ralph Richardson, the keeper of the world's knowledge, was the right casting, and John Houseman was the right casting. I mean, there were some wonderful actors in this piece. And I was at my peak, stylistically, as far as being able to work again without any interference. I had no creative interference. I was terrified every day that someone was going to be killed or hurt on the set. We had one accident in California even before we started the film, when the stuntmen were developing the idea. That was the only injury.

# F.I.S.T. (1978)

*Sylvester Stallone; Rod Steiger; Peter Boyle; Melinda Dillon; David Huffman;*
*Kevin Conway; Tony Lo Bianco; Cassie Yates; Peter Donat; John Lehne;*
*Henry Wilcoxon; Richard Herd; Tony Mockus, Jr.; Ken Kercheval; Elena Karam.*

Stallone thinks I'm one of the best directors he's worked with? That's an unusual observation coming from Sly Stallone, because he and I didn't get on too well. I got him right after *Rocky* and he had become an American folk hero. You know what films are like. They create gods and heroes. I kept reminding him that this was a story about Jimmy Hoffa. This was a story about the betrayal of the ideals of the American labor movement. This was my opportunity to make a film about unions, about unions challenging government, about the working man and big business.

I reached out again to Rod Steiger to play the role of Senator Kennedy. Indeed, President Kennedy's confrontation through Bobby, who was the attorney general, with Jimmy Hoffa is well documented. Again I was reminded that maybe this was a film that I shouldn't make. That if I went ahead with it, there would be repercussions. I think that's the reason Universal pulled out of the film. There was a lot of pressure. Arthur Crimm and United Artists really didn't want to make this film because of these political repercussions. It was certainly a film that America didn't want to see. I don't believe Americans were interested in the labor movement. I was. I was interested in the corruption and the betrayal of the ideals. I was interested in where's Jimmy?

Stallone was tough; tough to work with from the standpoint that at times he wanted to play Rocky. I tried to explain to him that this wasn't a story about Rocky. But I got a good performance out of him. We had a lot of disagreements about the end of the film because I rubbed him out at the end. Of course, he didn't like that. He wanted to go to be a heroic, mythical figure. I told him that was not the film we set out to make. Jimmy Hoffa is probably somewhere under the New Jersey Turnpike, I don't know, but he was rubbed out. That's the way the film had to end. Our relationship wasn't easy but I think he gave a very good performance. *F.I.S.T.* is a picture that I am proud of. But I must confess I think the timing of it wasn't right.

# . . . And Justice for All (1979)

*Al Pacino; Jack Warden; John Forsythe; Lee Strasberg; Jeffrey Tambor;*
*Christine Lahti; Sam Levene; Robert Christian; Thomas G. Waites; Larry Bryggman;*
*Dominic Chianese; Craig T. Nelson; Victor Arnold; Vincent Beck; Michael Gorrin.*

I guess you get obsessed looking for ideas to make films about because it's the idea behind the film that interests me. In other words, I'm a storyteller. That's all I am. But there has got to be some depth to the story. There has got to be some meaning to the story. Why are you telling the story? In *And Justice for All,* I wanted to attack the judicial system. I wanted to examine it. I wanted to examine plea bargaining. I wanted to examine this obsession that's developed in America about winning. Where is justice? Is there separate justice for the rich, for the poor, for black, for white? So I wanted to make a film about the judicial system and its problems. It's about a lawyer that realizes he can't defend a guilty person and he wants to tell the truth. Of course that's explosive as far as the judicial system is concerned. I came under attack by the Bar Association. But Al Pacino gives a brilliant, brilliant performance in that film. You know he's got a lot of anger in him. He's like unleashing a doberman pinscher. You think he's totally out of control, but he's an actor. He's totally in control. I just think he was wonderful in that film.

# A Soldier's Story (1984)

*Howard E. Rollins Jr.; Adolph Caesar; Art Evans; David Alan Grier; David Harris;*
*Dennis Lipscomb; Larry Riley; Robert Townsend; Denzel Washington; William Allen*
*Young; Patti LaBelle; Wings Hauser; Scott Paulin; John Hancock; Trey Wilson.*

*Soldier's Story* is a film that I'm perhaps the most proud of making simply because it's a film that again takes me back to the fifties. Takes me back to

World War II, the forties actually, in which I could deal with a segregated America. And so it's one of my favorite films because it tells the story from a black point of view. I think Charles Fuller's play was just totally brilliant.

It was very difficult to find a studio to make that film because I couldn't explain to them that I felt the film would be successful commercially. But I felt that it was a film I had to make and so I offered to make the film for nothing. During our meeting, Frank Price at Columbia leaned forward and said, "You'll make the film for nothing?" I said, "Yes, sir. You wouldn't mind if I had just a tiny, tiny piece of the gross just in case someone comes to see it? Maybe I could get my salary back." And he said, "With that kind of commitment I'm going to give you $5 million to make the picture. You go make the picture without any stars. Just go and do it." And so again, you see the courage that does exist within the Hollywood system that allowed me to make a film about a period in American history, perhaps something that we don't want to examine, but here again was a film that the timing was right.

The black audiences throughout America embraced the film because in many ways it was their story. Young black people could understand what their grandfathers and their uncles were telling them about an America that did exist, and you had to go and give your life in defense of your country but wouldn't allow you to be led by black officers. I think it's a powerful film. I'm very proud of that film.

# Agnes of God (1985)

*Jane Fonda; Anne Bancroft; Meg Tilly; Anne Pitoniak; Winston Rekert;*
*Gratien Gélinas; Guy Hoffman; Gabriel Arcand; Françoise Faucher;*
*Jacques Tourangeau; Janine Fluet; Deborah Grover; Michele George;*
*Samantha Langevin; Jacqueline Blais.*

When I wanted to make *Agnes of God*, the president of Columbia Pictures asked me what the film was about. I said it was the struggle between logic and the Catholic faith. It was the struggle between those two forces and Agnes is in the middle. She is the Lamb of God and she is being pulled apart. Now if you can look at it from that aspect it's something that people go through every day. Every day, I'm sure, no matter what your religion, you question the existence of God. Whatever your faith. On the other hand, you have Freudian logic that says there can't be any God. We're just animals— just a higher form of animal life. At the end, life is over and the circle is finished. Here, on the other hand, you have a woman who believes in miracles. Here you have a divine conception. It was a very unique opportunity for me to examine that idea.

I brought cinematographer Sven Nykvist into the mix because he understood what it was about. Sven was the source of a lot of inspiration behind Ingmar Bergman's work. The cast was perfect—Jane Fonda representing logic with both feet planted on the ground, as Jane can be, and Anne Bancroft, who is a Catholic and wanted desperately to play Mother Superior, and in the middle Meg Tilly, this Lamb of God. I mean, the innocence, the pure innocence. Meg got a nomination for an Academy Award. She should have won the Academy Award.

That was a very strange little film. We shot it all in Quebec and Ontario, Canada. Again, it's a film that went on to surprise people and justify Columbia's involvement.

# Moonstruck (1987)

*Cher; Nicolas Cage; Vincent Gardenia; Olympia Dukakis; Danny Aiello;*
*Julie Bovasso; John Mahoney; Louis Guss; Feodor Chaliapin, Jr.; Anita Gillette;*
*Nada Despotovich; Joe Grifasi; Gina DeAngeles; Robin Bartlett; Helen Hanft.*

John Shanley was a playwright in New York. He had only written one film, called *Five Corners. Moonstruck* read like a play and was originally called *The Bride and the Wolf*. It sounded like a horror film. I had kind of followed his career because John writes about Catholic families and the relationships within the family. I thought that this script was just wonderful. It had coffee stains all over the cover. When you get a script that's got a lot of coffee stains on the cover you know it's been around.

I went to meet Shanley in New York and he said, "You want to make my script?" I said, "Yeah," and he said, "Well, present your credentials." So I explained to him what I wanted to do. This was an Italian family in Brooklyn and I told him what I felt his film was about. I said, "You're very theatrical, you're not really a film writer. Can I sit and work with you on this?" So he came to Canada and we spent a lot of time on my farm and we made a lot of changes and called it *Moonstruck*. I explained to him how the moon affected all of our lives. How the moon has been used as a romantic symbol by writers and poets for the last three, four thousand years. And then into this mix I was lucky enough to hire people like Vinny Gardenia and Olympia Dukakis and, of course, Danny Aiello and Cher.

I went and spoke to Cher. I said, "You are my first choice. And if you want to make this film we will do this." She said, "Well, what is the film about? I don't even understand this film, and I've got something else to do called *Verdict*," or something. And I said, "Well, I promise you we will make this film in twelve weeks." All through the picture, Cher kept looking at me and saying, "Who was your second choice?"

I think Cher was perfectly cast and it was one of those films that was so totally romantic because at my age I'm going through a romantic period obviously—my last gasp of romanticism. And so *Moonstruck* to me was a mythical kind of romantic moment where I could deal with something that I thought was very poetic and lyrical. I spent a lot of time with Italians and with the family atmosphere that exists and the strength of the family which is the core of Italian society and the religion. So it was a film I was familiar with. I knew what it was about. I had great joy in making *Moonstruck*. It gave me a chance to make it like an opera. Music was a very important part of the film. But I never believed, like I did with *Soldier's Story* or many films I've made, I never believed that the audience was going to embrace it like they did. But as Bobby Kennedy says, the timing is right. So the timing was right for a romantic film at that point in our lives. It went on to drive the Academy Awards that year.

It's a film that seems to be international in its scope. By living in Europe for nine years it was possible for me to understand that films have no borders. They are not American, they are not British, or German, or French, they are truly universal. Boy, when you see *Moonstruck* in Spanish it's terrific. The Spanish version for some reason was even better than the English version. I can't tell you why. It had an edge to it, but the casting is so right. The Italian version is good but the French I don't like at all. It was a film that seemed to reach out to Europeans and throughout the world in a different way. It's about a family, it's about us, and it's about people regardless of nationality.

> *The fact is that with Norman you always know where you stand, you know. There is no fussiness about the work. If you feel like you need to do something and you make it your own, he will let you try it. That's a unique thing, to find a director who trusts the people that he's hired. You are not just a piece of cattle to him. You are an intricate part of the process.*
>
> *Whoopi Goldberg—Actress*

# Bogus (1996)

*Whoopi Goldberg; Gérard Depardieu; Haly Joel Osment; Andrea Martin; Nancy Travis; Denis Mercier; Ute Lemper; Sheryl Lee Ralph; Barbara Hamilton; Al Waxman; Elizabeth Harpur; Fiona Reid; Kevin Jackson; Richard Portnow; Mo Gaffney.*

As I get older I think I reach out for ideas which I have been living with for a number of years. When I was a child, as I told you earlier, I spent a lot of time with imaginary friends in an imaginary world. When a child gets to be seven or eight years old, we keep telling them that what they see and who they're talking to are not real. We pull them out of an imaginary world into a world of reality. I think the idea of *Bogus*, where a little boy who has lost his mother and is alone in the world—when he reaches out for his imaginary friend and I can go into his world and his relationship with his imaginary friend—gives me the opportunity to explore things that I haven't dealt with on film before. So we are talking here about *Wizard of Oz*. We are talking here about an unreal world, a world of imagination, of daydreams.

I had never driven across America. I've flown across it thousands of times. As a matter of fact I've never driven across my own country, Canada. I bought a car and met writer Alvin Sargent in Buffalo, New York, and we drove to Las Vegas like Thelma and Louise. We worked every day on this story and by the time we arrived in Las Vegas we thought we had most of it licked.

Las Vegas has always had a strange attraction to me. It's like a squashed orange in the middle of the desert. It deals with greed and things that are rather unworldly. It's a spacey kind of place. There's nothing real there. It's strange. It's like a dream factory. The purpose of it is for you to go and lose your money, so it's very real. The idea behind it is obscene.

What we ended up with in the script was this little boy who lives in Las Vegas and his influence is magical, an illusion, and he believes what you see is not necessarily real. We follow his story and he's sent to his godmother in Newark, New Jersey. His godmother is Whoopi Goldberg. His mother was a foster child who grew up in a mixed foster home. On the way he creates this imaginary friend who is French because his surrogate father in Las Vegas is a magician called Monsieur Antoine. I talked Gérard Depardieu into playing Bogus, the imaginary friend.

We're still in the middle of shooting the film and we're getting further

---

NOTE: This interview was conducted in Toronto, Canada, during the filming of *Bogus*.

and further away from reality into an unreal world which has got us all crazy. It's going to be very interesting to see how it turns out. I never believe anyone will come to see a film. There's a lot of me in this film. There's a lot of my childhood in this film. It's a very personal film.

Whoopi Goldberg is the most delightful actress I've ever worked with. I've never found an actress this supportive of the storytelling process. I think that comes from the fact she started out in the theater, alone, on center stage, in control of the whole story. She has this wonderful ability to kind of step outside herself and realize the story we're telling. Gérard Depardieu is probably one of the most talented, intense actors I've ever worked with. He's like a child. He's totally filled with wonder and imagination in his performance. I have this little boy playing the lead role that I was lucky to find, that I think is just an extraordinary talent. We'll see what comes out.

## What Does the Future Hold for Norman Jewison?

What destiny has in store for me or any of us no one knows. But right now what the future holds for me is will I ever finish this goddamn picture! Will I ever get out of here without collapsing physically or mentally? There is a point in making a film where all the things that you dreamed of fall by the wayside and all you want to do is finish it. It's like fighting a war.

I would think the future holds time for me to spend at the Canadian Film Center, which is similar to the American Film Institute. I founded it nine years ago and it's now producing young filmmakers. Two of the films that were produced by the Center were invited to the Cannes Film Festival so we're pretty excited about what we've achieved in nine years. I hope that in the future I'll be able to spend more time nurturing the young filmmakers of tomorrow, those people who have the dreams, the guts, and the desire and the commitment to muddle their way through this terrible business.

I live on a farm. I always wanted to live on a farm. My ancestors were all farmers. It's like I have the best of both possible worlds. I've got my farm in Canada. I've got my little house in Malibu. I've got an apartment in New York. Come on, what more could one ask for?

I'm so in love with filmmaking that it's all a high to me. The low points in my life have probably been between films. Maybe the lowest point in my life was before I left America in 1970, when I felt abandoned by the political system. I was going through a period of great disillusionment because I believed I had lost every battle I tried to fight. I believed that everything I believed in was being challenged and was being defeated. So I think that was a low point in my life. I think going to Europe and making five or six films there gave me a different perspective. I realized that I was still an optimist and I could still remain an idealist and still find the child in myself, because it's when we're afraid to be childish and lose our faith in what is right, when we don't do the right thing, that we're in danger. As an artist, I worry that if I ever lose that I'll lose my sense of humor. If I become defeated in what I believe in, I'll lose everything. I'm not upset about rejection. I've been rejected before.

If a film doesn't work and no one comes to see it the only low point is that some people will say you wasted a year and a half of your life. We only have so many films in us. Film is forever and that's what makes it important. Outside of my children, that's all I'll leave behind.

# Director Filmography

*Forty Pounds of Trouble* (1963)
*The Thrill of It All* (1963)
*Send Me No Flowers* (1964)
*The Cincinnati Kid* (1965)
*The Art of Love* (1965)
*The Russians Are Coming! The Russians Are Coming!* (1966)
*In the Heat of the Night* (1967)
*The Thomas Crown Affair* (1968)
*Gaily, Gaily* (1969)
*Fiddler on the Roof* (1971)
*Jesus Christ Superstar* (1973)
*Rollerball* (1975)
*F.I.S.T.* (1978)
*…And Justice for All* (1979)
*Best Friends* (1982)
*A Soldier's Story* (1984)
*Agnes of God* (1985)
*Moonstruck* (1987)
*In Country* (1989)
*Other People's Money* (1991)

*Only You* (1994)
*Bogus* (1996)
*Lazarus and the Hurricane* (1999)

# Awards

**Academy Awards, USA**
Irving G. Thalberg Memorial Award, 1999
*Moonstruck*, Best Director (nominated), 1988
*Moonstruck*, Best Picture (shared with Patrick J. Palmer, nominated), 1988
*A Soldier's Story*, Best Picture (shared with Patrick J. Palmer & Ronald L. Schwary, nominated), 1985
*Fiddler on the Roof*, Best Director (nominated), 1972
*Fiddler on the Roof*, Best Picture (nominated), 1972
*In the Heat of the Night*, Best Director (nominated), 1968
*The Russians Are Coming! The Russians Are Coming!*, Best Picture (nominated), 1966

**Berlin International Film Festival**
*Moonstruck*, Best Director, 1988

**British Academy Awards**
*In the Heat of the Night*, UN Award, 1968
*In the Heat of the Night*, BAFTA Film Award (nominated), 1968
*The Russians Are Coming! The Russians Are Coming!*, UN Award (nominated), 1967

**Golden Globes, USA**
*Fiddler on the Roof*, Best Director—Motion Picture (nominated), 1972
*In the Heat of the Night*, Best Motion Picture Director (nominated), 1968

In 1982, Mr. Jewison was made a companion of the Order of Canada by the Governor-General, the Queen's representative in Ottawa. The order is Canada's highest civilian decoration.

# The Films of John Carpenter

John Howard Carpenter was born in Carthage, New York, on January 16, 1948. He attended Western Kentucky University and the USC film school in Los Angeles. While he was there he began work on *The Resurrection of Bronco Billy,* for which he won an Academy Award for Best Short Subject (live action).

A movie buff and amateur filmmaker since childhood, producer/writer/director John Carpenter was taking film study courses at the University of Southern California when he turned out a short sci-fi satire, *Dark Star,* with fellow student Dan O'Bannon. Utilizing such economical props as a beach ball (standing in for a "space alien") and a muffin tray (representing a "life support system"), *Dark Star* was endearingly goofy enough to spark the interest of a distributor. Expanded into a sixty-thousand-dollar feature, the film quickly entered the repertoire of the cult-film circuit. Carpenter's first mainstream film was *Assault on Precinct 13,* an admitted "steal" from Howard Hawks' *Rio Bravo* plunked down in a contemporary urban setting. The director's next film proved to be a hit beyond his wildest dreams: *Halloween,* a beautifully constructed "slasher" film which managed to incorporate homages to virtually all of Carpenter's boyhood idols.

John Carpenter has worn the hats of director, composer, writer, actor, producer, and editor. That makes him an all-around filmmaker.

In an interview in the *Directors Guild Magazine* in 1996, Carpenter had this to say about his filmmaking: "I'm happy if a movie is finished. You've done something that most of the rest of the population never gets a chance to do. The percentage of movies that actually move an audience is minuscule. And if you move an audience and it also affects them, then you've really done something."

*Great directors have a vision. They have a particular, specific vision.*
*They don't just direct traffic. They don't just bring people into scenes*
*and out of scenes. They don't just tell them what they'd like to see.*
*They have a vision. They've got the movie in their head. There's just*
*nobody else that would do the movie that way. I think in terms of ap-*
*preciation, that's what I appreciate most about John as a director.*

*Kurt Russell—Actor*

# The Conversation

My early surroundings were kind of unique. My parents were from northern New York. My dad was a music professor. He got his Ph.D. at the Eastman School of Music in Rochester, and got a job in a little tiny estate college in Kentucky. So we moved from the north to the south, right to the middle of the Bible Belt.

I grew up in a facsimile of the log cabin that Abraham Lincoln grew up in and was born in. And I grew up in a log cabin on the museum grounds and it was a very strange kind of magical environment. My parents, you have to understand, were Northern Liberals, and here we were in the middle of this kind of Bible Belt situation. It gave me a great sense of isolation. I was not clear as to what was going on with these people and what was going on in the community around where we lived because there was tremendous racism, I mean just tremendous in those days. It was huge. This was way before any of the civil rights movement in the fifties took hold. It was a bizarre situation.

I think the first time I knew I wanted to be a director was back in 1956 when I saw the movie *Forbidden Planet*. I was eight years old at the time. It was so well done that I said, "Whatever this director guy does, I want to do that. That sounds like a good job. I really would like to do that."

My dad gave me his 8mm movie camera and somewhere around that time I began making films with my friends. I don't really want to discuss those movies with you because they were pretty bad, but I did learn some. I did learn how to shoot a scene. In those days I had an 8mm camera and I would point it at the actor. He would come up and look off screen. Then I would turn around and point it at what he saw. Then I would turn back around to the actor and get his reaction. And all of a sudden my father slipped me this editing kit. And I figured out that I could do the whole scene with the actor coming up and looking off screen, reacting, and then I can turn around and shoot what he sees. As a matter of fact, it doesn't have to be in the same place. And that was kind of my beginning awareness.

In 1968 my father said to me, "Look, you've got to make a decision. What do you want to do with your life? Either you stay here in Kentucky or do something." And I wanted at that point to try out movies. I was in a rock and roll band, having a great time. We were making a lot of money. We were becoming very successful. It was a great way to meet girls. But it didn't seem like a career choice. So my dad was nice enough to send me to film school. And this was around the time of a great explosion in cinema.

I can't begin to tell you what it was like to go to USC in 1968. This would have been the year after George Lucas and John Milius were there. Our lecturers, the directors that came down and spoke to us, included Howard Hawks, John Ford, Orson Welles, Roman Polanski, and Robert Wise. All the great classic American directors were my teachers in a sense.

The production program at USC was extraordinary at the time. Basically, they said, look, you're here to make movies and this is an art school. This is not just a training school. You have to learn everything. You have to learn the camera, you have to learn sound, and you have to learn the editing. You have to even project the movies. But what you have to do is make personal films. It doesn't matter if someone else writes it, it doesn't matter what it is, make it your own. And that was the basis of my training.

1969 and 1970 I was in the senior production workshop. We all got together and decided to do a more Hollywood-oriented film rather than the student-type, experimental films that were being done at the time. And we came up with a story called *The Resurrection of Bronco Billy*. We shot it in black and white and we put our own money into it. It ended up winning an Academy Award for the Best Short Film in 1970.

But it was a rather embittering experience, because the school at the time had a distribution system where they distributed these films and made money off them. We put our own money into *Bronco Billy*, but we were not to share in any of the profits of the movie. They kind of confiscated it. I remember the director of the department came down and had the Academy Award in a brown bag and let me look at it. It made them a lot of money over the years, and I became rather pissed off.

# Dark Star (1973)

*Brian Narelle; Cal Kuniholm; Dre Pahich; Dan O'Bannon;
Joe Saunders; Michael Shaw; Miles Watkins.*

I made *Dark Star*, which began as a student film and then turned into a feature. It took me four years to make it with Dan O'Bannon, a collaborator, who has now gone on to his own career as a writer. When we finished *Dark Star*, the film department said, "That's our movie. We want it." I said, "You prove it's your movie. I didn't sign anything that said this is your movie. I paid for it. I own the negative." And I was right.

My biggest recollection about *Dark Star* is that we got hooked up with a producer and distributor by the name of Jack Harris who, basically, gave us money to complete the film. It was actually released in theaters in Los Angeles, a big wide release, just like a real movie. But I recall my horror at reading my first bad review in *Variety*. It was totally unexpected. I thought the movie would come out and they would pull up in a limousine and say, "Mr. Carpenter, we want you on the set." It didn't happen.

# Assault on Precinct 13 (1976)

*Austin Stoker; Darwin Joston; Laurie Zimmer; Martin West;
Tony Burton; Charles Cyphers; Nancy Loomis; Nancy Kyes;
Peter Bruni; John J. Fox; Marc Ross; Alan Koss; Henry Brandon;
Kim Richards; Frank Doubleday; Gilbert De la Pena.*

After *Dark Star* I couldn't get a job. So I began writing screenplays and I managed to sell a treatment and wrote a screenplay for Jon Peters called *The Eyes of Laura Mars*, based on an original idea of mine. That gave me some financial freedom. It also attracted the interest of an investor in Philadelphia who wanted to put up some money for a feature for me to write and direct. That film was *Assault on Precinct 13*.

I wanted to make it an action/exploitation film, but I based it on one of my favorite old films, *Rio Bravo*, directed by Howard Hawks and starring John Wayne and Dean Martin. They're in jail and the bad guys are outside.

We shot it in twenty-five days in Panavision [wide screen]. I personally did the editing and the music. And again it was actually released theatrically in theaters. And again when the reviews came they were just devastatingly bad reviews. They called me all sorts of names. I said, what's going on here? Why don't people appreciate my work?

It was only when I took the movie to England and saw it played at the British Film Institute that all of a sudden they said this is a great film. I got this reputation over there as being some kind of a new, young director and that reputation kind of preceded me back to the United States. That's how my career kind of got started.

When I think up storylines I think in terms of keeping people in suspense or frightening them. We're all afraid of the something. Fear of death, fear of a loss of a loved one, fear of the unknown, and fear of the future. We all have the same nightmares. So fear and suspense are kind of universal emotions in people. Tapping into it intellectually is not difficult. But how do you do it so the audience really responds to it? That's the artistry of it and a lot of it is instinct.

I would go for the isolation I felt as a kid growing up in that log cabin looking out at this strange world, and in my view a kind of dangerous world. That's how I saw the police station under siege in *Precinct 13*—isolated and looking out at this dangerous world. I've used themes of isolation before. It's kind of a thing with me. Goes back to my childhood. Other than that, I make it all up.

But in *Assault on Precinct 13*, I was basically using the structure of *Rio Bravo*. I wanted to indicate that to anybody who was interested so I used the name John T. Chance instead of my own for my editing credit. John T. Chance is John Wayne's name in *Rio Bravo*. It was kind of my tip of the hat, as if to say this is what I'm doing. I am doing a low budget Howard Hawks' picture with a little bit of this and that added, but it owes its origins to *Rio Bravo*.

## Someone Is Watching Me! *(1978, TV movie)*

*Lauren Hutton; David Birney; Adrienne Barbeau; Charles Cyphers; Grainger Hines; Len Lesser; John Mahon; James Murtaugh; J. Jay Saunders; Michael Laurence; George Skaff; Robert Phalen; Robert Snively; Jean Le Bouvier; James McAlpine.*

In 1977 there was an article in the paper about a woman who had been basically stalked by a man in an apartment building across from where she lived. He had a telescope. And he began to terrorize her, watching her every move. I thought this would be an interesting movie to make. It might be a kind of Hitchcock *Rear Window*. So I made a development deal with Warner Bros. to make the film. I wrote the script and the feature department at Warner's decided it wasn't good enough. Maybe we'll do it for TV, they said, so that's what we did.

The original name of the story was *High Rise*, but they changed it to *Someone's Watching Me!* It starred Lauren Hutton, Adrienne Barbeau, and David Birney. I had a great cast and crew and just had a great time making it. I don't think it scored a big rating and unfortunately it was never released as a feature overseas, but I think it was pretty good.

Directing for TV is not my favorite thing to do because you don't have any time. You have to work really fast. And it's interrupted by commercials and there's nothing you can do about it. It's a commercial venue. That's distressing. That's not the way you want to have your work presented.

> *John Carpenter single-handedly gave me a movie career. I mean, there's just no question about that. You never know what would have happened had I not been given an opportunity by someone. I'll never forget the experience as long as I live of getting that call for that job.*
> *Jamie Lee Curtis—Actress*

# Halloween (1978)

*Donald Pleasence; Jamie Lee Curtis; Nancy Loomis; P.J. Soles; Charles Cyphers; Kyle Richards; Brian Andrews; John Michael Graham; Nancy Stephens; Arthur Malet; Mickey Yablans; Brent Le Page; Adam Hollander; Robert Phalen; Tony Moran.*

*Halloween* was a very quickly put together idea. The money was there. Irwin Yablans had released *Assault on Precinct 13* and came to me and asked if I would like to make a horror film for $300 thousand. He said he had this idea about these babysitters who get stalked by a killer. He wanted to call it *The Babysitter Murders*. I said I would do it if he would give me cut. He agreed and Deborah Hill and I wrote the screenplay. During the writing of it Irwin called me up and suggested we set it on Halloween night. "As a matter of fact," he said, "why don't we call it *Halloween*?"

*Halloween* was the most successful independent film of all time for a while because it was made so cheaply and its profit was so big. But I think it was the style of the film. The film made people scream. It was the first horror film in a long time that was kind of a roller coaster ride. The last film of that particular genre that worked as well was *Psycho*. *Halloween* was basically a good old-fashioned haunted house movie. There's something awful in this dark house and these poor people are walking around not paying attention. It began a cycle of kind of teenage slasher movies, which in many ways imitated the style of *Halloween,* but took the gore to an extreme. In *Halloween* all the violence is really off screen. You never really see anything. It's what you think you see that's so scary.

We started shooting *Halloween* with a $320 thousand budget. We had Donald Pleasence for a total of five days. Casting Jamie Lee Curtis was Deborah Hill's idea—kind of an echo back to Janet Leigh in *Psycho.*

The main street we used in *Halloween* is right off of Sunset Blvd. It's Orange Grove Avenue. There's a Blockbuster now across the street from Kentucky Fried Chicken, which wasn't there when we shot the film. Haddonfield, Illinois, right in the middle of Hollywood, folks.

The odd thing about all of these movies is that when people look back on them they see them with kinder eyes than the movie was received at the time. *Halloween* received terrible reviews. Just absolutely awful reviews putting it down, calling it a turkey, saying it wasn't scary. But audiences were going to see it so it was making money. It was only when the review came out in the *Village Voice* did things start to turn around. They called *Halloween* more than just a good film; they called it a groundbreaking film. And all of a sudden it was re-reviewed all across the country. Now they thought it was always this darling film. But for a while I thought that maybe I needed to find something else to do for a living.

There are many legendary stories that go along with certain films. Here's one that is true. We thought about what kind of a mask our killer was going to wear. The most obvious thing would be some kind of bizarre clown mask. But that didn't seem appropriate. The screenplay called for a mask that looked like the pale features of a human being. So the production designer, Tommy Lee Wallace, went out to Bert Wheeler's magic shop and picked up a full head mask of William Shatner from *Star Trek.* It was a Captain Kirk mask. And what he did was cut the eyeholes a little bit bigger, spray painted the whole thing white, and put it on. It was terrifying. So I guess I owe it all to Shatner.

Jamie Lee Curtis was one of the last contract players at Universal Studios, so Jamie was a loan out from Universal to our company. Jamie was nineteen at the time, just a young child. It was Jamie, P.J. Soles, and Nancy Loomis. The girls were just fantastic actresses.

My secret technique to directing on *Halloween* was to talk to the actors from behind the camera and talk them through everything. In the final scene Jamie is struggling to not break out laughing because I was saying some outrageous things from behind the camera. Like, "Stab the son of a bitch!" And other things I can't mention here. But I would talk them through everything almost like a silent movie. But Jamie's just a terrific actress. She rose to it and off she went.

When the sequel idea for *Halloween* came along I went along with it because of business considerations. I mean, when you have partners saying we'll sue you if you don't let us make this film, it's a kind of an uncomfortable situation. I didn't want to stop anyone from making money. Since they were going to make it anyway I thought I'd have something to do with it. But I didn't feel, as a director, there was any more story. I didn't want to remake the same movie again, which is basically what the audience wanted to see. The same movie over and over and over again. I thought that was the way to oblivion. Although now I could probably think of two or three good ideas for *Halloween*.

# Elvis *(1979, TV movie)*

*Kurt Russell; Shelley Winters; Bing Russell; Robert Gray (II); Season Hubley;*
*Pat Hingle; Melody Anderson; Ed Begley, Jr.; James Canning; Dennis Christopher;*
*Charles Cyphers; Peter Hobbs; Les Lannom; Elliott Street; Randy Gray.*

*Halloween* hadn't been released yet and my agents were showing it around town trying to get me a job. My agent called me and said there was a TV movie that every director in town had turned down. "Great," I said, "I guess that's why you're sending it to me." It turned out to be the story of Elvis Presley from the beginning of his career through 1969.

Dick Clark and the producers were looking desperately for a director and they saw *Halloween,* of all things, as an example of my work. But they figured since I did the music for *Halloween* I understood music so maybe I could understand Elvis, who I never did figure out. But I took the job anyway.

When I came aboard *Elvis* there were two choices to play Elvis. One was a guy who looked exactly like Elvis Presley. He was stunning but he could act about as good as this typewriter. Zero! Nothing!

Then I saw some tape on Kurt Russell. I didn't know who Kurt Russell was. I had never watched Disney movies. Here was this guy with these cab door ears, these giant ears, and no hair. He came to the office one day and I said, "This is the guy who's going to play Elvis?" I look at him and I don't know how to shoot him as Elvis. He doesn't look like Elvis. So I said to Kurt, "If you think you can play this role, I guess I can direct it."

It turns out he was just absolutely stunning. He nailed it. And it's because Kurt Russell is a natural born mimic. He can do me. He can do anybody. His imitations are unbelievably realistic. This guy is unreal. He inhabits whoever he's playing. And the odd thing about Kurt is he doesn't really think about it too much. He doesn't agonize over it. He doesn't give it more than five seconds thought and then he does it. He's just a natural born actor. That's how he came to be cast and was nominated for an Emmy. And it was a really great experience.

*Elvis* was my baptism as a director. I had never gone through an experience like that before. We had thirty days to shoot a three-hour television movie with 88 speaking parts, 150 different locations, and a period movie that took place from the 1950s to the 1960s. We shot in Nashville and locations around Los Angeles. All I can tell you is, I have never worked so hard in my entire life. I didn't know it was going to be that grim. I didn't know how tough a director's job was. That was my boot camp.

# The Fog (*1980*)

*Adrienne Barbeau; Jamie Lee Curtis; Janet Leigh; John Houseman; Tom Atkins;*
*James Canning; Charles Cyphers; Nancy Loomis; Ty Mitchell; Hal Holbrook;*
*John F. Goff; George "Buck" Flower; Regina Waldon; Jim Haynie; Darrow Igus.*

*The Fog* was the second feature after *Halloween*. Deborah Hill and I had made a deal with Avco Embassy to make two films for them and that was the first one. It was an idea that I came up with when I was in England driving around Stonehenge. Deborah and I were driving to Bath on a vacation, and we looked out and saw this fog creeping across and it looked like kind of a movie thing. I think *The Fog* was really influenced by an old movie I saw when I was a kid called *Crawling Eye*.

As easy and fun as *Halloween* was, *The Fog* was horrible and gut-wrenching. A ghost story is very difficult, because to make the audience believe in ghosts is a more difficult task than making them believe a guy could come after you with a knife. That's very primal. The ghost part was very hard for us.

*The Fog* was the first film that I shot the way it was written, cut it together, mixed it, looked at it, turned to my partners, and said, "This is a piece of trash." And so a month and a half before release we re-shot twenty or thirty minutes, re-cut it, re-scored it, and released it the way you see it now. All I can tell you is that I learned my lesson about the differences between certain genres. When you get into fantasy you're on a lot more difficult ground than you are in a reality-based film. Reality-based films are very easy to do. They're actor dependent. Basically, people sitting in a room talking is not hard to direct. What's hard to direct is that which the audience knows cannot exist. And once the audience knows it can't exist, there aren't really ghosts on that ship floating out in the harbor. You have to work ten times harder. All I can say about *The Fog* is that I did the best job I could at the time.

# Escape from New York (*1981*)

*Kurt Russell; Lee Van Cleef; Ernest Borgnine; Donald Pleasence; Isaac Hayes; Season Hubley; Harry Dean Stanton; Adrienne Barbeau; Tom Atkins; Charles Cyphers; Joe Unger; Frank Doubleday; John Strobel; John Cothran, Jr.; Garrett Bergfeld.*

After we released *The Fog* I had one more picture on my Avco Embassy deal. I started writing *The Philadelphia Experiment*, which was a famous folk tale about this WWII invisibility experiment in a navy shipyard where this ship disappears. I had a great two-act movie, but no third act. I couldn't end it. Bob Rainey, who was the head of Avco, wanted another picture from me, so he asked what else I might have. So I reached down in the trunk and came up with this thing I'd written right out of film school called *Escape From New York*. And Bob said, "Great, let's make it."

    *Escape* was the story of this hero, kind of bad guy, on a mission to rescue the President of the United States who is being held inside New York City. In the film, Manhattan island has become a maximum-security prison. It's the most dangerous, evil place in the universe.

    The first thing we decided was that we couldn't shoot it in New York because there was no way to get the look I wanted. We were even thinking about using studio backlots. Then someone scouted St. Louis, Missouri. St. Louis had a tremendous fire in the seventies that had burned out the entire downtown section of the city. I mean it was gutted, blackened. The city was in such trouble at the time that they gave us whatever we needed. The only way we got to make that movie was by going to St. Louis, which stood in for New York City.

    We had no money for special effects. So we went to Roger Corman's New World special effects department. Jim Cameron was working there then and he painted us a little map. They did an incredible job of effects for very little money. I think the total cost for the effects was something like fifty thousand dollars. We were lucky on that film all the way around. I had a lot of talented people working with me.

    That was the first film to use high-speed Panatar lenses from Panavision where you could shoot wide open in the middle of the night in the street and get an exposure. And the only way we got the kind of depth you saw in the film was to use those lenses. The problem is when you're opening up a lens like that you have no depth of field. So if you're shooting a close-up and the focus puller is off at all, it's out of focus. There were a few shots that were troublesome but we managed to cut around them and the movie worked.

# The Thing (1982)

*Kurt Russell; Wilford Brimley; T.K. Carter; David Clennon; Keith David; Richard A. Dysart; Richard Masur; Donald Moffat; Charles Hallahan; Peter Maloney; Joel Polis; Thomas G. Waites; Norbert Weisser; Larry J. Franco; Nate Irwin..*

When you come to *The Thing*, you come to one of my favorite films. But it was one of the most painful experiences I went through as a professional. Probably changed my professional life.

We went back to the original source material rather than the Howard Hawks 1951 version, which was called *Thing from Another World*. The original source material was written by John W. Campbell and was called *Who Goes There?* It was about a creature that could imitate other life forms and nobody knows what anybody is, creature or human. It was a very compelling, Agatha Christie *Ten Little Indians* kind of thing.

We had been given a decent budget from Universal and our special effects guy came up with a really novel concept for the creature. He suggested The Thing could look like anything. It could look like all the life forms it's imitated throughout the universe. So it could constantly keep changing. And we could do things on the screen that had never been seen before.

We shot the movie on a glacier in British Columbia in the wintertime, and it was incredibly cold and difficult. I've never seen such locations. I can attribute my skin cancer to being up on the Janeau Icefield and not protecting myself, because of the glare that comes from the sun and bounces off of the snow. I mean, basically, it was a real tough shoot.

Let me back up a minute. Two weeks before our movie comes out, they released this other movie called *E.T.* And there's this burst of love all around this movie. I guess the country was going through a recession and there were tough times. Audiences wanted an up/cry and *E.T.* gave it to them.

Two weeks later, out comes my movie. And my movie is exactly just the opposite of *E.T.* It is not an up/cry. It is a downer. It is the grimmest thing you have ever seen. There's a transformation scene where these dogs suddenly turn into this horrible creature, and during the first preview one audience member jumped up and ran into the bathroom and threw up. The executives thought we had a hit. Unfortunately, they were wrong. I was criticized heavily for the gore. The critics called me a pornographer of violence. I've been called a lot of names before but I got called the most names on that film.

Here I thought I had made this really great movie, right? But even during the preview stage I knew something was wrong because I had this sixteen-year-old ask me what happened at the end—which one of them was The Thing? I told her she had to use her imagination. She told me she hated that. So I realized I was in deep trouble with that film. And I was right. The industry turned against me because they thought I had gone too far with the gore. I think it probably changed my career.

I had made a deal during the filming of *The Thing* to make another film for Universal called *Firestarter*, a Stephen King novel. A friend of mine, Bill Phillips, had written a great screenplay and we already were scouting locations. Universal was so upset and shocked by the reviews and the fact that *The Thing* had not made the kind of money they expected, I lost the directing job on *Firestarter*, even though they had to pay me my salary.

I was in shock. I didn't work for about eight or nine months. I didn't have anything. I thought my career was going to end. But all of a sudden from heaven drops this book called *Christine*, a novel by Stephen King. Stephen had written this gigantic book about a haunted car. A producer I had known over at Warner Bros., Richard Kobritz, got the rights to the book and suggested I do it. I needed a job so I did it.

# Christine (1983)

*Keith Gordon; John Stockwell; Alexandra Paul; Robert Prosky;*
*Harry Dean Stanton; Christina Belford; Roberts Blossom;*
*William Ostrander; David Spielberg; Malcolm Danare; Steven Tash;*
*Stuart Charno; Kelly Preston; Mac Poppel; Robert Darnell.*

*Christine* was an interesting experience for me. It was a mixed bag. I think that when I was directing it my heart was still broken from the negative reaction to *The Thing*. So I don't believe I did a very good job with *Christine*. I had some terrific actors and enjoyed working with them. Keith Gordon, Alexandra Paul, Robert Prosky. Great people. The screenplay was very good and written by Bill Phillips, again from a novel by Steven King.

But somehow in the end I didn't capture what the novel had captured. I didn't get what King seemed to have gotten through his words.

People have asked over and over again what it is about a Stephen King novel that doesn't seem to translate to the screen very well. I suppose the best of his books made into a movie was *Carrie*. Brian De Palma made it his own film. With *Christine*, we remained faithful to Stephen's story and structure, and I really don't know what happened. I think King is scary when you read his words. But I don't know that when you put the images on the screen they're that scary, at least in terms of *Christine*. That's all I can speak for. I didn't really think a haunted car was all that frightening. But I needed a job, and I did it. It was not unsuccessful. And there are some champions of the film, but I'm lukewarm about it. I take responsibility for it not being better because maybe I wasn't better as a director

# Starman (1984)

*Jeff Bridges; Karen Allen; Charles Martin Smith; Richard Jaeckel; Robert Phalen;*
*Tony Edwards; John Walter Davis; Ted White; Dirk Blocker; M. C. Gainey;*
*Sean Faro; George "Buck" Flower; Russ Benning; Ralph Cosham; David Wells.*

I made *Christine* for Columbia and they had this other picture that they developed that nobody wanted to make. It was called *Starman*. It was this very sweet love story that pre-dates *E.T.* in terms of it being about a benevolent alien. To me it was suddenly a chance to make something different than I had been making. It was a chance for me to make a kind of *It Happened One Night* type of a film. A love story on the road.

In a way it was an antagonistic love story. It was a terrific screenplay and I think I jumped at it because it was romantic. I had not been known for doing anything like that. I'd done it in *Elvis*, but that was the only time. I cast Jeff Bridges and Karen Allen and it just worked. It was originally written as a woman's picture, but Jeff took it over and made it his.

We started shooting the film and of course you shoot it out of continuity. The crew was watching Jeff perform the role as Starman and they couldn't understand what he was doing. They thought he was way off base in his approach to the character. It was only when you saw it all together that you realized his genius. He had figured out this character from beginning to end. He had figured out every stage of *Starman* and every stage of the alien. I'm very proud of his work and my work. It earned him an Academy Award nomination. People loved the movie. And it's not only because it's written so very well, but also because Jeff is a brilliant actor.

It was a nice little love story and I wanted to show I could do it. I had a good time making it.

# Big Trouble in Little China (1986)

*Kurt Russell; Kim Cattrall; Dennis Dun; James Hong;*
*Victor Wong (III); Kate Burton; Donald Li; Carter Wong; Peter Kwong;*
*James Pax; Suzee Pai; Chao Li Chi; Jeff Imada; Rummel Mor; Craig Ng.*

Kurt wanted to do *Big Trouble in Little China*. It was a comedy/action picture and had a lot of martial arts in it. The idea was an inversion of your typical story. Usually you have your typical Caucasian hero and his ethnic sidekick. And of course, the male Caucasian carries the day and the sidekick is along for support. In this one, the male Caucasian is a complete idiot. He's incompetent. He cannot fight. Can't do anything right. And his sidekick is the one who is the tough guy. We thought that was a great idea. So we made the character a complete fool. He's always out of it. He's just a blowhard. If you watch the movie you'll see that Kurt is doing a John Wayne imitation. But he's an idiot John Wayne, a John Wayne who is incompetent. He just talks too much, swaggers around, and can't find his ass with two hands.

Strangely enough, out comes the movie and once again, bad reviews. They said it was terrible.

Now, I had a terrible time on *Big Trouble* in terms of the management at the studio. It was a new age in Hollywood. The agents had firmly taken hold. This was back in 1985, 1986. Management at Twentieth Century Fox had come from Paramount and they were pretty tough guys and we hit head on. There was a lot of bad blood. I became extremely fed up with the studio system after that picture.

We killed ourselves to make that movie only to find out that the policy at the studio was to spend only $3 million on its opening weekend in terms of publicity and advertising. They limited it. And I said, "Wait a minute. What's this limit? We just killed ourselves to make this film. You should be splashing it everywhere." But it wasn't their corporate policy at that time.

And they tried to get involved creatively. Basically, here's the kind of person that I am. If you ask me to do something, I'll do anything for you. If you tell me to do something, you're never going to get anyplace. Do not tell me to do something. Don't force me to do it. And that's the problem that we had. If they just had been a little nicer and not treated me like help you don't trust. I prefer to be treated like a professional. And I prefer to be treated with a little bit of dignity as a human being. And that didn't happen. So that was another turning point in my career. Interestingly enough,

I've had several. Because of that one I said adios to the studio system. I didn't want to deal with those guys anymore. Goodbye.

Basically I left the studio system in 1986 and then made two movies for Universal. One was the *Prince of Darkness* in 1987, and one was *They Live* in 1988. Both were $3 million budgets. One was basically a straight horror movie about physics and the anti-god who lives on the other side of the mirror. A very tough horror film.

# Prince of Darkness (1986)

*Donald Pleasence; Jameson Parker; Victor Wong III; Lisa Blount; Dennis Dun;
Susan Blanchard; Anne Marie Howard; Ann Yen; Ken Wright; Dirk Blocker;
Jessie Lawrence Ferguson; Peter Jason; Robert Grasmere; Thom Bray; Joanna Merlin.*

In the two-picture deal with Universal, *Prince of Darkness* came first. It was a straight out horror movie in a church, and I wanted to work with Donald Pleasence again. I wanted to work with some of the Asian actors from *Big Trouble in Little China*, and I wanted to make a real scary movie. I saw it with a preview audience and they were screaming, yelling, and going crazy. But it was not well received by the critics. They were angry that I went back to horror. You see, there's a condemned/redemption thing in American society. We want to destroy all of our heroes. We want to build them up, then destroy them. When they come back and redeem themselves, then we accept them. But if the hero that is built up and destroyed and then comes back, and then leaves again and does something bad, we can't tolerate it. So nobody could figure out why I wanted to go back and make a horror film. It was because I was so sick of the studio system.

# They Live (1988)

*Roddy Piper; Keith David; Meg Foster; George "Buck" Flower; Peter Jason;
Raymond St. Jacques; Jason Robards III; John Lawrence; Susan Barnes; Sy Richardson;
Wendy Brainard; Lucille Meredith; Susan Blanchard; Norman Alden; Dana Bratton.*

A short story called *Eight O'Clock in the Morning* kind of inspired *They Live.* It's about a guy who discovers that the human race has been hypnotized to believe that everything is normal, when in fact aliens have already taken over. At that particular point, probably because of my experience with Twentieth Century Fox in 1986, and seeing how far right the country had come, I decided to make a little political science fiction movie. And I decided to go after unrestrained capitalism.

My political philosophy is kind of in the boring middle, but all of a sudden there were a lot of homeless people out there, and a whole lot of people getting richer, and a whole lot of people getting poorer. The makeup of the country had changed. I saw things I wasn't very happy with. So I made the aliens Republican capitalists who had taken all of us over by hypnotic signals through television sets. And basically a pair of sunglasses was developed that if you put them on you could see the truth. The aliens were consumers. They were basically capitalists from outer space. They were raping our resources for their own planet, for their own good. It's all about money.

The studio didn't understand what the hell the movie was about and wanted me to make a film about some basic science fiction thing. I had final cut, so I went ahead with it. It was made for very little. It has the longest fight scene in movie history, about ten minutes long. And it's a real cool idea.

Back in the old days, when there was such a thing as B movies and A movies, A movies were straight. They usually were made from a novel written by somebody famous. You attach A stars to the project and you go make it. The B films were called budget films, and you were allowed to do movies with more subversive material, things that you could slip in between the cracks that the audience understood. A little more edgy material than some of the A stuff. So *They Live* was a kind of old fashioned B movie with a lot of subversive messages basically shoved into a science fiction film.

## Memoirs of an Invisible Man (1992)

*Chevy Chase; Daryl Hannah; Sam Neill; Michael McKean; Stephen Tobolowsky;*
*Jim Norton; Pat Skipper; Paul Perri; Richard Epcar; Steven Barr;*
*Gregory Paul Martin; Patricia Heaton; Barry Kivel; Donald Li; Rosalind Chao.*

Basically, *Memoirs* came to me as a finished screenplay from Warner's that Chevy Chase was already involved with. I had always been a fan of his and I always wanted to work with him. I thought he was very funny.

Chevy was a producer on the film. It was a modern re-telling of the old *Invisible Man* story, but this new version had some different issues involved. I thought that as a comedy it's fine, but it really talks about the invisibility of the generation of men that are now kind of yuppies. They have no lives, they are invisible. It was kind of a metaphor for the times. It was also a big studio film. And I thought, why not. I'll go back and give it another try. I got to work with William Fraker, who is one of the greatest, dearest friends of mine and a terrific cameraman.

I can't say it was the most pleasant experience. It made me never want to make movies again because of the movie making process in this particular case. The movie making part was pretty bad. I won't go into why. The film was not particularly well received. I don't know if it was sold wrong or what. I don't know that I did a great job with it. But as I look back on it, I'm very happy with it. I think it worked out particularly well.

I went up to ILM and worked with Bruce Nicholson on special effects and he came up with a way to shoot the invisibility that was later used in *Forrest Gump*. We developed that first and won the Academy Award for it.

I got to work with some great people on the film, like Shirley Walker, who composed the score. She had worked with many composers in Hollywood and it became a relationship that I utilized later on in *Escape From L.A.* She is just terrific.

I have a number of unusual stories about the *Invisible Man*, but I don't think it's really appropriate for me to discuss them (*laughs*).

# Body Bags (1993, TV)

*John Carpenter; Tom Arnold; Tobe Hooper; Robert Carradine; Alex Datcher; Peter Jason; Wes Craven; Sam Raimi; David Naughton; Stacy Keach; David Warner; Sheena Easton; Debbie Harry; Mark Hamill; John Agar; Roger Corman; Molly Cheek; George "Buck" Flower; Lucy Boryer; Roger Rooks.*

*Body Bags* was a kind of *Tales from the Crypt*, with a dead guy who gets up in the morgue and tells stories of the dead people who are there and how they met their ends. The whole idea was for me to play the guy who gets up from the body bag. So I would direct one and ended up directing two of them. Tobe Hooper, who is a friend of mine and another horror director, directed one.

We strung the episodes together with my narration. Makeup to make me into a corpse was done by Rick Baker, who is one of the best makeup men in the business in terms of special effects. He developed this kind of look for me. The problem was I didn't realize what it would take to get into this makeup every day. So every morning for about two to three hours I would sit in his trailer and he would make jokes at my expense, painting on this stuff. It's very uncomfortable and not fun but I did look like a dead man.

Acting in *Body Bags* gave me an appreciation for actors. But mainly it's an appreciation for actors that have to undergo torture to get into their makeup. In terms of doing a scene, I think that acting's pretty easy for me as long as I have a teleprompter with some of the lines on it and I can go to that if I get in trouble.

## In the Mouth of Madness (1995)

*Sam Neill; Jürgen Prochnow; Julie Carmen; Charlton Heston; Francis Bay; Wilhelm von Homburg; Kevin Rushton; Gene Mack; Conrad Bergschneider; Marvin Scott; Katherine Ashby; Ben Gilbert; Dennis O'Connor; Paul Brogren; Sharon Dyer.*

Right after *Body Bags* I got involved with *In the Mouth of Madness*. And luckily for me, Sam Neill, one of my favorite actors, was going to be in it. He's a consummate professional and just an absolutely brilliant actor. I can count on one hand the actors I can depend on. Jeff Bridges, Kurt Russell, and Sam Neill are in that category.

The movie had kinetic elements to it and was another fantasy film, like *The Fog*. It's a movie where you know the stuff that's going on cannot possibly exist. We shot it in Toronto and believe it or not, for the first time in years I got rave mainstream reviews. It was a big shock to me. When I say mainstream reviews, I'm talking about *The New York Times* and *Los Angeles Times*. When you get these big newspapers saying, boy, is he good, it's kind of a big shock.

The movie initially opened at number three, but didn't do particularly well overall because it was more of an intellectual horror film. I don't know if it was as visceral as the audience wanted, but I'm extremely proud of it. It was made for $10 million, and that included everything in there. And we had a great time making it.

## The Village of the Damned (1995)

*Christopher Reeve; Kirstie Alley; Linda Kozlowski; Michael Paré; Meredith Salenger; Mark Hamill; Pippa Pearthree; Peter Jason; Constance Forslund; Karen Kahn; Thomas Dekker; Lindsey Haun; Cody Dorkin; Trishalee Hardy; Jessye Quarry.*

After *In the Mouth of Madness*, I did *Village of the Damned* to end a commitment to Universal. I got a great cast together. But the story is very serious. It asks the question, what happens when you find out that your children are killers, murderers, and essentially evil? We took it seriously, as opposed to a rollicking horror film where there's a lot of jokes and humor tossed around.

This was Chris Reeve's last movie before his accident. As a matter of fact, I was with him in New York promoting the film two weeks before he had his accident. He was very happy with the movie and looking forward to its release. It just shows you what can happen.

The film received some strangely mixed reviews. I got really good mainstream reviews from like *The New York Times* and the *L.A. Times*. Then from the popular press I got just the reverse. Some called it the worst ever seen. I was compared with Ed Wood by some of the reviewers. It was from like one extreme to the other. That's when I began to develop my theory about the kind of reviews I get.

My career is basically genius or bum. I am both genius and bum and sometimes I am both simultaneously. To some people I am the worst director and I can't be expected to make a good movie. And to some people I'm this genius. You know neither is particularly true. The truth lies someplace in between. So I've come to accept a little more philosophical approach to my reviews.

I'm often surprised by descriptions of the "cinema of unease" and my relationship to it. People say that I can make you feel uncomfortable in a film through cinema techniques. That's true within the context of a theatrical motion picture. But I'm in the Hollywood game, unfortunately, and there are certain limits as to what you can do. If you go beyond the limits, as I have discovered in my career, then they won't let you work. You have to stay within a certain area. If the country was a little bit different, embracing a kind of open, free speech, anything goes attitude, I could really scare you. But the country won't allow it. We're too scared in our personal lives these days. But just imagine . . .

# Escape from L.A. (1996)

*Kurt Russell; Stacy Keach; Steve Buscemi; Peter Fonda;*
*Georges Corraface; Bruce Campbell; Valeria Golino; Pam Grier;*
*A. J. Langer; Michelle Forbes; Jeff Imada; Cliff Robertson; Ina Romeo;*
*Peter Jason; Jordan Baker; Caroleen Feeney; Paul Bartel.*

*Escape from L.A.* began after Kurt and I finished *Big Trouble in Little China*. We were returning from New York and I suggested that it would be great to go back and meet that character again, because Snake Plissken was Kurt's favorite character.

I thought it would be fun to do to L.A. what we had done to New York, which was basically send it up and make it an evil place. But at that point we had no story. There was actually a screenplay written but it didn't work out very well. Kurt and I decided there was nothing frightening about L.A. It's the beach, it's sunny, it's daytime. It was really only in the nineties that we began to experience some disasters here in Los Angeles. The riots in 1992, the earthquake in 1994, the mud slides, the fires, the rains, the storms. Also the crime began to grow and the unease grew because we had become a real ethnically diverse population. All of a sudden, in 1994, 1995, we took over from New York. We became the baddest place in the United States. And all of a sudden it became viable to do a sequel because there was a story. And so Kurt got Deborah Hill and me together and we came up with this story and Paramount Pictures bought it. The sequel was born.

*Escape from L.A.* was a big challenge to make because all of it took place at night. I had seventy straight nights of shooting. I was up for ninety nights in a row without seeing the daylight, in the worst weather. And it gets pretty cold out here sometimes. So it was an emotional and physical challenge, but once again I had Kurt Russell. He was a great collaborator. We wrote part of the screenplay together. We developed the character together. We dealt with the problems together. He was a great friend. I love him very much. I've never had as much fun on a film and we were both really pleased with the result.

Anytime you have a film where you're taking something familiar like Los Angeles and destroying it, you have to create the entire thing from nothing. Because L.A., no matter what we say, is gorgeous. Even at night in some of the worst sections it's hard to understand what the danger is about.

In our story there's been a big earthquake and Los Angeles has become an island. So basically we had to build everything. There were a few locations in Northridge at the site of the earthquake of 1994 that we used, but primarily everything was built from scratch. We based it on some of the real severe earthquakes in South America, China, and India. Pictures of them. So the production designers got together and created this destroyed world.

It's interesting to look back on the films that I've done. I have no idea what I'm doing next [in fact, he has since completed *John Carpenter's Vampires*]. Part of me would love to stop directing because the business has changed so much. It's not the same business I got into when I made *Dark Star* in 1970. The dynamics have changed—the people have changed. And in another way it's a very exciting time to be in the movie business. There's so many outlets now. There's cable television, video, and laser disc. The industry is really cranking out lots and lots of films. Unfortunately they're all formulaic. At this particular time, not as many horror films are being made. It's a downtime for horror, although that may come back. It's a cyclical business.

I just don't know that it's a joy to make films anymore. You know, you get to be a certain age and it's not fun to stand out in the middle of the night in cold and rain all night long. You'd rather be doing something else. But the thing that keeps one going is the joy of cinema. That's where I started. I started as a kid going to see a movie and just being in awe of what I saw; seeing *Forbidden Planet* in 1956 and wanting to be the guy who made that. And in a sense that's what keeps me directing films. Maybe if I had been the guy who directed it and knew what it took to direct it, I would have had second thoughts.

Sometimes it's better not to know what it's really like. To come into a situation and be yourself without limitations, without knowing any of the problems, and just go ahead and make something. Not have to deal with the studio politics, the censorship issues, the rating issues, and all the business end of it. That can be a very destructive thing. It's the old story of the art and commerce battle. Somehow, one has to keep walking through this minefield without losing the pure joy of cinema. For myself, when I lose it, that'll be it. That'll be the end of it—when the joy of it is diminished by the reality of commerce. Then it's time to move on. I don't know when that time will come.

The world is changing to a globalized economy along with the information revolution and the computer revolution. Everything is realigning itself in terms of the old order of the world. It's a whole different ballgame. And, unfortunately, there's some real negative sides to this. The clichés have been talked about for years. The rich are getting richer; the poor are getting poorer. And unfortunately, in the United States, there's a right-wing conservative pall hanging over all of us.

We're going to have to face a lot of problems in the next century. Overpopulation, diminishing natural resources. We all know what the problems are going to be, but we don't want to face them. We want it to be this fantasy world, where everything's going to work out okay. I think there's a lot of wish fulfillment going on in movies now. Movies today tend to be about good times.

Labeling me is tough. I would say that I'm John Carpenter. I do things that other people don't do and other people do things I can't do. I do musical scores, write, and direct. I can light a film; I can photograph a film. It might not be very good, but I can do it. I can edit a film. Filmmaking is part of my blood. I may not be the best at it but when all is said and done, these are my films from top to bottom; with very few exceptions, every frame is what I wanted it to be. And that's about as close as you can get to having pure creative expression in a collaborative medium. The more control you can seize of every aspect of it, the more it's going to be your film—a personal film.

This leads us back to my training at USC when I was a twenty-year-old kid arriving on an airplane from Bowling Green, Kentucky. They said, doesn't matter who writes it, doesn't matter who's in it, but make it your movie, make it a personal film, make it John Carpenter's movie. So that's what I've done for twenty-six, twenty-seven years.

How would I like being remembered? He was just John Carpenter, a guy who lived for a while. He directed these movies. And then he went away.

The only parting words I could say is what Salvador Dali said to a group of people when he won an award. He said, "God save the train station at St. Sebastian."

Who knows what he meant, though?

# Director Filmography

*Dark Star* (1973)
*Assault on Precinct 13* (1976)
*Someone's Watching Me!* (1978, TV)
*Halloween* (1978)
*Elvis* (1979, TV)
*The Fog* (1980)
*Escape from New York* (1981)
*The Thing* (1982)
*Christine* (1983)
*Starman* (1984)
*Big Trouble in Little China* (1986)
*Prince of Darkness* (1987)
*They Live* (1988)
*Memoirs of an Invisible Man* (1992)
*Body Bags* (1993, TV)
*In the Mouth of Madness* (1995)
*Village of the Damned* (1995)
*Escape from L.A.* (1996)
*John Carpenter's Vampires* (1998)

# Awards

**Academy of Science Fiction, Horror and Fantasy Films, USA**
*Vampires*, Saturn Award, Best Music, 1999

**Cable Ace Awards**
*El Diablo*, ACE, Writing a Movie or Miniseries (TV, shared with Bill Phillips), 1991

**Edgar Allan Poe Awards**
*Someone's Watching Me!*, Edgar, Best Television Feature or Miniseries (nominated), 1979

**Los Angeles Film Critics Association Awards**
New Generation Award, 1979

# The Films of
# John Frankenheimer

John Frankenheimer was born February 19, 1930, in New York City. In his youth he wanted to become a professional tennis player. But a few twists and turns, as well as the air force, changed that. He applied for and was accepted in the Motion Picture Squadron of the air force, where he realized his natural talent behind the camera. After his military discharge, he convinced CBS to hire him as an assistant director, which consisted mainly of working as a cameraman at that time. He eventually started to direct the show he had been working on as an assistant. Strangely enough, Frankenheimer never had any intention of directing feature films. He liked directing live television, and he would have continued to do so if the profession itself hadn't ceased to exist.

Frankenheimer first turned to the big screen with *The Young Stranger* in 1957. He claims he hated doing it because he felt he did not understand movies and was not used to working with only one camera. Disappointed with his first feature film experience, he returned to his successful television career, eventually directing a total of 152 live television shows between 1954 and 1960. In 1961 he took another chance on the cinema industry, working with Burt Lancaster on *The Young Savages*.

As a filmmaker Frankenheimer has had an extraordinary career. Many of his films express his views on important social and philosophical topics and he has never hesitated to tackle controversial subjects as he did in such classic films as *The Manchurian Candidate* and *Seven Days in May*. Frankenheimer's films reflect the care and integrity with which he creates his projects. Whether working on location or in Hollywood, his actors soon discover that he believes "The very process of crafting a show is a comment by the director."

*John is known as a man's man. And he really makes a woman feel like a woman. He has this heightened awareness that translates so easily onto the screen. There's quite a bit of mystery surrounding him and all that comes through in his films.*

*Ann-Margret—Actress*

# The Conversation

Ever since I was a little boy I loved going to the movies. I was a very shy kid and I found that I liked to escape by going to the movies. I went almost two or three times a week when I was a child, and I was continually drawn to creative things, whether it be drawing, whether it be acting. I acted in a lot of school plays at Williams College. I hated Williams College; I really hated it when I went there in the late forties and fifties. Out of my tremendous feelings of rejection there I went into the theater at Williams and found tremendous peace and satisfaction. I found the kind of home that I was looking for in the theater and I realized that that's what I wanted to do.

When you are a kid you have movie stars that you really go to see and I think my favorite movie star was Robert Mitchum. God, I'd go to see every Robert Mitchum movie. I also loved Jeanne Crane. I was madly in love with Jeanne Crane. I thought she was the most beautiful woman I ever saw, with this long brown hair. I guess I saw *State Fair* fifteen times. As I got older I just got more interested in movies by people like Alfred Hitchcock and George Stevens, William Wyler, Carol Reed, David Lean, and, obviously, Orson Welles.

I went to work for an insurance company one summer when I was in college and I can honestly tell you that I think that if I had to do that kind of thing all my life I would have committed suicide. I really hated it. I just cannot tell you how much I hated it. I found myself in a position where I knew what I didn't want to do but I didn't know what I wanted to do. I had a long list of what I didn't want to do. I thought I wanted to be an actor. I went into summer stock when I was in college and did a lot of plays at college.

Because it was during the Korean War and I had gone to military school and had gotten a commission in ROTC I went into the air force almost immediately after getting out of college. I was stationed in Washington, D.C., where I did some theatrical projects, like the American Theater production of the movie *Blue* and things like that. Then I applied for and was accepted into the motion picture squadron of the air force that was stationed in Burbank, California. And it's a funny thing because later on Fred Coe, who was one of the best producers I ever worked with, defined talent as doing easily what other people find difficult. And as soon as I started fooling around with the camera in the air force, I can't explain it to you, but it was not difficult for me. I kind of instinctively knew where to put the camera in this film squadron and I was very at ease with it and it became kind of an extension of me. It was really wonderful training because we had no unions or anything so you could learn everything. I learned how to operate the camera and I learned how to take it apart and put it together again.

I eventually became a director for the air force doing training films. When I got out I was supposed to work with John Ford as an assistant, but he went into the hospital with a cataract operation. But before he did he told me that I should try and get into television. So when I got out of the air force I went back to New York. I knew some people that I had acted with that were now working in television in a production capacity. They were very glad to see me until they found out what I wanted was a job. Then they didn't have any time for me at all. I went through all the things that one does—I tried to get in to see people and I got all the usual rejections.

In California I had been offered a job as a parking lot attendant at CBS, as a page at NBC, and as a scenery construction coordinator at ABC, which really wasn't a network at that time but they had a few stations. So I was considering going back to California to take this ABC job. But before I did I went into CBS at 485 Madison Avenue and went up to the employment office and said I wanted to be an assistant director. I was filling out this form and suddenly I heard, "Send that damn fool back here." I went back to this office and there was a guy sitting there with an electric fan blowing all over him. His name was Richard Stanley and he was head of employment for CBS. He said to me, "I just wanted to see what kind of nerve it took for someone to walk in here and ask for a job like that."

We sat down and we talked and I don't know why but he liked me. And after about fifteen minutes he said, "Look, there's a guy you should see and his name is Hal Meyer. He is down on 41st Street and Vanderbilt Avenue. Do you think you could get your résumé down there if I called?" I said, "I think I probably could, yes." Well, it was about 4:30 in the afternoon and it was about 102 degrees out and he suggested I take a cab down there. When I went out I couldn't find a cab so I ran all the way down to Vanderbilt Avenue and when I got there I was soaking wet. I went up to the secretary, a Miss O'Neal, and gave her my résumé and she said Mr. Meyer could see me in about three weeks. I don't know what possessed me to say this, but I said, "I can't do that." Then she said, "How about this weekend?" and I said, "No, I can't do that because I have to go back to California." And she said, "Well, what about in two days at 10:00?" And I said, "Fine, I'll be there."

So I came back to see this guy and he looked exactly like the actor Lloyd Nolan. Oh, and Miss O'Neal said to me before I went in that if he doesn't spend much time with you please don't get upset because he's very busy. So I went in and he looked at my résumé and he saw that I'd been in the Fifth Photographic Squadron in the air force. He told me that he too had been with the Fifth Photographic Squadron during World War II. We talked and I was there for about half an hour and finally he said to me, "Look, I have this tremendous stack of résumés in front of me. All these people have all this experience in the theater and the movies so what makes you think that you are qualified for this job ahead of these people?" And I don't know why, but I just said I wouldn't have to unload any bad habits. Finally he said, "I know that you've heard this before but I really will call you one way or another as soon as anything happens, if anything happens. But regardless, you'll hear from me in the next four weeks."

So I went back to this lousy little hotel that I was living in that had no message service. What I would do is go out in the morning and buy a sandwich and then sit in the room and wait for the phone to ring because I didn't want to miss this call if it ever came. I did this for about two and a half weeks. I was running out of money when finally the call came and it was Hal Meyer and he said, "Look, we have promoted one of our assistant directors to director for eight weeks so we've got an eight-week job, do you want it?" I said, "Yeah, sure I want it. When do I start?" He said, "Tomorrow."

I became an assistant director at CBS and things started to go very, very well for me. I mean, I was good at it. An assistant director at CBS in those days was mainly a cameraman. In other words, you helped the director get the shot that he wanted. I didn't want to be a director so none of the directors felt threatened by me. I was there to help them. Then one day one of these guys just threw up all over me and said, "Take anything, save me, save me!" We had to get him out of the control room and I somehow or other got the show on the air.

The next day I talked to the head of CBS and I said, "You know, that was just an awful experience." I said, "The guy threw up all over me. I could direct the show better than he did." And he said, "Well, why don't you?" I was totally thrown for a loop by that because that's not what I wanted to do. He said, "You try this and if you don't like it you can have your old job back as the assistant director." So with that kind of promise I said okay.

The first show I did was a show called *You Are There* with Walter Cronkite as the host. I had been the assistant director of that with one of the best directors that I ever worked with—Sidney Lumet. I had been Sidney's assistant on that show and I learned a lot from Sidney. Sidney was wonderful to me. And I've never forgotten that. He really taught me so much and he was so patient with me. And I did that show and then I went on to do *Danger*, which was a half-hour show also, and from there I went out to California to do *Climax*—I did a lot of those. And then from there to *Playhouse 90*. In between there were some *Studio Ones* and things like that, but that's a long answer to a very short question.

Rod Serling and I did an awful lot of shows together. As a matter of fact, Rod Serling wrote the second show I ever directed, which was a half-hour danger show called *Night of the Dark* with Paul Newman, and I happen to have a kinescope of that and I've run it recently and it was pretty good. It was a pretty good show. Paul Newman got about $300 for acting in it; I got my $250 for directing it and Rod got $200 for writing it and the budget of the show was $17,000. But it was a good show. And I went on to do a lot of stuff with Rod and we became very good friends. Really very good friends. And he did *Seven Days and Nights* with me, also as a movie. And he was a man that I respected a great deal and we worked well together. We worked very well together. I think I did somewhere around ten shows of his.

Martin Manulis was a huge influence on my career because I did so much work with him. In the first place, he took me from relative obscurity from the *Danger* show to California to do *Climax* and later to do *Playhouse 90*. I think we did somewhere around sixty to seventy shows together. And Martin was an extraordinary man, he still is, but Martin had the capacity to function terribly well in a crisis and I think I learned a lot about how I function in pressure situations from Martin. Martin was able to put things in perspective, I think, better than anyone I've ever known. He was brilliant handling people. He was just an ideal producer, certainly for live television, because he was very good with script, he was very good with juggling all kinds of things around, and he handled pressure better than anyone I've ever known. And he encouraged me, Martin Manulis encouraged me, Martin Manulis gave me the confidence to do arguably the best work I've ever done. Because I knew that he would protect me and I knew that he would help me and I knew he was there for me. And Martin Manulis is still today one of my closest friends.

I would not have a film career if it had not been for my television work. I worked with wonderful writers, wonderful actors, and really great producers on so many different shows. I had all these different scripts, all these different tasks, all these different situations. I was able to do almost everything because I was very young—I was in my twenties—I was twenty-four when I became a director. I was thirty when I did my last television show. It was a whole career from age twenty-four to thirty and I did like 140 some-odd shows during that time. But I never wanted to be a film director. I think it's important to say that. I was divinely happy directing live television and later taped television. I would have continued to do that if the profession itself had not ceased to exist.

# The Young Stranger (1957)

*James MacArthur; Kim Hunter; James Daly; James Gregory;*
*Marian Seldes; Whit Bissell; Jeffrey Silver; Edith Evanson.*

Well, *The Young Stranger* came about because it was based on a television show that I had directed on *Climax* called *Deal the Blow*. The movie was written by the same person who wrote the TV show, who then expanded it another fifty minutes into a feature film. In fact, we used the same young man, James MacArthur, in the lead. It was the story of a young boy and his father and was based on a kind of autobiographical incident in the life of the writer, Robert Dozier. His father was William Dozier, who was head of production for CBS and later became head of production for RKO. When he became head of production for RKO he took this property and reworked it into a feature film and wanted me to do it. I did it in the summer when I was on a hiatus from my television work.

I hated doing the movie. I really hated it. Number one, I didn't understand movies. I didn't understand the whole business of working with one camera. I didn't understand the business of the waiting. I didn't understand how to pace yourself. I tried to use one scene to get into another like I did on live television and it didn't work at all. I didn't understand how to do things out of sequence. By that I mean I didn't know how to do the end of the movie at the beginning of the shooting schedule. Things like that. I was very uncomfortable with the crew and for me being comfortable with the crew is so important, because I have a crew that I work with now that I'm totally devoted to and we feel like an extension of each other. On that movie it was a crew that was very hostile to me because I was very young.

I was twenty-six. I was, by almost twenty years, the youngest person on the crew. I was trying to do a quality movie with a very low budget and a very short shooting schedule. The crew was used to big studio pictures. They hated being on this picture. The cameraman and I clashed continually. It was a miserable, miserable experience and I really hated it.

## A Small Bump in the Road

I waited four years to make my next film and I only made it because live television as I knew it had stopped. A man named James Aubrey had come in and taken over CBS and taken off the air all the shows that I did. So being what I was, which was a live television director, was like being the village blacksmith after the invention of the automobile. There was no need for my services. I was out of a job. I was thirty years old, I was getting a divorce, and I had been fired from a picture called *Breakfast at Tiffany's* without ever directing a frame of it. I had been hired to do that picture with Marilyn Monroe. George Axelrod was writing the script, and overnight the producers went to Switzerland and they cast Audrey Hepburn. Audrey Hepburn and her then husband, Mel Ferrer, said they never heard of me and they insisted that I be paid off and then hired another director, Blake Edwards, to direct the film. I was out of a job with no prospects and my personal life was absolutely in pieces—in shreds.

## The Young Savages (1961)

*Burt Lancaster; Dina Merrill; Edward Andrews; Vivian Nathan; Shelley Winters; Larry Gates; Telly Savalas; Pilar Seurat; Jody Fair; Roberta Shore; Milton Selzer; Robert Burton; David J. Stewart; Stanley Kristien; John Davis Chandler.*

My agents, who had not protected me at all in the *Breakfast at Tiffany's* situation, called me and told me that there was this picture with Burt Lancaster being produced by Harold Hecht. They wanted to do it very inexpensively and would I go over and see Harold Hecht, who was Burt Lancaster's partner. I went over there and I found out that their company had gone broke and that they owed United Artists a lot of money. In order to pay off the debt they had agreed to do three pictures at very modest budgets and Lancaster would take a greatly reduced salary and this was to be the first one. It was called *A Matter of Conviction* from a novel by Evan Hunter. Hecht and his production manager really only asked me one question about the whole thing—could I shoot this picture in thirty-five days?

Not could I shoot it well, not could I do this, could I do that, but could I do it in thirty-five days. And I said, "Yes, I could"—not knowing if I could or not. But I said yes and they hired me. So *A Matter of Conviction* became *The Young Savages*. My two movies to date were *The Young Stranger* and *The Young Savages*. I always think I took *The Birdman of Alcatraz* because they couldn't possibly put "young" in the title.

I insisted on using actual juvenile delinquent gang members for the picture. The producer, Harold Hecht, wanted Paul Anka as the head juvenile so that he'd have Paul sing the title song. I told him that just was not an option and we had a long, long and very heated argument over a period of two or three weeks, but I finally won. Working with those young boys was very interesting but it was also very time consuming. I was doing my first picture with a major movie star, Burt Lancaster, and I wanted to spend as much time as I could with him. So I called in this young actor, who had been my assistant on the Ingrid Bergman television show I directed called *Turning the Screw*. He was very good with actors and he was a good friend of mine and his name was Sydney Pollack. He came out to New York and worked with these kids and did a great job. Burt Lancaster liked him a lot and got him an appointment with Lou Wasserman. Burt and I tried to convince him that what he should do was become a director and the rest, as they say, is history. He turned out to be a pretty good director.

## How Does he Select his Projects?

It's very eclectic, the way one chooses subjects in the movie business, especially in the commercial movie business. You need to develop material yourself or material is presented to you as an assignment to direct. I've always been attracted to rather controversial material and have always been attracted to material that has characters go through some kind of a crisis. I try to choose material based on the fact that when I go to see this movie that somebody else may too. That's really my criteria for all of that. I look for the kind of stories that interest me; whether they are sociological or psychological, it doesn't really make any difference, it's just, do they interest me.

## The Secret to Casting

What you have to try and do is get yourself familiar with a great many actors' work so that you don't miss somebody. I try and cast the best actor for the roles, but at the same time the actor/director relationship is a very close personal relationship. I think it's very important to cast someone with whom you think you'll get along. Casting is an arduous and painful process because I honestly think that casting is probably 70 percent of directing—to cast the right people is 70 percent of your job. You need to hire the best casting director you can and one that really works well with you and understands you and understands the kind of actor that you like to work with. There is no hard-and-fast rule to my casting. I just like to work with good actors, but I imagine any director would tell you that. I don't have any formula for it.

I find that one of the most difficult things in this business is communication, because basically it is a business of communication. Once you've worked with someone and you're able to communicate with them well, the temptation is to want to work with them again because you don't have to go through the whole process of how to communicate with them. In the case of Burt Lancaster, Angela Lansbury, Roy Scheider, or other actors that I've worked with a lot I hardly have to say anything. They know and we talk in a minimal way. We understand each other and that's a wonderful feeling. Frederic Forrest and Clarence Williams are two actors that I work with now that I have a great relationship with.

# The Birdman of Alcatraz (1962)

*Burt Lancaster; Karl Malden; Thelma Ritter; Neville Brand; Betty Field; Telly Savalas; Edmond O'Brien; Hugh Marlowe; Whit Bissell; Crahan Denton; James Westerfield.*

*The Birdman of Alcatraz* was a unique movie in that there were no logistical problems. The movie was shot in sequence from beginning to end like you would do a play. Burt Lancaster at that time was one of the most powerful actors in the business and he could pretty well have what he wanted. Because of the tremendous makeup changes that he would have to go through we shot in sequence. It was a very demanding film to make.

Another thing we learned is that there is no such thing as a trained bird. There are only hungry birds. We tried to get them to fly off the pipe down onto Lancaster's hand. We would tape bird food to Burt's fingers. Now, in those days we did not have silent hand-held cameras. We had the Mitchell BNC and the NC. The BNC was the silent camera and it held one thousand feet of film, and we'd put one thousand feet in that thing and wait for the birds. And sure enough, time after time, as we were changing film, that's when the birds would fly. It took hours to do this stuff.

I had wanted to do *The Birdman of Alcatraz* on live television, if you can imagine that. It would have been a disaster, having these birds fly all over the studio, but I was young enough and I suppose just so full of myself in those days that I didn't think there was anything I couldn't do. But that would have certainly been one of them. Halfway through the filming of *The Young Savages* I was told that there was no chance of my ever doing *The Birdman of Alcatraz* because Burt Lancaster hated me and thought that I was very defensive and I didn't listen to him, and so forth and so on. All of which wasn't true. Burt gave me a very, very hard time because I just didn't knuckle under to him. He just wanted to get in and get out and get it over with so he could pay off his debt to United Artists and go on to something else, which in this case was *The Birdman of Alcatraz*. When we were finished with *The Young Savages* he never even said goodbye to me, he was gone.

I went back to New York after cutting the picture together and I got a call from Harold Hecht and he said you've got to come out to California because we've got this problem with *The Young Savages*. And I said, "Harold, you haven't got any problem with *The Young Savages*. If you just leave the picture alone the way I cut it instead of trying to improve it, it'll be just fine." He said they had tested it the night before and there was a big problem. Well, I was getting a divorce at this time and the last place I wanted to be was California because of the community property problem. I was doing just fine in New York. I agreed to go out there under another name for the weekend to look at the picture if they would guarantee me a return ticket.

So I went to Los Angeles International Airport and who meets me at the airplane but Burt Lancaster. Well, I knew something was very, very strange because he had not even said goodbye to me. So Burt says, "I just want to tell you something. I knew that if I asked you to come out here you wouldn't have come." He said, "I saw *The Young Savages* last week. It's a brilliant movie. I think you did a great job on it and I want you to direct *The Birdman of Alcatraz*. Will you do it?" Well, I was overwhelmed, just absolutely overwhelmed, because I knew the property very well and I had always wanted to do it. I read the script, told them that it was long and warned them that it would run over four hours, but they insisted I shoot that script or they would get someone else.

So we start to shoot the picture. And we shot and shot and shot. So now we cut the picture together and I called Harold Hecht and tell him I have a cut to show to him and Burt. He called me back and said they had booked a screening room for 3:00 at Columbia Studios and then he had a cocktail date at 6:00 at The Brown Derby that was just up the street. I said, "Cancel it, Harold, and cancel dinner while you're at it." And he said, "What are you talking about?" I told him that the picture ran 4 hours and 45 minutes long. As you can imagine, there was panic after the screening, and Harold asked if I could cut it. And I said, "Well, you can't cut it. The name of the picture is *The Birdman of Alcatraz* and in this script he doesn't find the birds for 1 hour and 50 minutes." We went back and forth, and to make a long story short he said, "Well, what do we have to do?" And I said, "What you have to do is re-write this picture and we have to re-shoot the first half of the movie." After a long period of discussion, everybody realized that that's what had to be done.

Burt Lancaster went off and made *Judgment in Nuremberg* for Stanley Kramer while the writer and I re-wrote the first part of the picture. Well, the problem was that by the end of the picture Lancaster was totally bald because he was supposed to age. So we had to make a toupee for the first part of the picture to match the hair that we chopped off. There were about two shots in the whole movie of Lancaster with his real hair, and we shot the picture so that we got to the birds in the first ten minutes. We put the picture together and it is what it is. But we shot one and a half times.

# The Manchurian Candidate (1962)

*Frank Sinatra; Laurence Harvey; Janet Leigh; Angela Lansbury; Henry Silva;*
*James Gregory; Leslie Parrish; John McGiver; Khigh Dhiegh; James Edwards;*
*Douglas Henderson; Albert Paulsen; Barry Kelley; Lloyd Corrigan; Madame Spivy.*

*The Manchurian Candidate* came out of a collaboration between George Axelrod and myself. He asked me if I had ever heard of a book written by Richard Condon called *The Manchurian Candidate* and I never had. We went across the street from his apartment, which was at 64th Street and Madison Avenue, and we picked up two copies of the book, and he went in one room and I went in another and we read it. Both of us came out about three hours later loving the book. We called George's agent, Irving Lazar, and he optioned the book for us. Luckily for us, Frank Sinatra wanted to do that picture.

Now to get Sinatra and firm it up we had to go down to Miami to the Fountainbleau Hotel where he was appearing. This was a little bit of a problem because I had not worked after *All Fall Down* and money was a problem. But somehow we did it. We got down to Miami and George Axelrod said to me, "Look, we've got to get this guy Sinatra. Don't say anything that could conceivably put him off. Don't offend him, don't do anything that's gonna give him any doubts whatsoever." So we got to Frank Sinatra's suite at the Fountainbleau. We knocked on the door, and there was that great Sinatra smile greeting us. Sinatra says, "God, I'm glad you guys came down because I really want to do your project."

Well, anything we said from then on would have gotten us in trouble because he had already said he wanted to do it. The best thing for us to do was to get out of there, you know, to thank him and leave. But we couldn't because he had tickets for us to the fight the next day between Johansen and Patterson, so we had to stick around for a day and a half. But it was really that simple. Once we had Sinatra then everything went fine. We got Laurence Harvey to play Raymond Shaw. Sinatra wanted Lucille Ball to play the mother, but I wanted Angela Lansbury. But Sinatra was extremely gracious to me. He said, "I've wanted to work with you and you're the director, so if you want Angela Lansbury, we'll have Angela Lansbury."

There was one interesting thing that happened. About two weeks before we were going to actually start to film it, George Axelrod and I realized that we were making a movie where Frank Sinatra, our hero, orders the murder of the mother, played by Angela Lansbury. That's the way Dick Condon wrote it in the book. We just realized, good God, this is a terribly immoral movie, and we can't do this. The solution we came to was that the Sinatra character could not know what the overall plan was. So we interrupted the Raymond Shaw story before he could tell who his American operator was and what the plan was. And then the problem became: How do you find Raymond Shaw in Madison Square Garden if Sinatra didn't know he was going there? So we had all the lights in Madison Square Garden turned off during the Star Spangled Banner except the one in the booth, where Raymond Shaw was, and that's how Sinatra found out where Raymond was and that's what happened.

As I said, at first every studio in town had turned down *The Manchurian Candidate*. Nobody wanted to make it. But John Kennedy wanted the movie made. He loved the book. Sinatra and John Kennedy were very close at the time. Once the United Artists people heard that the President wanted the picture made there was no further resistance to it whatsoever. In fact, John Kennedy just wanted to know who was playing the mother. That's all he wanted to know.

*I think* Seven Days In May *is one of John Frankenheimer's best directed movies*

                                        *Kirk Douglas—Actor*

# Seven Days In May (*1964*)

*Burt Lancaster; Kirk Douglas; Fredric March; Ava Gardner;*
*Edmond O'Brien; Martin Balsam; Andrew Duggan; Hugh Marlowe;*
*Whit Bissell; Helen Kleeb; George Macready; Richard Anderson; Bart Burns.*

Edward Lewis, who was Kirk Douglas's partner, called me about doing a television show for the American Civil Liberties Union. During the course of that conversation he told me that he had just bought this book with Kirk Douglas and they thought of me as the director. It was *Seven Days and Nights*. The book opens on a Sunday morning in the parking lot of the Pentagon. The Kirk Douglas character is the duty officer, and he goes in and is greeted by this young naval officer who tells him that all these generals and admirals are betting on the Preakness the next week. And that gradually starts the plot going. I didn't want to do that. I wanted to open the picture with a riot in front of the White House then go into the President's office and show that the President was in terrible shape in the polls which meant starting the picture on a Monday instead of a Sunday.

There was no horse racing in this country on Sundays for years and years, and so the Preakness was always run on Saturday. I realized about three weeks before we starting shooting that I'd lost a day in May. Suddenly I had a picture called *Six Days in May* because I started my picture on Monday and the Preakness was on Saturday. Well, there was this wonderful rewrite guy in town who made these ridiculous bets that always involved hours of his time instead of money. He owed me twelve hours of his time for tennis bets that he had lost. So I called him up and I said, "Charlie, I want to get my twelve hours worth of your time," and I told him what my problem was. He said, "Here's what you do. You have this scene in the Washington Airport where the Senator is leaving and the Colonel, Kirk Douglas, comes to see him. Stage that scene next to a wall and on the wall put a poster that says 'First Sunday Running of the Preakness.' And that's your solution," he said. And that's what I did. And nobody ever picked it up. Nobody. And the picture got great reviews. And even today nobody knows that, but that's how we got the seventh day back.

Kirk Douglas was very friendly with Burt Lancaster and he wanted Burt to play General Scott in the film. I had already done two movies with Burt Lancaster. I didn't want Burt Lancaster again. The whole business of having to cut *The Birdman of Alcatraz* was very painful and he and I had not gotten along that well on either of those two pictures. I wanted Paul Newman to play Colonel Casey, and Kirk to play General Scott. But Kirk really felt very strongly about the fact that he worked very well with Burt Lancaster and he begged me to reconsider and to take Burt Lancaster on as the general. After a lot of talking I agreed to it. Well, it turns out that Burt Lancaster and I got along magnificently well on the picture, and it turned out that it was a very good experience and Burt and I became very good friends.

I have to tell you that I met a man on that film who was to become a lifelong friend and who is, in my opinion, the finest actor I ever worked with and probably the finest man I have ever known, and that was Fredric March. I have never, ever had an experience like working with Fredric March and I probably never will again. I mean, there's just nothing superb you can't say about that man. He came out of retirement to do *The Iceman Cometh* for me, also. That was kind of a highlight in my career, to have worked with him.

# Grand Prix (1966)

*James Garner; Eva Marie Saint; Yves Montand; Toshirô Mifune; Brian Bedford; Jessica Walter; Antonio Sábato; Françoise Hardy; Adolfo Celi; Claude Dauphin; Enzo Fiermonte; Geneviève Page; Jack Watson; Donald O'Brien; Jean Michaud.*

A great love of mine has always been cars. From an early age I wanted to be a racecar driver. I was in France directing a movie called *The Train* and I went to LeMans. I saw people at LeMans screaming and cheering and I also went to a few other Formula One races and realized that I wanted to make a movie about Formula One racing. By this time I was in partnership with Edward Lewis, and he and I put together *Grand Prix*, which was about one season of Formula One racing.

The picture was extremely difficult to make because we were filming on real locations during the actual races. We had our own cars on the circuit and the difficulties were huge but the rewards were great. We were able to take advantage of the huge crowds that they had on race day and we were able to get a tremendous feeling of realism into the movie. We actually were filming the real event, and then cut our cars right into that to match certain things in the real race.

We sent all our drivers to driving school. James Garner was a great athlete and he came out of it a very, very good driver. Yves Montand came out of it very well, as did Antonio Sábato. The only one who didn't was Brian

Bedford, who couldn't drive at all, and we had to double him all the time. But the other guys were really driving their own cars and they did very well. They were very gutsy, those three actors. They really did it.

There were no accidents. That's the wonderful part of that movie. I really take credit for that because I continually talked about safety to the race drivers and to the actors. We had a great crew and we continually checked and double-checked so that nothing bad would happen. We realized that if some terrible accident happened and it was our fault, we would have been thrown off the race tracks and the picture would be over. I mean, when you consider the risks we took to make that picture, if something awful had happened, the picture would have been canceled and MGM would have been out all that money, because it was a very expensive movie.

That picture was a great labor of love for me. It was the best time I've ever had making a movie. I'll never have a time that's that good again, because I love the sport itself. This is something I've wanted to do with my life, and in my next life I hope I am a race driver. I just loved every day of making that movie. It was a great, great feeling.

Robert O'Brien, the chairman of the board at Metro, came over to see me in August and said, "Look, I'm having problems with my board of directors. I've got to have this movie in the theater by December and I'll give you all the support you need because I need this film completed." I arrived back in the United States October 2 with 1,250,000 feet of uncut film. We went to Metro Golden Mayer in Culver City. We had four teams of editors and we worked twenty-four hours a day, seven days a week. We finished the movie, we got it in the theater on December 21 and we won the Academy Award for film editing—and for sound and for sound effects. So it was really back to live television for me.

# The Gypsy Moths (*1969*)

*Burt Lancaster; Deborah Kerr; Gene Hackman; Scott Wilson; William Windom; Bonnie Bedelia; Sheree North; Carl Reindel; Ford Rainey; John Napier.*

*Gypsy Moths* was a project that Edward Lewis found. It was from a novel by a man named James Drought and we got William Hanley to adapt it into a screenplay. We had seen Gene Hackman in *Bonnie and Clyde* and thought he was brilliant, and one of the keys was casting Gene Hackman in that picture. If you look at that movie, Gene Hackman is really the engine that makes that movie work. He's brilliant in it. I think, parenthetically, that Gene Hackman and Fredric March are the two best movie actors I've ever worked with. Gene Hackman is a brilliant movie actor and he was fabulous in that picture.

Burt Lancaster, again because of the relationship I had with him, played the part of Mike Rettig. The mistake we made is that we kill Burt off twenty-five minutes before the movie was over, which we shouldn't have done. But I love that movie. Deborah Kerr was just a joy to work with. We had very good cast. I had an excellent time making that movie in Kansas.

# The Horsemen (1971)

*Omar Sharif; Leigh Taylor-Young; Tom Tryon; Mark Colleano; David De Keyser;
Peter Jeffrey; Jack Palance; Eric Pohlmann; Mohammad Shamsi; Alan Webb.*

*The Horsemen* is about the men who played a game that came down to us from Genghis Khan called buzkashi. The only guy I felt who could really do the part was Omar Sharif and we were very fortunate to get him. We got Jack Palance to play Tursen, Omar Sharif's father. For me it was a reunion of sorts with Jack Palance because we had done several television shows together, including *The Last Tycoon* on *Playhouse 90* and I had great, great admiration for Jack.

We filmed a great deal of the movie in Afghanistan and it was a thrilling place to be. It's so magnificent and so beautiful and yet so savage. Once you got there, you realized why nobody had ever been able to beat these people. I mean, if the Russians had ever asked me, I would have told them, "Don't go in there, because, boy, they're a kind of people that are just unbeatable." It's absolutely amazing.

The sequence involving the horses is a game called buzkashi. Genghis Kahn used this game to get his warriors ready for battle. The object of the game is that a carcass of a stuffed goat or sheep is placed in a circle. One of the riders lifts that carcass out, rides it around the pole which is like five miles away, comes back, and drops it back in the circle. The one who does that wins the game.

About a year before I got to Afghanistan they had finally agreed to outlaw knives in this game because too many riders were dying. So knives were illegal but the whips were not. And the violence—I have never ever been involved with anything that violent. The guys are huge. I mean, they all look like defensive linemen for the Pittsburgh Steelers. I mean, they are about 250 to 300 pounds—the strongest men I've ever known. They could pick up this 250-pound carcass stuffed with sand just like you or I would pick up a small stone or a paper cup.

Edward Lewis arranged for us to film in Afghanistan. We got there in June and it was very hot, so we had to start early in the morning, quit during the middle of the day, and come back in the afternoon. Now, when I needed spectators in *Grand Prix* I held a raffle and thirty-five thousand Italians came out because I was giving away two cars. I tried to use the same technique in Afghanistan but the Afghans told me it would never work there. It may have worked in Italy, but it will never work in Afghanistan. We were gonna give away a Volkswagen as first prize. We hauled it through the streets and we had announcements on Afghan radio and loudspeakers all over the place.

One day I left my house at 4:00 in the morning to get to the buzkashi but I couldn't get near it. The road was wall to wall people. Three hundred thousand people showed up. Three hundred thousand! We couldn't get near the actual film location. We had to call the army out to disperse the people. There were no telephones so I couldn't even communicate with Columbia Pictures to tell them what had happened. We waited for a day so the army could get some order restored and then we went back in to film.

We had these huge savage men on these horses and none of them spoke English. I had four interpreters, two who spoke English and two who spoke French. I would say what I wanted these men to hear in both English and French, but it didn't make any difference because when it was translated they had no idea what I was talking about. None of these men had ever seen a movie, let alone been in one. They had no idea what we were talking about. They had no idea why they had to pick up this calf and then stop. To them they were there to play a game, and that's what they did—they were professional buzkashi players. It was impossible to explain to them what we wanted to them to do and they couldn't understand all the Panavision camera equipment. But I'll tell you something, those men were the toughest and fiercest men and probably the nicest that I've ever known. I have always maintained that if you got eleven of those guys over here and put them in American National Football League uniforms and told them that they had four plays to get the ball over the goal line, there is nobody that could stop them. They were just that tough.

## The Love of His Life

I think I should start off talking about my wife, Evans Evans, by saying that we've been together on a regular basis since 1961, which in this business is a very rare thing. I think I'd give 75 percent of the credit to her. I was doing a play in New York in 1959 and I was married to somebody else at the time, unhappily, I might add. There was a part in this play for a very vivacious, beautiful girl, and I had seen Evans in *Dark at the Top of the Stairs* the year before, where she won an award for the most promising newcomer on Broadway. The producers kept saying to me, "Well, what we need in this part is somebody like Evans Evans." And I said to them, "Well fellows, I have a better idea for you, why don't we get Evans Evans?" And they said, "Well, do you think that she'd do it?" Evans was in Jacksonville, Florida, and she came up and she read for the part and she did it. And she was wonderful. Unfortunately the rest of the play was not as good as she was and the play closed in Boston.

She and I saw each other when she got back from Boston but it was one of those things that just didn't seem to have any future to it. She went to England to do a play, and I went to California to do a television show of *The Snows of Kilimanjaro* and later on film *The Young Savages*. In the meantime, I left the person to whom I was married and Evans came back to the United States and we saw each other briefly in New York. Then I went on to do *The Birdman of Alcatraz*. I called her and she came out to California for the weekend in January 1961, and, for all practical purposes, never left. For me, it's obviously the most important relationship I've ever had in my life. She's an extraordinary woman.

I want to say a bit more about Evans. Being married to a movie director is really a tough go for anybody. I mean, she's had to pick up and move to all these various locations. She's had to go through really great times and really terrible times, and she's had to be the backbone in this relationship a lot. There have been great moments of happiness, but there have also been great periods of despair, and through it all she's been there, she's been a constant. I think she's really one of the big reasons I'm here today. I just wanted to add that.

## The French Connection II (1975)

*Gene Hackman; Fernando Rey; Bernard Fresson; Jean-Pierre Castaldi; Charles Milot; Cathleen Nesbitt; Pierre Collet; Alexandre Fabre; Philippe Léotard; Jacques Dynam; Raoul Delfosse; Patrick Floersheim; André Penvern; Ed Lauter; Daniel Vérité.*

Regarding *French Connection II*, after Bobby Kennedy's death I went through a very bad personal period. I went to live in France and I took about a year

---

NOTE: When Senator Robert Kennedy was shot at the Ambassador Hotel in Los Angeles on June 5, 1968, it was his good friend John Frankenheimer who had personally driven him there that day.

and a half off from the movie business. I went to cooking school, and I wanted to just fully live my life and I had a wonderful time doing that. I loved France, I loved living there, but it was not very good for my movie career.

*French Connection II* was proposed to me by Gene Hackman, who asked me to come up with a story. They had the title and they had the actor and I came up with the story with a writer named Robert Dillon. The idea was very simple, which was to make Popeye Doyle a dope addict and to bring him to France and he'd be like a fish out of water. At the time I wanted to go back to France and make another movie so it worked out well. I had a wonderful crew there, I spoke the language, and it seemed a natural thing for me to do, so I went over and I did it. I'm very glad I did.

# Black Sunday (1977)

*Robert Shaw; Bruce Dern; Marthe Keller; Fritz Weaver; Steven Keats; Bekim Fehmiu; Michael V. Gazzo; William Daniels; Walter Gotell; Victor Campos; Joseph Robbie; Robert Wussler; Pat Summerall; Tom Brookshier; Walter Brooke.*

*Black Sunday* was a very difficult movie to make, much like *Grand Prix*, because we had to go and film this real event, in this particular case the Super Bowl, and we didn't have any chance to redo it. There was that whole element of the blimp and the Super Bowl. I think the movie as a thriller works very, very well, and it was based on a novel by Thomas Harris.

## Working with Crowds

One of the problems we had was working with large crowds. One of the secrets of working with large crowds is to have a great assistant director, and I had a great assistant director named Jerry Ziesmer on *Black Sunday*. I also had Enrico Isacco on *Grand Prix* and James Sbardellati on *Andersonville* and *The Burning Season*. I find that these three men have been invaluable to me. I could not have done *Black Sunday* without Jerry Ziesmer. He was just incredible dealing with the crowds. You have to figure out what you want the crowd to do and then shoot enough film so that you're sure you have it. You have to get the crowd working with you, and you have to know where it fits in terms of the story. Certainly that was true in *Black Sunday, Grand Prix,* and *Andersonville*. Those are three movies that could not have been done without huge crowds because they're the background to everything that happens. It's difficult working with huge groups of people because, again, if they don't feel like cooperating with you there's absolutely nothing you can do about it.

*John's a very intelligent director and respects the intelligence of the people he works with. I think he expects the actor to expand, experiment, and do more with the part than what's written on the page. Some directors don't encourage that, but John does.*

*Roy Scheider—Actor*

# 52 Pick-Up (1986)

*Roy Scheider; Ann-Margret; Vanity; John Glover; Robert Trebor;
Lonny Chapman; Kelly Preston; Doug McClure; Clarence Williams, III; Alex Henteloff;
Michelle Walker; Philip Bartko; Tom Byron; Harvey Cowen; Ron Jeremy.*

I read *52 Pick-Up* on a trip from London to California, and I immediately called my agent to find out who owned it. It turned out that Cannon Films owned it and it turns out that they wanted me to do the picture.

The first thing I did was to cast the very talented and beautiful Kelly Preston as the girl who gets shot. I kind of did it exactly the way Elmore Leonard described it in his book and shot it on 16 mm. I put it on videotape and played it on the television screen and reflected Roy Scheider off the television screen as he was watching. It was a brutal scene to watch, but critical to the story.

I had some extraordinary actors in that picture. I had John Glover, who was just absolutely brilliant as Alan Raimy, and Clarence Williams as Bobby Shy. I couldn't have asked for a more cooperative and professional actress than Kelly Preston. We shot that whole killing sequence in a couple of hours. And the Elmore Leonard dialogue is so well written and the situation was so highly charged that I can honestly tell you that it was not a difficult scene to do. It was a difficult scene to watch, but not a difficult scene to do. I think the key to it was putting that board in front of her chest, where you really saw what those bullets do. Yeah, that was very, very vivid. And again, that was straight from Elmore Leonard's book.

Roy Scheider is one of those very special people. He's a wonderful actor and he is equally a wonderful guy. Crews love Roy. He sets an example for everybody on the set. Roy Scheider makes one's life better. There are certain people you are privileged to know in life that are life givers. Roy is a life giver. He just makes you a better person by the very fact that you know him. He tries everything he can to make the picture better, to make the picture as good as it can be.

# The Fourth War (*1990*)

*Roy Scheider; Jürgen Prochnow; Tim Reid; Lara Harris; Harry Dean Stanton;*
*Dale Dye; Bill MacDonald; David Palffy; Neil Grahn; Ernie Jackson;*
*Ron Campbell; John Dodds; Richard Durven; Harold Hecht, Jr., Alice Pesta.*

In the case of *The Fourth War*, we had a wonderful story which was based on the fact that there was terrific tension on the East German/Czechoslovakian border. Unfortunately, by the time the picture was released it became a historical movie, because there was no East German/Czechoslovakian border. So the picture was not about anything that anybody could relate to that was happening at the moment because it had all been resolved by the time the picture came out. Also, I don't think that the distribution company, in this particular case Cannon, spent nearly enough money to promote the picture. So the picture never really had a chance because they never really did the publicity necessary to make the public aware that the picture existed. It's a great disappoint to me because it's a good movie.

# Against the Wall (*TV, 1994*)

*Kyle MacLachlan; Samuel L. Jackson; Clarence Williams, III;*
*Frederic Forrest; Harry Dean Stanton; Philip Bosco; Tom Bower;*
*Anne Heche; Carmen Argenziano; Peter Murnik; Steve Harris;*
*David Ackroyd; Mark Cabus; Bruce Evers; Joey Anderson.*

*Against the Wall* was a huge turning point in my career. When I was asked to do *Against the Wall*, things had not been going well for me. I had made a picture called *The Year of the Gun* that came out and did no business. I had done a couple of pictures before that, including *The Fourth War*, which for one reason or another did not do well. I was getting older and I was very acutely aware that there was not that much demand for me. It was a period that I referred to earlier as a period of great despair. Because I don't mind the idea of retiring but I don't want to be told that I'm gonna retire. I wanted to work.

Jonathan Axelrod, George Axelrod's son, was a young man in 1968 to whom I gave a job on a movie I did called *The Fixer*. I took him to Hungary with me as an intern. He was sixteen and it turned his life around and he proceeded to pursue the motion picture business and the agency business. He was a quite well-known television producer with a contract to do a picture for HBO. He called me and he said, "Look, we've got this cable movie, you probably won't do it because it's for far less money at a far less budget than anything you've ever done, but we think it's a great script and we think you would be fabulous for it. Would you read it?" So I read it and it was the best material that I had read in a long, long time.

I called this friend of mine to whom I'm very close and I said, "Clancy, I've just been offered this television movie for no money and no budget. I really don't think I should do this, do you?" And he said, "No. You should turn it down. And then what you should do is sit by the telephone, wait for it to ring, and think about the good old days." He said, "That's what you should do." Well, I immediately picked up the phone and called HBO and said, "I'm your man." So I set out to do this movie.

I had worked with a young cameraman by the name of John Leonetti on the HBO series *Tales from the Crypt*. And I took an art director that I'd never worked with before, by the name of Michael Hannah, and set out to make the movie. We had thirty days to shoot the whole movie and no budget. But what we had was a good script and we had people that really wanted to work.

I had wanted to work with Clarence Williams again after *52 Pick-Up* and *Tales from the Crypt,* so he was the first person I cast. I was very lucky to get Sam Jackson, Fred Forrest, Kyle MacLachlan, Harry Dean Stanton, and Anne Heche, as well as some of the other actors that we got. We went to Tennessee to shoot it and I decided, quite honestly, that I was really just gonna go for broke with this thing. I had nothing to lose. I tried to get a tremendous amount of energy into it. I tried to make it with the same kind of style, almost, that I had made *Grand Prix* and *Seven Days in May* and *Black Sunday.* I tried to get as much reality into it as I could. I tried to get as much tension and I tried to get as much drama into that whole Attica episode as I possibly could. Did I mention my editor, Lee Percy, who I had collaborated with before?

It was one of those classic cases of a group of people coming together, much like happened in *Manchurian Candidate.* A group of people who came together at a certain time in their lives and did some of the best work that they've ever done, because a movie is an ensemble thing. A movie is not one man going out and making a movie. It can't be done. I think that it's a group of people coming together, dedicated to work together and to do their best work together. And luckily, like *Manchurian Candidate,* that happened with *Against the Wall.* It turned out that we made a movie that I think we're all very, very proud of. It was a huge turning point in my life. I mean the HBO executives were wonderful—Bob Cooper and Hutch Parker were terribly supportive and the whole thing really was a very pleasant experience.

There was another element that has to be mentioned in this and that was the writer, Ron Hutchinson. He wrote the script of *Attica*, *Against the Wall*, and he wrote the script of *The Burning Season* after some other writers had tried it. Ron Hutchinson and Rod Serling are the two writers that I have had the best relationship with. Ron Hutchinson's probably better than Rod Serling and he is a very important element in my life.

# The Burning Season (*TV, 1994*)

*Raul Julia; Sonia Braga; Carmen Argenziano; Kamala Lopez; Luis Guzmán;*
*Nigel Havers; Tomas Milian; Esai Morales; Tony Plana; Marco Rodríguez;*
*Edward James Olmos; Gerardo Albarran; Terrence Beasor; Carlos Carrasco;*
*Jonathan Carrasco; Alberto Isaac; Jeffrey Licon; Loló Navarro; Tony Perez;*
*José Pérez; Briana Romero; Valentin Santana; Jorge Viteri.*

Working in Mexico was horrible. But it was the only place that we could make the movie. We had to have the rain forest and it was impossible, for political reasons, to shoot the movie in Brazil. The locations existed in Mexico and we went down and did it. But you knew, when you signed on to do a picture about the rain forest and about the rubber tappers in Brazil, that you weren't gonna end up at the Hotel de Paris in Monte Carlo. You knew that. So we were prepared for the worst and we got the worst. It was very primitive, it was horrible conditions, but we nevertheless did not lose track of the fact as to why we were down there. We were dedicated to making that movie and dedicated to doing the best job we could. Luckily, Raul Julia never lost track of why he was down there because I think his performance is very special. He was a great man and there's no doubt about the fact that without Raul we would not have had nearly the movie that we ended up with.

Roy Scheider is a very dear friend of mine. Roy and I spend quite a bit of time together whenever we can. I told him that this was my next project and I told him that there were three people whom HBO was discussing for the part of Chico Mendez. One of these three was Raul Julia, and Roy said to me, "Well, by far and away the best actor of all these guys is Raul, and you really should go out of your way to make sure that you get him." So I took his advice and I got him.

# Andersonville (*TV, 1996*)

*Jarrod Emick; Frederic Forrest; Ted Marcoux; Carmen Argenziano; Jayce Bartok; Frederick Coffin; Cliff De Young; Denis Forest; Justin Henry; Tony Higgins; Kris Kamm; Andrew Kavovit; Olek Krupa; William H. Macy; Matt McGrath.*

*Andersonville* was a project that was written by David Rintels, and it's based on true incidents that happened at this prisoner of war camp during the Civil War. It was a huge undertaking and a very difficult subject because it certainly does not have a happy ending. When you do a picture about Andersonville you try to do a picture about human dignity, courage, nobility, and hope. I think that's what we did. I think you end up caring a great deal about those characters.

We had extraordinary actors—Frederic Forrest, Jarrod Emick, Ted Marcoux—actors that are not terribly well known but I think will be after this picture comes out. And Michael Hanan, the production designer, did a monumental job in reproducing this prison camp. The set itself was nine acres in diameter, which was immense, and of course we had to have thousands of extras in order to film this, and just from a budgetary standpoint and from a production standpoint it would be extremely difficult to make under any circumstances. The Turner Entertainment people were very supportive and the verdict is not in on that picture. I hope that it's as good as we all think it is. But again, that still is to be seen.

## Making Movies for Cable

There were good things and bad things about making cable movies. Like somebody once said, there's no free lunch. The good things far outnumber the bad things. The good things, certainly in the case of HBO and lately with Turner, are that the subject matter is so good. These companies are doing movies that major studios will not make. They're doing controversial material and the only market for that is cable. It's material that is attractive to me. And the people with whom we've been working at these networks have just been great and very supportive. I've had very good relationships with these companies. I've had complete creative freedom, complete artistic control. There's been no interference. Those things are very important to a director.

---

NOTE: This interview was conducted after filming of *Andersonville* had been completed, but the film had yet to premiere on TNT.

The bad side is that you have very limited money to work with and the shooting schedules are usually very short, so you cannot make a mistake. You cannot go out and mess up the scene and hope that you're going to have the time to go back and re-shoot and fix it. You have to be right the first time. And for me that's like going back to live TV. I like making movies for cable or for studios. I love making movies and that's what I want to continue to do. The climate seems to be very receptive to that right now. And I'm very grateful for what I do. It's been a wonderful business for me. I've had a ter-rifically long run at it. I've been able to do things and be places and meet people and just have a life that I would have never had at any other busi-ness, doing anything else that I might have chosen to do. Nothing would have ever been like this. We all bitch and moan about this business but there is no other business where I could have had the kind of life that I have.

## Is the Industry Changing?

Quite honestly, I don't believe it's changed at all. It's always been difficult to get movies made. It's always been a business and it's always been run by very strong people. I don't think there is really that much of a change. Look at John Calley, Mike Marcus, Frank Mancuso, and Sherry Lansing. These are very creative people and they love movies. Just as Harry Cohn and Jack Warner were monsters, lest anyone forget. A lot of those guys treated peo-ple really badly. There's this great kind of romantic lure attached to these men now, but a lot of them were really horrible human beings and I don't think there's anybody like that running a studio today. Most of the people that I know that are running the studios are really kind of nice people. They're the kind of people that in most cases I'd like to go out and have dinner with. And I think they genuinely, for the most part, there are always exceptions, but for the most part these people want to do good movies. No-body wants to go out there and make a bad movie.

## How Do I Get a Job in the Film Industry?

This is a young business. You walk into any studio and most of the develop-ment executives are in their twenties. How they get these jobs, I don't know. I have no formula as to how to go get a job in the movie business. But I do find that many of the young people that are in responsible positions are very bright. If I had one complaint, it's that a lot of them have no sense of history whatsoever. They have no sense of what went before. They have no sense of who the great directors were before their generation. And I'm not just trying to be self-serving by saying that, but they really have no knowledge of

William Wyler or Fred Zinnerman or Carol Reed, some of the great men that made movies. Those men influenced the way movies are made today.

The object for somebody like me making a picture today is to make it a picture that appeals to a crossover audience, not only the kids, but also to the people in their twenties, thirties, forties, fifties, and sixties that will come out of their houses and take a look at a movie that I make. That's what I hope to be able to do. But it's a very unforgiving audience. It's an audience that has a very short attention span. Today's audiences are very visually oriented from MTV and from constant exposure to television and visual things from the time they were infants. It's a tough audience to play for.

## His Parting Words

I feel that my job is to create an atmosphere where creative people can do their best work. In other words, I have to create an atmosphere where these people feel safe, where they feel respected, and where they feel that they can contribute. I cannot work with hostility around me. I can't do that. That first movie I did, the crew hated me and I hated them. I never wanted to go back and I never wanted to do another movie. I have to have people around me that want to work hard, that I feel care as much as I do about what we're doing. Once I find those people I want them to do their best work and I want to encourage that and make them feel safe and make them feel respected and make them feel that their contribution is important, which it is.

I can't predict the future of the industry. I can't even predict what's gonna happen tomorrow. I am not some pundit that people ask what's gonna happen five years from now. I have no idea. To me, there is always gonna be an audience for a good story and that's really what I'm interested in. My business is not predicting the future. My business is not trying to forecast what's going to happen electronically or digitally or anything like that, because a lot of that's out of my hands. What's in my hands is the ability to sharpen my skills, which will enable me to tell the story that I'm hired to tell in the best possible way. That means learning to deal with all the tools that are at my disposal, whatever they might be. So I have to be a chameleon with that stuff but I can't predict what's gonna happen.

An amateur is someone who does something when they want to and only when they want to. A professional is somebody that does something when they don't want to do it. Okay? That's the difference between an amateur and a professional. There are many times on a movie set when I have gone out there when I haven't wanted to go out there. I'm a professional movie director so I had to do it. There's no time I have ever cooked a gourmet meal when I didn't want to. I only do that kind of stuff when I want to do it. Nobody pays me for cooking. Nobody pays me for playing tennis. I cook because I want to cook. I like to cook. But I'm an amateur cook.

# Director Filmography

*The Young Stranger* (1957)
*The Young Savages* (1961)
*Birdman of Alcatraz* (1962)
*The Manchurian Candidate* (1962)
*All Fall Down* (1962)
*Seven Days in May* (1964)
*The Train* (1964)
*Seconds* (1966)
*Grand Prix* (1966)
*The Fixer* (1968)
*The Gypsy Moths* (1969)
*The Extraordinary Seaman* (1969)
*I Walk the Line* (1970)
*The Horsemen* (1971)
*Story of a Love Story* (1973)
*The Iceman Cometh* (1973)
*99 and 44/100% Dead* (1974)
*The French Connection II* (1975)
*Black Sunday* (1977)
*Prophecy* (1979)
*The Challenge* (1982)
*The Holcroft Covenant* (1985)
*52 Pick-Up* (1986)
*Across the River and Into the Trees* (1987)
*Riviera* (TV—as Alan Smithee, 1987)
*Dead-Bang* (1989)
*The Fourth War* (1990)
*Year of the Gun* (1991)

*The Burning Season* (TV, 1994)
*Against the Wall* (TV, 1994)
*Andersonville* (TV, 1996)
*The Island of Dr. Moreau* (1996)
*George Wallace* (TV, 1997)
*Ronin* (1998)
*Reindeer Games* (1999)

# Awards

**Bodil Festival**
*Seven Days in May*, Best American Film, 1965
*Seven Days in May*, Best Film, 1965

**Directors Guild of America, USA**
*George Wallace*, Outstanding Directorial Achievement in Dramatic Specials (nominated), 1998

**Emmy Awards**
*George Wallace*, Outstanding Director for a Miniseries or a Movie, 1998
*George Wallace*, Outstanding Miniseries (shared with Mark Carliner, Julian Krainin, Ethel Winant, Mitch Engel, James Sbardellati; nominated), 1998
*Andersonville*, Outstanding Individual Achievement in Directing for a Miniseries or Special, 1996
*Andersonville*, Outstanding Miniseries (shared with Ethel Winant, David W. Rintels, Diane Smith; nominated), 1996
*The Burning Season*, Outstanding Individual Achievement in Directing for a Miniseries or Special, 1995
*The Burning Season*, Outstanding Made for Television Movie (shared with David Puttnam, Thomas M. Hammel; nominated), 1995

**Ft. Lauderdale International Film Festival**
President Award, The Robert Wise Director of Distinction Award, 1998

**Golden Globes, USA**
*Seven Days in May*, Best Motion Picture Director (nominated), 1965

**Razzie Awards**
*The Island of Dr. Moreau*, Worst Director (nominated), 1997

**San Diego World Film Festival**
Lifetime Achievement Award, 1998

# The Films of Lawrence Kasdan

Lawrence Kasdan was born January 14, 1949, in Miami, Florida. He was raised in West Virginia and grew up in a family in which writing was encouraged. He attended the University of Michigan, supporting himself with a series of writing awards while he studied English literature. He then went on to earn a master's degree in education.

For the next five years, Kasdan worked as an advertising copywriter in Detroit and Los Angeles while trying to sell his screenplays. The sixth screenplay he submitted, *The Bodyguard,* was the first to be purchased, in 1977.

His next screenplay, *Continental Divide,* caught the attention of Steven Spielberg, who introduced the writer to George Lucas. Spielberg and Lucas asked Kasdan to write the screenplay for *Raiders of the Lost Ark.* When screenwriter Leigh Brackett died before finishing the script to the *Star Wars* sequel, *The Empire Strikes Back,* Kasdan was asked to take over as writer. He went on to co-write *Return of the Jedi* with Lucas.

Kasdan made his critically acclaimed directorial debut with *Body Heat,* in which he cast two little-known actors, William Hurt and Kathleen Turner, in the lead roles. Next he directed *The Big Chill,* which he co-wrote with Barbara Benedek, and which was nominated for three Academy Awards, including Best Picture.

Kasdan made his theatrical debut in the fall of 1995 as director of John Patrick Shanley's *Four Dogs & a Bone.* This dark comedy, an ironic look at the seamier side of Hollywood, starred Elizabeth Perkins, Martin Short, Brendan Fraser, and Parker Posey, and was the inaugural play of the newly renovated and renamed Geffen Playhouse.

Kasdan chooses his film projects very carefully, preferring to direct material that he himself has authored. His attention to detail is evident in each of his films and his love of language is clear in the dialogue he so eloquently writes.

*He doesn't spend a lot of time talking in a conversation at lunch or whatever. He spends a lot of time asking questions. He keeps pursuing tough questions and there's a side of that that's very charming and yet very searching, and I like that quality that I see in his movies. There's a lot of ways in which he's really enamored with human nature and human behavior and human eccentricities.*

Bill Pullman—Actor

# The Conversation

I was born in Miami Beach, Florida, but my family moved to Pittsburgh and then on to West Virginia when I was very young. So my childhood was really in West Virginia. It was a small, regular, American kind of steel town. I felt very fortunate to have had a regular American childhood in the fifties. It was a safe place, where you owned the town if you had a bicycle. I saw only American movies there.

My family had a history of writing. My father had written in college and my mother had also wanted to be a writer. Neither were able to make a career of it, but there was a feeling in the household that writing was the legitimate thing to do. It was a legitimate way to express yourself. You take the feelings you're having, and every child, every person, is boiling with those feelings, and in our household there was an understanding that writing was a way to deal with those feelings. So from the time I was very young it was considered the legitimate thing to do.

When I was thirteen years old, I went to see *Lawrence of Arabia* with my brother, who was already very interested in film. He was five years older than I was. He was about to go off to Harvard. I was already taken with American movies at that time. American films about men bonding, doing brave things together. Those things stirred and touched me. And I was seeing all other kinds of American movies. I just loved being in a dark movie theater. When I saw *Lawrence of Arabia* in 1962, it struck me in a way the other movies did not. I began to think that that was how I would like to spend my life.

I went on and had a normal high school life in West Virginia. I continued to write, as I was encouraged to do around my house. In high school

I got a lot of recognition and approval of my writing. When I came to choose a university, I chose the University of Michigan, where Arthur Miller had gone to school and had won an award. I had no money. I thought that maybe these awards would help put me through school. I was already a pretty decent writer. So I chose to go where Arthur Miller had gone and entered that same contest and won it enough times to really make it possible to go through school with a combination of scholarships and loans. But the writing award, which I won four times, really made it possible for me to afford college.

Very early, I shifted from writing short stories and theater writing to screenplays, because I already knew I wanted to make movies. In the late sixties, many screenwriters in Hollywood were getting to be directors. I thought, well, that will be the route I'll take. I didn't want to be a cinematographer; I didn't want to be an assistant director. I thought, I can already write and I'll see if I can turn that into directing. So I began to write screenplays while at the University of Michigan. I didn't get any response to them, really. I had no way to get them read. When they were read, they weren't well received. But I continued to write them.

I graduated from the University of Michigan and I couldn't decide what I wanted to do. Actually, I was accepted to UCLA, in the film school, not in the directing program, but in the writing program. I came out to Los Angeles alone and my girlfriend went to New York. I did not like being in the writing program. I had no money and it was a struggle anyway, so I thought if I couldn't be in the directing program, I can write anywhere. So I went back and worked in a record store. I continued to write screenplays. My girlfriend came back and lived there and then we were married.

The time came when I had to make a living. I had gotten a masters degree in education, thinking I would teach high school to support myself. But there were no high school English teaching jobs. It was almost as hard to get that kind of work as being a movie director. So I took a job in an advertising agency through someone I had met in Detroit. The work, which was copy writing, came easily to me. I had success right away. But after six months I was very frustrated doing that kind of work. I wound up doing it for another four and a half years, in Detroit and eventually in Los Angeles. I had a son and I had to support the family.

All during this time I was writing screenplays without success. Eventually I wrote a screenplay called *The Bodyguard*. I wrote it in 1975 and I was able to get an agent after a long time trying. At the same time I got a job in Los Angeles and moved my family out here but was still working in advertising. *Bodyguard* was sent around town by the agent and was rejected sixty-seven times over a two-year period. I did not want to work in television, which my agent had suggested. I felt I was already doing work I didn't want to do and I didn't want a new version. So I continued to write screenplays without success.

After two years, someone finally got interested in *The Bodyguard*. John Calley, who was then the head of Warner Bros., paid a small amount of money to option the script for a year. It was enough money for me to quit my job. I had written two more scripts in the meantime. The second of those scripts was called *The Continental Divide*, and unlike everything else I had written, this script became very popular. There was a bidding war for it. Steven Spielberg wound up as the person who bought *Continental Divide* to produce but not direct. He paid a lot of money for it. Now I was really free to write and have some security for my family.

When I met Steven, he said, "I'm going to do an adventure film with George Lucas. We don't know all that much about it, but I'd like you to come meet George. I've shown him *Continental Divide* and he's very interested in you writing this adventure film for us." George and Steven and Frank Marshall, who wound up producing the film, all got together for the first time. George said, "We're going to do a movie that's like the old serials. I don't know too much about it but the hero is named after my dog, Indiana. I know the hero wears a fedora and a leather jacket and carries a whip."

Phil Kaufman, a wonderful director, had told George a story his dentist had told him thirty years earlier about the Lost Ark of the Covenant. At one time Phil was involved with this movie and he had come up with the Lost Ark of the Covenant as being the piece that our hero would be chasing in this adventure.

Lucas said, "I know what it's called. It's called *Raiders of the Lost Ark*. That's about it. That's everything I know. Steven and I would like you to come work with us and figure out the story and write the screenplay." I, of course, was thrilled. George had just made *Star Wars* and Steven had just made *Close Encounters*. So we went off to a house in the Valley, and wrote *Raiders*.

The truth is the first five scripts I had written were not very good and after I became a selling screenwriter I had no desire to bring them out and sell them. But when you write something, you think it's great. The day you finish, you think it's wonderful. So I couldn't understand why from 1968 to 1977 no one seemed interested in what I did. After a while you begin to think that maybe they know something you don't, that there's a reason for it. The truth of the matter is, which I know now, there is no reason for it. It's completely arbitrary. The hardest thing that anyone in Hollywood ever does is take a chance on an unknown quantity. Because I was unknown, it was very easy to dismiss it as just another screenplay. Once I started to sell things, everything I wrote was of interest to people. So it's not always based on the work itself. It's based on a lot of factors.

But I was desperate to make this move into the business and I knew it had to be through writing. So when *The Bodyguard* finally attracted the attention of Warner Bros., it was a great moment in my life, because it meant that all this frustration would come to an end. It meant I could write movies during the day. I had written only at night or during the weekends and it was a terrible life because it left very little free time. I had a young boy and wanted to spend time with him but I felt guilty if I wasn't working on the screenplays.

I should back up a bit. When I met Steven Spielberg he was not that much older than I and he was already one of the biggest directors in the world. It was very easy to relate to him. I met him on the backlot of Universal, where Bob Zemeckis was making his first film, *I Want To Hold Your Hand*, which Steven produced. Bob was Steven's protégé. To this day, I always have a thrill when I'm allowed onto a studio lot. This was one of the first times I was allowed on the backlot and they were shooting. It was very exciting to me. Bob Zemeckis was actually a year or so younger than Steven and Steven was only a year older than I was and had already made *Jaws* and *Close Encounters*.

Steven said, "I love *Continental Divide* and we want you to write this adventure film, but don't let George steal you away because I'm afraid he's going to get you to do the sequel to *American Graffiti*." I had been desperate to do anything for years, so to say I wouldn't let George distract me and make me write a sequel to one of my favorite films of all time . . . But I was dutiful and said, "Don't worry, I won't be distracted." So that was when I entered the world of Steven and George. I worked on *Raiders* alone, pretty much, in Steven's office for six months while he went off to do *1941*.

When I was done with it, I took it to George and he put it on his desk and said, "Let's go out to lunch." Leigh Bracket, who had been writing the first draft to the *Star Wars* sequel, had died just then. George now had no one to write it, and he wanted me to come in and work on it. I said, "You haven't read *Raiders* yet." He said, "Well, I'll read it tonight and if I hate it,

I'll call you tomorrow and withdraw this offer. But," he said, "I just get a feeling about people and it's definitely right." He called me the next day to say he'd read *Raiders* and he loved it, so he wanted me to go ahead on *Empire*. So, much to my surprise, I wound up working with George for about a year and a half, solid, between writing *Raiders*, writing *Empire*, and doing revisions on *Raiders*.

Empire was actually made before *Raiders*. That was my first credit. *Empire* came out in 1980. Steven didn't get around to making *Raiders* until 1981. But it was an intense exposure to George, more than Steven, because we spent so many hours writing the two scripts. George's world is special and separate from Hollywood. He has a certain attitude about Hollywood and movies. He was about to give up directing, in fact. He didn't like it as much as he thought he would. He was more interested in getting certain kinds of movies made than he was with the day-to-day arguing with actors and with production problems.

But I couldn't relate to that. All I wanted to do in this world was direct. But George was a wonderful influence. He was very strong about the rights of a director. He had a terrible fight with Universal about the release of *American Graffiti,* where they had cut seven minutes out of the film and he never forgave them or the guy who was running Universal at the time. I asked him once where he had gotten the confidence to argue with the head of a studio when he had not had a hit yet. His only previous picture had been *THX 1138*. And yet he had been violently, wonderfully strong in his argument with the head of Universal. But he said to me, "You know, you have to act as though you have the power even when you don't, because it's your work. When they said to me that I had to take seven minutes out of *American Graffiti*, it's as though they said to me, that's a cute baby but we don't like its pinky so we think we'll just chop it off. You have to have that fierce protectiveness about your work. They have no right, just because they paid for the movie."

That made an enormous impression on me and has affected me ever since. So when I made my own first picture several years ago—in fact, George was the sponsor for it—the head of the studio said I had to have the hero shave his moustache the day before we started shooting. I said, "Why?" They said, "Because he looks sleazy." I said, "He's supposed to look sleazy." They said, "Look, we don't want to argue about this. It's our movie and your first film and we want the moustache shaved off." I said, "Well, I can't do that." They said, "Let's not talk about it anymore," and hung up.

I started shooting the next day without shaving the guy's moustache, because I believed that it was my movie and my responsibility and it was my name on the movie and that the moustache was correct, and I never heard a negative word from the studio head. It made a huge impression on me because I saw, in fact, it *was* my writing and if I felt strongly enough about it, it would be okay. It all comes from George. George was very generous with me creatively and with his ideas and his philosophy, and generous with the deals that he gave me even though I was an unknown writer on *Raiders* and *Star Wars*.

And after I had made my first film, *Body Heat*, George asked me as a favor to come back and write *Return of the Jedi*. I had no desire to do that because I no longer wanted to write for anyone else. I had been very lucky with the directors that made my screenplays and yet I found even that very frustrating. I didn't want anyone changing my work. I wanted only to write and direct my own films. So when George asked me to come back as a favor and write *Return of the Jedi*, I was reluctant to do it. But he'd been so helpful to me that I did it as a favor and it turned out to be a bit of a lark and good fun. We put the script together in a very short amount of time.

George was an enormous influence on me. He had an inside Hollywood feeling about him that was very useful to me. He was very free and fair with his collaborators, something that I've tried to do in my career. He's a fun-loving person that makes the films a real joy. That's been terribly important to me. And Steven and I have continued to be friends all these years. He has been an inspiration in his sheer ambition for filmmaking. And I'll always be grateful to him.

# Body Heat (1981)

*William Hurt; Kathleen Turner; Richard Crenna; Ted Danson; J.A. Preston; Mickey Rourke; Kim Zimmer; Jane Hallaren; Lanna Saunders; Carola McGuinness; Michael Ryan; Larry Marko; Deborah Lucchesi; Lynn Hallowell; Thom Sharp.*

I had just begun to sell the screenplays *Bodyguard* and *Continental Divide* when I was sucked into this world of George Lucas and sort of disappeared for a year and a half while I worked exclusively for George in northern California. But the word got out and I was very much in demand as a screenwriter. Not only had I sold two original screenplays but I was working on two very high-profile projects for George. And so, the situation I had dreamed of for many years happened while I was sort of otherwise engaged.

It became very clear to me that I had no interest in being a hot screenwriter, that I would never have a period where I would cash in on my screenwriting heat. That everything I had intended from way back would now come true. It had nothing to do with being a hot screenwriter. It had everything to do with parlaying screenwriting into directing. So I began to turn down every offer. I refused to write anything for anybody. Alan Ladd, Jr., the head of Twentieth Century Fox, who was very involved with *Star Wars*, had submitted many things for me to write. I had turned them all down. He called me in and said, "What is it that you want?" I said, "I want to write and direct my own films." He said, "What, particularly?" I explained *Body Heat* to him. I said, "I want to do a film noir, but I want it to be of my generation." He said, "Sounds good, go ahead," and he gave the deal to write the movie. By the time I had finished, Laddy had left Fox and Sherry Lansing had taken over the studio. She came around and greeted us all and hugged us all. Barry Levinson was in the office next to me and Franc Roddam was there making a picture at the time. Sherry put us all in turn-around. We all left Fox and had to find new homes.

Laddy, who had now started his own film company, said, "Come to me with the script you wrote and I will make it." So I was able to make *Body Heat*. He said, "I will do this and let you direct it, but you need to get a director who will sponsor you." He knew I had a relationship with Steven Spielberg and with George Lucas. He was not blind to who I might go to. I went to George and said, "Look, Laddy's insisting I have some back-up, some mentor to make him feel confident about me directing *Body Heat*, and would you do that? Would you produce the movie?" And George said to me, "Look, I just started Lucas Films. It's about family films, and *Body Heat's* a very provocative, sexual movie. I don't think it's a good idea for me to put my name on it. But what I will do is sponsor you without any credit." What I did not know is that he went to Laddy, and said, "I will sponsor Larry, and I will back him up, and if there's a problem, I'll be helpful. I will take a fee for doing that, but I will not take any credit. But if Larry should go over budget, you can use my fee for any overages." It was an extraordinarily generous thing to do. He did it in the best possible way, which is he told me nothing about it.

There's an old saying, do good and go away. It's a hard thing to live in your life—to do a good deed and not to take credit for it. But George did that in the purest sense. He did good and he went away. In fact, he went away so much that he was barely involved with the movie. He spent one day with me in the editing room, going over what we'd done, and made wonderful suggestions. Essentially, I had the best possible first directing experience.

I had been thinking about and fantasizing about and reading about directing for probably ten years by the time I actually walked on a set. All that thinking about it paid off in some weird way because I felt totally at home the first day shooting *Body Heat*. There was very little nervousness. There was no fear. It helped that we had shot screen tests three months earlier in Los Angeles. I had had the experience of having a full crew around me and saying "action" at the proper time and saying "cut" at the proper time. I felt I had finally come home to the place where I was supposed to be, rather than having the feeling I was in some new place. I had truly lived it in my head before the actuality of it.

That's what screenwriting really is. You make all these movies in your head. The frustrating thing about screenwriting for other people is that they're not made the way you imagined it in your head.

Then an odd thing happened, which was probably a mistake in scheduling. *Body Heat* is an incredibly explicit sexual film. Even though we had rehearsed for two weeks, everyone was nervous about the sex scenes. You're asking two actors, no matter how skilled, to do something in public which is very rarely done in public. You try to create as private and sensitive atmosphere on the set as you possibly can.

But here I was a first time director. Kathleen had never made a film before—she'd worked exclusively in television. Bill had just completed his second film. We had to do this incredibly intense sexual material. It was laced throughout the schedule so there was never a time where we thought, "Oh, that's behind us." But on the very first day of filming, the way the schedule had worked out, it made sense for us to do one of the most explicit scenes in the movie. It took place in a boathouse, away from the main house. So in the afternoon we found ourselves on the first day doing this incredibly explicit sexual scene with both of them completely nude.

I had laid down the rules about how the crew would treat it, how limited we would make access to the set during actual shooting, and how close the wardrobe people would be to cover up the actors when they were done. And everything sort of worked. I knew that that was as difficult as anything was going to be in the picture. There were frustrations, there were troubles, there were problems, as there are on every picture, but I had somehow jumped the biggest gully right away. It felt great.

I wanted *Body Heat* to be a very sexy film. What had happened in the late sixties was Hollywood had been able to deal with sexuality in an open way that had never been achieved before. Part of it was the influence of foreign films, which were much more explicit, mature, and sophisticated than American films. Nudity was now accepted for the first time in American films in a way that had never been since the beginning of Hollywood. The problem was that in the twelve years between the onslaught of that kind of freedom in the late 1960s and 1980, when I was making *Body Heat*, it had almost become a dead cinematic language to show lovemaking. There had been so much lovemaking on the screen it was hard to find new ways to do it to wake the audience up and have them see it as anything different.

The challenge of *Body Heat* was to make that love affair seem fresh and hot. All of the writing had been aimed at that—to come in on the sex scenes either before or after or right in the middle of them in such a way as to jolt the audience. My struggle with each of the sex scenes was trying to make them fresh and alive and true in a way that the audience could see, after being a bit jaundiced by a decade of sex on screen. I felt that some of the sex that had been portrayed in film during the seventies had taken away a lot of the eroticism. Movies are a very sexy art form because they control what you see and how much you know. I wanted to play with that in the sex scenes of *Body Heat*.

I've always been bound to wonderful actors. I've been very lucky and have had a large group of friends and actors that have repeated with me, and there's always new people coming into the circle. I expect people to come back. When I like someone, I want to work with them again. It's true of the crew and the actors. But I'm drawn to a very strong, non-fussy, hopefully a non-self-absorbed, kind of acting. I want great listeners. They aren't in competition with the other actors in the frame. They're there to support and to make the other actor better. I'm interested in people who are interested in submitting themselves to roles, to a story, to knowing that sometimes the grander action is the wrong action, the showier action is the wrong action. Sometimes repose is the most appropriate response to something. My movies are cut and acted on the reactions, not the actions. I think that's where the secrets of life are revealed. Not necessarily in what we say, but how we react to what we hear.

The filming of *Body Heat*, in some ways, was the most vivid experience for me because it was so new. Now that I've directed eight films and been involved with sixteen, there's a tendency for things to start to blend. *Body*

*Heat* was extremely intense because it was so new. One night in particular, during a night shoot, we started at dusk and shot until about three o'clock in the morning, and there was a screw-up in the production. I was new enough not to see it coming or to even worry about it. But we made a big company move in the middle of the night and it was not necessary. We didn't get much work done because it's hard to light at night, and we were doing traveling shots, and when you're lighting for traveling shots you have to light the whole block you're shooting on. It's very time consuming. You don't get much footage.

When we got back to the hotel at about two or three in the morning, I went into the bar, which was being kept open for us. They told me that John Lennon had been shot. I was devastated by it. Bill Hurt came in and sat beside me. We sat there for several hours drinking and talking about Lennon and what he meant to us. We are essentially the same age and we experienced the Beatles and that era in the same way. We were in this kind of limbo in the middle of the night talking about the impact that this man had had on our lives and our desires to make art. It put a certain perspective on the film. It didn't seem less important because of this tragedy; it just seemed to fit the process of filmmaking right into the texture of life, somehow. Lennon was an important artist to us. We hoped we were doing something that was important. We were making a movie about life and death and the kind of choices we make.

> *I think he was always optimistic about* The Big Chill, *but I think there were circles of people, if I can remember back to 1983, that thought we were doing a special film. I think it was surprising to some people, the breadth of its appeal.*
>
> Jeff Goldblum—Actor

# The Big Chill (1983)

*William Hurt; Tom Berenger; Glenn Close; Jeff Goldblum; Kevin Kline;*
*Mary Kay Place; Meg Tilly; JoBeth Williams; Don Galloway; Jamie Gillis;*
*Ken Place; Jake Kasdan; Ira Stiltner; Jake Kasdan; Muriel Moore.*

When I was cutting *Body Heat* and thinking about what I would do next, I had this idea about a group of friends that would get together. I thought I wanted to do an ensemble piece, because I found the intense working relationship with Bill and Kathleen and myself just a little claustrophobic and I wanted a change from that. I wanted to use more actors. I wanted to deal more directly with some of the things I was feeling about my generation. We were the children of the sixties. *The Big Chill* is about ten years after the fact and what happens when they get together and are reminded of what they thought ten years earlier and what their hopes were and what they had thought their lives would be like.

The origin of the picture was the thought of telling the story and ending it with a flashback that showed us what they were really like in 1970, after having watched them for an hour and a half in 1980. I wanted to see them as kids and where their memories were reinforced and validated and where they had fantasized about their previous lives.

My lawyer's wife, Barbara Benedict, was just starting to write on her own. I said to her, "Let's write a movie together." She was shocked. So when I finished *Body Heat*, Barbara and I sat down and wrote *The Big Chill*. Barbara was enormously influential to the tone of the piece. We were able to deal with people who were composites of people we knew. For each of us, there was a little bit of ourselves in each of the characters.

*The Big Chill* used the longest rehearsal period that I've ever had because I wanted all the actors to get to know each other and I wanted them to play friends. So I arranged to have four weeks of rehearsals. That's unheard of in the movies. It was an extraordinary experience for a bunch of young actors and for me. It was really exciting and much more lighthearted than *Body Heat*. It was much more fun and not so intense.

*The Big Chill* was a terribly difficult movie to get set up. Even though everyone wanted me to direct and write for them after *Body Heat,* no one wanted to make an ensemble film. No one believed that an ensemble film could be commercially successful. Hollywood always wanted you to have a protagonist, hopefully a white male who the audience could invest in, and possibly a sidekick or possibly a woman that he was involved with. When I presented them with a movie that had eight protagonists, they were only confused. I pitched the film to around seventeen different places. Even though all these producing entities were offering me pictures to write and direct, no one wanted to do this ensemble picture. They just couldn't get it. They couldn't understand how it could work for an American audience. Finally, Marsha Nasatir, who was working for Johnny Carson, who wanted to make films, went to him and said, "This is the film we should make." Carson had a deal at Columbia. They finally agreed to make the movie.

I loved the challenge of shooting an ensemble piece, where you have an enormous amount of coverage because everyone's important, everyone needs a signal, everyone needs to be grouped in two-shots or with various other important characters or you had to cover the whole thing. It was a whole new set of issues for me. I worked with cinematographer John Bailey, who was married to my editor from *Body Heat*. So now we had a sort of family thing going on. A lot of children were around. It started a tradition for me of having a very open set, having a lot of family around, which I feel increases the richness of the experience for me. The house that I used in *The Big Chill* had been used in *The Great Santini*. Since then, *Forrest Gump* was shot there, and about thirty other movies. But at that time it was all fresh to us.

I asked my wife, Meg, to come up with the music. I knew I wanted to use the mood of the music that we liked best in the sixties. These people in their thirties were still totally slaves to the music of the sixties. Meg took on the job of assembling that soundtrack with enormous energy and we were able to use some of our favorite songs. When the movie came out, the album went platinum. It was so popular because we had touched, I think, something that was very real for people. In fact, no one had used that music at all. The closest anyone had come was George Lucas, who had used previous decades of music in *American Graffiti*.

*The Big Chill* was not only a joyous, exciting, very current experience for all of us making it, but the public received it that way. It opened at the New York Film Festival and received the kind of media attention that lifted it above the other movies, because it was a social kind of document. It was very well received in some quarters and brutally attacked in others, because it was not politically correct to some people. It was a kind of a lightning rod to controversy. I think I was surprised by everything that happened to *The Big Chill* because it was so personal. It was so much out of my life, Barbara's life, and my wife's life that when it became very popular I was surprised. I didn't realize this would happen.

> *He creates an atmosphere that is pleasant, where the actor, having been cast, has been cast for a combination of strengths he has naturally, plus something that will challenge him in a stimulating way. He then lets you go and encourages you to bring your thing in and then he just sort of gently edits or makes suggestions.*
>
> Kevin Kline—Actor

# Silverado (1985)

*Kevin Kline; Scott Glenn; Kevin Costner; Danny Glover; Marvin J. McIntyre;*
*Brad Williams; Sheb Wooley; Jon Kasdan; John Cleese; Todd Allen; Kenny Call;*
*Bill Thurman; Meg Kasdan; Dick Durock; Gene Hartline; Rosanna Arquette;*
*Jeff Goldblum; Brian Dennehy; Linda Hunt; Jeff Fahey; Lynn Whitfield.*

I had loved westerns since I was very young. *The Magnificent Seven* had had an enormous impact on me. I loved the way it looked, I loved the way the guys related to each other, I loved the clothes they wore, and I loved the horses and the landscape and the music. I was totally enamoured of what westerns could be and the freedom you had to tell any kind of story within that context. I wanted to go out to that land, which I had had only limited experience with, and choose among all the beautiful settings and places that are out there to make my movie. My brother and I wrote a kind of post-modern western. We didn't call it that at the time. I don't know that that's what we intended but we knew always that it had a modern viewpoint on several sorts of classic situations. That we would assemble a group of heroes and they would go on a certain kind of journey and would encounter many of the basic themes and issues that all the westerns we liked involved. It meant that the movie would not be as serious as some westerns I admired, but it would have all the kind of exuberance and fun that many of my favorite westerns had.

I cast it full of wonderful actors. We built a town on an empty space, which now is still the biggest land-based movie set in the world, actually. I used it again on *Wyatt Earp* and made it even bigger. I was able to now frame and stage action using a wide-screen format in a way that I had never been able to before. I fell in love with the format. I was able to play with many of the genre conventions of the western. You could do physical action, which I had never done before, and play with the tone and the humor of the thing. It was a great experience for me.

I started shooting, insanely, in November, right before a brutal winter in New Mexico. I was so impatient to make the picture and so worried that if we put it off, the movie would never be made. The location is five thousand feet above sea level, so it was very cold. We shot some of the coldest scenes I've ever been involved in. You can see in the picture that it's truly cold. There's a lot of beautiful snow work and in many of the scenes you can see everyone's breath. We had problems with hypothermia with some of the cast and the extras. But it was exactly that kind of vigorous, full-bodied undertaking that I was looking for. I had made two films that were essentially room-bound. Talking heads. I like talk. I don't mind that. But I wanted to do something that would allow me to break out. To see a horse ride fast across the plain. To see men draw guns and fall down and jump and run and shoot.

You're flooded with so many memories from these films. Every day is a kind of adventure. All your feelings about the films are mixed up with what happened outside the frame. Not just in the production, but in the location. We had blizzards where the crew could barely get back to Santa Fe, where the roads were impassable, where the situations were very dangerous for the people and the animals. We had rainstorms and flash floods. We had heat. By starting the movie in November and shooting throughout the year, we encountered every kind of weather possible. So it was like a military undertaking. It is a kind of battle against the elements, the light, the shortening days. An undertaking like *Silverado*, which for me was the biggest up to that time, has a special adventurous feeling to it, and you assemble the people you think can most take the difficulty of it.

The release was moved up and damaged the reception the movie got enormously, not so much because of the critical reception, but because there was no marketing in place. What happened was we took the picture to Seattle and it played through the roof. It was the hottest numbers Columbia Pictures had ever received on a preview, and the studio was being run at that time by a bunch of amateurs who Coca Cola had placed in charge, and they said, "Well, we should release this movie right away because it's so popular." And I said, "But there's no advertising, there's no trailers, there's no TV commercials." They said, "This movie plays through the roof. You don't have to worry about any of that stuff." The proper merchandising and marketing was not done and the movie didn't do a fraction of the business it should have done, which was terribly disappointing to me.

*When I got nominated for the part we, of course, were at the Oscars and Larry was there. He said, well, you got nominated and then you won. That's so much better than getting nominated and not winning. Yeah, it did work out really good.*

*Geena Davis—Actress*

# The Accidental Tourist (1988)

*William Hurt; Kathleen Turner; Geena Davis; Amy Wright;*
*David Ogden Stiers; Ed Begley, Jr.; Bill Pullman; Robert Hy Gorman;*
*Bradley Mott; Seth Granger; Amanda Houck; Caroline Houck;*
*London Nelson; Gregory Gouver; William Brown.*

I had considered, and almost made, a picture written by Carol Eastman. She'd written a script called *Man Trouble*, which was eventually made with Jack Nicholson and Ellen Barkin. That picture did not work out. Carol and I and the producers could never agree on where the script should go. And when I finally let it go, after getting Robert DeNiro and Jessica Lange both involved, we had to give up on the project.

Then I was submitted this Anne Tyler book which I was not familiar with. I read this book and fell in love with it. And by coincidence, it was about a female dog trainer, a sort of working class female dog trainer and a middle class, very uptight man. So it was kind of the reverse of *Man Trouble*. In ways it touched me much more deeply than *Man Trouble*, because it was about trying to control our universe, which I think is central to all my movies and my life.

*The Accidental Tourist* is a story about a man who's suffered the worst kind of tragedy. He's lost a child to exactly the kind of uncontrolled evil that exists in the world, the chaos that he most fears. He makes his living writing guidebooks, telling travelers how to go out into the world and not be affected by the world. He writes a series of books called *The Accidental Tourist* and the whole idea is that you could travel without ever knowing you're traveling, never experience the things that you're brought in contact with. It's a very controlled, tight view of the world.

But the uncontrolled part of the world has come in and altered his life horribly by taking his son and breaking up his marriage. He has a dog and he gets involved with a woman who is as uncontrolled and chaotic as the world. They fall in love and she introduces to his life all the possibilities of joy and unpredictability that is also inherent in that chaos. It was an extended metaphor brilliantly worked out by Anne Tyler. In fact, it's the same story that Anne Tyler has told again and again in her novels, which is about chaos and control, and also about families and how they work to try to insulate people from the world. How they can be a harbor of safety and a suffocating cocoon.

Bill Hurt and Geena Davis play the two lovers. The other characters are the family that Bill Hurt is trying to break out from, which represent an insulated world that Geena represents a release from. So you have this widescreen, beautifully photographed story of this very claustrophobic world that Bill lives in, and this slightly freer but much more chaotic and enlivened world that Geena lives in, in a working class district of Baltimore. It's a movie that's very much of its place.

I always think that a good director is a great casting director. Once you cast the parts most of your work is done, if you've cast it correctly. Just to get to the point where you cast someone and you see that they have an understanding of that character. They have a physicality that is right for your image of that character. They have a body of work, or instincts, which you relate to as being correct for your way of working.

I screen-tested four women for *Accidental Tourist*. When I looked at the screen tests, it was clear to me that Geena was the right person to play that part. All of her instincts were right. What little I had to tell her, she responded to very completely, fully, and quickly. That's what you're looking for in an actor. When you make an adjustment, you can do it with the least amount of effort because they're so in tune with the character. So if you cast correctly, there's very little directing to be done. Then you're just doing fine adjustments. That's the way it is with good people of any kind. The better the actor, the better you are as a director.

They say you should never work with children or animals. *Accidental Tourist* is very much about the dogs. We had this one dog that had to be doubled. It's very odd when you start framing for a dog who's eight inches tall with a six foot two actor. The dog sometimes behaves and sometimes doesn't. The dog is central to most scenes in the movie. And so, as difficult as it is to play the scenes and get the tone exactly right, at the same time you have to deal with a dog who has to do this or that and it was a very interesting challenge to be sort of on a leash.

# I Love You to Death (1990)

*Kevin Kline; Tracey Ullman; Joan Plowright; River Phoenix; William Hurt;*
*Keanu Reeves; James Gammon; Jack Kehler; Victoria Jackson; Miriam Margolyes;*
*Alisan Porter; Jon Kasdan; Heather Graham; Michelle Joyner; John Kostmayer.*

There's an enormous amount of humor in *Accidental Tourist*, but the central issues are so serious for me. In fact, I found it very difficult to deal with the parts of the story that had to do with the death of the son. It was a great fear of mine and touched deeply for me. So I was looking for something very light and irreverent to do. I was sent a script that was based on a true incident involving a working-class couple in Pennsylvania. The wife had tried to kill her husband. Not once, not twice, but about six different times, out of revenge for his infidelity. She failed to kill him. He survived, she and her accomplices were caught, and when she got out of jail, the husband took her back and forgave her and they continue to live together to this day. I was fascinated by that story. I thought it would make a wonderful film. I liked the screenplay quite a bit.

I assembled this truly wacky ensemble to play these characters. Tracey Ullman was the wife and Kevin Kline was the husband who wouldn't die. They're surrounded by these very strange characters, played by Joan Plowright, Keenau Reeves, and Bill Hurt. River Phoenix, a wonderful, talented young actor who's sadly gone now, played Tracey's confidant and best friend.

For the first time I was directing a film I had not written. I discovered what it must be like for an actor to try to understand the screenplay. I had never had that. The movies had always come from out of my head. But when I was directing someone else's screenplay, I found I had to work harder to understand each day what should this scene be? What should it sound like? What is the tone? In addition, it was not a straight movie in any way. It's a black comedy and probably the least popular American form. One of my favorite movies of all time is *Doctor Strangelove,* one of the greatest movies ever made. When it came out, it did no business. Couldn't find an audience. That's typical. There have been maybe two, three, or four black comedies that have ever been successful. It's a form that makes Americans very uneasy. This was a movie about a wife trying to kill her husband.

*I Love You to Death* was the biggest flop I had ever experienced. I had been disappointed by the commercial response to *Silverado* just because I thought we had been so badly marketed and had missed a great opportunity. *I Love You to Death* did not even get on the radar. It was a bomb commercially and critically at the same time. I had never experienced that kind of flop. But it didn't effect me emotionally like *Silverado* did, because I wasn't quite as invested in it and I knew it was a terribly difficult piece of material. I was amazed by how roundly it was rejected. I came out of it not so much shaken as bemused about what was my proper work. I felt that I should write my own scenes and I should understand them fully, and I also knew I wanted to talk about things I related to very closely as opposed to something separate from my life.

# Grand Canyon (1991)

*Kevin Kline; Danny Glover; Steve Martin; Mary McDonnell; Mary-Louise Parker; Alfre Woodard; Jeremy Sisto; Tina Lifford; Patrick Malone; Randle Mell; Sarah Trigger; Destinee DeWalt; Candace Mead; Loren Mead; Simon Baker.*

My wife and I had been talking for years about doing a movie that dealt with some of the things we were feeling at the time about our country and our city, Los Angeles. In the fifteen years we had been living in Los Angeles, the quality of life had deteriorated terribly. Our feelings of safety, security, and peace of mind had been hacked and threatened. The relations between the races had deteriorated rather than improved. Our sons were growing up and we were worried about the effect on them. All these things were weighing upon us. We used to take walks around the neighborhood and talk about it, and soon it became clear that we could make a story out of those conversations.

To tell that story we could draw to us all the people we most valued in our creative life. We could do the kind of thing I had done in *The Big Chill*. We wrote that story very much out of our own lives and our feelings about the city and the country and race relations, about the haves and have-nots, about the possibility of joy and of pain no matter what economic situation you're in. We were trying to deal with all these things that you wake up with every day in Los Angeles or America. How do you have positive, hopeful, what I call humanist contact with the other people in your world, whether you know them or not? When does a stranger become a friend? What is the first moment of a friendship? To what extent do luck and fate play a hand in that?

So we created this story in which luck and fate play a large hand in bringing two very different protagonists together. That's the Kevin Kline character and the Danny Glover character, who rescues him in a desperate situation. As they come together, their worlds are brought together. We see separately and together the people that inhabit their worlds. The goal was to use these people's lives to try to look at what was happening in Los Angeles and America at that time. It happened that much of the tension that was dramatized in the movie was manifested a year after the movie came out in the riots in Los Angeles.

There was an enormous amount of press about the fact that *Grand Canyon* had predicted the explosion of rage and violence. Of course, anyone could have predicted it. It was all there. Anyone walking around L.A. at that time could feel it. The riots were a natural kind of explosion that anyone could have predicted. When there's as much anger and rage in any American city, like there is now, then the possibility of explosion is always there. *Grand Canyon* is the possibility of hopefulness, of contact, love, caring, and generosity. Here I had written a film with my wife about our lives and our sons, about our city.

The reviews were actually better than I anticipated, given how personal it is. The movie did very decent business. It won the Golden Bear at the Berlin Film Festival as best picture of the festival. So in many ways you're getting all the positive things you can possibly have from having a career like mine, which is I get to write and make movies about anything I wish. And if I pull it off, I get to go on. I worked for a fraction of my salary and so did the actors. In that way we were able to keep the budget down. If you want to do something more ambitious in Hollywood, then you have to make sacrifices. Everyone did and it all paid off, so it was the best kind of experience you can have.

## About Life, People, and Trusting

You get into a situation where you get to make your art the way you want to. It's unusual in Hollywood, but I've been lucky. So then you're drawn to the people you trust and like and you think are talented. My brother had introduced me to westerns and to movies, to some extent, so it seemed natural to write *Silverado* with him. Barbara Benedict was a friend when I chose her to write *The Big Chill* with me. She had a particularly funny point of view about people of our generation. When I wanted to do a story about my life with my wife and our marriage and our place in this society, it seemed perfectly natural to have her write it with me. That's the great gift of having some success, where people are willing to let you make these movies as you see fit. It's a miracle to me to be able to do this work that I love and be well paid for, and at the same time get to work with the most wonderful people around.

> *Larry's the best listener I've ever met. When he first meets you, he's kind of like an investigative reporter. He wants to know everything.*

*He absorbs people. He just absorbs them entirely, and he seems to find vitality in staying involved with people.*

Mary McDonnell—Actress

## *The Bodyguard* Comes Full Circle

*The Bodyguard* had come to life and had gone back to sleep many times between 1977 and 1992, when I produced it with Kevin Costner and Jim Wilson. Kevin Costner had heard about it when we were making *Silverado* in 1984, and had never let go of the idea that he would be in it. At the time we were making *Silverado,* he was not a star. There was no way that any movie was going to be built around him. But *The Bodyguard* never got made, and by 1991 or so Kevin was a huge international star, and he asked me if I would direct it with him in it. I had messed around with *Bodyguard* in so many different versions over the years that I felt really burned out about it. It was also at the exact moment that Meg and I had decided to do *Grand Canyon,* so I told Kevin that I did not want to direct the film but I would produce it with him, and we hired Mick Jackson to direct it.

I had some problems with Mick Jackson's direction, but I think it had nothing to do with Mick Jackson. I think it had to do with the fact that I'm not a good person for having other people direct my screenplays. I was very unhappy when the movie came out. I didn't like the tone of the movie. It's the same problem I had with *Continental Divide* and other pictures that I had written, where no matter how good the director was or how fine the work he had done, there is no pleasing me. I'm just not a good one to have other people do my work, and so I was very unhappy with *The Bodyguard.* Kevin and I got very involved in the editing, which is not something I would normally do with any other director. I don't want people messing with my movie. But we were the producers and we had serious problems with it.

The movie came out and it was never what I thought it should be. I had written the part for Steve McQueen long before I was in the movie business. I adored Steve. And Kevin, to some extent, had carried on the McQueen tradition. He never let go of the idea of playing *The Bodyguard* because he wanted to play that McQueen-like character. And I think he achieved that fully. The rest of the movie is not too satisfying to me. The reviews were probably the worst reviews I've ever had, even worse than *I Love You To Death.* I didn't realize at the time part of it was with the movie, which had serious problems, and part of it was the start of a backlash against Kevin, which lasted for a couple years. He just had too much success for the media and they were ready to put him in his place.

The reviews were totally irrelevant to that movie. It was a smash beyond anyone's expectations and predictions. Not only did it do $120 million in business in the United States, but also it did $240 million overseas. It was an extraordinary hit. I mean, it wound up doing $400 million worldwide when all things were counted in. That's just in the theaters. So it was an enormous hit. It was the fourth time I was able to do one of the biggest movies of all time. I had written *Jedi, Empire,* and *Raiders,* and that part was exciting. It was exciting to have a big, popular hit, but it was frustrating, too, to have it not be the movie I thought it should be.

I must say, if I had directed that film it probably wouldn't have done anything like that business. I have a feeling that by nature I will never make a film that popular because there's something about popular films and the simplicity to them that I may not be able to achieve. I wish I could. All of my objections were personal. The movie did work on some level that I did not anticipate. I have a good friend who called me up after seeing *The Bodyguard* and said, "You know, I think that's my favorite one of your movies." Well, I was terribly insulted because I didn't like the movie and I didn't like him saying, by implication, that all my other movies were crap. I said, "What is it you liked so much?" He said, "There's something heart-breaking to me about their relationship and this love that can never be satisfied. He's willing to do anything for her but they can never be together." And I thought, "Well, you're giving it a lot more weight and feeling than I think the movie deserves," but in retrospect, there was something about that relationship that spoke to people, mainly to women, but to people all over the world, everywhere it went. It was a huge success. The critics said it was a piece of crap.

## He's a Hard Man to Please

There was a moment after I first saw *Raiders of the Lost Ark* where the difference between what I had imagined and what was on the screen was great enough that I was actually disappointed. I'm much older now, much more experienced, and I look at *Raiders* now and I'm very proud of it. I think it's a terrific movie and I think Steven did a magnificent job with it. As I say, I think I'm a bad person to have other people direct my work. My dissatisfaction at the time was because of my youth and this sort of purist mentality. But yes, no matter how well you're served by a director, for me as a writer it's never satisfying.

# Wyatt Earp (1994)

*Kevin Costner; Dennis Quaid; Gene Hackman; David Andrews;*
*Linden Ashby; Jeff Fahey; Joanna Going; Mark Harmon; Michael Madsen;*
*Catherine O'Hara; Bill Pullman; Isabella Rossellini; Tom Sizemore;*
*JoBeth Williams; Mare Winningham; James Gammon;*
*Rex Linn; Randle Mell; Adam Baldwin; Annabeth Gish.*

I love westerns and I had always been drawn to the story of Wyatt Earp and the gunfight at the OK Corral. I don't know that I should have made the movie *Wyatt Earp*. What happened was I was about to do another picture and I went to see Kevin Costner. He had tried to get me to do this *Wyatt Earp*. He had a six-hour script for a mini-series that he was going to do as a pay-per-view event. I was not interested and I didn't like the script. I told him that I was about to commit to another picture. He said, "Why are you doing that? Why don't you do *Wyatt Earp*?" I said, "I don't like the screenplay." And he said, "Well, then, write a new screenplay." I said, "Well, I could do that if you would commit to making this movie next summer," because I was ready to go to work. He said, "You can write a new screenplay and I'll make the movie." And we decided right there on the spot to do this movie.

We knew that there were inherent problems in it commercially, in that Wyatt Earp is not a particularly appealing or sympathetic character. I did write a screenplay that I liked very much, and I gave it to Kevin and he was very upset by it, and I didn't know why at first. Then I realized that this six-hour mini-series script he had presented to me he was more invested in than I had thought. At that point we probably should have called the whole thing off, but we didn't. Instead, we reached a kind of compromise script. I had never had that experience before, because everything that I had ever written I had just gone out and shot as is. Here I had this kind of hybrid. It was my script plus elements from his previous script and I think it confused the whole situation, and if I had my wits about me I probably would have said, "Kevin, look, because we're very good friends let's preserve our friendship and not do this movie." Well, we have preserved our friendship, but unfortunately we did do the movie.

Now, it was a very good experience in many ways. Making the film was great. Kevin and I are very close. It was a big adventure to make the film. Twice the number of people as *Silverado* and five times the number of cities. It's an epic film on an epic scale. It shows the building of the railroad and a span of Wyatt's life. So in many ways it presented the challenges I was looking for. It's a big bite of a movie and there are things in it that are as good as anything I've ever done. And certainly the cinematography is magnificent. There's great work from the set designers and the score and the actors are wonderful. But the movie is not satisfying to me, and I hate that I worked that hard and gave that much to it and did not figure out a way to make the movie the one I wanted it to be. It has to do with this initial step about us not being able to agree about how the script should be. Kevin and my friendship survived and we're as close today as we've ever been, but I wish that we had come to real understanding of what the movie should be or that we had just backed out. I spent two years on that movie. It's terrible to have feelings of dissatisfaction like that.

It was almost universally panned when the movie came out. But then there were these odd reviews that were wonderful. The fact that it wasn't popular was not a surprise to me. We knew before the movie opened it would have commercial problems. It opened in the middle of the summer. Another movie called *Tombstone* along the same subject matter had opened six months earlier, and it had done very well. We were doomed commercially. But when it was critically destroyed too, it was a big load to take. Any director you interview will tell you how hard it is to take that double-barreled disappointment and that you come out of it changed. What you hope is that it doesn't make you fearful or cautious in a way that makes it harder to do good work.

Dennis Quaid, who played Doc Holliday, was a joy to work with. I had met him socially before that and when I offered him the part of Doc Holliday he responded with enormous enthusiasm and went on a medically controlled diet that led him to lose forty pounds. He's an incredibly fit, handsome fellow and to take forty pounds off a body that was already pretty cut and buff was really difficult, but he did it with medical supervision and you see the results in the movie. He was an emaciated skeleton. He totally entered the character. That Doc Holliday is very close, I believe, to the truth about Doc Holliday, and, in fact, I think I wrote that character better than I wrote Wyatt and some of the other characters in the movie. That's the most satisfying part of the movie for me. Aside from its great look, I am pleased with Dennis' performance as Doc.

# French Kiss (1995)

Meg Ryan; Kevin Kline; Timothy Hutton; Jean Reno; François Cluzet; Susan Anbeh; Renée Humphrey; Michael Riley; Laurent Spielvogel; Victor Garrivier; Elisabeth Commelin; Julie Leibowitch; Miquel Brown; Louise Deschamps; Olivier Curdy.

Meg Ryan and I had been looking for something to do together. We had gotten to know each other a little better through her husband, Dennis Quaid, during the filming of *Wyatt Earp*, although I actually knew Meg before that, too. I was a great fan of Meg Ryan and her comic ability and her charm. She came to me with this script that she had commissioned, and I thought it was a good part for her and would be fun to do. I wouldn't have to write something new. I'd just done this really difficult movie and I thought, well, I'll go to France with my family for a while. I love France. And it was all those things put together.

Kevin Kline is an amazing collaborator and as smart as anyone I've ever met. He's fast and he's funny. He's one of the funniest people on earth. We've worked together five times so we don't have to say all that much to each other. There are so many references about tone and about level of humor and about the size of the character and how can we fill in the details better. He comes from a musical background. He wanted to be a concert pianist and gave it up when he thought he wasn't good enough. He had won two Tony Awards by the time I met him. He was just a little over thirty. He's an astounding stage actor. He has had a wonderful film career that sometimes people underestimate, because he hasn't been the traditional kind of superstar. But his movies have done extraordinarily well. He's had a lot of big hits.

## On American Films in General

American films seem worse than ever in my memory. The situation in Hollywood is dreadful—the way the media deals with movies and the obsession about box-office grosses, the constant feeding to the public of the lowest form of movies with the least characters and least challenges. It's barely recognizable as the same industry as it was in 1973 or 1974, when the public was being presented with *M*A*S*H*, *Shampoo*, and *The Last Detail* and *The Last Tango*, and *The Godfather* and *American Graffiti*. Compare that to the movies we've had in the last two or three years and it's barely recognizable as being the same industry. So there's a deterioration of quality, a lessening of standards in the movie business.

There's a new generation of people making decisions in Hollywood who are the worst kind of prodigies of television. They don't even remember *Midnight Cowboy*. Their references are the hits of the last five years and they're trying to duplicate those hits. It's a dreadful time. You could say it's a dreadful time for American culture. But it's more obvious in the movies than anywhere else to me. There is some hope. The independent film scene has taken on the burden of doing decent movies and there are great films coming out of the independent world. It's a shame that Hollywood has given up the effort, for the most part, to do serious work. You'd never believe it in the summer, but as we approach Academy Award time, the studios tend to release their more serious material. That's insane. The approach is to say, "Well, in the summer we'll make money and at Christmas we'll throw in a few classy items that will make money and if they win an Academy Award, they'll make even more money." It's nothing about a general level of quality.

From 1968 to 1975 there was enormous excitement in America about what films could be. They were the best films in the world. They were dealing with the society within and dealing with our history. There was startling social insight and moving drama and wonderful comedy. How many movies of the last five years could qualify as any of those? It's a terrible time for movies and the people making the decisions are probably the least qualified in almost fifty years. Even the moguls, who always came out here to make a buck, always believed that the money would come if they told good stories. The people in charge now are working for multi-national corporations that also make cars and candy bars. They have absolutely no feel for story, no background in story, don't know what narrative is. It's not hard to put beautiful images on the screen, but it's very hard to tell a story.

We have an era in which everything is deteriorating. Sometimes we blame the writers, but the fact is the writers write to the market and the market is for mindless, TV-like entertainment. Directors are given so much power. They have the power over the script and they will sometimes mold and simplify and ruin the screenplay into some shape that reminds them more of a TV commercial or music video that they're more comfortable with. The studio executive that is making the decision about when the script is ready to be made comes from the same background.

I think it's a good time for independent films. Almost by necessity. People who want to do good work have turned to other sources. They've given up on Hollywood movies. It's too bad, though, because my audience and many of the people that I care about don't want to go to Hollywood movies.

They won't even give a Hollywood movie a shot. They've been disappointed so many times. They've given up even checking the listings.

## He Feels Lucky to Be Doing What He Is Doing

When you get to do work that's the only thing you've ever wanted to do, and you get to do it with enormous freedom, and you're even paid to do it, you feel blessed and lucky. But then your goals change. Once you've achieved the right and the ability to do this work, then what happens is you want to keep raising the bar, and you have to figure out how do you do better work. Not more superficially serious work, or more expensive work, or with bigger stars, but how to do better work. Whenever we're startled or delighted at the movies, it's always about something touching our hearts and our minds in a new way or in a very familiar way that seems fresh. It has nothing to do with budget or stardom, commercial or critical success. It has to do with the startling insight, the moment of blinding truth. It's what we hope for most from art. It stirs us up in some new way. So what do I want? Since I already know the work I want to do, the only thing left for me is to try to do it better.

I've thought about what else I would do besides directing many times and I always come up empty-handed. That, I think, is what got me here, and that's probably my salvation, and it would be a terrible problem for me if I had to do anything else. I've been so completely single-minded about this. I could tell you a few careers that seem possible but it'd be a charade, a joke. I'd probably sit in a room and twiddle my thumbs if I couldn't direct movies, because it's the only thing I like.

## What Does the Future Hold for Lawrence Kasdan?

I don't know what the rest of my day will be like, much less the rest of my life. Pretty much of what I've worked on has been about how unpredictable life is. I've been very lucky to be able to do work I like for so long because I had a long period when I couldn't. I'm very appreciative of it. I think it's one of the great gifts. I've been very blessed with family and my circumstances. In a way, I feel I've been so blessed that whatever happens now, I hope that I can deal with it because I can't believe my good luck will continue. But, hopefully, it will, and I'll continue to make movies until I don't think I can say anything useful in them anymore.

---

NOTE: Since the completion of this interview Kasdan wrote and directed *Mumford*, starring Mary McDonnell; David Paymer; Martin Short; Alfre Woodard; Priscilla Barnes; Arell Blanton; Jane Adams; and Ted Danson.

# Director Filmography

*Body Heat* (1981)
*The Big Chill* (1983)
*Silverado* (1985)
*The Accidental Tourist* (1988)
*I Love You to Death* (1990)
*Grand Canyon* (1991)
*Wyatt Earp* (1994)
*French Kiss* (1995)
*Mumford* (1999)

# Awards

**Academy Awards, USA**

*Grand Canyon,* Best Writing, Screenplay Written Directly for the Screen (nominated, shared with Meg Kasdan), 1992

*The Accidental Tourist,* Best Picture (nominated, shared with Charles Okun & Michael Grillo), 1989

*The Accidental Tourist,* Best Writing, Screenplay Based on Material from Another Medium (nominated, shared with Frank Galati), 1989

*The Big Chill,* Best Writing, Screenplay Written Directly for the Screen (nominated, shared with Barbara Benedek), 1984

**Berlin International Film Festival**

*Grand Canyon,* Golden Berlin Bear Award, 1992

**British Academy Awards**

*The Accidental Tourist,* Best Adapted Screenplay (nominated, shared with Frank Galati), 1990

*The Big Chill*, Best Original Screenplay (nominated, shared with Barbara Benedek), 1985

## Edgar Allan Poe Awards
*Body Heat*, Best Movie (nominated), 1982

## Golden Globes, USA
*Grand Canyon*, Best Screenplay—Motion Picture (nominated, shared with Meg Kasdan), 1992

*The Big Chill*, Best Screenplay—Motion Picture (nominated, shared with Barbara Benedek), 1984

## Razzie Awards
*Wyatt Earp*, Worst Remake or Sequel (shared with Kevin Costner and Jim Wilson), 1995

*Wyatt Earp*, Worst Director (nominated), 1995

*Wyatt Earp*, Worst Picture (nominated, shared with Kevin Costner and Jim Wilson), 1995

*The Bodyguard*, Worst Picture (nominated, shared with Kevin Costner and Jim Wilson), 1993

*The Bodyguard*, Worst Screenplay (nominated), 1993

## ShoWest Convention, USA
Director of the Year, 1992

## USC Scripter Award
*The Accidental Tourist* (shared with Anne Tyler & Frank Galati), 1990

## Writers Guild of America, USA
*The Big Chill*, Best Screenplay Written Directly for the Screen—Comedy (shared with Barbara Benedek), 1984

# The Films of Mark Rydell

**M**ark Rydell was born on March 23, 1934, and raised in the Bronx in New York City. There he majored in English and philosophy first at New York University and later at the famous Juilliard School of Music, where he gained his life-long passion for jazz piano. This Oscar-nominated director—and well-trained scene-stealing actor—is an accomplished storyteller, which makes him one of America's most prolific filmmakers.

As an actor, Rydell performed many roles both in feature films and television, including a six-year stint as one of the leading characters on the soap opera *As The World Turns*. Producer Matt Rapf encouraged Rydell to make the move to Hollywood, where he eventually directed more than fifty episodes of dramatic television, including an award-winning episode of *Gunsmoke*. He also directed episodes of *Ben Casey* and *I Spy*.

In 1968 Rydell directed his first feature film, the controversial production of D.H. Lawrence's *The Fox*. For his second film, he seized the opportunity to work with Steve McQueen in bringing William Faulkner's last novel, *The Reivers*, to the screen.

In 1979 he introduced Bette Midler to moviegoers with *The Rose*. Her powerfully emotional performance as a declining rock singer brought her an Oscar nomination as Best Actress.

His critically acclaimed production of *On Golden Pond* received ten nominations, for Best Picture, Best Actor, Best Actress, Best Supporting Actress, Best Adapted Screenplay, Best Cinematography, Best Editing, Best Sound, Best Music Score, and one for Rydell as Best Director. Actor Henry Fonda and writer Ernest Thompson won Oscars.

*Mark created a great spirit among the members of the cast and crew, which I think is really important. Because if that kind of attitude is at the helm, it's going to filter all the way down to even the guy carry-ing the rubbish bins. And you are going to get the best from everyone.*

Mel Gibson—Actor

# The Conversation

I spent the majority of my youth in the Bronx, where I actually lived across the street from the maternity hospital where I was born. I was a little boy and was smaller than most of my compatriots. I also was the youngest in my class, for some odd reason. I graduated all of my schools at an earlier age than most so I was always the youngest and the smallest, which I would say in some way is the source of personality compensation. You develop entertainment skills and instincts because you feel you don't measure up to the other developing students, particularly around the age of puberty. Everybody was into puberty before I was and so I became kind of an entertainer, a comic, an emcee, and a mascot. It was a difficult time for me. I would say all of my childhood was relatively tormented.

My father was a stockbroker on Wall Street and my mother was, and still is, the quintessential Jewish mother. Woody Allen would have a great time creating a character portrait of her. She's full of energy and pizzazz and she was a pianist, and so I inherited some of my musical skills from her and much of my entertainment skills from her. My father also was a pianist in addition to being a stockbroker. And I have a younger sister, five years younger than I, with whom I'm very close, so I have a good heritage of personality juice that came from my family and to whom I'm eternally grateful. But it was a tough time.

I wanted to go to the high school of music and art. I would sketch and I was a pianist, but my father felt that that was kind of suspicious. He wanted me to be more of a man's man. He was a very strong figure and he managed to seduce me into going to the Bronx High School of Science—a brilliant school whose curriculum was all science—but it held no interest for me. I took a test to get into this very distinguished school and got 98 in English and 31 in math. My father used his influence to get me in, which was a nightmare because I was a fish out of water. I would go to the school and once I was registered I would sneak out and get on the subway, go down to 42nd Street, put my books in a locker, and go into the Paramount Theater and watch Woody Herman or Tommy Dorsey. In those days, they would run the movie and then there was a show in between the movies. I used to watch these bandleaders come out of the pit and I'd dream that I was going be a bandleader in a white suit. Then at the end of the day I'd go home. When it came time for testing at the school I used to work four or five nights in a row and learn enough to get me through the Regent's examinations so they couldn't fail me.

## He Is a Great Storyteller

There is an incident that I have never discussed publicly which will probably be censored and edited for this tape, but I'll tell it to you anyway. I went into the army at seventeen in order to escape from my family circumstances. I wanted to get away but didn't have the emotional courage to go without enlisting in the army. My mother and father signed, allowing me to go in at seventeen. Unfortunately, at seventeen I looked like I was twelve. I've always looked younger than I am.

It was right after World War II and I was sent to Japan. It was not uncommon for the guys between seventeen and twenty-two to want to have sex. The whorehouses in Tokyo were off-limits to American GI's but they managed to frequent the off-limits areas. One night I was arrested along with about twenty other young men in a very elaborate Japanese geisha house and was taken to a prison. It was horrifying. Your shoes and shoelaces were removed along with your tie so you couldn't kill yourself. We were treated like the infraction was murder. We were forced to stand at attention for something like five hours without moving, and if you moved they would hit you with a billy club. The idea was to terrify you and indeed they did.

Then you were marched down three or four flights of stairs and brought into a circular, two-tiered prison and you were put in a cell that was five feet high so that you couldn't stand up. It was three feet wide and maybe ten feet deep. There was a toilet without a seat and the bunk was filthy and the floor was covered with urine and it was wet and you were barefoot. I stood there because we were not allowed to lie down on the cot.

After some hours we were taken to an area where they were conducting a mass court-martial. I was maybe twentieth in a line of twenty-five people. Each guy would go through the door and face the court-martial. It took three minutes and out they came and they walked down the line and each one announced his punishment—like six months hard labor. I came close to the door and I said, "I've got to figure a way out of this." I walked through the door and there I saw, seated behind this desk, a gray-haired, distinguished man looking down. He looked like Judge Hardy. He looked up at me and he saw this infant. I must have looked fourteen or fifteen years old. He said, "How did you get involved in this kind of horrifying situation, son?"

As he said "son," something clicked on in me—I hate to admit it—but I thought, my only way out of this was to pretend that the other guys had intimidated me. I pretended to be a virgin, which was not true, of course. Then I started to weep, half out of anxiety and half out of a certain kind of pleasure. I saw him looking at me with great compassion and he said, "That's terrible that you did that." I said, "I know. I'm so ashamed but I was so embarrassed to be the only virgin in the company," and so on and so on. And he said, "Ten dollars." A great wave of relief came over me. I thanked him and I left and at that moment I knew that I should be an actor. It's a horrible, horrible confession but I promised you I'd tell the truth.

As soon as I graduated high school I went to Juilliard and studied for a while with Teddy Wilson, a great jazz pianist. Then I went into the army and by that time I was a reasonably good pianist. Another story comes to mind. (I assume you edit these things out.) When I went into the army I was assigned to ordinance. I was placed in a barracks in Yokohama and I was assigned to a tire repair barge in Yokohama Harbor. They woke me at midnight and they took me out in a boat to this tire repair barge where these ovens were vulcanizing rubber. It as a nightmare! I was there for an hour shoveling coal in the fires and vulcanizing rubber and I knew that if I stayed there I would go mad.

I slipped over the side of the ship at two o'clock in the morning and swam to shore, got on a train from Yokohama to Tokyo where I knew the Special Services were. I stood near the stage door of the Ernie Powell Theater waiting for the people to come in that morning. When they arrived I said, "I have to play for you." They were so stunned. Here was this bedraggled young kid in an army uniform and I went upstairs with them and I literally played for my life. As a matter of fact, there's a woman named Kay Medford, the late Kay Medford—wonderful actress—who was touched by me and I became her accompanist and I was assigned to Special Services. I found a way of saving my life.

When I left the service I went to the Chicago Musical College at the University of Chicago. I was playing jazz piano around Chicago. Now, jazz musicians were the drug addicts of the day and that frightened me. I saw many of my friends destroy their lives. Some even died as a result of heroin addiction, and I was frightened because I have a kind of addictive personality. I was afraid I was going to be tempted and so I tore up my union card and went back to New York University. The reason I got into acting was that I was in a class called "Latin and Greek in current usage," and the professor asked us to etymologize the word ornithology, which is a very famous Charlie Parker song. I began to hum under my breath and someone behind began to do the same thing. It turned out to be Marilyn Katz, who is now Marilyn Bergman of Alan and Marilyn Bergman, the great songwriters. We became fast friends. She said to me, "You have to become an actor." She is the one who is responsible for sending me to the Neighborhood Playhouse.

I knew nothing when I went to the Neighborhood Playhouse, but I was suddenly exposed to Sanford Meisner, who in my mind, was the greatest living teacher of acting. My dance classes were conducted by a middle-aged woman who absolutely thrilled me. It was Martha Graham. I eventually became a member of the Actor's Studio, where my teachers were Kazan and Lee Strasberg. I'm still deeply involved with the Actor's Studio. I'm a member of their Board of Directors along with Sydney Pollack and Marty Landau. I am an executive director of the Actor's Studio West and a member of the Board of Directors. I've been the beneficiary of really great training, more so than is available to most people today.

An actor has to remain, in the most distinguished way—there is no pejorative intent in this remark—has to remain, in some sense, a child. He has to peel away all the insulation that culture teaches us to make him or herself responsive to situations, to relationships. We learn through culture to protect ourselves, to cover up, to take of this kind of situation, take care of that situation. Well the actor's task is a heroic one. He has to peel away all of those layers and he has to expose himself. I have great admiration for actors. But when I was a musician, I wanted to be a conductor, and when I was an actor, I always wanted to be a director. I felt it was a natural evolution for me toward a more leading, paternal role.

## Directing Comes into His Life

I learned about movie directing by accident. I went to the Lexington Translux Theater on Lexington Avenue and saw *The Killing* by Stanley Kubrick. It's a film that's full of directing, full of interesting cutting. The film is about the robbery of a racetrack and there is constant, recurrent cutting back to the race. During the race there's a horse that's killed and it draws everybody's attention. These crooks all steal the money from the racetrack during this time, and it was the picture that showed me what is possible as a director. What you can do, how you can change things, how you can organize things. I sat in that theater all day long watching *The Killing* and decided to become a director.

I did some minor directing in New York at the theater. Sydney Pollack, who was a very good friend of mine at the time, had come to California and had begun directing. It was the beginning of his career. He came to New York and he asked me to help him with a show that he was going to do. He was still very focused on learning the camera and things like that and asked me if I would help him. I did because he was a friend and it was exciting for me to learn. Matt Rapf, the executive producer of *The Ben Casey Show,* after hearing of my skills from Sydney, invited me to leave the television show that I was acting in. I was kind of one of the leading characters on *As the World Turns* for some six years. He invited me to come to California and to learn about directing and become an assistant. I knew that this was my chance so I abandoned a very lucrative career and came to California for, I think, three hundred dollars a week for some three or four months.

I did everything on *The Ben Casey Show,* from helping with scripts to watching shooting and dubbing. One day this heroic figure, Matt Rapf, with the support of Vince Edwards, who played Ben Casey, said to me, "Here's your script; you direct this next one." The network went crazy but both Matt Rapf and Vince Edwards said, "If you don't allow him to direct we will quit." So they stood up for me and I became a director that day and I haven't stopped.

This was back in the sixties. Television was different then. You never heard from the sponsor and you never heard from the network. It was a much freer period, creatively, than it is now. It was a very exciting time because you were handed a crew and a screenplay that you had to develop into forty-nine, fifty, or fifty-two minutes, because the commercials were much shorter in those days. You had six days to shoot it and six days to rehearse it and it forced you into a kind of guerrilla filmmaking. In those days the director was a transient. You knew the real bosses were the executive producers and the cast who remained week after week. The director moved from show to show and was really there just to execute the show and to leave.

I loved my early days of television. I thought it was terrific. I worked with great actors. I was suddenly in charge of brilliant, talented people. I had a lot of freedom. I even cut all my television shows. I remember coming to the cutting room and they were shocked that I came into the cutting room at all. Directors didn't do that. I used to go to the dubbing stage and make sure the dubbing was right. I directed many *Gunsmoke's*. I must have done fifty or sixty hours of dramatic television. I treated every show like it was my last chance to direct ever, whether the material was of good quality or not. I always found something in it that I thought was worthy that I could invest my enthusiasm in, which, I must tell you, is the secret of directing.

# The Fox (1968)

*Sandy Dennis; Keir Dullea; Anne Heywood; Glyn Morris.*

By the time I was offered the opportunity to direct *The Fox*, I had been offered a number of other pictures. There were always a lot of producers who were looking for hot young television directors that they could get for nothing because everybody was trying to get into the movies. When *The Fox* came to me I had rejected a number of film opportunities with the knowledge that if you don't make a success in your first film, you go back to "Go," don't collect two hundred dollars, start from the beginning again.

I loved the material that *The Fox* was based on. I loved D.H. Lawrence. I love the idea of turning a rather long short story, maybe some thirty-six pages, into a movie. I loved the fact that I really had control of it. I loved the fact that it was daring and sexual and that I felt that I could tell the truth on screen in a way that had been, prior to this date, forbidden to me. So I went after it like a dog grabs a bone and I worked on it for eighteen months for twenty-five thousand dollars. That was my salary and the movie was, fortunately, very successful. It won the Golden Globe as the best film of the year and my career was launched.

I must confess that probably the intimacy of that film had never been seen in American films before. It kind of blew a wind of freedom across America because it was so successful. There was a masturbation scene in *The Fox* that never had been seen on American screens before, except in foreign films like *The Silence*. *The Fox* was a very personal and very sexual film, full of sexual tension. Of course the fact that I was in my twenties and had enough sexual tension for the whole room didn't hurt.

The producer's wife, Anne Heywood, played one of the leads in the picture. I kept putting off the masturbation scene with her, which was really a scene of desperate loneliness. It wasn't supposed to be an erotic scene, although it certainly appeared to be erotic when you watched it in a big popular American movie. It was a scene of a desperately lonely woman. She had taken a bath and was drying herself off and finally, in a deep sense of loneliness, she tries to relieve her anxiety by masturbating. It was not very graphic but it was shot in the nude. I was terrified of it. I kept putting it off and putting if off until almost the end of shooting.

Finally the day came that we had to do it and Anne Heywood, who was a very sweet lady, was in her dressing room. I turned to the cameraman, Bill Fraker, and I said, "Listen, we'd better go back there and talk to her and relax the situation and make it tolerable." We had everybody off the set and there were curtains all around. Anne had been getting body makeup and she had a robe on and so I said, "Anne, we have to do this now." We had, by the way, rehearsed it with a nude model so we knew exactly what to do. I knew exactly where she had to go, where she had to stand when she got out of the tub, and how she went to the sink and how she went to a mirror. It was all worked out.

I finally said to her, "I'd like to walk you through it and I think in order to get over this tension and anxiety you have to take off your robe now and we have to become comfortable with your nudity." And she went, "Oh, I can't believe it, no!" I said, "Well, there's no other way." So she took a deep breath and dropped her robe and then we began to talk about the scene, pretending that she wasn't nude. This all took place in her dressing room. Now she puts on her robe and we go out to the set. I get everybody out who's not absolutely critically essential to the scene and we walk her through it with her robe on. Ultimately it comes time to actually shoot and she drops the robe and we start to shoot the scene. She was so comfortable in her nudity that she refused to put the robe on for the rest of the day. We would be shooting close-ups where she didn't need to be nude and she would insist on being nude. It was both exciting and thrilling and honest.

# The Reivers (1969)

*Steve McQueen; Sharon Farrell; Ruth White; Michael Constantine; Clifton James; Juana Hernandez; Lonny Chapman; Will Geer; Rupert Crosse; Mitch Vogel; Diane Shalet; Pat Randall; Diane Ladd; Ellen Geer; Dub Taylor.*

The success of *The Fox* was extreme. I didn't have to go through climbing the ladder. In my second film I replaced both John Huston and William Wyler, who were supposed to direct *The Reivers*. John Huston had dropped out because he had another commitment in the middle of preparation and William Wyler finally decided that it was too arduous a film for him to do. I had a very enterprising agent who got on a plane with Steve McQueen and made sure he sat next to him. Steve was shooting *Bullitt* in San Francisco and by the time their plane landed, I had the film. Steve and I, by the way, had gone to the Neighborhood Playhouse School together and, as a matter of fact, I introduced him to his first wife, Neile, a wonderful singer and actress.

I saw that script and I knew that I had to do it. I was passionate to do it. It was a really exciting experience to work with Steve, who was the biggest star in the Hollywood pantheon at that time. Insane and paranoid and lunatic though he was, he was magically talented and brilliant. And this William Faulkner, Pulitzer Prize-winning tale just touched me very deeply. It was a tale of a boy's movement through puberty and exposure to the realities of life. It was a very sweet and touching and a wonderful period piece. I was desperate to do it.

Steve McQueen was a brilliant, brilliant actor and a very well-trained craftsman. You bring up a very interesting issue because I was confronted with an extremely difficult problem. I had hired the late Rupert Crosse to play McQueen's best friend in the picture. Rupert was a six-foot, five-inch brilliant black actor who had never been in a major film before, and I had to overcome Steve's paranoia about working with a very tall actor. Steve was a guy who was about five-nine or five-eight and because of many personal and emotional problems didn't like the idea of working with a big guy. But I managed to convince him.

There was another problem with working with Steve and Rupert. Rupert was an actor and you have to work with every actor differently. That's the first thing you must learn as a director. Every actor has his own personal needs and has to be dealt with in a different manner. Rupert Crosse was the kind of guy who got better on the third and fourth take and by the sixth or seventh or eighth take he's really swinging. Steve, on the other hand, was a guy who would look at the script once and never again. On the day before he'd shoot, or the day of the shoot, he would quickly look at the lines. He didn't even want to walk onto the set until it was ready because he was very improvisational. He wanted to feel what it was like—oh, here's the chair, here's how I sit down, you know. It was all very organic and after two takes Steve was finished. He lost his spontaneity.

But it took nine for Rupert to get to the place where it was good. I finally solved it by acting myself in the first nine takes with Rupert and when Rupert was hot, I would call Steve in. I would do it with Rupert because I was an actor and I was capable of doing that without any problem. I knew where everything was and I knew the blocking so I would play the scene with Rupert. We would shoot, often without film, pretending we were shooting, then we would bring in Steve and Steve would come be improvisational and alive and vital and Rupert by that time was ready.

It is of course extremely difficult to reduce a novel of some five to six hundred pages to a screenplay of one hundred and twenty pages. But we did it with the help of a couple of writers whose wisdom and intelligence and taste permeated that adaptation. They were able to reduce this massive novel to a successful screenplay. Of course we tried desperately to be faithful to the original and I think we were, in spite of McQueen's resistance. William Faulkner is full of dialogue and full of language. Steve played a character named Boon Hogganbeck who was described by Faulkner as a man who would have been arrested out of any crowd, which was very much like the real Steve, by the way. He wanted to cut out the dialogue all the time and just do his looks. He was able to deliver a great deal with a moment of behavior but I forced him to do all the dialogue. He didn't really forgive me during the making of the film. I must tell you that later, when he saw the finished movie, he apologized to me.

I believe my accuracy with dates is not something to be admired but I would think that *The Reivers* was done in the late sixties or early seventies [1969]. It was certainly prior to the Civil Rights revolution. We shot in Mississippi, which was the seat of some of the ugliest racist behavior. I remember we all lived in a motel in Greenville, Mississippi, and traveled to another small town that we had turned into a wonderful set for the picture. There were police in the motel courtyard protecting our interests. When Rupert arrived, Sharon Farrell, who was a young, voluptuous, blonde actress in the picture, rushed to greet him and threw her arms around him. The officers took their pistols out when Sharon and Rupert embraced. I mean, the tension was that strong during the making of that picture.

I also take great pride for being able to hire Will Geer, who played the grandfather in *The Reivers*. Will had been blacklisted for many years and when I offered him this part, I was told I couldn't use him. I was so horrified that the residue of the blacklist was still present that I threatened to hold a press conference and announce this blacklist. I was in a sense responsible for the resurgence of his career because he hadn't worked in some fifteen years. He was a blacklisted actor, a victim of the fifties horror and McCarthyism and I was in some sense responsible for the resurrection of his career, for which I proudly accept responsibility.

# The Cowboys (1972)

*John Wayne; Roscoe Lee Browne; Robert Carradine; Lonny Chapman;*
*Matt Clark; Bruce Dern; Colleen Dewhurst; A Martinez; Slim Pickins;*
*Alfred Barker, Jr.; Nicolas Beauvy; Steve Benedict; Norman Howell, Jr.;*
*Stephen R. Hudis; Sean Kelly; Clay O'Brien; Sam O'Brien; Mike Pyeatt.*

*The Cowboys* was one of the great experiences of my life. I found the novel, which was unpublished, and I sold it to Warner Bros. Warner's asked me if I would use John Wayne. I had George Scott in mind. I was a Jewish liberal, rebel, left-wing kind of guy and I knew John Wayne to be what he was. His reputation was well-known. He was a strong right-winger, very much a part of the blacklist of the fifties and responsible in some senses for that. When John Calley of Warner Bros. and I took the Warner plane down to Mexico to meet with him I was waiting for anti-Semitic remarks. I didn't really want to work with this monster. Well, he was in Mexico shooting a picture and he couldn't have been more gracious. It was a great lesson for me, by the way, which I'll get to in a moment. He was warm. He was deferential. He was intelligent. He was committed. He read the novel and told me he would love to try and do his best in the part if I'd give him a chance. I told him I wasn't looking for a director or a co-director or co-producer, because his reputation was very strong for swallowing directors for breakfast. I was going to produce and direct this film. He said, "Wonderful."

I went home stunned, and subsequently learned, during the making of *The Cowboys*, that he was indeed one of the most gracious, charming, available, professional men I had ever met. He could quote Shelley for half an hour and did so regularly with Roscoe Lee Brown, a great black actor who played opposite him. If you went to a restaurant with John Wayne it was like walking in with Abraham Lincoln.

I'll tell you a quick story that I suspect you'll enjoy. I was on a crane and had five different cameras working. We were shooting the scene at the beginning of the cattle drive. There were fifteen hundred head of cattle and one hundred horses. There were ten kids between the ages of eight and fifteen on horseback handling this cattle drive. Roscoe Lee Brown was up running the wagon and all the families of the children who were supposedly going on this cattle drive are there in the background. We have to roll the film when I think it's ready because to start fifteen hundred head of cattle moving you don't just say "go." Somebody has to nudge the cattle in the back and they begin to push the ones in the front and you begin to see a rippling effect and slowly, when all the cattle are going, I could roll the shot.

John Wayne was sitting over there on his horse and his first line to Roscoe Lee Brown is, "Let's move 'em out." So I'm waiting until I think the cattle are ready and he—John, "Duke"—decided that it was time. He rode up to Roscoe Lee Brown and started his lines. I became enraged with the rage of a child who had been challenged and I stood up and I said, "Duke, don't ever do that! Don't ever do that! You are an actor here, go back to your place, I'll tell you when we're starting!" Now I'm thinking I'm fired for sure. There were a lot of people watching and I humiliated John Wayne. I attacked him for crossing the line as an actor. Well, he turned around and walked back to his spot. Now I'm quivering, but I yell "Action" and we do the shot that had taken eight hours to get ready. When the shot was over it was the end of the day so he got in his car and left. The crane gets lowered and the crew all walked up to me one by one and shook my hand proudly, but as if to say goodbye. I just knew that the next day there would be a director down there from Warner Bros. to replace me.

The writers came over to me and said, "How could you have done that?" I said, "I'm so ashamed and I hate myself. I lost my temper. It was a terrible thing to do." We drove home to Santa Fe horrified and expecting at any moment to get word that I was being replaced. We get back to the office and sure enough, there were four calls from John Wayne. I screwed up my courage and I called him and he invited me to dinner. I thought, "This is it."

We went out to dinner at some wonderful restaurant called Nirvana. I don't know if it's still there. And, like I said before, it was like walking in with Lincoln or one of the great figures of history. The whole place went crazy but he was gracious to everybody who came over to him. He would sign autographs without hesitation and he was just sensational. But I'm waiting for the axe to drop. Now we begin to drink tequila. I hardly drink at all. Two drinks of tequila and I'm helpless. At one point he gets up and goes to the bathroom and hasn't said a word yet about the incident earlier in the day. When he comes back from the bathroom I noticed that one side of his trousers is soaking wet. I asked him what had happened. Wayne said, "It always happens to me. I'm standing there and I'm peeing and some guy next to me turns and says, 'You're John Wayne,' and pees all over me." To this day I don't know if that story is apocryphal or if it's the truth, but I believed it. In any event, this terrific guy, bigot though he was—this wonderful, warm, loving man—never said a word to me about the incident. He called me sir for the rest of the picture. He, in some sense, respected my confronting him, much like John Ford confronted him. I treasure the moments I spent with Wayne.

It was a physically arduous shoot. We shot in Santa Fe and in the mountains of Colorado. We shot for one hundred days and the entire budget, including the cattle and Wayne and everybody, was $5 million. That wouldn't pay for one actor today. It was a glorious and difficult shoot, but well worth it.

We also had to find ten boys who were actors who could do all the physical activities that were necessary. We hired five rodeo boys and five actors. The actors had to be trained because they had never been on horses before. By the time we started shooting you couldn't tell the difference because these kids quickly adapted to the glory of being cowboys and they rode, full speed, anytime we wanted. It was just thrilling to watch. It's a boy's dream, I'd imagine, being ten or eleven years old and told you're going to be a cowboy and you're going to do a man's job and be in a movie with John Wayne. It was a dream come true for these kids. And it was, as a result, a dream come true for myself.

> *Mark's movie* The Rose *is a very, very insightful study of a woman singer.* Something for the Boys *is a very interesting movie about the war.* On Golden Pond *is a beautiful, lyric film about growing old. These are all things that intrigue Mark as a director and I think Mark is a master of that.*
>
> Eli Wallach—Actor

# Cinderella Liberty (1973)

*James Caan; Marsha Mason; Kirk Calloway; Eli Wallach; Burt Young; Bruno Kirby; Allyn Ann McLerie; Dabney Coleman; Fred Sadoff; Allan Arbus; Jon Korkes; Don Calfa; Ted D'Arms; Sally Kirkland; Diane Schenker.*

*Cinderella Liberty* was a novel by Darryl Ponicsan that came to me by way of Twentieth Century Fox. It was a massive novel of social protest, but there was one chapter in the novel that was the inspiration for the screenplay. *Cinderella Liberty* is the story of a sailor and his relationship to a whore and her black son and the sailor's effort to make a family out of this unlikely group. That idea seemed very touching to me so we developed a screenplay based on that chapter of the book.

Many, many great actresses wanted to be in *Cinderella Liberty* because it was a wonderful part. Once I had hired James Caan, who I consider one of the best and most distinguished American actors, I went to look at various navy bases to use in the picture. I was in San Francisco and I decided on an impulse to go to the Geary Street Theater, where they were putting on a production of *A Doll's House*. That's where I saw Marsha Mason. I was so stunned by the brilliance of her talent. I went backstage to introduce myself to her and to tell her that I thought I had a leading role for her. She thought I was a masher or something. I had to convince her that I was really a director.

I met with her again the next day and then called Twentieth Century Fox and told them that I had found this girl. They were outraged that I had even thought of using an unknown. They cut my budget in half, but after one week's dailies, they sent me a wire saying that if I had the choice of any actress in the world they would have chosen her now. And she received an Oscar nomination for Best Actress.

There are endless stories about *Cinderella Liberty*. I'll tell you some. Marsha Mason's character is pregnant and delivers a child during the movie, so we decided to photograph a real delivery. We had hired three or four women who were relatively her size who were due to deliver during the period of our shooting. We paid for their delivery, all their expenses, and gave them some money. We always had a station wagon ready while we were shooting in case we would hear that somebody was in labor. We would be able to jump in that station wagon, that was all loaded with camera equipment, and race to the hospital.

Vilmos Zsigmond was our cameraman, a genius whose work I revere intensely. He's one of the most creative and stimulating partners that I've ever had. We got word that there was to be a delivery so we raced to the hospital and quickly donned our gowns. We had two hand-held cameras and Jimmy and Marsha stood in the background, out of the shot, watching so that they could reenact after the delivery was complete. This poor woman was screaming in pain. Her contractions couldn't have been more monumental. Vilmos is standing on a ladder changing the operating room lights to ones that were appropriate for filming and we managed to shoot a delivery of a child. It was one of the most extraordinary, exciting experiences that all of us could ever have. It took Jimmy and Marsha an hour to recover before we could shoot them and cut it into the stuff that we had. Jimmy was helpless from the miracle. There is no greater moment that I can think of than to watch this miracle occur. It was great.

# Harry and Walter Go to New York (1976)

*James Caan; Elliott Gould; Michael Caine; Diane Keaton;*
*Charles Durning; Lesley Ann Warren; Val Avery; Jack Gilford;*
*Dennis Dugan; Carol Kane; Kathryn Grody; David Proval;*
*Michael Conrad; Burt Young; Bert Remsen.*

I wanted to make a picture that was much more comedically oriented, almost a farce, and I really loved this screenplay. So I decided to make a kind of Laurel and Hardy comedy with James Caan and Elliott Gould as Laurel and Hardy, and Diane Keaton and Michael Caine and various others to be their supporting players, or actually playing large enough roles to be considered starring roles. It was a departure for me. I loved the film. I cannot watch it to this day without being hysterical. The film did not enjoy a great, enormous success, as most of my pictures prior to that had done, but I just loved it.

I know what you're about to say: "Tell me an interesting story about *Harry and Walter.*" I'll tell you a good one. We shot in the Ohio State Penitentiary, which was a maximum-security prison. We were shooting amongst quite difficult prisoners and it was somewhat dangerous. Everybody was scared that they would grab one of the actors and kidnap them for ransom or worse. A wire came in from David Begleman at the studio, who had a real sense of humor. The wire said: "If they get Caan, stall and negotiate. If they get Gould, stall and negotiate. If they get Caine or Keaton, stall and negotiate. If they get Rydell, stall until we can get another director."

As I said, the film was not very well received. There's nothing like failure to jolt you into unemployment. This town is not very tolerant of failure. The picture was not a real big box office success and I languished for a couple of years trying to find the right material to do and finding an environment that was conducive to my making a picture. Very often the director is the guy in the hot seat because, indeed, a director is responsible for every frame of the film. There's nobody else who can do it. It's one of the attractions of the job. You could put on every frame exactly what you want and if it doesn't work, you can fix it. And do it again until it's exactly as you want. And I must tell you that I do that in all my films and I must take responsibility for their failures—and their successes.

# The Rose (1979)

*Bette Midler; Alan Bates; Frederic Forrest; Harry Dean Stanton; Barry Primus;
David Keith; Sandra McCabe; Luke Andreas; Victor Argo; Jonathan Banks.*

*The Rose* languished for perhaps fifteen years. When it was first offered to
me I suggested Bette Midler play Janis Joplin. In those days, it was *The Janis
Joplin Story.* I had seen Bette in the Baths in New York. At that time Twentieth Century Fox didn't know who she was. Nobody knew who she was.
They wanted me to use an actress and dub in a singing voice. I told them
that was not acceptable to me. I told them that Bette should play the part
and they looked at me like I was crazy and suddenly I was out of the picture. Marvin Worth, the producer, stayed with it. Any number of directors
worked on it. Fifteen years later the studio became aware of who Bette was,
and they realized that I was the one who had suggested Bette in the very
beginning, so they came back to me with the project. I still consider doing
*The Rose* to be one of the great experiences of my life.

   Bette Midler is a truly remarkable talent. I don't think that the movie industry knows what to do with her. Occasionally they find a picture that
comes up to her talents—hopefully. *The Rose* was a good example. She had
never acted before but had a kind of vital and exciting talent that was incomparable. It was the first performance she had ever given as an actress.
She was very intimidated by having to act with Alan Bates and Fred Forrest
and all those really wonderful actors. She was, after all, making a film that
was inspired by a genius, Janis Joplin, although it was a fictionalized film,
which was my contribution to it. I insisted that it be fictionalized because
if you make the Janis Joplin story, you are bound by the circumstances of
her life and while we used many of those circumstances, this was a fictionalized version.

   I don't know of any performer that I've ever worked with who is able to
turn herself inside out with as much skill as Bette. There are some who can
turn themselves inside out and when you look at the inside, it's not worth
it. That's not so with Bette. What's in there is gold all the time. It was a really great privilege to be the one who guided her and I am eternally grateful to her for the generosity with which she turned herself over to me. Not
having any real craft as an actress, she really listened and delivered every
single moment that I ever required and in an extraordinary way, with

power that still astonishes me to this day. I am her devoted slave; I will make any picture with her at any time.

I'll give you an example of Bette's perfectionism. We had to do a series of concerts. She rehearsed with the band on the stage at Twentieth Century Fox for a month or two to develop the character of The Rose. She had a very successful act independently of *The Rose* which she performed all the time, but suddenly she was playing a rock 'n' roll singer doing a lot of songs that she had never done before and she was thrust into an almost impossible situation. She took an act that had never been previewed into a theater with fifteen hundred to two thousand people dressed in sixties wardrobe. There was no way to anticipate whether or not they would like this act. It was like taking a play to Broadway without taking it on the road to Boston and Philadelphia and New Haven and trying it out and fixing it.

All I told the audience was that this was a very big rock star that you will love, but if she is no good, then don't pretend. If you enjoy her, let it happen. We announced her and she came out and did this act and she mesmerized this audience. She paralyzed everybody that was present. We shot with nine cameras, each one operated by a very distinguished cameraman. We had every major cameraman come down and pick up a camera and I assigned them positions—everybody from Conrad Hall, Haskell Wexler, Laslo Kovacks—it was an endless group of geniuses who were operating the cameras, all under the supervision of Vilmos Zsigmond and myself.

It took hours to shoot this concert, but then we wanted another take. This was all done live, by the way. All the music in *The Rose* is live. There's no pre-recording and there was very little post-recording. Essentially it was a live twenty-four-track performance—we got what we got. She was exhausted at the end of her performance but we had to get her ready to do a whole other performance for take two. The audience was also exhausted but we managed to do it again. Bette got herself up and was brilliant. The audience was inspired and thrilled with her second performance and we shot it brilliantly, I thought. So now we've finished and it's four in the morning and I walk into her dressing room to embrace her and tell her that it was a miracle, what had happened, and I'd see her tomorrow. She said, "What do you mean? We're not gonna do it again?" I said, "Bette, my God, I've never seen anything like this, and we have enough for twelve movies." She was furious that I wouldn't give her a chance to do yet another concert. That was Bette.

## On Actors in General

I probably have said this here before, that every actor is a different case. I have a real deep and abiding love for actors and for the profession of acting. I think it's an extremely courageous profession because it requires really letting yourself go in front of many people. If you want to do it properly, you have to be out of control, in some sense. You have to put yourself in the circumstances of the material. You have to allow yourself to be surprised by what happens to you. You have to call upon your unconscious and it's a very denuding experience—you're like naked. And it requires a lot of willpower and dedication to do it well. I think actors sense that I appreciate them and I appreciate their task. They know that I have been an actor many times myself and I think that I can talk to them in ways that many directors find difficult. I'm compassionate to their problems, I understand what they're going through, and I appreciate it. And they know that I wouldn't ask them to do anything that I can't do. I think that reassures them. I do respect them very highly. I think the profession of acting is a noble one and a very difficult one and actors deserve enormous credit and the enormous fees that they get all the time.

## On Golden Pond (1981)

*Katharine Hepburn; Henry Fonda; Jane Fonda; Doug McKeon;*
*Dabney Coleman; William Lanteau; Christopher Rydell.*

Directing *On Golden Pond* was one of the great, great summers that I will ever spend in my life. It was an enchanted summer. It was a real honor that Henry Fonda, Kate Hepburn, and Jane Fonda wanted me to guide them. It was very intimidating, I must tell you, to realize that you are directing perhaps the greatest living actor of the time, Henry Fonda, and certainly one of the great actresses of all history, Katharine Hepburn.

I must tell you that every day was a lesson to me. You would have thought that actors of their stature would have a certain kind of confidence that what they were doing was always right. But they were like twenty-year-old actors. An actor, if he's doing it properly, doesn't know what happened in the sense that if you watch yourself when you're acting, if you're judging yourself as you act, you are, to that extent, not really acting. You are being the judge and the performer at the same time. They knew that instinctively. They knew that. You didn't have to teach them that. They would surrender to a scene and at the end of the scene they would turn to me with the innocent faces of children to see my approval, to see if it was all right. And it was the thing that reassured me the most because I was very intimidated by the responsibility of directing these geniuses. I watched Henry Fonda; I stared at him day after day from under the camera. I never ever saw him do a false moment. A wrong moment, yes—a moment that I would have to adjust because he made the wrong choice. But I never saw him do anything false. Even a wrong moment he would do perfectly. And I would have to say to him, "Perhaps this is a better idea, Henry, maybe this might be a better choice," and he would try it and do it immediately.

How do you describe Kate Hepburn? Katharine Hepburn, Katharine Hepburn, Katharine Hepburn. How many people have had the privilege of having directed her, who are alive, who had the privilege of directing her in a performance that won her the Academy Award? She is an incomparable woman. She's enthusiastic, passionate, and brilliant. You know, if she watches this, she'll go like this [sticking his finger in his mouth]. She'll be horrified that I'm giving her all these accolades, but I treasure every moment that I've spent with her. She's a great raconteur. Is that the right word? She tells stories better than anybody.

Three weeks before shooting she broke her shoulder serving in tennis so I went to the hospital where she had surgery. She was lying there with all kinds of bandages and I said, "Can you do the picture?" And she said, "Don't be ridiculous!" There was nothing that would stop her from doing the picture. To this day she's still furious with me because of one scene I had to cut. Early in the picture she and Henry Fonda are in front of a fireplace and they talk about going canoeing. She goes out and picks up the canoe by herself, a canoe that must have weighed one hundred pounds, lifted it over her head, walked down to the dock, and put it in the water. When we put the picture together I realized it would be good to cut from the fireplace to them canoeing, which required me to cut the scene of her holding the canoe. She never forgave me. She was enraged that I didn't show her carrying that heavy canoe.

She required a lot more attention in a certain way. Let's see, I have to say this, Kate, so that you don't get offended. She has a tendency to be larger than life. The performances needed containment and I found a good way of containing her by telling her to whisper. I would say to her, "See if you can whisper this thing," and then she began to understand the nature of a certain kind of intimacy that I thought was required for the material. But she never failed me at any moment.

She's always wearing those high collars. Everybody says she has to wear those collars because of her neck. There's a scene in the gazebo where she's sitting alone and Henry Fonda comes up and kisses her on the neck. So I thought, "Here's my chance." I said, "Kate, what is this thing with the high collars? Can I see your neck?" I figured I might as well bore right in. So she showed me her neck, which was glorious and beautiful, but it was a habit, a style that she developed with the high collars. She wasn't hiding anything. I told her that I would like the relationship between her and Henry to be sexual. I would like to have the feeling that they still are intimate at night and go to bed together. She was shocked that I would dare ask her, but she loved it, of course. I thought that was a big element of the relationship. There was almost a sexual intimacy between the two of them that I thought was wonderful in the picture.

During rehearsals Kate told story after story about Spencer Tracy. She loved telling stories about him and adored Spencer. (I say "Spencer" as if I knew him, but I didn't. Mr. Tracy would have been more graceful.) She told these wonderful stories but I sensed that Henry was beginning to feel somewhat left out so I went to her and I asked her if she could do something about this. I asked if she could do something to include Henry because he was now her husband in the film. She looked at me and understood immediately what I was saying. On the first day of shooting she brought Spencer's hat and gave it to Henry and said, "You're my man. Here's Spencer's hat, would you wear it?" Well, I mean Henry wept uncontrollably for five minutes. And of course it did what was necessary to transfer her relationship.

Kate was a great supporter of the underlying reality of the picture, that was Jane's effort to repair her relationship with her father, which was mirrored in the script. But it was also a reality in life. Jane indeed bought the play for Henry. She used it as a device to repair their relationship and that was what was going on during the summer. So it was an exciting thing to be part of and to help guide toward conclusion. I felt that I was doing a good thing and they were doing a good thing because by the time the picture ended they had resolved all of the problems and they were very close.

I must tell you that, not unlike all of the pictures I've ever made, I have always had to beg to get my pictures made. Pictures that aspire to a certain kind of quality are not always the easiest pictures to finance. There is a certain kind of commerce that interferes with that. I begged to get this picture made, even after Henry Fonda, Katharine Hepburn, and Jane were committed to it. All of them worked for very little money. But I had to beg to get the picture made.

I hate to seem arrogant, I'm often accused of it, but I knew from word one that we had a hit picture. When we had an argument over my salary in the picture, when I was negotiating my deal, I offered to take no salary and a certain amount of money for every nomination that the picture got. Fortunately, all that did was tell them how much I believed in the picture. They paid me the salary I asked for because if they had done the deal that I had proposed, it would have cost them ten times as much, because the picture received ten Academy Award nominations.

## His Opinion of Awards

The Academy Awards becomes a kind of blank spot. You go to the Academy Awards and you're in kind of a state of emotional paralysis. You can hardly hear, not because it's not loud enough, but because you're emotionally deaf. I must tell you that I am not a great fan of awards. This is something that will not endear me to the profession. But this is the most self-congratulatory profession. Every night you're turning on another awards show on television where we're giving recognition, and it gets a little bit uncomfortable for me. There shouldn't be winners. To pick them against one another is absurd. It becomes like a popularity contest and it has nothing to do with the fact that some of the great performances and pictures are not recognized for any number of reasons. So I am not a great fan of awards shows. On the other hand, I would miss them, I'm addicted to them, and I'm thrilled to be nominated. I was so excited when I received my nomination and when the picture received ten nominations. It's almost unheard of and it happens so rarely. It was a great honor and an exciting evening. But if it were up to me there would be no awards shows.

> The River was at a time in my career when I was very young. I think it was my first American film, so I was like very intimidated, and Mark was very generous and I think he sensed that and he wanted to put his actors at their ease. In fact, I heard him say something one day. We did a take and it worked all right for me but the camera guy said, "Oh, gee, it was a bit of a shaky frame for me." Mark said it didn't matter that the frame looks like shit so long as what happened within it was okay. Given the choice, he would rather have the frame look great and what's happening in it look great too, but being an actor I think he could understand that we didn't need to do another take. That was great.
>
> Mel Gibson—Actor

# The River (1984)

*Mel Gibson; Sissy Spacek; Shane Bailey; Becky Jo Lynch; Scott Glenn;*
*Don Hood; Billy Green Bush; James Tolkan; Bob W. Douglas; Andy Stahl;*
*Lisa Sloan; Larry D. Ferrell; Susie Toomey; Kelly Toomey; Frank Taylor.*

The making of *The River* was an extraordinary experience for me because I come from the Bronx. That's one of the reasons I was attracted to making *The River*. It dealt with areas of life with which I wasn't automatically familiar and I had to do a lot of research. It's one of the adventures of being a director. You never know what area you're going to be in and it's like a constant education. Suddenly you're dealing with rock 'n' roll of the sixties and then you're at a lake in New Hampshire or you're making a picture about farmers or cowboys. Life is so exciting. Art is so exciting. Curiosity keeps you alive and keeps you young.

So *The River* was a challenge. It was a challenge in the sense that I had to expose myself to a life with which I was not familiar. And it was very difficult to create a flood. *The River*, for those of you who never have seen it, is about flooding of farmlands. We had to create every drop of water in that picture. We had to find the right river that we could control with the help of the Army Corps of Engineers and build a levee in which there were hydraulic doors so that we could raise the river. I learned about reverence for the land and about what the farmers of this country experience and the difficulty of the life of those people who are responsible for agriculture in our country.

I turned Mel Gibson down out of hand when he was offered to me. I thought it was absurd, this actor whom I thought was Australian. I subsequently found out that he lived in upstate New York and moved to Australia. But he insisted on coming to see me. It's one of the things I admire most about people, enthusiasm, a commitment, a kind of determination—later I'll tell you about Sharon Stone's determination. But Mel Gibson demonstrated his determination. He came to my house and said he wanted to play this part. I was polite to him and I said, "Listen, I think it's a very interesting idea but I don't think really that you're right for it." He told me that he was American. I didn't quite believe it. He was on his way to England to do *Mutiny on the Bounty* and he said, "Promise me that you won't cast it until I have a chance to read for you." I said, "Of course."

Now he goes to England and shoots for ten or twelve weeks and then has to go to Tahiti, but he flew back through L.A. to get there. He called me up and said he was coming over and he comes to my house to read. I figured by this time he had worked on the screenplay with a dialogue coach and was going to show me a Tennessee accent. I said, "Do you have your accent taken care of?" He said yes. So that he wouldn't read the lines from the script, I said, "Here, take this *Time* magazine. Read me an article from *Time* magazine." He took the article and he proceeded to read for me. It was astonishing! His transformation into a Tennessee farmer just blew me away. I told him right then and there that he was my man. I admire that kind of pursuit, that kind of determination, that kind of love of acting that makes a guy want to play a part. It's that kind of enthusiasm, it's that kind of affection for material that makes the difference. When someone needs to play a part, you're halfway home.

I will tell you that I told Sissy Spacek that she was my farm goddess. I fell in love with her during the making of that film. Sissy is one of the most remarkable women. She's had a wonderful career and I hope it continues with the same kind of fervor which has existed in the past. She has warmth and a depth and solidity and she's a mother. She has a sense of the earth and of the American that's inbred in her. I've been lucky in my life. I've worked with some of the best actresses alive and I continue to do so. And she stands very high on that list.

Sissy had this scene where she had to repair a tractor. She gets under the tractor to repair it, and, as written, her arm gets caught between a gear and a chain and it really catches her, digs deeply into her arm, and she's trapped in an empty field with nobody around for miles. There was the danger of bleeding to death. It was quite a horrifying scene. Nearby there's a bull that she induces to attack the tractor so that she can free herself. That's the way it was written.

We found a passive bull to play the easy shots. But then, when we needed the bull to attack the tractor, we had to get a ferocious bull. So ferocious, indeed, that a full tractor had to be embedded in the earth with spikes or the bull could take the tractor and toss it twenty feet. Then there was a stunt girl that had to lie down under the tractor. We dug a pit underneath the tractor for the camera and the crew and myself. The stunt girl did these horrendously dangerous shots where Sissy throws a shoe at the bull. And he snorts. Then she throws another shoe at the bull and then we brought the bull that had indeed killed some people. That's how ferocious it was.

The stuntwoman gets in place and next they prod this bull and the bull hurtles his twenty-five hundred pounds—or whatever it was, it seemed like it must have weighed twenty thousand pounds, the way it looked at me. I was six inches from it when it attacked the tractor, which was being held down by spikes or else it would have flown away. It was so alien to my experiences, you know, a Bronx jazz musician. This bull put dents in a metal tractor that had everybody shocked. The sequence is a really good sequence, in my estimation. Ninety percent of it is Sissy except for those final moments where the bull attacks the tractor. Where are you gonna get that experience in life?

## Disappointments along the Way

I spent five years developing a picture called *Nuts*, which was eventually made with Ms. Streisand. She and I did not enjoy the healthiest of relationships. She's a genius. But she likes to control things and I must tell you that I didn't enjoy that situation. I feel that there's only room for one leader on a picture and I feel that that leader has to be me. So that is why, with all due respect—because I think she is one of the most extraordinarily talented people that our industry has ever produced—I withdrew from that project. After five years it was a grave disappointment because I had developed the screenplay. It hurt me personally and emotionally. I felt like I had been run over by a truck. I felt like something that had been mine, that I had nurtured from its inception from a stage play through five drafts of a screenplay—suddenly somebody else was doing it. Marty Ritt, one of my early closest friends, ended up directing it with Barbra. And that hurt me.

Then I spent a lot of time developing a picture with Marshall Brickman from a novel called *Fifty*. We developed that one with Richard Dreyfuss for a number of years. We were two days away from shooting the picture and, for reasons that I'd rather not go into, personal complicated business reasons, the plug was pulled. There was one great experience that came out of that project and that was my relationship with Marshall Brickman, who I consider to be one of the most enjoyable and brilliant people in the business. He subsequently has written quite a few pictures for me. That relationship was established during the preparation of *Fifty*.

Both of those things happened one after the other. I brought two pictures to the point of shooting and then for various reasons they didn't go. One because of my relationship with Ms. Streisand, and on the second, because of business reasons, Tri-Star felt that the Dreyfuss picture should be cancelled. Both of those experiences were deep emotional disappointments to me. But whatever disappointments came from that were balanced out by my relationship with Marshall Brickman, who wrote the next two pictures that I did.

# For the Boys (1991)

*Bette Midler; James Caan; George Segal; Patrick O'Neal; Christopher Rydell; Arye Gross; Norman Fell; Rosemary Murphy; Bud Yorkin; Dori Brenner; Jack Sheldon; Melissa Manchester; Karen Martin; Shannon Wilcox; Michael Greene.*

Bette Midler had been developing this idea about a show biz couple. The story spanned many years in their relationship. The opportunity of working with Bette again was really exciting. I immediately saw the opportunity to make a kind of portrait of America over a fifty-year period and how this country has changed in its attitude towards wars. After all, the picture dealt with World War II, the Korean conflict, and Vietnam, so you had a chance to really examine this nation's change during that fifty-year period. If you remember, the picture began with Bette as an old lady being seduced into coming to an award dinner for her previous partner, played by Jimmy Caan, from whom she had been estranged. She didn't want to go to the dinner and the guy who came to take her got her talking about her life. What she remembered is what we got to see in the picture.

I'm very proud of that picture. I thought that in some ways it was done a disservice by its marketing approach. It was marketed as a Bette Midler musical comedy, which it was not. It was a serious picture. But those in charge felt that our triumph in the Persian Gulf was so patriotic that to do a picture whose clear intention was to expose the absurdities of war was not the way to go. I felt that the picture was marketed too lightly. Although the studio stood behind it and spent quite a bit of money marketing that picture, they marketed the wrong picture. They were afraid that American patriotism would reject an anti-war theme picture. So they advertised the picture without the soberness and seriousness of its intent. I think anytime you lie to an audience about what you're going to present, you're putting yourself in danger of having less of an audience than you were capable of getting.

I was thrilled with the picture. Every audience who saw the picture loved it. The picture will appear on network television finally in its full, uncut version. I refused to allow them to cut it and I was lucky enough to have a contractual clause that said that they could not cut the picture for television. So you're gonna see the picture as it was intended, with the possible exception of a few curse words that networks won't allow. But essentially you're going to be able to see the picture as it was intended and I'm delighted that it's going to be seen probably by more people in one night than all those who have seen it in all of its theatrical release.

As for Jimmy Caan, I have a special relationship with him. Jimmy is, in my estimation, one of the greatest actors in America. He's had a very turbulent life and he is now reappearing on the scene, and he deserves all of the affection and respect of anybody who admires great acting because he is indeed a great actor.

The great glory and joy of that picture is the fact that my real son, Christopher Rydell, played the adult son of Bette Midler in the Vietnam sequence. The opportunity of working with my son was so wonderful and he was so fabulous in the part that I weep when I think about it. There's a scene in Vietnam where he is killed and I had to photograph this scene and it shook me to my toes to do it. To have to execute one's own son is no pleasure, even though it was just in a movie. The additional pleasure that I had in that picture was that my daughter is a very good dancer and she played one of the dancers in the fifties' television. I got a chance to have the major portion of my family in the picture. My eight-year-old son, Alexander, has yet to be in a picture. My wife played George Segal's wife in the picture, so nepotism does exist.

# Intersection (1994)

*Richard Gere; Sharon Stone; Lolita Davidovich; Martin Landau;*
*David Selby; Jenny Morrison; Ron White; Matthew Walker;*
*Scott Bellis; Patricia Harras; Keegan MacIntosh; Alan C. Peterson;*
*Sandra P. Grant; Robyn Stevan; David Hurtubise.*

Sherry Lansing was a producer at Paramount prior to becoming the big cheese at Paramount. She sent me the original screenplay by David Rayfiel, which was subsequently enhanced by the work of Marshall Brickman because Rayfiel was not available to do the rewrites. I loved the idea of doing *Intersection* because it dealt with problems that I felt were common to any marriage. It seemed to me a deeply personal story. The drama came from the interaction of real, interesting characters as opposed to car chases or bank robberies or other melodramatic issues. It was an adult story about a man's torment in leaving a wife and a child and moving on to another life with another woman.

The picture begins with a car accident. The car starts to spin out of control and you spin into the story and pick up the few days prior to the accident that leads you back to the accident and the end of the picture. The idea of breaking conventional linear form and moving rather fluidly from scene to scene in a nonlinear manner was adventurous for American movies. It had been done brilliantly by the French but this was an American adaptation. It was a terrific exercise in filmmaking to make those transitions work, to challenge an audience with a new form, a new style, forcing them to concentrate in a way that they're not used to.

Most TV audiences are used to five-minute segments and then they go and have a beer while a commercial is on. I think that's been some of the most destructive results of some of the lesser television programs. There are great things on television occasionally, but I think that one of the real disadvantages of television is its effort to reduce two of the most common denominators. It has stupefied audiences and makes them unprepared for adventurous films. On the other hand it's also true that you find that people are flocking to the theaters nowadays because they get a chance to get away from this little box and to see something of size and magnitude.

In any event, it's shameful to admit, but I like all of my pictures. I loved *Intersection*. I saw it the other night. I thought, it's on television and I'm going to watch the first few minutes. I couldn't stop. I watched it from beginning to end, unashamedly pleased with what I had done.

The accident was shot in slow motion, for the most part, and it was examined in the minutest detail. A car is speeding along and a little Volkswagen bus is stalled in the road. Richard Gere, who is driving the car, is driving rather fast in exultation of having made a commitment or a decision that we had been waiting for throughout the picture. When he tries to avoid the Volkswagen bus he swings around and there is a truck. He then has to swing again in the opposite direction and winds up in a spin and hits the Volkswagen bus, spins around and hits a truck and then another car, and winds up rolling over and over and over. It was a grotesque, horrific accident and we planned, as you must in preparing something like that, for months and months. Every detail of the accident was precisely manufactured and we were able to invent equipment that enabled us to do things that you couldn't do otherwise.

For example, we built a car on the chassis of another car that was driven by a stuntman. They put on top of the chassis a Mercedes Benz with Richard in it. The car was actually being driven by stuntmen, so that when the car is zooming along Richard is pretending to drive. You don't see the lower car underneath. They were able to spin the Mercedes on top of its chassis so that you saw the trees and everything moving behind it but underneath the car was continuing in the proper direction and was in full control. We photographed the spinning and tumbling of a car many, many, many times.

Then we had to put Richard in that car as it was rolling down the embankment. Well, how do you do that? How do you photograph somebody spinning around 360 degrees in a car and see a close-up of his face as the car tumbles over and over and over? Well, we developed another piece of equipment, which was a kind of armature that stuck out from a truck and we impaled the car on this armature. Then, as the truck rolled along, the Mercedes revolved under controlled circumstance. Then we shot at very high speed and spun Richard around many, many times. It was like a ride at Disneyland. It was like being on a roller coaster. And it produced the reality of that accident.

I had originally wanted Sharon Stone to play Lolita Davidovich's role. She is a quite remarkable human being. I think she is underrated in this industry. She's achieved enormous stardom in the past few years. People don't credit her appropriately for the immense achievement of that character she played in *Basic Instinct*. People tended to say that it was eroticism and exposure of her pubic hair that made her a star. Don't let anybody fool you, she's one of the best actresses we have. She walked away with that picture because of her acting and because of her ability to play that role as brilliantly as she did.

Anyway, she wanted to play the wife in *Intersection*. I had the normal conventional thought that she should play the lover. I fell into the trap, as many people do, of typecasting her as the sexual object. She, with her infinite wisdom, insisted that she wanted to try out for the role of the wife. And as I've mentioned in a number of newspaper interviews, she was like a little schnauzer pursuing that role. She grabbed hold of my pants and wouldn't let go. She wanted to play that part. She was shooting *Sliver* at the time and she and Richard Gere came in and we read all of her scenes and she was spectacular. Brilliant! I was stunned with the depth of her talent because she is a very well-trained actress. She's so beautiful that it's hard to look at her without falling in love. The opportunity to let her play a very classy, Grace Kelly type of a part made it impossible to refuse her. I think her performance in *Intersection* is astonishing. Richard loved working with her. Lolita loved working with her. Everybody loved working with her. She's an amazing creature. I hope I get a chance to work with her again because every moment was a joy.

## Directors Must Read

You know, the real profession of a director is reading. What you do between pictures and during pictures is expose yourself to material. I have one test of material that I use all the time. When I read material, it must move me. I believe that art is not worth its salt if it doesn't reach in and move you. If the hair stands up on the back of my neck when I'm reading something, I know that there's something in the material that's hooked into my unconscious and that I will have an endless creative source for directing a film. I know I have hooked into something deep, significant, beyond the material. When the response is visceral, the hair literally stands up on the back of your neck and suddenly tears are streaming down your face because you're reading something that moves you. That's the time when I'm assured that I will not run out of skill to make the picture because I'm hooked into that endless source of talent which is your unconscious. Once you hook in there, you're okay.

## How Have the Studios Changed?

How have the major studios changed over the years? Well, people are quick to attack motion pictures nowadays because of the blockbuster mentality that I believe has hurt the motion picture industry. The weekend-gross syndrome didn't exist ten or fifteen years ago. You open a picture now on Friday night against three or four other pictures that are opening that same weekend. By eight in the evening, through the miracle of computers, you know what you're going to do over that weekend. It's all about dollars and cents. It's rarely about quality.

There are pictures now that are enormously successful that produce hundreds of millions of dollars and that's a difficult thing for studios to resist. But what it does is damage the ability of filmmakers to make pictures of quality that might not have quite as broad an audience, but there must be room made for pictures of quality. The motion picture is the art of the twentieth century. It's a form that needs to be respected. The great filmmakers are still making great films, but great filmmaking is much more difficult to achieve because of the studios' wish to compete in the world of blockbusters—the $200, $300 million-grossing pictures. Not every picture can do that. Nor should it. That's why there's a PBS, because there's a home for certain kinds of quality that may not appeal to the broadest audience. But we have a responsibility to educate, to lead, to sharpen people's appreciation of art. It's the salvation of humanity.

For God's sake, if we didn't have art, which appeals to the highest qualities in human beings, we would be doomed. The other night on the Grammy show there was a speech made by the president of The Recording Academy in support of the National Endowment for the Arts and attacking Newt Gingrich's attempt to eliminate finances for the arts. During the speech he quoted Winston Churchill, who, during World War II, when asked to cut the budget for the arts, took a moment and then said, "Hell no! What are we fighting for?" That is a powerful and significant message. This is a noble profession. Its significance cannot be underestimated. We must not turn our backs on the world of art in any way. It's our salvation.

## His Parting Words

Parting words? Well, what can I say? I want to talk to the young people. I want to tell them not to be deterred by rejection but to believe in themselves. If you do believe in yourself, persist. You'll get your chance. And be ready for it. Train, train, and train so that you can be ready. God forbid you get your moment and you're not ready for it, so go prepare and study. Art is a vast subject of enormous interest. Keep your enthusiasm. Keep your curiosity. And work.

# Director Filmography

*The Fox* (1968)
*The Reivers* (1969)
*The Cowboys* (1972)
*Cinderella Liberty* (1973)
*Harry and Walter Go to New York* (1976)
*The Rose* (1979)
*On Golden Pond* (1981)
*The River* (1984)
*For the Boys* (1991)
*Intersection* (1994)
*Crime of the Century* (TV, 1996)

---

NOTE: Since the completion of this interview Rydell has directed *Crime of the Century* for HBO. The story about the Charles Lindbergh baby case starred Stephen Rea, Isabella Rossellini, J.T. Walsh; Jay Acovone; Allen Garfield; David Paymer; Gerald S. O'Loughlin; Michael Moriarty; Barry Primus, and Bert Remsen.

# Awards

**Academy Awards, USA**

*On Golden Pond*, Best Director (nominated), 1982

**British Academy Awards**

*On Golden Pond*, Best Direction (nominated), 1983

**Emmy Awards**

*Crime of the Century*, Outstanding Individual Achievement in Directing for a Miniseries or a Special (nominated), 1997

**Golden Globes, USA**

*On Golden Pond*, Best Director—Motion Picture (nominated), 1982

*The Fox*, Best Motion Picture Director (nominated), 1968

# The Films of David Zucker, Jim Abrahams, and Jerry Zucker

David and Jerry Zucker and Jim Abrahams grew up in Shorewood, Wisconsin, a suburb of Milwaukee. After graduation, David, Jerry, and their friend Jim rented the back of a Madison, Wisconsin, bookstore and created their own comedy troupe, Kentucky Fried Theater, a multi-media show that combined live improvisations with videotaped and filmed sketches. In 1972, they moved to Los Angeles and opened a new Kentucky Fried Theater, which soon attracted critical acclaim and a devoted following. In five years they performed to more than 150,000 patrons and became the most successful small theater group in Los Angeles history.

In 1977, the team of "ZAZ" released their first movie. Inspired by their stage show, *Kentucky Fried Movie* soon became a hit independent release. Their next project, *Airplane!,* became the surprise hit of 1980, and launched the trio on a streak of successful movies and TV shows, including the Emmy-nominated *Police Squad, Top Secret,* and *Ruthless People,* one of the top-grossing films of 1986.

> *I'll never forget when we did* Airplane! *and an interviewer asked the boys why they just pulled up stakes and left Milwaukee to come out to Tinsel Town to make movies. How did that happen? So David says, "Well, you have to understand that back in 1972 motion picture making in Milwaukee was at an all-time low." It's so ridiculous. Great line.*
> Leslie Nielsen—Actor

NOTE: Although the chapter includes the work of David and Jerry Zucker and Jim Abrahams, only David Zucker and Jim Abrahams were interviewed, both on separate occasions. David Zucker's interview appears first, followed by Jim Abrahams' interview.

# The Conversation with David Zucker

I guess my unique sense of humor probably comes more from my dad. The skepticism about what was coming across on the TV channels or in the movies came from my mom. I remember sitting in our den watching TV with the family. It was my mom who would talk back to the TV and criticize what was going on. That's kind of where the satire comes from. She was an actress from the time she was five. In fact, she was in some shows at Carnegie Hall in New York, where she grew up.

My dad has a very dry sense of humor, sarcastic. He would always put people on. His natural bent was just to make jokes. Around our dinner table at night, everybody was doing puns and it was a pretty funny affair.

Jerry and I were kind of the class clowns. I remember teachers saying to Jerry and me, "Zucker, someday I'm going to pay to see you, but for now, shut up and hit the books."

While we were in college, Jerry and I made some Super 8 student movies. One was a very funny ten-minute movie about Jerry running around campus trying to find a place to take a leak. So we showed that in our study session of twenty students and they laughed so hard the teacher's assistant wanted to take it to the professor to see what he thought of it. The professor liked it so much that he asked me if I would mind him showing it to the entire lecture hall of eight hundred students. I had never seen this stuff in front of a whole audience. I think that when Jerry and I saw that played we were hooked. Just to see that many people laugh at something we did on film was just great. We really didn't have that feeling again until we did a preview of *Kentucky Fried Movie* in 1977.

We ran a small theater called Kentucky Fried Theater in Los Angeles. Well, first on the campus of Madison for a year in 1971. Then we loaded up a U-Haul truck and Jerry and Jim and I drove out west in 1972. We set up the whole theater just as we had in Madison. In Madison it was about seventy seats and we had twice that many in California. We ran it until 1975.

Even before that we started writing scripts. The first script we wrote was *Airplane,* but we couldn't sell it. We had gotten to know John Landis and he suggested we do a movie based on our Kentucky Fried shows. We wrote a movie using all of the sketches from the Kentucky Fried Theater show. It was an hour-and-a-half show.

So we wrote the script and managed to get financed by putting our own money into a ten-minute sample of the film. That proved to United Artists Theater Circuit, who financed the production, that we could do it. We got Bob White to produce and John Landis to direct and we were the writers and producers at the same time. It was the first time we had ever been on a movie set. We learned a lot. We learned that if you really wanted a movie to come out the way you wanted it to, you had to direct. So on the next movie, *Airplane!*, we insisted on directing.

When I was in college, I used to love the Marx Brothers' movies, the Three Stooges and Woody Allen. But what made me laugh the most was seeing serious movies and throwing in my own lines. I think that's kind of how this whole thing evolved. We had this concept of creating these serious movies with actors like Robert Stack and Leslie Nielsen and then put our own lines in, almost as if we were taking the real movies and re-dubbing them.

We had the idea for *Airplane!* way back in the early seventies when we were doing the Kentucky Fried Theater. We used to leave the videotape recorder on overnight just to catch the late movies and to get the commercials so we could re-dub later and spoof them in some way. We would view the tape in the morning and see what we had gotten the night before.

> *I can say this in retrospect because Ross Hunter is no longer with us and he did* Airport, *as you know. Ross Hunter never got over* Airplane! *"What have they done to my movie?!" he would say. "An old man naked! God!"*
>
> Robert Stack—Actor

# Airplane! (1980)
*Robert Hays; Julie Hagerty; Lloyd Bridges; Leslie Nielsen;*
*Peter Graves; Robert Stack; Kareem Abdul-Jabbar; Lorna Patterson;*
*Stephen Stucker; Jim Abrahams; Frank Ashmore; Jonathan Banks;*
*Craig Berenson; Lee Bryant; Barbara Billingsley; Maureen McGovern.*

One night we recorded a movie called *Zero Hour.* It's a 1957 movie starring Dana Andrews, Linda Darnell, and Sterling Hayden. It was one of those "airliner in trouble" movies. Remember, this was during the time that Universal Pictures had come out with a series of *Airport* movies. And so we thought it would be a great idea to do a spoof of those films. And so we started writing it. Originally it was called *The Late Show*, with the plane-in-trouble movie being spoofed and commercials in between. People were reading the script and saying, "This airliner-in-trouble movie is pretty good, but could you make the commercials shorter?" So we kept dropping them to less and less until we had eliminated the commercials altogether. We now had this expanded airport spoof which we called *Airplane!*

To spoof something you have to have some affection for the genre. We really did like those Universal *Airport* movies. Just like we liked the police movies, the *Dirty Harry* movies and all those police shows we spoofed with Leslie Nielsen. We were watching these *Airport* movies and thinking, "Charlton Heston is just too funny." The trick was to cast serious actors like Robert Stack, Leslie Nielsen, Peter Graves, and Lloyd Bridges. These were people who up to that time had never done comedy. We thought they were much funnier than the comedians of the time were.

It wasn't easy getting these guys. Robert Stack was the most important one because he was the linchpin of the whole plot. We felt we needed someone of his stature to really anchor the whole thing and make it really funny. He was really reluctant to try it because we had never directed before. I was prepared to camp out on his front lawn and pitch a tent until he said yes.

With Peter Graves and Lloyd Bridges, I think it was because of their kids. Lloyd Bridges showed the script to his sons and they said, "Dad, you have to do this." They knew it was going to be funny. Leslie was the only one who needed no prodding whatsoever. Leslie needed to show it to no one. He looked at the script and said to his agent, which we heard later, "I don't care if you have to pay them. I want to do this movie."

We had a meeting with Peter Graves. He said that he had read the script and it was funny, but why did we want him? So we tried to explain to Peter that he was the joke. We told him it was going to be a new kind of comedy that didn't rely on comedians but relied on the jokes and the seriousness of the characters and the absurdity of the situations. And the straighter he could play it the better it would be. He said he had never done comedy and wasn't with it. I told him that didn't matter. He just needed to be comfortable with what he'd done for his entire career, which was to play it straight, do it serious, let the lines do the work.

Peter was a little uncomfortable with the scene where he asks the little boy if he's seen a grown man naked. He was a little bit uncomfortable doing it. There's that fine line between good and bad taste, not that I've ever aspired to good taste. So when we actually shot the scene I told Peter, instead of saying the line directly to the little boy, look straight ahead and say it. It made it funny for some reason.

We also told Peter, like we do everybody, that if it's not funny, it won't be in the movie. And if it's funny and people laugh that means it's okay. We have tried bits in movies where you just hear a gigantic sucking sound from the audience. That means it's not funny, we've gone over the bounds of good taste, if that's possible, and it doesn't end up in the movie.

We were very lucky to get Robert Hays. He had been on a television sit-com called *Angie*, but we didn't hold that against him. He had the comedy down without much direction at all. We just threw him in the water and he went with it. He even helped us get some laughs that weren't in the script with some of his reactions. He played it never trying to be funny, which was also true of Julie Hagerty. She just pretty much played herself and didn't try to put any spin on it.

I think *Airplane!* was the first of its kind where you had a comedy without comedians. That was hard to sell to the studios. We owe a lot of thanks to Michael Eisner, Jeff Katzenberg, and Barry Diller for at least seeing this was a good script, a funny script, and to trust us to direct it.

## The Three of Them Directing the Same Picture?

It's hard for me to imagine what it's like for other people to be on the set with us. Back when we used to direct movies together it was pretty businesslike. We even had fun sometimes. Part of the job is you have to be able to laugh on the set. When you play a scene back on the monitor, you have to be able to laugh even on the eleventh take to imagine what the audience is thinking as they're seeing it. But as far as it being madcap like the Marx Brothers, I don't remember that. You still have a job to do as the director and you're still responsible for millions of dollars on the production. You have to get the work done. It's work, but part of the work is you have to laugh now and then.

When Jim and Jerry and I would be interviewed and people would ask us how do three people direct a movie we would all start talking at once (*laughs*). How it really happened was the preplanning would take place before we came to the set. Once we were on the set we would designate Jerry to talk to the actors about what we wanted and in between takes, the three of us would confer back at the monitors. We would decide what to do to correct the next take because directing is mostly about solving problems. It's like in *The Right Stuff* when the plane is crashing. First you try plan A, then try plan B, then plan C before you actually press the ejection button.

On *Airplane!* we had a script supervisor that was always trying to make points. A friend of mine was visiting from New York, but we told her he was Lewis Friedman, a big, important Paramount executive. As soon as Lewis was on the set she started pointing out every little thing like mismatches and stuff like that. That was the most hilarious thing that happened on the set. Actually, there must have been more stories, but it's hard to think of any right now. We tried to keep the funny stuff happening on the screen.

When I see *Airplane!* now, I see all the mistakes. It's like seeing all those experiments they send up to Mars. You hope that 90 percent of them work. I think we did pretty well, though, because people hadn't seen anything like it before. In that way it really worked. I guess the test is if the movie still works twenty years later. We'll see in a couple of years if it's still funny.

## A Television Interlude

Everything we had done was aimed toward getting *Airplane!* done, so once we were there it was like landing on the moon. Once you've landed on the moon what do you do then? We couldn't think of anything so we did a television series called *Police Squad* with Leslie Nielsen. We couldn't think of a good plot to make it as a movie, so Michael Eisner suggested we do it as a television series. That's what we did between *Airplane!* and *Top Secret*.

## Top Secret (1984)

*Omar Sharif; Val Kilmer; Jeremy Kemp; Warren Clarke;*
*Tristram Jellinek; Lucy Gutteridge; Peter Cushing; Christopher Villiers;*
*Billy J. Mitchell; Major Wiley; Gertan Klauber; Richard Mayes;*
*Vyvyan Lorrayne; Nancy Abrahams; Ian McNeice.*

We always enjoyed watching old movies, so we started watching old Elvis movies, which was a genre we thought we could spoof. And those World War II spy movies where they always sneak up behind the German sentry and knock him over and infiltrate behind enemy lines. The movies were made during World War II and were as much for propaganda as entertainment. It was the most obscure genre you could get. So that became *Top Secret*. An Elvis-style character goes behind enemy lines. It was the French Resistance in East Germany and it was very surreal, like a Terry Gilliam movie.

Val Kilmer came in and read for the part and we thought he was pretty talented. He was just better than anybody else was. He made an audition tape singing the Jerry Lee Lewis song "Whole Lot of Shakin'." He was young and looked the part of a movie star, but it didn't really help the movie. If we had gotten young Tom Cruise, who knows?

When you run a tape back it sounds like Swedish so we thought of doing a whole scene in *Top Secret* backwards. It took us a whole day of rehearsal and a day of shooting because it had to be done in one take. We couldn't cheat. The actors appearing to be talking Swedish the entire time and we ran with subtitles. The whole movie was nothing but weird scenes. Like the German general walking up to the big phone in the foreground and the train station leaving the train instead of the opposite way. It was just all these weird concepts that were funny but didn't necessarily make for a hit movie.

There are a couple of scenes from *Top Secret* that are my favorites. The one where the armored car hits the Pinto and it just pings and then it explodes. That always gets a big laugh. Then there's the scene where the guy is singing but it turns out the horse is the one singing. There are probably more funny moments in *Top Secret* than any film we've done, but, as I said, it didn't really work as a movie. Ah, wait a minute. What I really should say is that the studio released it all wrong. It was their fault!

## How They Come up with These Goofy Films

We start by watching a serious scene from a serious movie and then figure out what can be done with it. Generally, we have two people talking in the foreground and the craziness is going on in the background. Or, if there's funny dialogue, then we keep everything else straight.

When Jerry, Jim, and I did films together, which was *Airplane!*, *Top Secret*, and *Ruthless People*, we all worked on everything. There was no one who didn't write or didn't cast or oversee the wardrobe or whatever. We all did everything together. When we were writing *Airplane!* we would all come up with the ideas and jokes equally, but Jim took on the additional duty of actually typing. Those were in the days when people had typewriters.

## Ruthless People (1986)
*Danny DeVito; Bette Midler; Judge Reinhold; Helen Slater; Bill Pullman;*
*Anita Morris; William G. Schilling; Art Evans; Clarence Felder; J. E. Freeman;*
*Gary Riley; Phyllis Applegate; Jeannine Bisignano; J. P. Bumstead; Jon Cutler.*

*Top Secret* didn't really perform well at the box office, although it made plenty of money for the studio so it wasn't a huge disaster for them. We regarded it as a huge disaster for us because we were used to a movie coming out and being a big hit, like *Airplane!*, I guess. We decided that maybe audiences didn't want satire any more. We wanted to do something completely different.

Jeff Katzenberg sent us the script to *Ruthless People*. It was written by Dale Launer and we thought it was very funny but needed a little work. We sat down with Dale and did several rewrites and added things to the plot. I think we really went to school on that movie and we kind of learned some things that we neglected on *Top Secret*. Like a movie needs a plot and it needs characters. It needs a beginning, middle, and an end, and a movie needs three acts. We applied that to *Ruthless People* and it worked.

*Ruthless People* turned out to be easier to direct because we were using actors who understood comedy. You just turn the camera on Bette Midler and Danny DeVito and they're funny because they were hired to be funny. As my brother Jerry told me when he directed *Ghost*, what he was doing was easier than what we were doing, because he had a script and was working with actors who were doing straight lines. It's easier than doing a comedy where everything depends on split-second timing of the jokes. That kind of movie is pretty difficult to do. Jim Abrahams pulled off the *Hot Shots* movies that way and it's quite a feat. The *Hot Shots* movies and *Naked Gun* movies are all jokes.

## Improvise? No Way!

I don't allow much leeway as far as improvisation goes. I insist that every line be said as written. When I write with someone like Pat Proft we argue over every word and sentence. We're very specific about scripts like *Airplane!*, *Top Secret*, and Jim's *Hot Shots* movies. The timing has to be very exact.

When Robert Goulet came on the set to do *Naked Gun 2 1/2* we were running lines in the rehearsal. I was looking down at my script and I didn't recognize any of the words he was saying. I asked Bob if he had the right draft. I thought maybe that he'd been given another draft of the script. He told me he was paraphrasing. Just about then I'm sure he noticed that I turned several colors.

We went back to my trailer and I told him he'd have to do the lines exactly as they were written, even if he had to read them off cue cards. Believe it or not, he was very relieved. Some actors don't memorize lines. Brando doesn't memorize lines. Some actors like to read them off cue cards and that's fine with me. The important thing is that the lines are read exactly as written. We don't do any improvisation. An actor might come up with an idea and that's just fine with me if it works. If an actor suggests a line or a piece of business we'll try it. But the audience is always the ultimate judge. We take the films out and preview them. Whatever gets a laugh stays in.

I love to take suggestions from the actors. On *Ruthless People* there's a scene with Judge Reinhold where he saves a bug from being stepped on. He takes it outside just to show that he wouldn't hurt anything. Judge suggested that he go back outside and stomp on the bug after he saved its life. He thought that would be funny. And I said, "Judge, that's just not going to be funny," but he wanted to try it anyway. I agreed to try it and if it worked we'd leave it in. We tried it with a preview audience and it worked. It got a big laugh. So that shows that sometimes an actor will come up with a good suggestion. Not often, but occasionally.

## The Times Begin to Change

After *Ruthless People* we all wanted to go off and do separate projects as directors. Jim was the first one. He did a movie with Bette Midler and Lily Tomlin called *Big Business*. That was way before he did the *Hot Shots* movies. I did the first *Naked Gun* and Jerry did *Ghost*. Since then we've all been doing separate projects. But often we'll read each other's scripts and give each other help and attend each other's premieres.

## The *Naked Gun* Films Beginning in 1988

For the first *Naked Gun*, we all sat down and everybody wrote thirty pages. Jerry, Jim, Pat Proft and me. That was the weirdest writing experience because we all wrote the first draft separately. We weren't even in the same room together. Pat turned in his thirty, Jim turned in his thirty, and Jerry his. I think I wrote one more draft with Jerry and then the next six drafts I wrote myself, probably in preproduction. Jerry and Jim were on the set a lot.

Of course, Leslie Nielsen was a natural casting decision because he had done our *Police Squad* television series. Our casting director came up with the idea of Priscilla Presley. She had been on *Dallas* and a couple of other television things. She was not funny in the least in any of these shows, but she had a very sincere quality about her. She was completely different from what I thought she would be like. I mean, having had an *Enquirer's*-eye view of what her life was like with Elvis I thought that she would be more of a racy personality. But she was so sweet. She was just the girl next door and perfect for the character of Jane.

For the villains in these films we needed people who hadn't made a name for themselves in comedy. Ricardo Montalban and Robert Goulet, for example, were just perfect for us. And then there's . . . I think O.J. Simpson had been in a sitcom, but I had never watched it so I figured he was safe. I will say that O.J. improved remarkably over his stint in the *Naked Gun* films. By the third *Naked Gun* he virtually needed no direction. He was very good.

I know you want me to tell you behind-the-scenes stores about the *Naked Gun* films, but I can't think of any. We're really more businesslike than you think.

OK, the most hilarious thing that happened on *Naked Gun* is when I turned into Drebbin myself. Everybody was laughing at me because I was complaining that I couldn't see the actor because someone was standing in front of the camera. Well, it turned out it was me. No one wanted to be the one to say, "David, I think you're the one standing in front of the camera."

People would also laugh because I could never find my way off the set. I would constantly take the wrong doors. We were shooting at Raleigh Studios across the street from Paramount and I would try to find the way back to my trailer and end up out on Melrose Boulevard. Tour groups would wonder what I was doing out there.

## Bring Back the ZAZ team!

I'd love to team up with Jim and Jerry again, but we'd have to find a project that we're all interested in and find a schedule where we'd all be free to do it. We've even thought of doing *Kentucky Fried Movie* again. But it's tough to sit down in a room and pick up where we left off. It seems that one of us is always off doing something and there's not enough of a desire to work together to make it really happen. There's just not one project that would interest all of us.

I always loved the collaboration. I don't know how anyone can write comedy in a room alone because you need that instant feedback. Jim is now collaborating with other people. Jerry is too. He collaborates with writers on the movies he directs and the ones he just produces. I don't subscribe to the one man, one film theory. So many people have their hands in the making of a film, although I think that the direction is the most important part. A good director can't save a bad script, but a bad director can wreck a good script.

## The State of the Industry

The most obvious thing is that it's become a star-driven business. You need a big star to open a picture. It seems more and more rare that you get a movie that can open and compete in the marketplace without a big star. I don't know if an *Airplane!* could do today what it did back in 1980.

There are huge budgets being spent on the technical aspects of films. I think if these big films have good stories, they've got a chance. But if they're boring, all the technical pizzazz in the world isn't going to save them.

There was a movie called *Daylight* with Stallone. Technically, it was spectacular, but I don't think people connected with the story. I think Stallone was good in it. Stallone is good in everything he does. But whether the audience will keep going to see movies that don't really involve them story-wise is something else. And that's also the responsibility of the director. Before you go on the set you better have a story that people will connect with and then you need to execute it in the way that will connect that story.

## How Would He Like to Be Remembered?

As a good environmentalist? I don't know. It's a hard question to answer. I suppose if I made a lot of movies that made people laugh, that would be good. I've received letters from families who had sick relatives in the hospital or something awful like that, and they all sat and watched *Police Squad* or one of the *Naked Gun* movies or *Airplane!* and they all got a good laugh. That has kind of a lasting meaning.

# The Films of Jim Abrahams

Although they still occasionally collaborate on some projects, Jim and the Zuckers have, in recent years, gone on to work independently. Jim has established The Abrahams Boy, Inc. Production Company for which he writes and directs feature films.

While he is best known as the creator of comedy films, Abrahams has, for very personal reasons, recently directed his vast talents toward tackling the serious task of curing pediatric epilepsy. In March 1993, Jim and Nancy's then one-year-old son, Charlie, was afflicted with severe epileptic seizures which could not be cured with conventional drugs or brain surgery. As a last hope, Charlie was brought to Johns Hopkins University to try the Ketogenic Diet—a little-known yet proven treatment for pediatric epilepsy. Since he began the diet in December 1993, Charlie has been drug and seizure free.

As an outlet for their gratitude, the Abrahams established The Charlie Foundation to Help Cure Pediatric Epilepsy. In addition, Abrahams produced and directed the made-for-television movie ... *First Do No Harm,* which aired on ABC. The movie, which starred two-time Oscar winner Meryl Streep, is a fictionalized dramatization inspired by actual events that chronicles the actions of a ferociously determined mother as she struggles to save her son from the torturous treatment of his epilepsy.

# The Conversation with Jim Abrahams

I grew up in Milwaukee, Wisconsin, in a very middle-class kind of background in a middle-class neighborhood in a time when it was a much simpler world than today's world. In the fifties and sixties things were black and white. Not just on television, because that's all I had. It just seemed that things were much clearer. I grew up in a time when Mom and Dad could say go out and play and be home in time for dinner and never give it any second thought. The television and media were very black and white too. There was just *Ozzie and Harriet* and *The FBI* and all those Quinn Martin productions and *Father Knows Best,* and there were no shades of gray in life. Everything was just crystal-clear and simple and that's sort of how we grew up.

I don't think any of us realized at the time that *Mad Magazine* had a tremendous influence on us, because the subtext of *Mad Magazine* was that things don't necessarily have to be taken the way they appear on the surface. We grew up in a world where everything was taken sort of superficially but *Mad Magazine* said wait a minute, you really don't have to take that at face value and there's really humor in that. At that level it had a big effect on us and I think later on, as we got into the movie business, it had a tremendous effect, too.

In particular I remember a column in *Mad Magazine* called *Scenes We'd Like To See.* They would always set it up where first you would see the movie they were spoofing. They would set it up very real, the way we were used to seeing it in the movie. Not with silly characters or silly sets or silly lines. Everything would be set up in these columns the way we're used to seeing it and then at the very end, in the last panel, they would make their joke. I think that when David and Jerry and I got into the movie business that was sort of the model we fashioned our comedy after, to set it up very seriously with dramatic actors, not comedic actors, and real sets, not silly wild sets, and serious music, not comedy music. So I think *Mad Magazine* just had an enormous effect on our sensibility and literally how we wound up making movies, comedy movies.

Me funny? Me? No, I wasn't a very funny kid at all. As a matter of fact, I was just home this last weekend for my nephew's wedding and my sister got up and gave this five-minute toast and she was hysterical. That's what I can remember growing up. My sister was really the comedian in the family and my other sister and I and my parents were kind of the audience.

What brought Jerry, David, and me together was a drug deal gone wrong. I'm just kidding. We didn't really meet that way. David, Jerry, and I knew each other from the time we were little boys. Our dads were business partners. A to Z Realty. I think David still has some of the stationary from A to Z Realty. Our families belonged to the same synagogue, so our parents were very friendly, so we were kind of thrown together socially as kids. I think I'm five years older than Jerry and three years older than David. Something like that. In that kind of age difference, when you're little it makes a big difference. So we didn't play together a lot as little kids other than when our families got together. After college we all kind of reunited and started working together.

I think back about the adventure we went through together and it was just a magical thing that went on in our lives. I ran into David in Milwaukee. At the time he was a construction expeditor in Milwaukee. Jerry was just finishing college and I was a private investigator. I just ran into David one day and he said, "You know, I've got access to this video tape equipment." And in those days it was a big deal. Not like today where everybody owns his own camera. That was kind of nifty. He said, "So why don't you come over and we'll play around with this video tape equipment." So David, Jerry, and I would get together in the Zuckers' basement and just started having fun, taping spoofs of commercials or whatever was popular in the movie theaters at that time. It was really just for our own entertainment.

After a while we started to show it to our parents and our friends and they laughed. And that was great. So then we opened this little theater. Jerry was just finishing college at the University of Wisconsin. So we opened this little theater just on the weekends at the University of Wisconsin and it was very crude, both in sensibility and the way it was set up. But it was fun and people laughed. Eventually they paid a dollar and they still laughed. Wow, that was great.

Then we got a little more sophisticated and we rented the back room of a bookstore called Shakespeare and Company on the University of Wisconsin campus. We would show our video tapes and we would actually get up on the little stage and act and interact with the videotapes and people kept laughing so we kept doing it. It was a wonderful time. During the weeks I had a very straight, normal job as a private investigator with a very conservative law firm. And on the weekends I would drive up to Madison and hang out with the hippies and do this Kentucky Fried Theater. It was just fabulous. We had success, and mercifully David and Jerry had this drive and ambition and goals. They had this idea that if this worked out so well at the University of Wisconsin, why don't we move out to California and try it in Los Angeles. And that was beyond anything that I could imagine. I tried to get them to compromise and we'd go to Chicago or something, but they'd have none of it. They had bigger plans, larger goals in life, so I kind of went along for the ride and we moved out to California and opened Kentucky Fried Theater.

I think pretty early on in our theater career we realized that we were very uncomfortable performing. You're either an actor at heart or you're not. And among my many blessings in life, I'm not. And I think David and Jerry feel the same way. Getting up there and performing and showing the video tapes every week was not something that I'd think, "Oh boy, I can't wait for the next weekend so I can get up there and perform again." It was something that I, and I think they, sort of dreaded. So we had to figure out something else to do. And again, I'm just talking from my point of view, because I really think that David and Jerry had more vision of the future and had aspirations and thoughts about a film career. For me, it was largely, "Gee, I just hate getting up there and acting." I'm so self-conscious.

Kentucky Fried Theater was very successful. I think we ran the theater for seven or eight years and there was never an empty seat in the house. It was always packed and we would turn people away. And I think part of the reason it was so successful was number one, it was funny, but, more than that, there was the sense that the audience had that these guys weren't actors. They don't really belong on stage, but somehow that was endearing and they identified with us or something.

About that time we met John Landis, the director. He was a very up and coming kind of wonder kid in Hollywood in the middle seventies, because he had just made a movie called *Schlock* for sixty thousand dollars and it was good and he finished it. So we called him up and he came over and visited the theater and we got to know him a little bit and he said, "Well, why don't you make a movie out of this Kentucky Fried Theater?" And we said, "How do we do that?" And he said, "You write a script." And we said, "How do you write a script?" So he gave us a script he had written just so we would know the form, dialogue and that kind of stuff. And it turned out that the script he had given us to pattern our script after was *American Werewolf in London,* which he later went on to make, which was a wonderful movie. So we wrote a script called *Kentucky Fried Theater,* kind of translating our theater into a movie, and eventually that got made into a movie.

Collaborating with David and Jerry was always fun. I think we had good days and bad days like anybody else. We spent years and years in a room with the three of us just looking at each other. So you can imagine some days were better than others were and some days we'd like each other more than other times. But there were three of us so you could always arrive at a decision because it was an odd number and you could vote. But there were some magical moments and we thought of a lot of good stuff. Together it was a tremendous adventure. We shared in all the decision making. It's not as though one guy was in charge of this kind of comedy or this skit or something. Everything was improvised. Even the business stuff that we had to go through together we all shared in equally, so it was a lot of fun.

A question asked of us a while ago was what were our influences. That kind of *Mad Magazine* mentality did influence us quite a bit. That whole kind of naughty boy, things-don't-have-to-be-taken-quite-as-seriously-as-we-take-them mentality had a big influence on us. If those comedies are about anything, they are about not really having to take them so seriously. And I think that's why probably the most fun aspect of the whole process is sitting in the movie theater when you're done with it and sitting with an audience and hearing them laugh. Because it's just the most wonderful kind of laugh. It's a self-effacing laugh. It's "look what I've been taking seriously all these years and I really didn't have to."

I think the most endearing human quality is the self-effacing sense of humor. Even the casting of our movies is about the ability to laugh at yourself. When Leslie Nielsen, Robert Stack, Lloyd Bridges, Richard Crenna, Charlie Sheen, or Priscilla Presley are in movies like this, we know, as the audience, that they're really having a laugh at their own expense. And that's very endearing. I think audiences like that. They say, look, they're rich and famous but they still have the ability to laugh at themselves. I could go down a long list of people who've been in the parodies and made them work because they were willing to laugh at themselves. I kind of like that.

> *"Have you ever seen a grown man naked"... has become one of the famous lines of all time. It goes along with my totally opposite one, "The secretary will disavow any knowledge of your actions."*
>
> *Peter Graves—Actor*

# Airplane! (1980)

You can tell the story of how *Airplane!* came together in a minute, but it really took six or seven years. Back in the days of the Theater we would leave our videotape machine hooked up to the TV all night long because that's when the silliest, cheapest, dumbest commercials would show up, and we used to make parodies of those commercials. But one day we got to work and what was on our tape that had recorded the night before was a movie called *Zero Hour* which was made in 1957 and starred Dana Andrews, Linda Darnell, and Sterling Hayden. It was the serious version of *Airplane!*

If you want proof during your life that there is a God, this was one of those proofs. There was this perfect movie that was sort of handed to us on this videotape. It was perfect because it was dead serious and even though it was written in 1957 and this was the early seventies, we found it right at a time when disaster movies were very, very popular. There was *Towering Inferno, Earthquake, Airport,* and *Airport '75.* Movies like these had complete stories. They had three acts. A first act, a second act, a third act, and character arcs, and all this kind of stuff we didn't have a clue about. And all of this was done very, very seriously. So we purchased the rights to *Zero Hour* and we wrote it as a comedy and that changed our lives irrevocably.

We were very, very fortunate on *Airplane!* to have Howard Koch, Sr., as our producer. He is a real elder statesman in Hollywood and he had worked with Lloyd Bridges and Robert Stack. Howard Koch had directed episodes of *The Untouchables* that Robert Stack had starred in. He gave us an enormous amount of credibility. I think Howard was very helpful in getting Lloyd Bridges, Robert Stack, Peter Graves, and Leslie Nielsen to get on board.

The Jive Lady was originally Harriet Nelson. As I remember, she asked her son Ricky to read the script, and they didn't think it was funny, and so she passed. Barbara Billingsley was our immediate next choice, and of course it worked out beautifully. She was fabulous. It couldn't have worked out better.

Somebody once said to me, it's not what you do but how you do it. And I always use that scene with Peter Graves and the young boy as an illustration of that. Because if you think of what that scene is about, it alludes to child molestation and there is no more despicable subject in the world. But in all these years, however many years since *Airplane!* has come out, no one has ever said to us, "Gee, wasn't that tasteless" or "wasn't that offensive." And I remember sitting in the audience when those scenes came on and people just laughed and laughed. What's really funny was at the premiere of *Airplane!*, my wife and I were sitting right in front of Peter Graves and his wife was on the floor, I mean literally on the floor, laughing during those scenes. She just had a ball. Like I say, it's not what you do but how you do it.

I remember Paramount couldn't get its mind around that kind of casting. "No, it should be Dom DeLuise," they would say. "Why doesn't Dom DeLuise talk the plane down? Why would you want Lloyd Bridges?" Once they saw dailies and then saw the movie they understood. We knew that nobody had done that before. I don't think we had any idea how it would sort of permeate Americana, because it's amazing how you can go almost anyplace and people will know not to call you Shirley. I don't know why it's held up quite so well for so long. David, Jerry, and I had this discussion not so long ago. I think a lot of it is just good jokes.

We always came to the set prepared. I think that we had spent so much time in a room together working on the movie that we all came to the set sort of with the same vision so there were very few arguments and when there were disagreements we tried to keep them private. We're all nice little boys and we all like to be liked. I think that on our sets it was always fun. I know that in the subsequent years, when we stopped directing together, Jerry and David and I try to work on sets where people get along and have a good time. After all, it's only a movie and it should be fun.

## How Do Three People Direct a Movie Together?

Well, it's too bad they're not here. In the years when we directed together, people would ask how three people direct together and we would all start to talk simultaneously. I think the key to directing is knowing what you want. We would spend hours and weeks and months in rooms together getting a single vision of what we wanted, and given that, we pretty much agreed on things by the time we went to work. In essence the director is three times as accessible. So one guy could be talking to a costume designer, one person could be talking to a production designer, about a set, and another could be talking to an actor. In fact, it's an efficient way to go about directing. And the stuff that we directed always came in on time and on budget and it wasn't problematic. And again, if there was a disagreement we could get a very quick decision. It was an odd number and we could vote and so we could come to decisions quickly.

I remember one of the hardest times I had laughed. There was a script supervisor on *Airplane!* We were young and complete novices and we didn't really know what everyone's job was on a set. And the script supervisor was a bit pompous and a little pretentious. It's not such a good story. I don't think I should tell this.

Okay, I'll tell it. The script supervisor who was on that movie was very pretentious and because we were novices you could tell she had very little respect for us. So one day a friend of David's, Louie Feldman, came to visit us and he had a suit on, so we told this script supervisor that Louie was the president of Paramount. And she'd suck up to him so bad. She was so blown away by having met the president of Paramount and Louie was so great about putting her on. I just remember we laughed a lot. It was fun.

Thinking back, the one event that sticks in my mind is the premiere. Paramount insisted that the premiere take place on the Paramount lot. They wouldn't let us go to any of the guild theaters or any of the big commercial theaters. Much to everyone's horror the projectionist put the reels up out of order. I was very nervous that night so before the screening I went out and had a couple of cocktails. So when the reels came up out of order—we were in reel five instead of reel four—I thought to myself, "You know this movie really does step along. Look, we're already at this part of the movie." That was my reaction.

David's reaction was, "Thank God. Now I have an excuse why they're going to hate it, why they're going to pan it." Jerry was the only one of the three of us who had the presence of mind to go running back to the projection booth and tell the projectionist. Jerry said to the guy, "I know it's wrong! It's my movie. I made it. I've been working on it for seven years. You put it up wrong." So they put the reels back in the right order but they finished screening the movie. I remember that as kind of a classic moment.

The first time you direct it's like any kind of first experiences. You can't duplicate it. I remember what we shot the first day on *Airplane!*. It was Leslie saying, "Don't call me Shirley." And I remember seeing it so big on that screen in that room, and oh my God, it was just wonderful. And then during halftime during the NBA playoffs that year they showed the scene with Kareem, because that was right before the movie came out. I didn't know they were going to be showing it. I was sitting in my living room and there was that scene on television that we had thought about for years and there it was. I just remember them as being such exciting moments. You just can't duplicate that. Working so hard toward your goal and then seeing it happen, come to fruition, was terrific.

# Top Secret (1984)

*Top Secret?* Gee, I wish you were interviewing me about *Top Gun*. That would be great. I was telling Tom Cruise one day, "I've got this idea for a flying movie. Do you want to be in it?" He said, "Sure."

Well, *Top Secret* is an interesting story because after *Airplane!* we were really full of ourselves. We thought, "Oh, gosh, we can knock one of these things off every six or eight months and it won't be any big deal at all." And so we went about writing our next movie, which was *Top Secret*. But we missed largely the message of what *Airplane!* was. As I mentioned before with *Airplane!* all we did was bought an Arthur Haley script of *Zero Hour* and rewrote it as a comedy. The nuts and bolts of a real good script were in place with characters that arced. Three acts. All that was in place so all we did was add jokes. But with *Top Secret* we had to start from scratch and we didn't understand the necessity of having a three-act structure, of having character arcs! We just didn't get it.

We went about writing *Top Secret* and what we did was take ten or twelve of our favorite jokes and wrote some sort of story that would weave them all together. Then instead of having a specific target like disaster movies, we tried to mush together Elvis Presley movies and World War II movies and so it was much more vague and unfocused. Of all the parodies that we've worked on, *Top Secret* was the least successful in terms of reviews and in terms of box office. And it was probably the most constructive experience in our comedy filmmaking because whenever we get together and think about our experience in the movie business, that's the one we talk about the most because that was the biggest flop.

We went to New York and saw a stage play called *Slab Boys*. Val Kilmer was in it with Sean Penn and Kevin Bacon. It was a pretty neat cast. Val was terrific. He came in and auditioned and he was great. Clearly he took it very seriously and he was a really hard worker. In his audition he did some Elvis songs for us and really worked at it. He was great so he got the part.

My favorite joke in *Top Secret* is one scene in particular where they're having a shootout. We couldn't figure out how to end the scene and kill the bad guys. So the bad guys are coming at them in a big jeep and the good guys shoot the tire on the jeep and the jeep kind of veers off and right before it comes to a stop, it rear-ends a Pinto car, a real soft tap, and then this huge explosion takes place. That was always such a good joke. I love that joke. I remember audiences laughing too.

# Ruthless People (1986)

How we came to direct *Ruthless People* is interesting. We had an overall deal with Disney and we pitched Jeffrey Katzenberg and Michael Eisner on an idea they hated. And they said, "We hate it, we can't do it, but we have this movie in development called *Ruthless People*." It was written by Dale Launer and at the time Madonna was attached to the project. *Ruthless People* was a great idea and a wonderful script. We loved it. It was a combination of things. Our careers were winding down after *Top Secret* and this wonderful gift was handed to us.

As I said, when we inherited *Ruthless People* Madonna was attached to play the Bette Midler part. So we went out and met with her, David and Jerry and I, and on the strength of that one meeting alone she decided she didn't want to do the part. I guess we weren't very effective. Very early on, we knew the part would be perfect for Bette if she was available. And the same was true with Danny DeVito. Those were very early casting choices. And it worked out. Jeffrey Katzenberg, who ran Disney at the time, was very helpful and influential in getting Bette and Danny.

## Let's Break Here for a Bit of Philosophy

I hope the atmosphere on movies where I work is very professional, but there's also room to have fun. When they roll credits at the end of the movie, those are all people. Those are all professionals. They all work really hard and have families and lives to support. And I think that all movie sets are populated by professionals who work really hard. That's the bottom line of a movie set. There is a fiscal responsibility to some company that's footing the bill. But after that, we're all people and we all live in this world together and it's nice to laugh at the stuff we don't have to take seriously.

# The "Naked Gun" Idea

I think we came up with the idea to do *Naked Gun* and went in and pitched it to Frank Mancuso who ran Paramount at the time. I think we had decided after *Ruthless People* that we didn't want to direct together any more because with *Airplane!* we were novices and didn't even know everybody's job and we really needed each other to help make decisions. But after a while each one of us had a little more confidence in his own decision-making ability and it became harder to lose arguments and harder to split the salary. So we decided to go on and direct individually. It wasn't done with any kind of malice or anger. Nobody overdosed. I think we were just growing as individuals.

We went in and pitched the idea of *Naked Gun* to Paramount and they said yes and we wrote that together, but at the same time each of us was pursuing other ideas, too. I don't remember all the details or sequence of events. But basically we started directing on our own. David wound up directing *Naked Gun.*

Sequels really don't happen until the original does well. The original *Naked Gun* did very well both in the United States and foreign markets, so Paramount was interested in a sequel, so we wrote that together, along with Pat Proft, and once again David directed.

I think Leslie Nielsen was a latent comedian his whole life. If you really want to have a good time, look at *The Poseidon Adventure,* where he played the captain. That was a dramatic movie and you can still watch that today and not keep a straight face. Knowing the comedian that he is there's only a nuance of a difference between the way he plays the captain in *The Poseidon Adventure* and the doctor in *Airplane!* or Frank Drebbin.

# Hot Shots! (1991)

*Charlie Sheen; Cary Elwes; Valeria Golino; Lloyd Bridges; Kevin Dunn;*
*Jon Cryer; William O'Leary; Efrem Zimbalist, Jr.; Kristy Swanson; Bill Irwin;*
*Heidi Swedberg; Bruce A. Young; Ryan Stiles; Rino Thunder; Mark Arnott.*

The first *Hot Shots!* came about because Pat Proft called me and asked what I thought of the idea as a movie. It seemed to fill the criteria for a parody. That is, it was representative of a huge genre of movies—flying and war movies—and that genre takes itself very seriously. Those are the two real criteria. Is there a genre and does the genre take itself seriously? And so we sat down and started to write. The second *Hot Shots!* came about the same way the second *Airplane!* and second *Naked Gun* came about. The first was successful so the studio was interested in a second.

Joe Roth ran Twentieth Century Fox when we made the *Hot Shots!* movies. He had worked with Charlie Sheen in *Major League* so he knew that Charlie had a very good sense of this kind of comedy. It was his suggestion that Charlie play the lead in *Hot Shots!* We got together and met, and I think Charlie was a little apprehensive because *Hot Shots!* was further out than *Major League* had been. But we persuaded Charlie to do it. I remember one great moment, about two-thirds of the way through shooting, the studio had cut a theatrical trailer, a teaser trailer for the movie theaters, and we had a video cassette of it on the set and we showed it and Charlie said, "Wow, I'm really glad I did this."

We spend a lot more time on story and plot than one would imagine. When you read the reviews, whether the reviewer likes it or not, they point out my top three jokes and they tell the jokes, and then they go on to say they won't even bother to tell you what the story is because it's so stupid. Well, that comment means they don't really understand that process because in fact we spent a lot of time on the story. That's sort of the message of the failure of *Top Secret*. In *Hot Shots!* we would spend a lot of time putting together the three acts and character arcs and all that kind of stuff. The jokes were the frosting. They come at the end of the writing process, not at the beginning of the process. And they're the easiest part. They come usually from just sitting and watching the genre of a whole bunch of movies that we're spoofing. But we spent 90 percent of the time just working on the structure of the story and the characters.

## Directing Can Be a Lonely Business

I don't think I enjoyed directing by myself. I remember looking around for David and Jerry. And I thought, "Oh God, how am I going to do this?" It's kind of a growing experience. You have to make a lot of decisions. If you're someone like me, who can go for years without making any decision, to be making a thousand decisions a day is daunting. But it has its moments. The first time that I was directing on my own I was directing Bette Midler and Lily Tomlin. They're not only very funny but also very smart and very opinionated so I couldn't fall asleep at the switch, ever. They always wanted to know not just what, but why, and I think I probably grew a lot during that experience.

## The Incredible Lloyd Bridges

Lloyd's fabulous. He was great in *Airplane!* and both the *Hot Shots!* and he's going to be great in *Mafia*. [One of his last screen appearances.] He is very smart and very professional and has a real sense of this parody humor. Lloyd is just a dear man and a consummate professional. One day when we were filming the first *Hot Shots!* he was filming a big scene and we could tell he was not quite up to snuff and it took him a little longer than normal to get through the scene. He left the set that day and was in the hospital for three weeks with pneumonia. But he would never let on how sick he was. I could show you his performance of that day and you'd never have a clue how sick he was. But that's the kind of man he was.

## A ZAZ Reunion?

I doubt that we will ever direct together again. That's not in the cards. We might wind up working on a movie together again in some other kind of division of capacities. I think we will always be the dearest of friends. Each of us has an appreciation for the fact that none of us would be enjoying the life we have if not for the other two.

There's a mistake that people make about David and Jerry, that because they share the same last name they're the same person. They're considerably different guys. They have different senses of humor but both are hugely funny. I think they're the two funniest people I know in the world. But they're two different people and all the stuff that comes along with two different people. And that's important to recognize.

## About the Industry

I don't know too much about the movie industry. I just come in and go to work. Most of the time I'm home with my family. Things are a lot more expensive than they used to be. The movie that I'm working on right now, *Mafia*, has a budget of $35 million and it is the most expensive I've ever worked on by a lot. But it's considerably less than the average budget of the average Hollywood movie today by a lot. And it is by light years the cheapest movie Disney has right now.

When people ask David Zucker how he got his start in the movie business, or they ask, "how can I get my start in the movie business?" David tells them not to even try. He tells them to stay at home, to find some other career. And when people disregard that piece of advice, that's the first indication they can make it in the movie business.

How would I like to be remembered? I don't know. As a good dad and as a good husband.

# Director Filmographies

## Combined ZAZ Filmography

*Airplane!* (1980)
*Top Secret* (1984)
*Ruthless People* (1986)

## David Zucker

*Naked Gun: From the Files of Police Squad* (1988, TV)
*Naked Gun 2 1/2: The Smell of Fear* (1991)
*BASEketball* (1998)
*Toddlers* (1999)

## Jim Abrahams

*Big Business* (1988)
*Welcome Home, Roxy Carmichael* (1990)
*Hot Shots!* (1991)
*Hot Shots! Part Deux* (1993)
*. . . First Do No Harm* (1997, TV)
*Mafia* (1998)

## Jerry Zucker

*Ghost* (1990)
*First Knight* (1995)
*In Your Dreams* (1999)
*A Course in Miracles* (1999)

# Awards

## Combined

**British Academy Awards**

*Airplane!*, Best Screenplay (nominated), 1981

## Jerry Zucker

**Golden Satellite Awards**

*My Best Friend's Wedding*, Best Motion Picture—Comedy or Musical (nominated, shared with Ronald Bass), 1998

**ShoWest Convention, USA**

Director of the Year, 1991

# The Films of Sidney Lumet

Sidney Lumet, whose films have been nominated for more than forty Academy Awards, is recognized as one of America's most prominent film directors.

Lumet was born in Philadelphia in 1924. His father, Baruch, was one of the great stars of the Yiddish Theater. The family relocated to New York's Lower East Side when young Lumet was four years old, and his father began a series of dramatic broadcasts from a Brooklyn radio station. Young Lumet became a child actor, appearing for a number of years on the Yiddish stage before attaining his first Broadway role at the age of twelve in Sidney Kinsley's *Dead End.*

During World War II Lumet served in China, Burma, and India. On his discharge from the U.S. Army Signal Corps he organized an off-Broadway theater group and became its director.

In 1950 he joined CBS as an assistant director of live drama shows being televised regularly from New York City. A year later he started directing shows for such series as *You Are There, Danger, Best of Broadway, The Alcoa Hour, The Goodyear Playhouse,* and others. In less than ten years he amassed more than 250 television directorial credits.

In 1957 he made his film directorial debut with Reginald Rose's *Twelve Angry Men,* which was nominated for three Oscars. Since that time he has added forty-one films to his impressive list of credits.

> *He's interested in creating, he's interested in the exploration of human behavior and the ramification of moral and ethical choices within those inter-relationships, and that's what makes his movies about people and the dilemmas people are faced with on a daily basis.*
>
> Andy Garcia—Actor

# The Conversation

I was born in Philly and had the good sense to leave when I was four. Then right to New York and I was brought up here. I started as a kid actor in the Yiddish theater, then went over to Broadway at eleven in *Dead End*. As a Broadway actor, I did about fourteen plays as a kid. Enlisted in the army at seventeen and a half. I couldn't get into the navy or the marines because of my eyes, and the Army Signal Corps had a terrific program because radar was brand new at the time. So they sent you to a civilian school to learn electronics and mathematics, and then as soon as you turned eighteen you went right into the army, the Signal Corps, as a radar repairman. And it was wonderful because I had never had any scientific exposure before and I loved it. And then back, after the war, to New York as an actor for about four more years, then slowly began directing.

Like so many things, it was sheer luck. Unplanned. In fact, when I was a kid actor in the late thirties and early forties, the great snobbism was that movies were not an art form. Movies were for acts. The theater was the art form. I finally drifted into television, largely for economic reasons. Yul Brenner was a close friend of mine and he was directing television. He was a very good director, by the way. When he went into *The King and I*, I was his assistant. So I took over Yul's shows and there I was, directing. It wasn't a film; it was a TV show. These were the great days of live television. It was a half-hour melodrama every Tuesday called *Danger*. I did it for three years. And that was the show I took over from Yul.

## Twelve Angry Men (1957)

*Henry Fonda; Lee J. Cobb; Ed Begley; E.G. Marshall; Jack Warden; Jack Klugman; Edward Binns; James Kelly (V); Joseph Sweeney; Martin Balsam; George Voskovec; John Fielder; Robert Webber.*

*Twelve Angry Men*, again, was sheer luck, as always in these things. You know, whenever you get depressed and start thinking oh, this isn't working, or that isn't working out, you look back on your life in terms of the good stuff that happened, you see how much luck was involved.

When I was doing that television show, *Danger*, among the other writers was Reggie Rose. I did about four of Reggie's scripts. *Twelve Angry Men* had been a TV show on another network. I didn't do the television show. When it came time to do it as a movie, Reggie came and asked me to do it. He and Hank Fonda were the co-producers on it. Fonda had been in New York for a number of years doing *Mister Roberts*, and during that time, two of his cast members were in a workshop that I had downtown. It was called the Actors' Workshop, and it was just a place for actors to meet and work on scenes and so on. And at the end of each year, we'd do a full production. One of the cast members, a guy named Joe Bernard, asked Hank to come down and see the year-end production. He thought it was marvelous. So when Reggie suggested me for *Twelve Angry Men*, he had seen this play I had done and he said, "Terrific, let's go." And because there was no money in the movie, it cost $349 thousand, they knew they could get me cheap.

None of the cast members were stars at the time. Jack Warden, Ed Begley—Ed was somewhat known. Lee Cobb was not a major star. He was a character actor, and character actors were rarely major stars. Fonda was the only one who had any sort of residence as a star. They were all just young actors that I had worked with in TV and whom I knew very well. They weren't what they later became.

When I began to do *Twelve Angry Men*, everybody said, "You're crazy. How can you do a picture in one room?" And with complete arrogance and ignorance I never thought of it as a problem. If one simply made the camerawork a part of what the piece was about, emotionally and subjectively, it didn't seem to me to be a problem. I never had to force anything, never had to look for fancy angles. In fact, the only overhead shot I saved for the final credits.

I rehearse a lot and I rehearsed *Twelve Angry Men* for two weeks, completely staged it, everybody on their feet, lines learned. And the shooting came out of that. As I watched rehearsals I slowly worked out how I wanted to shoot it, put it all down in advance so there'd be as little duplication as possible and made the camera work an organic part of what the drama was about. And so it never turned out to be a problem. I never saw it as a problem and it didn't turn out to be one.

The Academy Award nominations were very heady, but you know, when you've been an actor for a long time, as I was by then, you don't get overwhelmed that easily. You know about the ups and downs. You know about the fact that you're going to have any number of careers. I knew it as an actor. The hot times and the less hot times. It was very exciting. You know a hit is better than a flop. Interestingly enough, by the way, *Twelve Angry Men* was not a hit in the United States. It got great reviews, but we didn't do any business. It was largely in Europe that the real impact of it was felt. So, even though it was thrilling and terrific, my ego didn't run away with it.

Making that film was such hard work. We had to do it so quickly. We did the movie in nineteen days. So once a chair was lit, everything that took place in that chair got shot. I shot it like one would shoot a television show today. And so there was very little time for socializing and chitchat.

The one thing that does stand out is Hank Fonda himself. It was the first time he was a producer. I'd always found him to be one of the best American movie actors. To me, the three best American movie actors of that time were Fonda, James Mason, and Spencer Tracy. He had taken on this job as producer and hated it. For example, he never watched himself. Even when a picture was over he wouldn't see it for maybe a year later. He couldn't bear watching himself. A lot of actors are like that. And he was a producer so theoretically he had to come to rushes. And he came the first day and was sitting in back of me. The first shot came up and he reached around and squeezed my neck and said, "It's brilliant," and walked out and never came again. He was that shy about himself. That's one of the most interesting memories for me—Hank trying to wear another hat.

# Fail-Safe (1964)

*Henry Fonda; Walter Matthau; Dan O'Herlihy; Frank Overton; Fritz Weaver;*
*Edward Binns; Larry Hagman; William Hansen; Russell Hardy; Russell Collins;*
*Sorrell Brooke; Nancy Berg; John Connell; Frank Simpson; Hildy Parks.*

It was a time of great tension about nuclear armament. There was no hint of any nuclear disarmament. It was not discussed I think. As a matter of fact, Kennedy began the first of what became the SALT talks. But that was the beginning. Nothing was signed. That negotiation went on for about six or seven years, at least. And as part of that, the whole problem of nuclear accidents was very prevalent in a lot of people's minds. Here were all these ICBMs and silos and SAC planes, always at least one squadron in the air with all these nuclear armaments, and so it was a subject matter that was very alive and important to a lot of people. And here was a perfectly good thriller about it. So, what better combination? To me, always one of the great combinations you can have is for a good melodrama, which is something that matters. I felt that the possibility of nuclear war was real and that nuclear disarmament was critical. So, all of those social factors were enormously important in the decision to do the movie.

I don't know whether a picture like *Fail-Safe* would make sense today. First of all, the nuclear situation is so different, especially with the breakup of what we called the Soviet Union, since that was the primary target. Now all the melodramas will be about the theft of nuclear devices and terrorists holding up the country and so on. I think you can expect four or five of those over the next couple of years.

The whole special effects question is very interesting. In *Fail-Safe* we could not get, of course, any Department of Defense cooperation, but even more than that, there was, I think—I could never prove this—an active attempt, not to stop the movie, but certainly not to help us in any way. For instance, there were always rental houses where you could get stock footage, shots of B-52s or a shot of an army tank. I started inquiring about footage, and all of sudden we couldn't even get any footage for rent. We had gotten a hold of one shot which was sent to us from some rental house, just as an example of what they had, and all you see in the final picture is various optical treatments of this one shot. Closer, farther away, placed way in the background. I mean we did the picture literally with one shot of the plane on exterior. Today I'm sure it would be filled with Industrial Light and Magic shots and a fine job they would do.

There was a terrific conflict about the movie because it was independently financed and therefore didn't have a distributor, and unbeknownst to any of us, Stanley Kubrick was making *Dr. Strangelove* at the same time. And a lawsuit was instituted by whoever wrote *Dr. Strangelove* against us claiming plagiarism. Max Youngstein, who produced the picture and had raised the money for it, and I were shocked. This suit started scaring off possible distributors. The way it resolved itself, Columbia Pictures which was making *Dr. Stangelove*, bought us as well. In that way they controlled the distribution of the two pictures.

We did not get a good release. I remember talking to Abe Schneider or Leo Jaffey, two very decent guys running Columbia then, about releasing our picture first. But they released *Strangelove* first. I told them they were going about it the wrong way. You release the drama first, since the plots were similar, then release the comedy version. Both pictures might do well that way. But Stanley Kubrick had a lot of clout. Well-deserved clout, I might add. They had bought us specifically to hold us off the market so they released *Strangelove* first and then *Fail-Safe* came out. The story of every picture, always, is the story of its struggle of one kind or another and that was the struggle on that one.

# The Pawnbroker (1965)

*Rod Steiger; Brock Peters; Jaime Sánchez; Thelma Oliver;*
*Raymond St. Jacques; Juano Hernandez; Marketa Kimbrell;*
*Nancy R. Pollock; Geraldine Fitzgerald; Baruch Lumet; Linda Geiser;*
*John McCurry; Charles Dierkop; Eusebia Cosme; Warren Finnerty.*

*The Pawnbroker* was an extraordinary experience. There hadn't been a film on the Holocaust in American movies at that point. I don't remember if *Judgment at Nuremberg* had happened yet, but I don't think so.

Coming from European Jews myself, that area of interest, you would think, would be automatic. But I am very much of Ellie Wiesel's opinion that nothing should be done about the Holocaust, that it's such a unique experience that I don't think paintings ought to be done of it, I don't think that movies ought to be done of it. Having said that, I think *Shindler's List* is one of the best pictures I ever saw. And obviously for every feeling you've got, or every rule that you make for yourself, there's always an exception, and Steven Spielberg's job on that is magnificent. But one of the things that I liked about *The Pawnbroker* was that it was about that, and the effect of that on a man's life, but it didn't take place there.

I remember, in the original script, there were indications of where newsreel footage should be used. Again, this was done with private financing, and I went to Eli Landau, who was putting up the money for it, and said, "Eli there's no way I'm going to do that. These people didn't die so I could make a movie out of it. What I just have to use is a few solitary instances where you flash back to it and I've just got to find a quick image that says it and we get out." From that point of view it was a good picture to work on because it was about really the effect of the past, about a man who couldn't get rid of his past. I also think it's one of Rod Steiger's best performances.

It's so hard to know how much I may have helped Rod with his performance because you never know when you say the magic word that makes it click and brings it alive for an actor. Sometimes actors arrive with the part complete. Then you just have to be a good editor. But on *Pawnbroker*, for the obvious reasons, the emotion was very complex. It was relentless. There was a lot of work to do. I remember Rod working very meticulously because the areas of emotion that he would have to go into eventually were so enormous. So it was very important to be very sparing early on until we got to the real revelatory parts of the character. It was a very tough molding job to make sure we weren't using fuel up at any point that we might require later on down the line.

I didn't know back then where I was beginning to fit in as a director any more than I know where I do fit in as a director now. I'm not introspective that way. I'm one of those people who just want to work and don't try to link the pieces. I do whatever interests me at the time. The subject matter can be very varied, the styles can be very varied, and the genres can be very varied. I go with what I respond to instinctively. I don't really know where I was at back then. Obviously, you immediately know after a couple or three flops. The offers start falling off.

# The Hill (1965)

*Sean Connery; Harry Andrews; Ian Bannen; Alfred Lynch;*
*Ossie Davis; Roy Kinnear; Jack Watson; Ian Hendry; Michael Redgrave;*
*Norman Bird; Neil McCarthy; Howard Goorney; Tony Caunter.*

My agent suggested I do *The Hill* and the producer liked the idea. I went over to London for a meeting with Sean. I don't know if he had director approval, but I imagine he did. We hit it off immediately. The people in England were worried that I knew nothing about the British Army, but the army is the army is the army. It doesn't matter if it's Pakistan or America. Armies are the same. The uniforms are different, we salute differently, we turn right and left differently, but those are the only differences. Everything else is the same.

I knew that Connery was a brilliant actor. But you know how people are. The Bond performances are charming, but people would say, "Can he act?" It is very hard, that kind of high comedy. Sean had many elements of it in his Bond performances. Those can only come from an actor. They don't arrive just as a quality. It's a real knowledge of acting, knowledge of what they're doing. So I knew he could act. I didn't have any doubts about it. Sean chose *The Hill*. The picture happened because of Sean. And he was obviously hoping to break the mold that the Bond pictures put him in.

There are two parts to Sean. He's very up; he's very energetic. Charming. Funny. He's also very serious about his work. Cares very little about the trappings. Doesn't want the limo, particularly. Loves the fact that the most he ever travels with is a backpack. Literally. He's also completely intolerant of people who don't know their work. If you've ever seen Sean on a set where there's technical screw-ups, or when he feels that the director is just floundering and not knowing what to do, he can get very rough. And he's quite right. He doesn't like to waste his time. He works very hard. He's an amazing man. He's self-made in every sense. He's self-educated, and he is educated. There are things people don't know about him. He sings like an angel. I always wanted him to do a musical. In fact, he was in the chorus of *South Pacific* in London in the theater. He's a giant in every way. The talent is enormous.

We did another picture together which was a big failure. I think it has some of his finest acting in it. It's called *The Offense*. He plays a cop who identifies with a criminal and it's an amazing performance. So I'm filled with nothing but love and admiration for him.

It was agony shooting *The Hill*. We were in a desert in Spain where they shot *Lawrence of Arabia*, and it was the most peculiar climatic spot I'd ever been in. It was unbelievably hot. A hundred and twenty degrees during the day. And yet, if you went over one set of dunes, there was the Mediterranean on the other side, so as a result you'd have these sea breezes all day. You were of course sweating like crazy, but because of the sea breezes you wouldn't get terribly wet. Yet the water in your body was being used up. After the third day, we had to be extremely careful that we kept going with the salt tablets and kept going with the intakes of water because by eleven, eleven-thirty in the morning you'd keel over. You know how they say that you shouldn't drink in hot weather. Well, I had eight Scotsmen in that movie. And they disproved the theory.

# The Group (1966)

*Candice Bergen; Joan Hackett; Elizabeth Hartman;*
*Shirley Knight; Joanna Pettet; Mary-Robin Redd; Jessica Walter;*
*Kathleen Widdoes; James Broderick; James Congdon; Larry Hagman;*
*Hal Holbrook; Richard Mulligan; Robert Emhardt; Carrie Nye.*

As far as I knew, very little had been done in movies about women. There was, of course, that Metro movie, *The Women*, that Metro did with Rosalind Russell and Norma Shearer in the late thirties, I think. Rosalind was a caricature. It was just a very broad comedy. There had never been, as far as I knew, anybody taking the time to really investigate women, and young women in particular. That is where *The Group* begins. They start in college. I found Sidney Buckman's script quite extraordinary. In many ways it was better than the book. So when Sidney sent it to me I was just thrilled. I jumped right in.

Candy Bergen was undeniable. I knew when she walked in the office that this was just going to go POW! And everyone else knew it too. Despite the fact that she's taken a real lambasting from critics over the years, she's a wonderful actress. There's a lot she can do. She was an experienced actress but she was an untrained actress, so she needed a director. But if you look at her work with good directors, whether it was me or Mike Nichols or the wonderful picture she did with Alan McClure, she's enchanting and funny and real and sexy and remote and yet available. All the good things. So Candy was quite apparent.

Shirley Knight is one of the best American actresses. American actresses constantly have the problem of what's going to happen to them after forty-five. They don't go on like the men go on. Paul Newman goes on, Redford goes on. The men go on, the women don't. It starts getting very tough. Sometimes, like Glenn Close, they play it brilliantly because Glenn keeps returning to the theater or a TV show that interests her. She keeps working and has kept her career alive. But most of them start having troubles. Shirley's career didn't work out, but Shirley is a superb, a superb actress.

As for the other women, Joan Hackett died and that cut a brilliant comedic career off. Two gave up the business and I think two others failed. The usual story.

I wasn't as happy with *The Group* as about my own work. There are certain pieces, certain movies and/or plays that need a comedic level to disguise what they're dealing with dramatically so that the garment slowly reveals itself. I felt that I didn't manage that style well enough. I didn't think it was funny enough. That was all directorial. It wasn't that I didn't have the talent. It was that I didn't know how to. I had the talent among the actors. They could have done it. I didn't know how and it took me a little while to learn.

> *I just think he's one of the greatest directors I've ever worked for. I don't think I've ever said that before, but he always made me feel safe and he always made me feel like I could make a fool of myself and it would be all right. He always made me feel like I could gamble and never come up losing. That's a pretty amazing thing for somebody to be able to instill in you.*
>
> Dyan Cannon—Actress

# The Anderson Tapes (1971)

*Sean Connery; Dyan Cannon; Martin Balsam; Ralph Meeker; Alan King;*
*Christopher Walken; Val Avery; Dick Williams; Garrett Morris; Stan Gottlieb;*
*Paul Benjamin; Anthony Holland; Richard B. Shull; Conrad Bain; Margaret Hamilton.*

*The Anderson Tapes* was, again, something that was up and about because of
the situation we were living in. It was right in the middle of the sixties.
There were a lot of radical activities in the United States. The civil rights
movement had begun. I don't know if Woodstock had happened. We were
in the midst of that whole upheaval. And we all knew that the government
had surveillance on everything and everybody. We couldn't prove it, but we
knew it. And here was a movie again, a very good melodrama, a good plot,
a good story, about the government's eyes and ears in on everything, so that
every one of the characters in that movie was being followed for one reason
or another. Sometimes just by accident—they lived over the headquarters
of the Black Panthers, who were on the floor below. Again, it was one of
those instances of getting a terrific, good melodramatic plot to go with
something that I felt very strongly about.

It was Christopher Walken's first film role. I had known Chris a long
time. He was a kid actor along with his brother, who was also a kid actor
who had worked with me in live television days. I don't remember whether
I had worked with Chris or not. Also, what's very interesting is how beautiful he was. A very sensuous face, a very arresting face. As an actor he never
does anything that's cliché in any way, it's always completely original, completely his own. I knew that about his work. I remember he came in and
read for the part and I said, "It's yours."

# Serpico (1973)

*Al Pacino; John Randolph; Jack Kehoe; Biff McGuire; Barbara Eda-Young;*
*Cornelia Sharpe; Tony Roberts; John Medici; Allan Rich; Norman Ornellas;*
*Ed Grover; Al Henderson; Hank Garrett; Damien Leake; Joe Bova.*

I think *Serpico* plays as well today as it did when we made it, because we're
in much greater corruption now than we were then. That story seems to
never stop. I don't know what the problems are in Los Angeles, but here in
New York we just had our dirty thirty up in Washington Heights. Thirty

cops caught framing suspects. Taking the drugs off the bad guys and selling it. Obviously a much more serious problem than taking free sand-
wiches, like in the Serpico story.

What we revealed in the NYPD Commission has not only not been resolved, if anything it's certainly as bad, very possibly worse today. So, again,
that problem of something we all knew about that is a big presence in our
lives coupled with a very good story, about a very interesting man.

I feel very obligated, when I do a story about a real person, to keep the
facts as right as possible. Obviously I can't get every fact right, every incident
right, because you're dealing with four years of a person's life and you've got
to fit it into two and a half or two hours. But it is extremely important to me
to stay dead true to the spirit of that person, that person's intention and to
what to me seems like the meaning of their lives up to this point. In the instances when Frank Serpico saw the picture, or when Bob Lucie came to the
screening of *Prince of the City*, I've never been so nervous. I was sweating because if they had disapproved or been disappointed or unhappy or felt ex-
ploited in any way, I would have felt terrible. Fortunately, both did not.

There is no behind-the-scenes stories on my movies because all we do
is work. I work very quickly and hard. Anyway, if there were stories, I
wouldn't tell you.

The main thing is to get the film done and as soon as possible. The streets
of New York are very, very easy to shoot in. You get tremendous cooperation.
They re-route busses for you, for example. On *Dog Day Afternoon*, they re-
routed a big bus line because the location I had picked was on a bus route,
and they diverted it by four blocks to help us. They're wonderful about it.
Much better than Beverly Hills, which owes its existence to movies.

# Murder on the Orient Express (1974)

*Albert Finney; Lauren Bacall; Martin Balsam; Ingrid Bergman; Jacqueline Bisset;*
*Jean-Pierre Cassel; Sean Connery; John Gielgud; Wendy Hiller; Anthony Perkins;*
*Vanessa Redgrave; Rachel Roberts; Richard Widmark; Michael York; Colin Blakely.*

I guess it was the producers who sent me the script and I fell in love with
it. I just thought it was the best plot I had ever read. I could not believe it
when I came to the end of that script. Talk about a who-done-it. Twelve
people done it. It just blew me away. And I said yes.

Then I went over to England to meet the producers. And I said, "Look;
there's been a whole bunch of Agatha Christie movies with Margaret

Rutherford. Kind of sweet little English country pieces. But this one is a study of nostalgia, glamour, and that time period, and Poirot as a character. This is just a whole existence that's just so rich." And I said, "I think there's a way of doing this so that we cast a star in every part—if we say, 'Look, this is the top money and you're all getting the top money. Billing will be alphabetical. The parts are fun, come along for the ride,'" and people did. Sean Connery was the first one to fall in line and that made it easy for everyone else. We just went from one to another and got yes, yes, yes, yes.

We had a week's rehearsal. We didn't do two weeks because the characters weren't that complex. Four of the actors were doing plays. Albert Finney, John Gielgud, Vanessa Redgrave, and Ingrid Bergman were in plays in London at the time, so they were shooting with me during the day. So I wanted to keep it a fairly easy rehearsal period because they all had performances to go to that night.

There were no difficulties on that movie whatsoever, except for the one sequence when the train left the station. That was a monster of logistics. The English railroad gauge is different from the European railroad gauge. Because of the people appearing in plays we had to be someplace near London.

We found this enormous railroad shed where they repaired the engines just outside of Paris. The set had to be built in London because there was a financing arrangement. At that time the English government gave you a certain subsidy if you spent a certain amount of money making a movie in England. So it was important to spend as much money as we could in England in order to get that subsidy. We built the set in London and brought it to Paris. I knew I would have only two days to shoot it because everybody had to be back in their plays on Monday, and so on Saturday I shot everybody but the people in the plays. Saturday night, after they finished their plays, they were flown over to Paris in a chartered plane, started working Sunday morning until Sunday night. We had to get the train leaving the station which meant that the shed had to be open, which meant that it had to be full night or you would have seen it was Paris, modern day, etc., etc., etc. As I said, it was a logistical nightmare but wonderful to work on.

As I said before, I was so disappointed with my own work on *The Group* that I knew that I had to learn a way, a technique, of lifting something off the ground so that it wasn't heavy and sobbing and boring. I just took a great lesson from the greatest high comedy writer of all time, Oscar Wilde, in a play called *The Importance of Being Ernest,* in which everything is important except the humanity of the people. As Lady Brackman says to someone, "Born in a handbag?" Not the fact that he was illegitimate is the problem, but the fact that he was born in a handbag is the problem. And that sense of what is important and what is not important. You just have to reverse it. In other words, you pay an awful lot of attention to whether it's going to be a white or green crème de menthe on a silver platter, and don't worry too much whether or not you're there for the emotion. The emotion will come along anyway. It's a question of shifting emphasis. It didn't hurt, either, having a bunch of actors who knew about that style of acting, too.

# Dog Day Afternoon (1975)

*Al Pacino; John Cazale; Carol Kane; James Broderick; Charles Durning; Lance Henriksen; Penelope Allen; Sully Boyar; Beulah Garrick; Sandra Kazan; Marcia Jean Kurtz; Amy Levitt; John Marriott; Estelle Omens; Gary Springer; Carmine Foresta.*

I don't know anyone who would have resisted the sheer story of *Dog Day Afternoon*. It was so wild. It was so nutty. Who could conceive of such a thing? A guy holds up a bank so he can get money for a sex change operation for his boyfriend. There had been nothing about gay life in an American movie except for *Boys in the Band*, which was very different. And here's this extraordinary story, and I was stunned when Pacino wanted to do it because no major American star had ever let himself in for that kind of a part. Not only the joy of working with Al again, because we get along really well and love working with each other, but that story was so perfect. The whole idea of dealing with what so-called normal people called freaks and doing a movie about the humanity of these so-called freaks appealed to me. In other words, what I'm saying is the so-called freaks are not the freaks we think they are. They are very connected to us and we are very connected to them. All our human attributes are the same. It was an extraordinary picture to work on. We did it with total passion and commitment and I think it shows in the movie. I think it's a wonderful movie.

I think the biggest thing I learned about Al was his confidence because he was out on such a limb. Not just from an emotional point of view and the complexity of the character, but just at the personal star level. So it was a question of shoring him up not only in the validity of the piece we were doing, but also in terms of his own performance. It was no struggle. We love each other and we never lie to each other so he knew I wasn't giving him any false confidence. I just gave him all the support I could and he felt it.

When you start dealing with sex or death, and *Dog Day* has both, you never know what an audience is going to do. I never know what an audience is going to do anyway; I should say that to begin with. But I sure in the hell wouldn't have known what they were going to do here. For the first time I was worried about what an audience was going to do.

I told the actors that we were never going to depart from the script structurally, each scene we would accomplish structurally, but that in order to make the characters closer to themselves, I wanted them to wear their own clothes and we didn't do any makeup, etc., etc. And then one of them asked me a question, the inevitable question, "What about words? Can we use our own words?" And I said yeah. It was very disciplined. It wasn't throwing the doors open for a situation of complete anarchy. Frank Pearson, who did the script, was present at rehearsals. And at the end of the day we'd take the improvisations, which were being recorded, and make the script up out of them. Three scenes were left for improvisation on camera.

It was a wonderful experience.

# Network (1976)

*Faye Dunaway; William Holden; Peter Finch; Robert Duvall; Wesley Addy; Ned Beatty; Arthur Burghardt; Bill Burrows; John Carpenter; Jordan Charney; Kathy Cronkite; Ed Crowley; Jerome Dempsey; Conchata Ferrell; Gene Gross.*

Nobody could resist doing a satire on television, especially with a Paddy Chayefsky script. Chayefsky is one of the finest American writers that has ever worked in movies. Not just *Network*, but *The Americanization of Emily* and *Hospital*. Marvelous movies. Paddy had a sense of the ridiculous and could write about it and write about it with humor. He also had great compassion and a fine sense of drama, so it's one of the best scripts that ever came across my desk.

*Network* is probably more timely than when we did it because everything that *Network* talked about has happened. I don't quite know whether anyone's been killed on the air yet, but I'm sure it will happen sooner or later. But other than that, it has all happened. People would say, "Oh, what a brilliant satire." We would say, "It's not satire at all. It's sheer reportage." And that's turned out to be true.

The big thing about doing *Network* was just being with Paddy. He's an extraordinary man. Very, very wise and very observant. However, we were very different people. Paddy was a night crawler. I'm a homebody. Paddy had wit. I have none. He was quite right wing politically. I'm quite left wing politically. But we had a common connection in the sense of futility about the way an awful lot of us behave. And this includes Paddy and myself. I'm not saying any of this from a superior position. We talked about just how ridiculous we can all be. So we laughed an awful lot.

# The Wiz (1978)

*Diana Ross; Michael Jackson; Nipsey Russell; Ted Ross;*
*Mabel King; Theresa Merritt; Thelma Carpenter; Lena Horne;*
*Richard Pryor; Stanley Greene; Clyde J. Barrett; Derrick Bell;*
*Roderick-Spencer Sibert; Kashka Banjoko; Ronald 'Smokey' Stevens.*

The idea of doing any musical was thrilling. When you talk about what this country created, we created musicals. We moved them from the European operetta to *Guys and Dolls*. *The Wiz*, while a kind of flawed piece of material, was nevertheless a chance to do a movie musical and musicals weren't being done a lot and haven't been since. Now that *Evita's* out, hopefully there's going to be some more. They're talking about doing *Chicago*.

If I had it to do over I would do it a lot differently. First of all, I would have educated myself. Computer graphics didn't exist then, but certainly matte painting and blue screens were available and I knew nothing about them. And I would have gotten myself a technical education. Technically, I'm very good in movies. I know the camera, I know lighting, and I know sound. But I knew nothing about what we now call special effects. I sure would have gotten myself grounding in that before I went into it because that's where I came a cropper. That's one of the places I came a cropper.

## What He Thinks of Critics

I've never learned anything from a critic. I don't know any director who ever has. I think the level of movie criticism in this country you can't even call criticism. It's either that kind of esoteric self-involved nonsense where everything gets so complicated or it gets to the level of mush like, "It was a wild, warm, wonderful movie." All that nonsense. At least four times a year you will read in some ad that this or that picture is the best picture ever made, or the best picture of 1979, or whatever.

The big thing I miss in movies is that critics don't know what they're talking about technically. You might say, well, why is that important? The reason it's important is if you're going to write about movies for the record, at least know what you're writing about.

When a music critic goes to a concert he can literally follow the score of what's being played. He can read music. There isn't anybody who knows anything about movies from a technical point of view because the technical is the artistic. That's how we make movies. We're a technical medium. There's a camera, there's film, there's light. That's how we do it. And if you don't know what the techniques were to achieve whatever effects there are in the movie and effectiveness in the movie, then it's just an opinion. In that case, the elevator man's opinion is as valid as yours or mine or anybody who plunks down $8.50. So the lack of knowledge reduces it all to absurdity.

# Prince of the City (1981)

*Treat Williams; Jerry Orbach; Bob Balaban; Carmine Caridi;*
*Tony DiBenedetto; Lance Henriksen; Richard Foronjy; Don Billett;*
*Kenny Marino; Anthony Page; Norman Parker; Paul Roebling;*
*James Tolkan; Steve Inwood; Lindsay Crouse; Matthew Laurance; Tony Turco.*

*Prince of the City* was just so appealing because of its complexity. I had never read Robert Daley's book. I had never read a book where people's motives were so obscure, complicated, where you couldn't trust anybody, where nobody told the truth. The government didn't tell the truth, Bob Lucie didn't tell the truth. Nobody told the truth. And everybody was, theoretically, pursuing the truth. And that's delicious because that's the way an awful lot of our lives go. Not deliberately, as in that case, but that happens an awful lot. So to me it was an irresistible story.

I didn't want competent actors in *Prince of the City;* I wanted marvelous actors. But I didn't want actors with whom the audience had previous associations. I felt the situation was so unique that I didn't want anybody bringing past associations into the theater. I wanted them just to look at the picture so they could deal with the moral dilemma.

This is part of what we were talking about before—critics not knowing what's going on technically. I once did a movie called *Long Day's Journey Into Night* with Katharine Hepburn, Ralph Richardson, Jason Robards, and Dean Stockwell, and it is the play. There was no screenplay. Eugene O'Neill's play is screenplay. And I think it's a tremendous picture and I think it's some of the best work I've ever done. And I remember it got marvelous reviews.

But I remember that some of the reviews, back when I was still reading them, said it's just a photographed stage play. Well, there's more sheer movie technique there than there is in any western. The complexity of the cameras, the lighting, lenses, everything shot the way it would be edited, etc., is a lesson in movie making. *Prince of the City* has that same kind of technical complexity about it. I don't know if it would be interesting to the audience what we did technically, because it involves a lot of movie terminology, but it was one of the most carefully worked out, complex techniques used on a movie. It only looks as if it's natural. It's not natural at all. We made everything happen. We created everything with painstaking care. I don't like when the audience sees my technique. I don't think it's any of their business. They just need to relate to the movie in whatever way they do. It's a well-disguised technique and boy, there's technique in that movie. Other directors knew about it. Kurosawa and I became friends because when he saw the movie he was bowled over by the technical mastery of it. Directors can see it. Critics can't.

# Deathtrap *(1982)*

*Michael Caine; Christopher Reeve; Dyan Cannon; Irene Worth; Henry Jones; Joe Silver; Tony DiBenedetto; Al LeBreton; Francis B. Creamer, Jr.; Stewart Klein; Jeffrey Lyons; Joel Siegel; Jenny Lumet; Jayne Heller; George Peck.*

I think the cast of *Deathtrap* was wonderful. By the way, this was Chris Reeve's first non-Superman part. And again, clearly a wonderful actor but nobody could get past the cape and see how good he was. And so I came to him with the script and a chance to play a real vicious but disguised heavy. He was thrilled about it. And Michael, of course, and Dyan are among the best comedic, light, gay in spirit actors that we've got. That doesn't mean they can't do drama as well because they can. They're both wonderful dramatic actors.

# The Verdict *(1982)*

*Paul Newman; Charlotte Rampling; Jack Warden; James Mason; Milo O'Shea; Lindsay Crouse; Edward Binns; Julie Bovasso; Roxanne Hart; James Handy; Wesley Addy; Joe Seneca; Lewis J. Stadlen; Kent Broadhurst; Colin Stinton.*

*The Verdict* actually dropped in my lap. David Brown and Richard Zanuck had been working on it for some time with another director and another star and it kept getting worse and worse. Well, by sheer accident the first draft of *The Verdict* had been written by David Mamet and I had read it. But they had thrown out that script and had gone on to a million more dollars of rewrites. Five other drafts to be exact. So when David called me to ask if I was interested in it I said yes.

David Mamet and I had been working on something else together and he told me they'd thrown out his first draft. That's how I got to read it. So when David Brown called me, I told him there was this marvelous Mamet version. And there's this pause for a moment over the phone. And he said, "Oh, we've gone on to a lot of other scripts since then." I said, "I've heard. But this is the one I'd love to do if you want to do it." He said, "Well, why don't you do me a favor? Read the other versions and we'll talk again." He sent me four other scripts, all of which I read. We talked three days later and I said, "No, it's Mamet's version. You're the producer but that's the one I want to do. Please, if you don't agree, find somebody else." Brown said, "No, no, we talked about it and we'll go back to the Mamet version."

Well, as soon as David and Richard wanted me to do it I recommended Paul Newman, and the script went to him. Forty-eight hours later he says, "Let's go."

It wasn't easy to find the keys to a character like Frank Calvin. First of all, the man is very complex. There's something about Mamet's writing that is one of the reasons it's endlessly interesting. He'll give you one line but he expects the actor and the director to fill in three unspoken lines. So you have to work out between you what has David left unspoken here, what is he not saying, and how do we play it. You're playing it unspoken all the time. It's one of the reasons that Mamet is a very difficult writer to act. And that's what we spent the time doing. And that's how we unearthed that character.

## Garbo Talks (1984)

*Anne Bancroft; Ron Silver; Carrie Fisher; Harvey Fierstein; Hermione Gingold; Steven Hill; Andrzej Bartkowiak; Howard Da Silva; Catherine Hicks; Dorothy Loudon; Mary McDonnell; Karen Shallo; Richard B. Shull.*

A lot of movies that I've done would not seem like movies that I would pick to direct. I'm just endlessly interested in other forms, other genres. Here's a completely sentimental, sweet piece about a dying mother who wanted to meet Greta Garbo. I thought it had charm in the writing. No great big important movie but what I hoped would be a charming movie and light in spirit. I don't know if we achieved what we set out to do or not. Obviously the audience did not feel we made it because it was not a very successful picture. But Annie Bancroft is a dream of mine. We used to work together in live television when her name was Ann Marno, a nice Italian girl from the Bronx, and so just to work with Annie was another reason to do the movie.

# Family Business (1989)

*Sean Connery; Dustin Hoffman; Matthew Broderick;*
*Janet Carroll; Victoria Jackson; Bill McCutcheon; Deborah Rush;*
*Marilyn Cooper; Salem Ludwig; Rex Everhart; James Tolkan;*
*Marilyn Sokol; Thomas A. Carlin; Tony DiBenedetto; Isabell Monk.*

*Family Business* was a big failure and I'm partially responsible. I think Vince Patrick also failed in the script to some degree. But it's always my responsibility because I didn't push him. I didn't know what the solution was until I finished the movie.

I wanted to do a fable. And fables always begin with "once upon a time," right? I'm not a fool. I know that Dustin Hoffman does not look like Sean Connery's son. And I know that Matthew Broderick does not look like Dustin Hoffman's son. But that was one of the joys of casting it that way, which was my way of letting you know, hey, this is not real, it's not to be taken that seriously. This is for you to have a good time with a hell of a good yarn, with what I hope is some good laughs. But it didn't work because the whole drama changed its tone just past 60 percent of the way in.

Once Matthew got caught by the cops and Sean got sentenced to jail, it just went into a dark area that the rest of the picture had not prepared you for. So it was neither fish nor fowl. It did not work. But again, I just wanted to do a fable.

Sean and Dustin are totally different in their techniques. Sean is no-nonsense. Dustin wants to investigate everything. Dustin's terrific. He is very, very bright. The questions he asks are not pain-in-the-ass questions. They are legitimate and he's using them to build the character he's playing. I know all the stories about how difficult he is. We didn't have that. I don't know what happened on other movies, but he's a very rich actor. And my feelings are always that the actor is the one that's up there. If he needs two hours of discussion to get this scene right, have the two hours of discussion. You might find out something, too.

# Q & A (1990)

*Nick Nolte; Timothy Hutton; Armand Assante; Patrick O'Neal; Lee Richardson;*
*Luis Guzmán; Charles Dutton; Jenny Lumet; Paul Calderon; International Chrysis;*
*Dominic Chianese; Leonardo Cimino; Fyvush Finkel; Gustavo Brens; Martin E. Brens.*

*Q & A*, I think, is one of my best movies. Marvelously acted. I can't remember many pictures that take an honest view of racism in America. And I don't mean racism in terms of "Hey, you dirty Jew." I'm not talking about that simplistic level. I'm talking about the racism that's built into the body of society. The people involved would say, "Hey, I'm not a racist." Most cops will tell you they're not a racist. But there is a mindset that they're not even aware of. It's maybe breaking down now. But I'm not so sure.

The Irish cops used to hang out together. The Italian cops used to hang out together, and the Jewish cops would hang out together, and the police organizations were based along ethnic and certainly racial lines. And certainly today in New York some of the black members of the PBA are all members of the Guardians. So that division is just there. And it's been there for so long that people have lost all awareness of what's going on.

That's what *Q & A* is about. It's really authentic. The book was written by Ed Torres, who was the first Latino judge appointed in New York State. He was a real tough mother, let me tell you. Ed is famous for looking down at a prisoner that he was about to sentence and saying, "Let me tell you son, your parole officer hasn't been born yet." That's Ed. He's no soft guy, he's not left wing, and he's quite right wing. He's one tough guy and he knows what he's talking about.

The book did not have the racial emphasis that I put into the script. That's why I wanted to write it myself. Also, when I know the language, when I know the sound of the person, like in *Prince of the City* or in *Q & A*, when I know that sound, I like writing it myself. I don't consider myself a writer on a Paddy Chayefsky or David Mamet level. Writing is a tremendous and separate talent. But when I know those people it becomes in a way almost simpler for me to write it.

I think my movies have a lot of reality but rather than investigate that word you can say they have a gritty feel. My movies seem real no matter how stylized the work is in making them. That's been said a lot. And therefore, like all things said a lot, it's kind of dismissive, in a way.

I remember saying that I thought Henry Fonda, James Mason, and

Spencer Tracy were three of the best movie actors ever but I got so tired of reading reviews of Hank saying that he gave another brilliant performance, as if that's just easy to come by. Not easy.

One critic said *Q & A, Serpico,* and *Prince of the City* completed the unofficial Sydney Lumet trilogy of New York police stories. Well, I guess calling them a trilogy is a fair statement. But what are they going to do now with my new one, *Night Falls on Manhattan*? What do you call it when it's not a trilogy, when it's four? I'm not bothered by that but I do question why things have to be put in such pretentious terms. To me it was another movie about New York and New York cops and I've got a fourth one coming out and I hope I have a fifth and a sixth. It's an endlessly interesting subject.

> *He's an artist. He's a true artist and he loves people, he loves actors,*
> *he loves the profession, and he loves the entertainment.*
> Melanie Griffith—Actress

# A Stranger Among Us (1992)
*Melanie Griffith; Eric Thal; John Pankow; Tracy Pollan; Mia Sara; Lee Richardson;*
*Jamey Sheridan; Jake Weber; David Rosenbaum; Ruth Vool; David Margulies;*
*Edward Rogers, III; Maurice Schell; James Gandolfini; Burtt Harris.*

People thought Melanie Griffith, who I think is a treasure and one of the best actresses we've got, was wrong for the part of Emily Eden. That's fascinating because Nick Paleggi and I were having dinner one night and he asked if I ever met—and he mentioned a woman's name—and I said no. He told me she was a real cop and she was just like Melanie in *A Stranger Among Us*. She has that little voice and that great body, even the same blonde hair. They were so much alike Mitch thought I had based the character on this woman. So the refusal to accept Melanie in that part was wrong. The picture clearly didn't work. Whether Melanie was the problem, or the script was the problem, or I was the problem, I don't know. The joy of that picture for me was working with Ms. Griffith. I would work with her tomorrow if the right script came along. I think she's just wonderful.

## Cops, Cops, and More Cops
Some critics have dared to suggest that they are getting a little bored with Sidney and his corrupt cop routine. The reason I'm interested in corrupt

cops is because it still goes on and is getting worse. I was once at a meeting in France when *Prince of the City* came out. There was a discussion on dope in Europe and corruption and dope in the United States. And this idiot French policeman stood up and said, "Well, we don't have those problems here." Like Marseilles is the cleanest city in the world. And that basic cop axiom that you can't have dope without having dirty cops is true all over the world, except in Holland where just about all drugs are legal.

So here we have this pervading force—drugs—which in my view can destroy this country. For the first time ever we have found little traces of corruption in the Drug Enforcement Agency which has never happened before. The money is just too big to resist. And as long as I keep seeing that up there, if I can get the financing, I want to keep making movies about it because I can't think of anything more pressing.

I think racism and drugs are the two things that can destroy this country. I don't think anything else can.

# Night Falls on Manhattan (1997)

*Andy Garcia; Lena Olin; Richard Dreyfuss; Ian Holm;*
*Ron Leibman; James Gandolfini; Shiek Mahmud-Bey;*
*Colm Feore; Dominic Chianese; Paul Guilfoyle; Bonnie Rose;*
*Norman Matlock; Sidney Armus; James Murtaugh; Melba Martinez.*

I hope the casting is perfect in *Night Falls on Manhattan*. The performances are marvelous. Andy Garcia is really a major actor and again, because of our unconscious racism and because of his name, he's always relegated to Latino parts. I've got him playing a black Irishman by the name of Sean Casey.

Richard Dreyfuss, of course, is a totally admirable American actor in a part that's a natural for him that's sort of loosely based on William Kunstler. He's something to watch, Mr. Dreyfuss.

# Critical Care (1997)

*Anne Bancroft; Albert Brooks; Helen Mirren; Kyra Sedgwick; James Spader;*
*Jeffrey Wright; Margo Martindale; Wallace Shawn; Philip Bosco; Edward*
*Herrmann; Colm Feore; James Lally; Al Waxman; Harvey Atkin.*

I hope *Critical Care* does for the health care system what *Network* did for television. I hope we kick the hell out of it. It's a black comedy. It's very,

very funny. But about two-thirds of the way through you start asking yourself what you are really laughing at. A very tough picture, stylistically, again, for all the reasons I've been talking about, how to get laughter and seriousness going at the same time. I hope it works as well as I think it does.

## Why He Loves to Shoot in New York

My love for shooting in New York was a way of keeping my personal life together. Once I couldn't take the kids with me because they were in school I had to make a choice. I didn't want to be separated from the family. I couldn't take them along. So it's composed of two things. I find New York endlessly stimulating and also it's terrific to have your work where your house is.

## How Does He Want to Be Remembered?

I haven't the foggiest idea of how I'd want to be remembered, or if I would be remembered, or if I want to be remembered. It seems to me that people who worry about that get themselves in terrible trouble. At least that's my opinion. You can't worry about history and posterity. Do your work and go home. What's going to happen is going to happen anyway. The very question, "how would you like to be remembered," implies that you're dead already, so what difference does it make?

It seems to be a useless pursuit. Fred Astaire said it best. "I don't take myself seriously, but I take my work very seriously." That says it all.

# Director Filmography

*12 Angry Men* (1957)
*Stage Struck* (1958)
*That Kind of Woman* (1959)
*The Fugitive Kind* (1959)
*Vu du pont* (1961)
*Long Day's Journey Into Night* (1962)
*Fail-Safe* (1964)

*The Pawnbroker* (1965)
*The Hill* (1965)
*The Group* (1966)
*The Deadly Affair* (1967)
*The Sea Gull* (1968)
*Bye Bye Braverman* (1968)
*Last of the Mobile Hot Shots* (1969)
*The Appointment* (1969)
*King: A Filmed Record* (1970)
*The Anderson Tapes* (1971)
*Child's Play* (1972)
*Serpico* (1973)
*The Offence* (1973)
*Lovin' Molly* (1974)
*Murder on the Orient Express* (1974)
*Dog Day Afternoon* (1975)
*Network* (1976)
*Equus* (1977)
*The Wiz* (1978)
*Just Tell Me What You Want* (1980)
*Prince of the City* (1981)
*The Verdict* (1982)
*Deathtrap* (1982)
*Daniel* (1983)
*Garbo Talks* (1984)
*The Morning After* (1986)
*Power* (1986)
*Running on Empty* (1988)
*Family Business* (1989)
*Q & A* (1990)
*A Stranger Among Us* (1992)
*Guilty as Sin* (1993)
*Night Falls on Manhattan* (1997)
*Critical Care* (1997)
*Gloria* (1999)

# Awards

### Academy Awards
*The Verdict*, Best Director (nominated), 1983
*Prince of the City*, Best Writing, Screenplay Based on Material from Another Medium (nominated, shared with Jay Presson Allen), 1982
*Network*, Best Director (nominated), 1977
*Dog Day Afternoon*, Best Director (nominated), 1976
*12 Angry Men*, Best Director (nominated), 1958

### Berlin International Film Festival
*12 Angry Men*, Golden Berlin Bear, 1957

### Bodil Festival
*The Pawnbroker*, Best American Film, 1966

### British Academy Awards
*Network*, Best Direction (nominated), 1978
*Dog Day Afternoon*, Best Direction (nominated), 1976
*Murder on the Orient Express*, Best Direction (nominated), 1975
*Serpico*, Best Direction (nominated), 1975
*The Deadly Affair,* Best British Film (nominated), 1968
*The Pawnbroker,* UN Award (nominated), 1967
*The Hill*, Best British Film (nominated), 1966
*The Hill*, Best Film from any Source (nominated), 1966

### Directors Guild of America, USA
D.W. Griffith Award, 1993

### Edgar Allan Poe Awards
*Prince of the City*, Best Movie (nominated, shared with Jay Presson Allen), 1982

**Golden Globes, USA**

*Running on Empty*, Best Director—Motion Picture (nominated), 1989

*The Verdict*, Best Director—Motion Picture (nominated), 1983

*Prince of the City*, Best Director—Motion Picture (nominated), 1982

*Network*, Best Director—Motion Picture, 1977

*Dog Day Afternoon*, Best Director—Motion Picture (nominated), 1976

**Gotham Awards**

Lifetime Achievement Award, 1998

**Los Angeles Film Critics Association Awards**

*Network*, Best Director, 1976

*Dog Day Afternoon*, Best Director, 1975

**National Board of Review, USA**

*The Verdict*, Best Director, 1982

**New York Film Critics Circle Award**

*Prince of the City*, Best Director, 1981

**San Sebastián International Film Festival**

*The Fugitive Kind*, Silver Seashell, 1960

**Venice Film Festival**

*Prince of the City*, Best Film, 1981

# Index

# About the Author

President and CEO of Media Entertainment Inc., **Robert J. Emery** has been a writer-producer-director for thirty-five years. He has written and produced a wide variety of screenplays and television shows, has taught film production, and has been the recipient of over seventy industry awards for his work.

# Books from Allworth Press

**Producing for Hollywood: A Guide for Independent Producers** by Paul Mason and Don Gold (paperback, 6 × 9, 272 pages, $19.95)

**Directing for Film and Television, Revised Edition** by Christopher Lukas (paperback, 6 × 9, 256 pages, $19.95)

**Making Independent Films: Advice from the Film Makers** by Liz Stubbs and Richard Rodriguez (paperback, 6 × 9, 240 pages, $19.95)

**Making Your Film for Less Outside the U.S.** by Mark DeWayne (paperback, 6 × 9, 272 pages, $19.95)

**The Filmmaker's Guide to Production Design** by Vincent LoBrutto (paperback, 6 × 9, 224 pages, $16.95)

**Get the Picture? The Movie Lover's Guide to Watching Films** by Jim Piper (paperback, 6 × 9, 240 pages, $18.95)

**Technical Film and TV for Nontechnical People** by Drew Campbell (paperback, 6 × 9, 256 pages, $19.95)

**The Art of Digital Filmmaking** by Gary Cooper (paperback, 6 × 9, 256 pages, $19.95)

**Documentary Filmmakers Speak** by Liz Stubbs (paperback, 6 × 9, 240 pages, $19.95)

**The Screenwriter's Legal Guide** by Stephen F. Breimer (paperback, 6 × 9, 320 pates, $19.95)

**The Screenwriter's Guide to Agents and Managers** by John Scott Lewinski (paperback, 6 × 9, 256 pages, $18.95)

Please write to request our free catalog. To order by credit card, call 1-800-491-2808 or send a check or money order to Allworth Press, 10 East 23rd Street, Suite 510, New York, NY 10010. Include $5 for shipping and handling for the first book ordered and $1 for each additional book. Ten dollars plus $1 for each additional book if ordering from Canada. New York State residents must add sales tax.

To see our complete catalog on the World Wide Web, or to order online, you can find us at *www.allworth.com*.

Videotapes and DVDs are available for many of the directors featured in this book. To order call (800) 414-1690 or visit *www.wellspring.com*.